A THEOLOGY OF HIGHER EDUCATION

In this book, Mike Higton provides a constructive critique of Higher Education policy and practice in the UK, the US, and beyond, from the standpoint of Christian theology. He focuses on the role universities can and should play in forming students and staff in intellectual virtue, in sustaining vibrant communities of inquiry, and in serving the public good. He argues both that modern secular universities can be a proper context for Christians to pursue their calling as disciples to learn and to teach, and that Christians can contribute to the flourishing of such universities as institutions devoted to learning for the common good. In the process he sets out a vision of the good university as secular and religiously plural, as socially inclusive, and as deeply and productively entangled with the surrounding society. Along the way, he engages with a range of historical examples (the medieval University of Paris, the University of Berlin in the nineteenth century, and John Henry Newman's work in Oxford and Dublin) and with a range of contemporary writers on Higher Education from George Marsden to Stanley Hauerwas, and from David Ford to Rowan Williams.

Mike Higton is Professor of Theology and Ministry at Durham University.

A Theology
of Higher Education

MIKE HIGTON

OXFORD
UNIVERSITY PRESS

OXFORD
UNIVERSITY PRESS

Great Clarendon Street, Oxford, OX2 6DP,
United Kingdom

Oxford University Press is a department of the University of Oxford.
It furthers the University's objective of excellence in research, scholarship,
and education by publishing worldwide. Oxford is a registered trade mark of
Oxford University press in the UK and in certain other countries

First published 2012
First published in paperback 2013

Published in the United States of America by Oxford University Press
198 Madison Avenue, New York, NY 10016, United States of America

British Library Cataloguing in Publication Data
Data available

Library of Congress Control Number: 2011942643

ISBN 978-0-19-964392-9 (Hbk)
ISBN 978-0-19-967795-5 (Pbk)

In memoriam
A.H.G.

Acknowledgements

In Chapter 7, I note that acknowledgement is a fundamental academic practice. It is also a pleasure—even when the acknowledger is beset by the worry that, for a project that has been nearly a decade in the making, he is bound to forget some of those to whom thanks are due.

I am grateful to all those who have discussed the subject matter of this book with me over the past several years, and whose voices have been echoing in my ears as I write: Nick Adams, Jonathan Barry, Siam Bhayro, John Blewitt, Luke Bretherton, Samantha Briggs, David Carter, Jon Cooley, David Cunningham, Stephen Dawes, Michael DeLashmutt, Jim Fodor, Regenia Gagnier, Chris Goringe, Sureka Goringe, Tim Gorringe, Dan Hardy, Jenny Hocking, Steve Holmes, David Horrell, Cherryl Hunt, Rob Innes, Tim Jenkins, Jeremy Law, Louise Lawrence, Morwenna Ludlow, John C. McDowell, Andrew McFarlane, Ian Markham, David Moss, Paul Murray, Ben Quash, Randi Rashkover, Esther Reed, David Rhymer, Chris Southgate, Francesca Stavrakopoulou, Jacqui Stewart, Adrian Thatcher, Susannah Ticciati, Ella Westland, and two anonymous readers for Oxford University Press. I owe a particular debt of thanks to those who have read (or listened to) and commented on draft chapters: Tom Greggs, Karen Kilby, Charles Matthewes, Paul Nimmo, Tom O'Loughlin, Mark Wynn, and participants in seminars in Cambridge, Exeter, Heidelberg, and Nottingham. And, as for Rachel Muers, who read more of the draft chapters than anyone, and who in that and other ways has had a bigger influence on them than any other colleague—well, having colleagues like her and conversations like that is one of the reasons why I love being an academic.

The other colleague who has done a disproportionate amount to shape this book is David Ford. At every turn in the writing, whenever I have been particularly excited to discover a new line of thought or hit upon a new concept, I have found David there ahead of me. I know of no more enthusiastic advocate of wisdom and collegiality in university life—and if this book does nothing more than demonstrate that his enthusiasm is contagious, I shall be more than content.

Even though I have already named many of the relevant individuals involved, I wanted to say a special thank you to the Department of Theology and Religion at the University of Exeter. I am writing these words about two weeks before I move from Exeter to Cambridge, and I am very aware that I will be leaving behind me a remarkable group of people, and a remarkable centre of academic life. My sense of the possibilities and excitements of university life has been deeply and happily shaped by the department's friendliness, its streams of conversation, and by the endless, endless jokes. If John Henry Newman was trying in his *Idea of a University* to capture what was best in the

Senior Common Room of Oriel College, I am not ashamed to be trying in this book to name something of what has been so fantastic about daily coffee breaks in the Amory Common Room.

I am grateful to Tom Perridge of Oxford University Press for holding onto the project when it looked as though it was slipping away, and to Hilary Walford for her patient and attentive copy-editing. An earlier version of some of the material in Part II was published in 2006 as a Grove Booklet, *Vulnerable Learning: Thinking Theologically about Higher Education.* I am grateful to the staff of Grove for their assistance and advice.

I am also more grateful than I can say to Brian and Cynthia Higbee, who have allowed me to work for much of the past year in a large caravan in their beautiful garden, looking out at views of Dartmoor, and who have been quite astonishingly hospitable. It has been a joy to be able to work without the interruptions of phones, emails, or small children, and there is no way that this book would have been finished on time without their limitless generosity. The only negative side has been the high levels of jealousy that descriptions of my Dartmoor idyll in the legendary Caravan of Seclusion have provoked among my colleagues and friends.

Thanks, too, to my family. I love my academic life, but family life is even better, and rather more likely to keep me sane. Time spent writing in the Caravan of Seclusion is good, but the days we have had this year at Sandymouth and Duckpool, up Cosdon Beacon, paddling in the East Okement, or simply at home in Sticklepath have been even better—and I will remember them long after I have forgotten what on earth I wrote about thirteenth-century Paris, or about openness to judgement in relation to research.

I want to finish with one final acknowledgement. My ideas for this book were shaped and sharpened by conversations with my father-in-law, Andor Gomme—but he died in September 2008, before even the first chapter was written. Among many other things, he was a quite remarkable academic, and he taught me more about what it means to be one than anyone else. I do not imagine, though, that anyone will ever say of me what must certainly be said of him: no one who met him could ever think the word 'academic' a synonym for 'narrow' again. With seriousness, with delight, with a vast store of carefully culled detail, and with spacious clarity, he wrote on Dickens, on D. H. Lawrence, on Jane Austen, on Shakespeare, and on literary criticism in general; he edited several Jacobean tragedies; he taught his way through the works of Doris Lessing and Paul Scott; he wrote standard works on the architecture of Glasgow and of Bristol, a masterwork on the architect Francis Smith, and (most recently) on the development of the English country house; he produced an edition of Bach's *St Mark Passion*—the list goes on and on. I am not sure universities make people like him any more, and this book is very much the poorer for not having been subjected to his acute but friendly criticism. It is, nevertheless, dedicated to his memory.

Contents

Introduction

This is a book about universities, and specifically about *secular* universities: universities that owe no explicit present allegiance to any Christian church or other religious group, and that do not knowingly encourage theological contributions to their policy discussions. It is, nevertheless, a theological book, and it develops a Christian theological account of higher education. It asks what I, as a Christian theologian, can recognize and celebrate as actually and potentially good about universities; it asks what I and those who share my theological commitments might do to help universities approximate to their proper good more fully; and it asks what openness there can and should be in such universities to theological voices like mine. My answers to all these questions circle around three core themes: higher education as training in intellectual virtue; the inherent sociality of university learning, reason, and knowledge;[1] and the proper orientation of higher education towards the common good—the *public* good.

The book was written to the accompaniment of a rising tide of anger in English universities, and as I finished that tide spilled over into sit-ins, marches, and violent clashes—a response to the announcement of dramatic cuts in government funding for higher education, and of the equally dramatic rise in student fees needed to balance them. The cuts were described by Steve Smith, vice-chancellor of the University of Exeter and president of Universities UK, as 'the abandonment of the state's role in funding higher education',[2] while Stefan Collini, a professor of English at Cambridge, described as breathtaking 'the scale of the . . . dismantling of the public character of higher

---

[1] I will use the words 'learning', 'reason', and 'knowledge' quite freely and informally in this book. Ch. 5 gives them a more precise meaning, but most of the time I use 'reason' simply to denote the practices of investigation and argument that academics are supposed to engage in, 'knowledge' the relatively stable intellectual results of such practices, and 'learning' the process of being inducted into those practices and into understanding of the results they yield.

[2] Steve Smith, 'Where is the Government's Mandate to Change the World of Higher Education?', *Guardian*, 19 Oct. 2010; www.guardian.co.uk/education/2010/oct/19/universities-change-world-government-funding (accessed 18 Aug. 2011).

education' involved.[3] In other words, while observers from countries with much higher student fees and a much lower reliance upon state funding might look on this as a little local difficulty, the underlying issue appears to be a deeply familiar, and a truly international one: the erosion of the idea that the existence of universities is, in some sense that goes beyond the economic, a genuine public good.

In such a context, it was deeply tempting to turn this book into a diatribe, or into the melancholy, long, withdrawing roar of retreating academic faith. I judged, however, that the world did not need yet another critique of the commodification of higher education, nor of the attendant fragmentation of the curriculum, nor of the bureaucratic managerialism that seems to afflict all universities become market-minded. Others have blown those trumpets, and have blown them clearly and well, and I find I do not have any interesting arpeggios of my own to add to their warnings.[4] I have, instead, set myself a different task: to answer the question 'What is (or should be, or could be) *good* about universities?', in the belief that answering that question, as clearly and convincingly as we can, is a more basic and a more urgent task than cataloguing all the ways in which that good is being eroded, denied, ignored, or discounted.

I have, therefore, tried to keep my focus on the good of higher education, even when I have found myself writing after the arrival of emails about new government cuts, intrusive quality-assurance practices, badly handled industrial disputes, perverse failures of academic vision, or—worst of all—annoying alterations to university car-parking provision. I have tried to keep central in what I have written my conviction that universities are worth fighting for, because there is a great deal that is good about them, and my conviction that there are all sorts of ways of imagining how they might realize that good more fully, and of working towards that fuller realization. To put it another way: I have tried to write in such a way that my love for the work that I do, and my love for the contexts in which I do it, come through at least as strongly as my worries, complaints, and criticisms. Anger certainly motivates some of the

---

[3] Stefan Collini, 'Browne's Gamble', *London Review of Books*, 32/21 (4 Nov. 2010), 23–5; www.lrb.co.uk/v32/n21/stefan-collini/brownes-gamble (accessed 18 Aug. 2011).

[4] As well as the Collini article just cited, see Gavin D'Costa's critique of higher education in *Theology in the Public Square: Church, Academy and Nation*, Challenges in Contemporary Theology, ed. Gareth Jones and Lewis Ayres (Oxford: Blackwell, 2005), or Stanley Hauerwas's in *The State of the University: Academic Knowledges and the Knowledge of God*, Illuminations: Theory and Religion, ed. Catherine Pickstock, John Milbank, and Graham Ward (Oxford: Blackwell, 2007), or Gordon Graham's *Universities: The Recovery of an Idea*, 2nd edn, Societas: Essays in Political and Cultural Criticism (Exeter: Imprint Academic, 2008), or the essays in Stephen Prickett and Patricia Erskine-Hill (eds), *Education! Education! Education! Managerial Ethics and the Law of Unintended Consequences* (Thorverton: Imprint Academic/Higher Education Foundation, 2002), among many others. You could even see my own 'The Research Assessment Exercise as Sin', *Critical Quarterly*, 44/4 (2002), 40–5, as a brief example of the genre.

things that I say, but I have tried not to luxuriate in it. I do not think our universities will be saved, or made to approximate more fully to the good that is already partly visible in them, primarily by anger.[5] It is when there is no vision that the people perish.

This book has grown in a particular context—or rather, two particular contexts. I spent half of the last decade running evening classes and distance learning courses in a beleaguered university department of extra-mural studies, the other half as a head of department in a university working its way into the upper ranks of the UK university league tables. As a consequence, I have also spent those years negotiating my way between numerous different discourses about higher education, from confident managerialism to nostalgic romanticism, looking for an account that would do justice to my colleagues' and my sense of academic vocation, while also allowing a serious, practical engagement with the constraints under which our institutions operate. This book has emerged, in part, from those negotiations. It is an attempt, in the tradition of Newman's *Idea of a University*, to set out a theologically informed account of university life, engaging with other attempts of the same kind, and exploring the kinds of settlement with the pressing constraints of the present that such an account might permit.

The other impetus for this book lies in my reading of contemporary theological and philosophical debates about the nature of secularity, and specifically about the nature of public reason in a secular and religiously plural society. In order not to float off into generalities, those debates require grounding in attention to the actual practices of reasoning that contribute to and partly constitute public life. My scrutiny of the dynamics and possibilities of university reasoning is intended as a contribution to that grounding. If university teaching forms reasoners, and forms them for public life, and if university research at least in part engages in reasoning for the sake of public life, then a theology of higher education should at the same time be a contribution to the theology of public life.

ARGUMENT

The book is divided into two parts, the first largely concentrating on other people's claims about the university, and the second on my own.

---

[5] I was partly cured of the desire to write in anger (though more slowly than I should have been) by reading Duke Maskell and Ian Robinson's description of their 'pure, aristocratic disdain, *desdeyn*' for some current academic practices—and recognizing myself a little too readily in their words (see Maskell and Robinson, *The New Idea of a University* (London: Haven, 2001), 134).

In the first three chapters of Part I, I explore three landmarks that dominate the horizon of many discussions of the nature and purpose of universities: the emergence of the medieval University of Paris in the twelfth and thirteenth centuries, the foundation of the University of Berlin in the nineteenth, and the publication a generation after Berlin's foundation of John Henry Newman's *Idea of a University*.

My discussions in these chapters serve four distinct purposes. First, they are intended to make the thematic foci of Part II—virtue, sociality, and the common good—more plausible by demonstrating that those themes are already clearly audible in university history. Discussion of the three themes is just what one might expect in an account of university life and purpose that orients itself by reference to Paris, Berlin, and Newman's Oxford and Dublin. Second, my discussions are intended to add richer harmonics to the ideas at the heart of those three themes, such that the idea of virtue in later chapters will come trailing echoes of monasticism picked up in Paris, the idea of sociality will come with echoes both of Berlin's Romantic salons and Newman's Oriel common room—and so on. Third, the three episodes provide foils against which I will develop some of my own distinctive claims. So, for instance, my account later in the book of the orientation of learning towards the common good will be set against Newman's account of learning as an end in itself.

Fourth, however, each of the three historical chapters will serve to advance the overall argument that holds the book together. At the risk of overemphasizing the methodological aspects of my account, I think it is worth setting down the overall argument in some detail here.

The chapter on the emergence of the University of Paris is directed against certain existing mythologizations of that episode. Specifically, I argue that the rationality or reasonableness of Parisian intellectual practice *cannot* be regarded as running in inverse proportion to the measure of its religiosity or devotion. Indeed, something closer to the opposite is true: Parisian intellectual practice is rational or reasonable *because*, and *in so far as*, it is devoutly Christian.[6] This argument prepares the way for my own claim, in Chapter 5, that reason is akin to discipleship, and that university education properly takes the form of induction into a spiritual discipline.

The second chapter, on the University of Berlin, will argue that the *Wissenschaftsideologie* that surrounded the new university's creation was, in part, an attempted repair of the broken and disputatious world of Christian learning. That is, the Romantic theorists of *Wissenschaft* appropriated a

---

[6] Of course, Parisian intellectual practice echoes, and might in some respects be influenced by, the intellectual practice of Islamic scholarship (see below, Ch. 1, n. 33). My claim is a local one about the nature of Parisian practice, not a global one about the only possible grounding of reason.

tradition-specific Christian vision of free, peaceable exchange (the economy of gift and reception in the Body of Christ) and sought to remake the whole world of learning on the basis of that vision. That remaking required, however, that they revise or abandon anything that could not be made to fit with the proper freedom of such peaceable exchange, including the heteronomous commitment of learners to particular traditions of religious thought and practice. The account they provided of the university—indeed, the account they provided of reason itself—was therefore inescapably both theological and anti-theological.

I will be arguing that these theorists' repair of their theological heritage itself needs repair. Far from requiring the overcoming of commitment to particular religious traditions, the kind of free sociality that they advocate actually requires the frank acknowledgement of, and argument about, such particular commitments. It may be true that a public university after Berlin cannot simply be exclusively Christian, but that does not mean that it can properly be exclusively secular. The vision embodied in the University of Berlin can be pursued more fully, I will suggest, in institutions that are explicitly secular *and* religiously plural.

Of course, one way of approaching such an account would be to modify the Berlin picture of a tradition-neutral scholarly reason, such that, while remaining neutral itself, it left room for tradition-specific voices. Such a solution, however, would miss the central lesson of my analysis of Berlin: the account of reason provided in Berlin is *not* neutral, but is an attempted repair effected within a theologically freighted tradition. To rethink that repair by rejecting the denial of tradition-specificity that distorted it means reopening the question of the compatibility between a tradition-specific, theological account of reason and a thoroughgoing commitment to free intellectual sociality.

Chapter 3, on Newman's *Idea of a University*, will argue that, for all its strengths, his vision of the university cannot provide the theological account of free intellectual sociality that the repair of the Berlin settlement requires. It certainly does have strengths, perhaps most notably in its picture of the intellectually well-formed graduate ready to navigate his way through a media-saturated world, but the problems are nevertheless substantial. Most notably, Newman was quite deliberately defending the idea of an exclusively Catholic university, secured over against secular or religiously plural forces. Crucially for my purposes, it turns out that Newman's account of this exclusivity relies upon a distinction between the natural end of intellectual formation and the religious end of ecclesial formation. The latter, the formation supplied by the Catholic Church, curbs, steadies, and supplements the former, but intellectual formation in and of itself is painted in non-theological colours. In fact, Newman's account of intellectual formation itself is, if anything, *less* theological than the account of *Wissenschaft* propounded in Berlin, and certainly less than the account of learning I have attributed to Paris. The intellectual aspect of human being is distinguished too neatly from the whole weave of human life before God, and the relationship between intellectual formation and Christian faith is as a consequence unnecessarily uneasy. In other words, the deepest problem I identify with Newman's account of university learning is not that it is too theological, but that it is not theological enough.

Part I finishes with a chapter that surveys contemporary Christian theological discussion about the university. Chapter 4 begins with various authors concerned to raise a distinctively Christian voice within a higher-education sector that is predominantly secular. For most of these authors, Christians can participate with a good conscience in the ordinary practices of secular academic reason, but will do so with distinctive motivations, with a special concern both about the wider implications and about the proper limits of their studies, and with a recognizably Christian ethos. The chapter moves on, however, to authors for whom the ordinary practices of secular academic reason themselves come into the theological spotlight. I examine, for instance, the work of Stanley Hauerwas, who raises serious questions about the supposed neutrality of these practices. His questions reinforce my earlier suggestion that any repair of the Berlin settlement will be inadequate if it continues to present the practices of secular academic reason as neutral territory, however hospitable to multiple tradition-specific voices that neutral territory might turn out to be. Taking his point in a more positive direction, I examine the work of a selection of Anglican theologians who have, in different ways, suggested that the ordinary practices of secular academic reason are already shaped towards God's purposes, and might be opened more deeply to those purposes—and who therefore set the scene for the second part of the book.

Part II begins with a resolutely theological account of learning, drawing on resources from my own particular ecclesial tradition (a certain kind of Anglicanism). I argue that, for one being formed in this tradition, learning means being invited as disciples to know God and the fulfilment that God has for God's creatures. I argue in parallel to the claims of Chapter 1 that such learning is inherently a spiritual discipline, in which participation in Christ's crucifixion and resurrection sets the basic dynamics. I argue in parallel to the claims of Chapter 2 that such learning is inherently sociable or ecclesial, and involves being drawn into an economy of gift and reception of the kind that constitutes the Body of Christ. And, in response to Chapter 3's discussion of the proper end of learning, I argue that education inherently takes the form of an interplay between wisdom and delight, in which wisdom seeks the flourishing of all God's creatures together before God, while delight registers the distinctive way of being of each creature called to share in this flourishing. I then argue that, seen from my tradition-formed perspective, *all* learning worthy of the name—indeed, all *reason* worthy of the name—takes this form, and has its proper context in worship and discipleship, but that it nevertheless takes place both in and beyond the church, and sometimes more truly beyond the church than in it.

The chapter finishes with a question. Can someone who holds to this account of learning (an account, I have just said, of '*all* learning worthy of the name—indeed, all *reason* worthy of the name') have anything good to say about universities, and in particular about the modern secular and religiously plural university? At this point in my argument, the implied answer might seem to be negative, and I might be thought to have laid the foundation for a call to an explicitly and exclusively Christian form of higher education. Yet my claim in the chapters that follow is that this theological account of learning in fact allows me to provide descriptions of and proposals for learning that are recognizably descriptions of and proposals for life in a secular and religiously plural university. To someone formed in my ecclesial tradition, I claim, the learning practices of secular and religiously plural universities can be seen to approximate, in significant part, to the good (or to be pregnant with the good), and participation in this kind of university life is therefore possible as a Christian vocation.

Of course, since these descriptions and proposals do not wear their theological origins on their sleeves, they can be taken simply as a scatter of contributions to discussions about university policy and practice, contributions that I hope are hospitable and attractive, and capable of helping me and other participants in university life recognize and pursue the proper good of higher education, regardless of whether their traditional provenance is made explicit. Yet I am after something more than piecemeal acceptance or rejection. Among the descriptions and proposals that I offer, there is the insistence that public universities can and should be involved in—indeed, be promoting—secular and religiously plural debate, especially about the common good, and in particular about their own good. Of course, my reasons for making this claim, and the precise form in which I make it, are no less determined by my particular theological tradition than any of the other descriptions and proposals that I offer—but the proposal is nonetheless for an open and free debate between multiple traditions. My proposal is therefore *not* for a university sector in which a Christian theological account has become the dominant account, but for a university sector formed by a renewed and serious argument about the good of university life—an argument that will include Christian theological voices like mine, and voices from numerous other religious and secular traditions, and in which the very form of the argument will be one of the items debated.

In the course of these chapters, therefore, I am offering neither a simple description of the present life of universities, nor a utopia unconnected to that present life. I am offering a way of construing presently existing university life. It can be seen, I am suggesting, as partially and falteringly pursuing a set of real goods—and to see it thus is to judge it: to affirm the respects in which it realizes those goods, and to condemn the many respects in which it denies them. I am offering this account to my colleagues in the university sector as a way of seeing and judging the institutions in which they work, and so of shaping their ongoing participation in those institutions. I claim that the goods that I delineate are already sometimes present in university life, when it is at its best; I claim that this is what university life should be and realistically could be—and that these are, therefore, the goods that we should be fighting to preserve and to pursue.

Chapter 6 focuses on the ways in which higher education provides a training in virtue. This is not primarily because universities inculcate virtue *alongside* training in reason. Rather, higher education provides training in reason, and reasoning is itself a virtuous discipline. If the university is to be a school of disciplined reason, it cannot but be a school of virtue, and the virtues inculcated will be directly constitutive of progress in any academic discipline. So, I argue that teaching will (if understood this way) primarily take the form of apprenticeship, and that the central virtues that the apprenticeship forms will be willingness to judge and openness to being judged—virtues already visible in all sorts of ways in the life of students, teachers, and researchers.

In Chapter 7, I argue that higher education properly provides an induction into a certain kind of moral community: a reasoning community united by forms of virtuous exchange. The members of that community call one another to account, try to take alternative views seriously, aim to review fairly and to critique robustly, and so on. There are, of course, plenty of vicious exchanges in academic life, but, far from such vicious exchanges being the true life of the modern university, they are in fact parasitic upon patterns of virtuous exchange. Patterns of virtuous sociality are the real structures that allow academic disciplines to function as practices of reason—and to take responsibility for the flourishing of the conversational ecologies of university life is the primary form that academic leadership should take.

In Chapter 8, I reject the idea of learning for learning's sake. I argue that it is not enough to send students formed in intellectual virtue out into the wider public world, but that universities have to take an active interest in the shaping and maintaining of virtuous and sociable patterns of reason across that wider world. I then argue, as already mentioned, that the university needs to be characterized by serious, socially inclusive, secular and religiously plural public arguments about the common good, and to promote such argument in the wider world by being thoroughly entangled in that world's conversational ecology.

In Chapter 9, I take this claim about secular and religiously plural debate one step further. I argue that the university's internal argument about its own practices and policies can and should take the form of such a secular and religiously plural debate. Once again, my grounds for making this claim, and the precise form in which I make it, are determined by my theological commitments, but the proposal is nevertheless for an open and free, multi-traditional debate. I back this claim up by arguing that the university is *already* constituted by a certain kind of multi-traditional conversation about its own virtues, forms of sociality, and ends, even if that fact is not widely recognized. University practices of reason are not determined in advance by well-defined principle, but are settlements between multiple different ideas of the university.[7] This book is, then, at once a particular contribution to this internal university conversation, and an account of why a conversation of this kind is a proper way for a secular and religiously plural university to determine its policy and practice—and I think I have good Christian theological reasons for thinking that the fuller realization of the vision of the university that I set out need not require the triumph of my Christian theological account to the exclusion of other religious and secular accounts.

I finish, in the Conclusion, with reflection on two limits to the argument that I have made. First, I note that a secular and religiously plural university is not, and should not be, the church. I ask what role explicitly Christian worship and discipleship—and the call to others to become Christian worshippers and disciples—can and should nevertheless play in such a context, and conclude that, while a public university is properly secular and religiously plural, practices of Christian worship and discipleship do fundamentally belong on campus.[8] Second, I examine another kind of limit: the inevitability that, despite all I have said, and despite the optimism and gratitude that I have tried to weave into my account, the university will remain an ambiguous and problematic institution, and that labour for its good will meet all too regularly with frustration. Despite all I have said about the good of university life, those who love the university like this will need to know how to live graciously with disappointment.

---

[7] Of course, even this claim is not neutral. My apprehension of the dynamics of university life is shaped by my tradition-specific intellectual formation, here as elsewhere. This turns out not to matter very much: I do not have to determine in advance the reasons that others might have for agreeing or disagreeing with me.

[8] I do not try to speak for other faiths. If analogous claims are made for those faiths (as I think, in several cases at least, they can and should be), they will be made on other grounds and in other ways. On the Christian side, there is something akin to 'ad hoc apologetics' going on here (see Hans W. Frei, *Types of Christian Theology*, ed. George Hunsinger and William C. Placher (New Haven: Yale University Press, 1992), and William Werpehowski, 'Ad Hoc Apologetics', *Journal of Religion*, 66/3 (1986), 282–301), and also something akin to Rowan Williams's 'communicative theology', 'experimenting with the rhetoric of its uncommitted environment' (Rowan Williams, *On Christian Theology* (Oxford: Blackwell, 2000), p. xiv). What there is not—as the self-confessed 'grumpy Barthian' among the friends who read my draft chapters will be pleased to hear—is any attempt to identify an apologetic *Anknüpfungspunkt*.

Part I

1

Paris

To say that one is writing a theology of higher education is, at least in some circles, to invite incredulity. Examine the roots of that incredulity, and one will often find it sustained by a belief that universities, and the forms of questioning reason that they represent, gained their proper identity and vitality precisely to the extent that they put away theological thinking. To write a theology of higher education is, in this view, like writing an astrology of the Hubble Space Telescope.

That belief itself feeds on a compost of mythologized history, and the story of the emergence of the University of Paris in the twelfth and thirteenth centuries is one of the key ingredients in the compost. As we shall see, the way the story is sometimes told suggests that the emergent university was able to move towards reason just to the extent that it attained freedom from captivity to religious tradition and devotion.[1] I shall argue, however, for a different construal of the story. University reason emerges not *over against* Christian devotion, but *as a form of* Christian devotion. The practice of reason in Paris may well have been uneven, but where it faltered the cause was not a surfeit of Christian faith and practice but a lack—and it may therefore not be so very strange an idea to write a Christian theology of higher education, speaking from within a tradition of Christian faith and practice to call the university to reason.

UNIVERSITY ORIGINS

In the twelfth century, a scholastic education was increasingly seen as the passport to a career (administrative, perhaps, or legal or medical), and more

---

[1] For instance, Hastings Rashdall (see below, p. 16) could write that the emergence of the university represented 'the reawakening of the European mind from the torpor of centuries' (Rashdall, *The Universities of Europe in the Middle Ages* (ed. F. M. Powicke and A. B. Emden), i. *Salerno, Bologna, Paris* (Oxford: Oxford University Press, 1936), 33).

and more people went in search of a good school.[2] Paris under the Capetian kings, a secure and prosperous city, was an attractive destination for such scholars, and royal and episcopal patronage enabled its schools to flourish.[3] In many other places, education fell clearly under a single jurisdiction: a cathedral school under episcopal control, perhaps, or a monastic school under the control of the abbot. In Paris, however, a variety of schools were able to emerge without a single effective jurisdiction uniting them all.[4] The control exercised by the bishops of Paris (through a chancellor appointed for the purpose) seems to have been at best uneven. It was not just that it had become customary for the canons of Notre Dame to let their houses to masters and students, allowing the establishment of multiple small schools close to the cathedral; the chancellors' rights of appointment and regulation might still have welded these into a unified system. Rather, it was the rapid growth of the city (it had a population of at least 25,000 by 1215) that stretched the chancellors' powers until they became purely formal: they increasingly exercised their monopoly simply by charging a fee to any master wishing to set up schools of his own. And even this attenuated form of control did not extend everywhere; there were gaps in episcopal jurisdiction, where the chancellor's power ceased to function altogether. It was possible, for instance, to step from the Ile de la Cité to the left bank of the Seine, to the purview of the abbey of Ste Geneviève, and to be outside episcopal jurisdiction. Academic life in Paris was therefore 'relatively free from control and regulation'.[5]

These conditions were enough to trigger a self-sustaining expansion. The favourable facilities and relative freedom attracted good masters; good masters attracted increasing numbers of ambitious students; the high number of students made it possible for multiple masters to compete for an audience; the jurisdictional variety made it possible for a number of competing schools to flourish. The city therefore filled with students and masters.

They were all, technically, clerics, but their clerical rights and duties could not straightforwardly be regulated by episcopal or monastic authority. 'Clerics by legal status but usually lacking the accountability or the obligations of the clergy, scholars collectively represented a new and distinct social group, one

---

[2] Stephen C. Ferruolo, *The Origins of the University: The Schools of Paris and their Critics, 1100–1215* (Stanford, CA: Stanford University Press, 1985), 93–7. For this section in general, see Walter Rüegg, 'Themes', in Hilde de Ridder-Symoens (ed.), *Universities in the Middle Ages* (Cambridge: Cambridge University Press, 1992), 3–34: 9–14.

[3] Ferruolo, *Origins*, 12–16; John W. Baldwin, 'Masters at Paris from 1179–1215: A Social Perspective', in Robert L. Benson and Giles Constable (eds), *Renaissance and Renewal in the Twelfth Century* (Cambridge, MA: Harvard University Press, 1982), 138–72: 140–2.

[4] Ferruolo, *Origins*, 17–25; R. W. Southern, 'The School of Paris and the School of Chartres', in Benson and Constable (eds), *Renaissance and Renewal*, 113–37: 119–21; John W. Baldwin, *Masters, Princes and Merchants: The Social Views of Peter the Chanter and his Circle 1: Text* (Princeton: Princeton University Press, 1970), 72.

[5] Ferruolo, *Origins*, 16.

that did not fit neatly into existing moral categories.'[6] Such ambiguity might have been sustainable had the numbers of people involved been small, but in twelfth-century Paris it posed a serious threat to social order. Rather than accept reabsorption under some existing jurisdiction, however, the masters of Paris began to seek—and to receive—royal and papal support for, and definition of, their rights and duties.[7] They became in the process a new jurisdiction of their own: a self-governing academic guild.

The term *universitas* originally designated only this simple fact: the academics of Paris were increasingly recognized as a legally constituted, self-governing corporation—a guild responsible for regulating the behaviour of masters and students, for defending their particular privileges, and for admitting and expelling masters.[8] That this particular guild was an academic one was not denoted by the term *universitas*, but by the term *studium*—or, as the thirteenth century progressed, by the term *studium generale*, which seems to have meant a *studium* that catered for more than local students, that had multiple masters, and that could admit students to at least one of the higher faculties (theology, law, or medicine). Eventually it also implied that, in principle though often not in practice, graduates from this *studium* had the right to teach in other schools without being re-examined; that is, it implied that the education provided in this *studium* was regarded as having a more-than-local currency, and as inducting its graduates into an international educational fraternity.[9]

The university that emerged was 'rooted in utilitarian soil',[10] serving 'the ecclesiastical, governmental and professional requirements of society'.[11] The

---

[6] Ferruolo, *Origins*, 206. Cf. Baldwin, *Masters, Princes and Merchants*, 73.

[7] Ferruolo notes a paradoxical element of the story of relations between the monastic orders and the university. Discussing the activity of various monastic critics of the secular schools, he says: 'In an indirect and quite unintended way, the reformers' persistent struggle to keep the monks and regular clerics out of the schools and to keep secular students out of the cloister seems to have contributed to the formation of the university. Not only had monastic opposition to the schools provided an additional impetus to the masters' effort to reform and to regulate their own affairs, but the exclusion of monks and regular clerics from the schools had also helped the masters to develop their own professional consciousness. Not bound by any strong ties to already existing orders, communities, or schools, the secular masters and scholars were motivated by their common professional identity and interests as teachers to form a single corporation' (Ferruolo, *Origins*, 314–15).

[8] Rashdall, *Universities of Europe*, 4–6; Alan B. Cobban, *The Medieval English Universities: Oxford and Cambridge to c.1500* (Aldershot: Scolar Press, 1988), 2; Jacques Verger, 'Patterns', in Ridder-Symoens (ed.), *Universities in the Middle Ages*, 35–74: 37–8.

[9] Rashdall, *Universities of Europe*, 6–17; Cobban, *Medieval English Universities*, 3–5; Verger, 'Patterns', 35–7.

[10] Alan B. Cobban, 'Reflections on the Role of the Medieval Universities in Contemporary Society', in Lesley Smith and Benedicta Ward (eds), *Intellectual Life in the Middle Ages: Essays Presented to Margaret Gibson* (London: Hambledon, 1992), 227–41: 227.

[11] Cobban, *Medieval English Universities*, 10; cf. Cobban, 'Reflections', 227; R. W. Southern, 'The Changing Role of Universities in Medieval Europe', *Historical Research*, 60/142 (1987),

average student sought to ready himself for future employment by gaining 'mastery of a challenging discipline, the sharpening of the critical faculties, the ability to expound logically, the careful digestion of approved knowledge'.[12] The kings who supported the emergent university sought 'effective intellectual and individual help in establishing and consolidating the governmental and administrative institutions they needed to overcome the centrifugal forces embodied in the landed and urban aristocracies'.[13] The popes who supported the university sought 'to strengthen the position of a rationally intelligible doctrine amidst the diverse and mutually contradictory beliefs of the various religious orders and scholars; they were particularly concerned to carry on a battle against the expanding heresies'.[14] All these forms of utility, however, depended upon the capacity of the new university to inculcate and sustain a commitment to rigorous and methodical enquiry in both masters and students, and so the university became the home for the refinement of the tools of such enquiry, and for the preservation and unification of its results.

THE TRIUMPH OF FREE ENQUIRY

This story of the emergence of the University of Paris (a contingent one that would need to be told rather differently were our subject Salerno, Bologna, or Oxford) is simply the skeleton on which the flesh of the myth of university origins is disposed. The great historian of university origins, Hastings Rashdall (1858–1924), provides the clearest and most influential example: for him, this is the dramatic dénouement reversing the tale of learning's decline in the 'darkest age in the intellectual history of Europe',[15] an age in which 'all culture that was not obviously and immediately useful was doomed to extinction' (p. 27), and in which classical education had been 'completely swept away' (p. 26).[16] Admittedly, in the narrow and exigent cells of the monasteries, and in the Carolingian cathedral schools, some of the traditions of classical learning 'for a time survived' (p. 26), and 'there were at least a few monasteries

---

133–46; and F. M. Powicke, 'The Medieval University in Church and Society', in *Ways of Medieval Life and Thought: Essays and Addresses* (London: Oldhams, 1949), 198–212.

[12] Cobban, 'Reflections', 230.

[13] Rüegg, 'Themes', 18.

[14] Rüegg, 'Themes', 15–16.

[15] Rashdall, *Universities of Europe*, 26; subsequent page references in text.

[16] In Rashdall's narrative, Islam is almost wholly absent, except in so far as the Arabs were the passive transmitters of Aristotelian texts, and in so far as the threat of Islamic invasion made for the fortification of Italian towns and so helped generate the new civic context in which south European universities would flourish. The possibility of a broader Islamic influence is mentioned in a footnote by Rashdall's later editors, F. M. Powicke and A. B. Emdem, only to be dismissed (Rashdall, *Universities of Europe*, 3 n.1). Cf. n. 33 below.

or cathedrals which kept alive a succession of comparatively well-educated ecclesiastics' (p. 30). In other words, all had not quite been lost: despite the surrounding darkness 'the torch was handed on from one generation to another' and 'seeds...had been sown' (p. 30) that were lying dormant and hidden until the weather changed. Twelfth-century Paris provided the spring in which those seeds could germinate: with the re-establishment of 'order and peace, leisure and security', says Rashdall, 'passion for inquiry took the place of the old routine' (p. 32), and the 'reawakening of the European mind' began (p. 33).

For Rashdall, the hero of this reawakening is undoubtedly Abelard (1079–1142), 'the clear-headed logician, the bold and independent moral philosopher, and the daring theologian' (p. 63).[17] Originally destined by his family 'to the profession of arms', he took up instead the 'warfare of the schools', and dared 'openly to combat the principles of his teacher' (p. 50). He was 'the true founder of the scholastic theology', and it was he who 'inaugurated the intellectual movement out of which [the universities] eventually sprang' (p. 43). Above all in the method of his enquiry and of his teaching, in his 'spirit of free inquiry' and 'individual loyalty to truth' (p. 59), he was the champion of 'that principle of free inquiry which it is the highest function of a university to enshrine' (p. 62), and so 'the intellectual progenitor of the University of Paris' (p. 44). 'In Abelard...[the] consciousness of the power of thought, which now began to take the place of the timid dialectic and conventional theology of the Dark Ages, found its fullest and most brilliant exponent' (p. 49). In him we see 'a mighty striving of the human spirit' (p. 63).[18]

The heart of Abelard's achievement, and the heart of the intellectual movement that he inaugurated and represented, is to be found in dialectic,

---

[17] Marcia Colish notes that this tendency to idolize Abelard is widespread. 'As a theologian no less than as a logician, Peter Abelard has been hailed as the father of scholasticism. Both in the rules for critiquing authorities laid out at the beginning of his *Sic et non*, and in his challenge in the *Dialogus*, that believers need to bolster their creeds with rational arguments, he takes to the field as the emblematic opponent of Bernard of Clairvaux, their standoff representing the last ditch effort of monastic obscurantism to halt the advance of scholastic enlightenment' (Marcia L. Colish, 'Abelard and Theology', in Stephanie Hayes-Healy (ed.), *Medieval Paradigms: Essays in Honour of Jeremy Duquesnay Adams* (New York: Palgrave Macmillan, 2005), i. 3–12: 3; repr. in Colish, *Studies in Scholasticism* (Aldershot: Ashgate, 2006), §VII). She might have had Rashdall in mind: 'not all the efforts of his malicious persecutor St Bernard could succeed in putting out the conflagration which the teaching of Abelard had kindled' (Hastings Rashdall, *Ideas and Ideals: Comments on Theology, Ethics and Metaphysics*, ed. H. D. A. Major and F. L. Cross (Oxford: Basil Blackwell, 1928), 161).

[18] Of course, Abelard's story is not a straightforward one. He did indeed suffer 'a moral downfall which...gave some colour to the arguments of men to whom that spirit of rationalism which Abelard represented seemed a direct inspiration of the Evil one', and he became the victim of 'undeserved persecutions' (p. 54) at the hands of 'intolerant ecclesiastical imbecility' (p. 58). Nevertheless, 'it is evident that the intellect of the age was with Abelard' (p. 58).

'the one treasure snatched from the wreckage of a bygone civilization' (p. 39). Of course, his dialectical skill was expended on theological questions; after all, 'intellectual activity stimulated by dialectic, intellectual curiosity aroused by the glimpses of old-world philosophy . . . had no material on which to expend themselves, except what was supplied by the Scriptures, the Fathers, and the doctrinal system of the Church' (p. 42). Nevertheless, it is the method that matters, not the content; and in dialectic Abelard and his co-workers had access to a set of procedures for cleaning out the Augean stables of the Dark Age mind. Free enquiry and rationalism impose themselves on the positive and the traditional, ordering, ventilating, and cleansing.[19]

Rashdall's tone and vocabulary are very much of his time, but the myth he passed on is still alive and well. A clear but unexceptional example can be found in the introduction that Michael Markowski provides to his translation of the Prologue to Abelard's *Sic et non*. It is, he says, 'a ringing declaration of the "liberating" ethos of education. Universities, Colleges and the Liberal Arts were being invented at that very time in order to free people's minds, and to fix a failing educational system. Abelard's own contribution was so startling, so new, so full of possibilities, that it threatened the authoritarian and tradition-based ruling classes.'[20] Abelard is, for Markowski, a hero of educational reform, opposed to authority, tradition, and obscurantism, and the ideal that his reform embodies is one that may still guide the university today.

A more sober example of something like the same storyline can be found in Edward Grant's *God and Reason in the Middle Ages*. Intent upon demonstrating that the medieval period was, in its own way, an age of reason,[21] Grant

---

[19]   For all that Rashdall insists that Abelard's spark found dry tinder in the twelfth century, such that he can truly be called the father of the university, he also makes it clear that the full potential of Abelard's method and spirit was not realized immediately. Certainly none of his immediate followers had anything like his spark—Peter Lombard, for instance, may have championed the form of dialectic, but he wholly lacked Abelard's spirit. 'In Abelard we must recognize incomparably the greatest intellect of the Middle Ages . . . in the Lombard we descend from the mountain to the plain' (pp. 58–9). In fact, Rashdall's narrative has a much longer timescale in view: 'in his advocacy of the rights of private judgment', he says at one point, Abelard was 'anticipating the sixteenth century' (p. 63); implicitly, it is clear that Rashdall actually saw Abelard as a hero for the late nineteenth century and the early twentieth. P. E. Matheson, *The Life of Hastings Rashdall D.D.* (Oxford: Oxford University Press; London: Humphrey Milford, 1928), 78 n. 1, records that Rashdall was known as the 'Socrates of the Cornmarket', whose students, gathered in a dedicated group around him and taken on long walks 'talking philosophy and Biblical criticism all the time', learnt to think of him as a 'great and fearless seeker after truth' (p. 80). It is hard not to feel that Rashdall had adopted Abelard as the patron saint of his own ideals.

[20]   Michael Markowski, 'Peter Abelard's *Sic et Non*: The Master Key to Wisdom' (2005) <http://web.archive.org/web/20101203203627/http://people.westminstercollege.edu/faculty/mmarkowski/Hall/Abelard.htm> (accessed 23 July 2009). The other texts Markowski provides to illustrate this intellectual vision are Kant's *What is Enlightenment?*, and (intriguingly) an extract from Athanasius' *Life of Antony*, on giving up everything for the sake of the Kingdom of Heaven.

[21]   From the twelfth century: 'In a real sense, Western Europe became a society obsessed with reason, which it consciously employed in many, if not most, of its activities. Nothing like it had

insists that the twelfth century saw a newly self-conscious, intensive, and institutionalized application of reason (p. 9). Admittedly, this reason was on the whole restricted to agreement with revelation and with Christian tradition (a restriction that was not to be lifted until later centuries), but within that boundary it nevertheless flourished. Abelard himself may not feature as Grant's hero, but Grant's description of the reason that the new universities embodied, and that flourished in the subsequent centuries, has very much the scent of Rashdall's patron saint: reason provides—in an implicit triumph over the obscurantism prevailing before the twelfth century—a method for freeing thought from the constriction of purely individual or sectarian perspective; it is a method that can be used by all, that can convince all who are rational, that yields truth that is truth for all; it therefore provided the occupants of the medieval university with a proper methodological impersonality, allowing them to aspire to a God's-eye view of the world.[22] Other examples are not hard to find; Rashdall's mythic narrative is a resilient one.

THE DECLINE OF WISDOM

Of course, this myth of university origins has generated counter-narratives. One of the most powerful of these is presented in C. Stephen Jaeger's *The Envy of Angels*. To sum up in a slogan, where Grant sees the triumph of impersonal reason, Jaeger sees the loss of personal learning.

Jaeger guides his readers through the secular schools from 950 to 1100, in the period before the changes that presaged the establishment of the university. The curriculum of those schools, he says, was a matter, on the one hand, of manners or *conversatio*, 'the discipline of conduct',[23] training in virtue and nobility (p. 25), and, on the other hand, of letters or *eloquentia*, the 'study of prose and verse composition based on classical models' (p. 3). This curriculum was profoundly *personal*: 'The vitality and continuity of secular learning in the period 950–1100 are not to be found in texts and artifacts, but in personalities and in the cultivation of personal qualities' (pp. 3–4); its product was 'the controlled body with all its attributes—grace, posture, charm, sensuality, beauty, authority' (p. 7); its mode of teaching inherently embodied and charismatic: 'The physical presence of an educated man

---

ever been seen' (Edward Grant, *God and Reason in the Middle Ages* (Cambridge: Cambridge University Press, 2001), 18).

[22] Grant, *God and Reason*, 11, drawing on Stephen Nathanson, *The Ideal of Rationality* (Atlantic Highlands, NJ: Humanities Press International, 1985), 10.

[23] C. Stephen Jaeger, *The Envy of Angels: Cathedral Schools and Social Ideals in Medieval Europe, 950–1200* (Philadelphia, PA: University of Pennsylvania Press, 1994), 3; subsequent page references in text.

possessed a high pedagogic value; his composure and bearing, his conduct of life, themselves constituted a form of discourse, intelligible and learnable' (p. 80).

Jaeger agrees that a deep cultural shift was under way as the eleventh century gave way to the twelfth, noting some of the terms in which this shift has been described by others: it was a shift from authority to reason (as in Rashdall and Grant); a shift in Eucharistic theology from real presence to symbolic; a shift in philosophy from realism to nominalism; a shift in politics from itinerant to administrative kingship; a shift in ecclesiastical polity from charismatic leadership to canonical procedure; a shift more generally from orality to textuality. For Jaeger, however, the connecting pattern is a transition from the embodied to the symbolic, or from performance to representation—a transition he sees epitomized by the transition from *actual* bodily training in the presence of masters who were taken to be the embodiment of the goal sought, to an educational goal only verbally represented, in the fictionalized and aestheticized 'perfect man' of Alan of Lille or Bernard Silvester (p. 14), or the 'wise virgin' of Bernard of Clairvaux (p. 13).

In Jaeger's reading, then, the twelfth century does not echo to the noise of bold steps forward for the human spirit, but with *nostalgia*.

The greatness of its art, its sculpture and its architecture, its literature, its learned humanist allegories, is in part a response to nostalgic desire, the testimony to a vast project aimed at capturing in symbolic representation the fading charisma that the previous age enjoyed—real, full, vital, embodied, and functioning as bearer of cultural ideals ... The results of that striving in the intellectual and artistic realm are what we call the 'twelfth-century renaissance'. (p. 9)

The works of the humanists of the twelfth century are simply 'shoring to stave off the inevitable collapse of a culture passing out of existence'.

One particular aspect of this transition is of central importance for my purposes: a transition from peace to violence. The educational ideology of the eleventh century stressed the necessity of a shared life of students and masters (p. 24) shaped by humility and, above all, by friendship (p. 37); it saw individual ambition as a threat, disputatious defeat of one's masters as unthinkable. 'In the eleventh century', Jaeger writes, 'it was perilous to contradict and argue with the teacher, to doubt and to assert the value of one's own opinions over the authority of the text and the teacher. It was a violation of the rule of love and peace' (p. 193).

Jaeger takes us to a school in Würzburg in 1030, whose students idealized it as 'an Elysian realm, an academy of poetry and virtue, its students a harmonious community of loving friends, knit together as "by a single vow"' (p. 72). In the twelfth century, however, 'the days of loving and emotional colloquies in cloister gardens between a revered master and a handful of socially and intellectually elite disciples were past, and in their place was an atmosphere of strident contention idealized and described in the language of military combat' (p. 241).[24]

It should not be surprising to find that Abelard plays the role not of hero but of villain in Jaeger's narrative. Abelard explicitly rejected the veneration of his charismatic teachers, breaking what the previous century would have seen as the rule of love binding master and student; he gloried in the disputatious, the martial; he cut at the conceptual underpinnings that held the old order together, the thrust of his ethical thought being 'to abolish the outer man as the textbook and artwork of moral training' (p. 234). He epitomizes the breakdown of the personal, peaceable order.

Abelard provides ample ammunition for this characterization in his *Historia calamitatum*. His father had intended him to become a knight, but, he says, 'I renounced the glory of a military life . . . I preferred the weapons of dialectic to all the other teachings of philosophy, and armed with these I chose the conflicts of disputation instead of the trophies of war.'[25] Speaking of his arguments with William of Champeaux, he says,

The argumentative clashes [*conflictus disputationum*] which followed William's return to the city between my pupils and him and his followers, and the successes in these battles [*in his bellis*] which fortune gave my people (myself among them) are facts which you have long known. And I shall not go too far if I boldly say with Ajax that *If you demand the issue of this fight / I was not vanquished by my enemy.*[26]

Under Abelard's feet, the schools turn into a muddy battlefield.[27]

[24] This is in part a matter of numbers. A small group gathered around a master could sustain the kind of charismatic education Jaeger sees as characteristic of the earlier period; once classes have grown to become crowds, the model is inevitably available only as a nostalgic reference point.

[25] Peter Abelard, *Historia calamitatum* 1 in *The Letters of Abelard and Heloise*, ed. and tr. Betty Radice and M. T. Clanchy, rev. edn (London: Penguin, 2003), 3.

[26] Abelard, *Historia* 2, in *Letters of Abelard and Heloise*, 6, translation slightly altered; Latin text available at <www.thelatinlibrary.com/abelard/historia.html> (accessed 27 Aug. 2009). See M. T. Clanchy, *Abelard: A Medieval Life* (Oxford: Blackwell, 1999), 145, for questions about Abelard's 'victory' in these battles.

[27] Herrad of Landsberg's *Hortus Deliciarum*, written between 1167 and 1185, provides an apt symbol of the new age ushered in by Abelard. In a famous image of *philosophia* surrounded by the seven liberal arts, *diale[c]tica* (the art on which Abelard's fame and the distinctiveness of the new scholasticism were based) appears as a woman carrying a dog's head; around her, the motto reads: *argumenta sino concurrere more canino*—I allow arguments to collide in the manner of dogs. See *Herrad von Landsperg, Aebtissin zu Hohenburg, oder St Odilien, im Elsass, in zwölften Jahrhundert und ihr Werk: Hortus deliciarum*, ed. Christian Engelhardt (Stuttgart: J. G. Cotta, 1818); reproduced online at the Bibliothèque Alsatique, <bacm.creditmutuel.fr/HORTUS_ PLANCHE_8.html>, and in higher resolution at Wikimedia Commons <upload.wikimedia.org/wikipedia/commons/7/71/Septem-artes-liberales_Herrad-von-Landsberg_Hortus-deliciarum_1180.jpg> (both accessed 26 Aug. 2009).

DEVOUT REASON

Both Rashdall's narrative and Jaeger's counter-narrative rely on versions of the same plot, in which the intellectual developments of the twelfth century (and the eventual emergence of the university in the thirteenth) are secured *over against* earlier patterns of intellectual life: that is, over against the personal, charismatic, and embodied or over against the traditional, obscurantist, and constricted, depending on your point of view. It is, however, possible to tell the story rather differently, by pointing beyond all the evident discontinuities to a significant line of continuity linking intellectual practices before and after the emergence of the university. Specifically, it is possible to see the emergence of the university as, in part, an experiment within an ongoing tradition of devout learning, and as involving the development of at least some practices of reason that were reasonable precisely *because* they were devout. Of course, the story of continuity that I will tell is only one, partially successful way of characterizing the emergence of the university: there were other aspects of intellectual development, and other aspects of devotional development, that my narrative does not capture. Even its partial success, however, is enough to disrupt the opposition between devotion and reason that powers standard versions of the Parisian myth. Reason and devotion cannot be unthinkingly taken to vary in inverse proportion to one another; in some respects at least they run hand in hand.

I have taken the cue for my account from a comment made by Hilduin, chancellor of the Parisian schools from *c.*1178 to 1193. He said that monks and scholars were both *contemplatives*, the former contemplatives devoted to prayer, the latter contemplatives devoted to study.[28] Versions of the same claim had already been made by his predecessor Peter Comestor (chancellor from 1168 to 1178) and would be made again by his follower, Peter of Poitiers (*c.*1130–1215, chancellor from 1193). Stephen Langton (*c.*1150–1228), who was a master in Paris until called to Rome in 1206, could even say that of the two types of contemplatives, each devoted to study, meditation, and prayer, the monks are devoted more to prayer and the scholars more to study *and more to meditation.*[29]

---

[28] Quoted by Ferruolo, *Origins*, 208, 351: '*Sunt autem duo genera contemplativorum. Alii enim sunt claustrales, alii vero scolares. Claustrales vacant orationi, scolares vero lectioni*' (from the sermon *Exsulta satis filiae Syon*, Cambridge UL Ii.I.24, fo. 168[vb]).

[29] 'There are two kinds of contemplatives, the cloistered and scholars; but, since contemplation consists in three things—study, meditation, and prayer—the cloistered are more frequently devoted to prayer, and the scholars more frequently to study and meditation. Also, the meditation of contemplatives can be divided in two. Some meditation strains itself to reach the heavenly court, to the state of the republic of that supreme city, and to the understanding of the incomprehensible mysteries of God, which cannot be understood in any other way; and this meditation is more familiar to the cloistered. The other meditation is occupied with divine law, and this is more suitable to scholars' (*Qui descendunt mare*, Paris BN lat. 3495, fo. 202[r]/BN

My attempt to repair the myth of university origins therefore begins by placing contemplation, or more specifically meditation, centre stage. What we find in the emergent university is a practice of devout reason, driven by a form of *meditatio* with striking continuities with monastic *meditatio*, despite all the obvious differences.[30] Such *meditatio* provides the bridge between the two dominant practices of scholastic learning, *lectio* and *disputatio*.[31] *Lectio* is 'meditative reading', both a route into *meditatio*, and itself already a form of *meditatio*; *meditatio* is the 'marking and learning' involved in *lectio*.[32] *Disputatio*, the conduct of public argument, testing the reasons offered for and against a particular claim, is one public form by which this *lectio*-driven scholastic *meditatio* proceeds.[33]

lat.14804, fo. 160rb; translated in Ferruolo, *Origins*, 208–9; he argues for the attribution to Langton at 351 n. 75).

[30] Were my concerns purely historical, I would probably avoid the use of the word 'reason' here and in what follows. In medieval terms, I am interested in *studium*, and in the practices of *lectio* and *disputatio* that are its primary forms. Nevertheless, given my wider concerns, it helps to name these as forms of the practice of reason, or as active forms of rationality—even though that usage is not one I have found in the primary texts.

[31] 'When the word of God is crushed by the millstone of *lectio*, ground by the pestle of *disputatio*, and then cooked in the pot of the mind by assiduous *meditatio*, "it teaches, corrects, reproves and trains" (2 Tim 3:16) and thus, like oil, it feeds, refreshes, lubricates, and illuminates' (Stephen Langton, *Legimus filios Israel*—his inaugural lecture as a master of theology—ed. Phyllis Barzillay Roberts in *Stephanus de Lingua-Tonante: Studies in the Sermons of Stephen Langton* (Toronto: Pontifical Institute of Medieval Studies, 1968), 226–37: 233; translated in Ferruolo, *Origins*, 256–7). For the place of lectures and disputations in medieval universities, see Rainer Christoph Schwinges, 'Student Education, Student Life', in Ridder-Symoens (ed.), *Universities in the Middle Ages*, 194–243: 232–3.

[32] 'Reading was an action of the whole person, by which the meaning of a text was absorbed, until it became prayer' (Benedicta Ward, 'Introduction', in *The Prayers and Meditations of Saint Anselm, with the Proslogion* (London: Penguin, 1973), 25–86: 43–4).

[33] My emphasis at this stage will fall primarily on the shape of reasoning as a practice or a way of life, or as the characteristic activity of a polity. That is, I will, on the one hand, not be focusing directly on the explicit accounts of reason (of truth or of epistemology, perhaps) that eleventh- to thirteenth-century authors produced, and I will not, on the other, be returning immediately to the complex story of the university's emergence as a legally recognized self-governing corporation. My approach bears some comparison to that of George Makdisi. He too attempted to repair the myth of university origins in order to expose an underlying and often overlooked continuity—in his case between Christian and Islamic scholasticism. Islamic scholars, he argued, get sidelined in the existing myth of university origins. 'It is standard procedure for the most part to limit their role to that of a conduit for the philosophy and science of the Greeks on its way to the West, through the Islamic East, by way of Muslim Spain. We readily grant that they passed Greek learning on to us. At best, we begrudge them a role beyond that of mere transmitters of a legacy; at worst, we blame them for having adulterated that legacy' (George Makdisi, 'The Scholastic Method in Medieval Education: An Inquiry into its Origins in Law and Theology', *Speculum*, 49/4 (1974), 640–61: 641). Cf. n. 16 above. While acknowledging that at the level of institutional polity the Islamic and Christian cases look very different, he identifies three core practices that connect Islamic and Christian scholasticism: *sic et non*, *dialectica*, and *disputatio*. I have simply broadened *sic et non* to *lectio*, and *dialectica* to *meditatio*. See also his 'Madrasa and University in the Middle Ages', *Studia Islamica*, 32 (1970), 255–64; *The Rise of Colleges: Institutions of Learning in Islam and the West* (Edinburgh: Edinburgh University Press, 1981);

The other step that I have taken in my attempt to reframe the myth of university origins is the location of a vantage point away from the university, from which its emergence can be seen differently. It is provided by a thoroughly monastic thinker who, though an innovator in the medieval practice of reason, was not in any direct way instrumental in the creation of the university: Anselm of Canterbury.[34] I will be focusing in particular on his writing of the *Monologion* and *Proslogion*, meditations that are clearly the work of a monastic contemplative, steeped in practices of prayerful *meditatio*, but that are also exemplary practices of devout reasoning.[35] It is precisely because they hold together reason and devotion that these works of Anselm provide the vantage point I need. From him, I will look towards the reasoning practices of the emergent university—the lectures and disputations—but also to the backdrop to those practices provided in the works of a group whom Stephen Ferruolo christened the 'Moralists': twelfth- and thirteenth-century Parisian preachers whose sermons to masters and students were influential in shaping the emergent university, and whose ideas are probably as close as we can get to plumbing the official ideology of learning in that university.[36]

---

and *The Rise of Humanism in Classical Islam and the Christian West, with Special Reference to Scholasticism* (Edinburgh: Edinburgh University Press, 1990).

[34] I have, as I say, not chosen Anselm as any kind of forerunner or hero of the university, but simply because he provides a vantage point outside the university from which university reason's distinctive features can be seen more clearly—but see Giulio D'Onofrio (ed.), *History of Theology*, ii. *The Middle Ages*, tr. Matthew O'Connell (Collegeville, MN: Liturgical Press, 2008), 164–70. Rashdall has no place for Anselm in his history of the emergence of the university, because Anselm's intellectual vigour was 'entirely subordinated to authority' (*Universities of Europe*, 42).

[35] The *Monologion* and *Proslogion* were written between 1076 and 1078, before Anselm became abbot in 1078. See R. W. Southern, *Saint Anselm: A Portrait in a Landscape* (Cambridge: Cambridge University Press, 2000), 113, 117. Anselm called the *Monologion* 'an example of meditation on the meaning of faith' (referring back to it in the *Proslogion* Preface, in Anselm of Canterbury, *The Major Works*, ed. Brian Davies and G. R. Evans, tr. M. J. Charlesworth (Oxford: Oxford University Press, 1998), 83). There are, of course, other works in the Anselmian corpus in which the continuities between monastic meditation and rigorous reason are far less evident— *De grammatico*, for instance. Once one has seen the fundamentally devout nature of the *Monologion* and *Proslogion*, however (once, for instance, one has seen the deep continuities with Anselm's other prayers and meditations), it becomes difficult to sustain the claim that *De grammatico* and other works are rationally rigorous *because*, or *in so far as*, they eschew the trappings of devotion—and easier to see how some of the ways in which those other works are rational (their dependence upon a process of attentive *lectio*, fuelled by a restless desire for coherent articulation of the order inherent in the material, and driven by interior *disputatio*) parallel the deepest patterns of Anselm's devotion.

[36] See Ferruolo, *Origins*, 184–277. He includes in this category two bishops of Paris: Peter Lombard (bishop from 1158–1160) and Maurice of Sully (bishop from 1160–1196); five episcopal chancellors of the Parisian schools: Odo of Soissons (chancellor from *c*.1153 or 1160–7), Peter Comestor (1168–78), Hilduin (1178–93), Peter of Poitiers (1193–1205), and Prévostin of Cremona (1206–9); and a number of prominent masters: Robert Pullen (d. 1146), Raoul Ardent (d. *c*.1200), Simon of Tournai (*c*.1130–1201), Alan of Lille (*c*.1128–1202), Alexander Neckham (1157–1217), Stephen Langton (*c*.1150–1228), and Jacques de Vitry (d. 1240).

LECTIO AND *MEDITATIO*

Richard Southern, in his discussion of the *Monologion*, argues that for Anselm *meditatio* was 'the central activity of disciplined spirits in this life', but that Anselm's meditation was unusual because it did not have its origin 'in the reading of an authoritative text—*lectio*'.[37] He contrasts this with the account provided half a century later by Hugh of St Victor: 'Meditation is frequent and mature thought about the cause, origin, nature and usefulness of everything. It has its origin in careful reading, but it is bound by none of the rules or constraints of reading . . . The *foundation* of doctrine, therefore, lies in reading; its *completion* in meditation.'[38] Southern's comment is, however, potentially misleading. When Anselm sent a copy of the *Monologion* to Lanfranc in Canterbury, asking for his approval (and for help in choosing a title), Lanfranc challenged Anselm to cite his authorities—that is, to name explicitly the tracts of *lectio* upon which his argument was built. Anselm responded by saying, in effect, 'It is all in Augustine.'

It was my intention throughout this disputation [*disputatio*] to assert nothing which could not be immediately defended either from canonical *Dicta* or from the words of St Augustine. And however often I look over what I have written, I cannot see that I have asserted anything that is not to be found there. Indeed, no reasoning of my own, however conclusive, would have persuaded me to have been the first to presume to say those things which you have copied from my work, nor several other things besides, if St Augustine had not already proved them in the great discussions in his *De Trinitate*. I found them argued at length in this work, and explained them briefly [*breviori ratiocinatione*] on his authority in my shorter chain of argument.[39]

The *brevitas* at which Anselm aims is, as Mary Carruthers has explained, one of the 'basic notions of monastic meditational practice': the division of an unmanageably large text into digestible chunks for the sake of easy and flexible recall and recombination.[40] Anselm's pursuit of *brevitas* stands in continuity with this practice: he has produced an extraction, rearrangement, and representation of the ideas that his ongoing *lectio* has unearthed in Augustine's *De Trinitate*. There is no reason to doubt the sincerity of Anselm's claim: the foundation of his meditation in the *Monologion* is *lectio*, and the process by which the *Monologion* was formed was a long, meditative steeping of the

---

[37] Southern, *Saint Anselm*, 79, 122.
[38] *Didascalion* 3.10, in *The Didascalion of Hugh of St Victor: A Medieval Guide to the Arts*, tr. Jerome Taylor (New York: Columbia University Press, 1961), 214–15; emphasis in original.
[39] Anselm, Epistle 77, translated in Southern, *Saint Anselm*, 71–2.
[40] Mary Carruthers, *The Craft of Thought: Meditation, Rhetoric, and the Making of Images, 400–1200* (Cambridge: Cambridge University Press, 2000), 63.

material garnered by *lectio*.[41] His method of *lectio–meditatio* certainly allows him considerable freedom (a potentially shocking, and certainly unusual, freedom in his day),[42] but it is a freedom funded by (rather than established against) his immersion in the authoritative texts of his tradition. As Southern puts it, 'his immersion in Augustine, as in the Bible, *gave* him freedom'.[43]

The raw material of the tradition harvested by *lectio* is not, however, always readily ordered; it is not immediately and wholly transparent. For Anselm, animated by a desire for order, for clarity, for a unification of the material of his faith, *meditatio* is the labour involved in disentangling and articulating the materials of *lectio*.[44]

He wrote in the Prologue to the *Monologion* that 'whatever the conclusion of independent investigation should declare to be true, should, in an unadorned style, with common proofs and with a simple argument, be briefly enforced by the cogency of reason, and plainly expounded in the light of truth'.[45] As Brian Stock explains,

Anselm means, in effect, to discuss, to comment upon, and to produce a new text... Through the interior dialogue [of meditation], a summary of biblical and patristic authority becomes a 'text' before actually being written down. The 'cogency of reason' to which he refers is in reality the text's principle of organization. Anselm, therefore, plays the role [*persona*] of someone in conversation with himself who both internalizes a textual methodology and anticipates a written product.[46]

---

[41] 'The thorough Augustinianism of his earliest work makes itself apparent not in quotations but in the deep structure of the thought and in the assumptions on which he works' (G. R. Evans, *Anselm* (London: Geoffrey Chapman, 1989), 38).

[42] 'He does not allow the texts [of his *lectio*] to shape the overall sequence of the thought. It is hard to emphasize sufficiently how unusual this was' (Evans, *Anselm*, 38).

[43] Southern, *Saint Anselm*, 73; emphasis added.

[44] It is not just his faith that he seeks to articulate, if that is taken to mark off some specific domain of his life and thought. It is the world. Anselm assumes that through faith's own legibility, the world as a whole becomes legible: the world is such that the mess of experience (of the world and of the self) *yields* to *meditatio*, to articulation. It lends itself to the articulated arrangement that memory can make of it. Mary Carruthers notes that the idea that the world is memorable is an approximate medieval equivalent of the modern claim that the world is measurable (Carruthers, *Craft*, 66–7). Cf. Southern, *Scholastic Humanism*, 31.

[45] Anselm, *Monologion*, Prologue, in Anselm of Canterbury, *Proslogium; Monologium; An Appendix in Behalf of the Fool by Gaunilo; and Cur Deus homo*, tr. Sidney Norton Deane (Chicago: Open Court, 1903); <www.fordham.edu/halsall/basis/anselm-intro.html> (accessed 3 Sept. 2009). This is the translation quoted by Stock, below; cf. Simon Harrison's translation in Davies and Evans' edition of *The Major Works*, 5–81: 5.

[46] Brian Stock, *The Implications of Literacy: Written Language and Models of Interpretation in the Eleventh and Twelfth Centuries* (Princeton: Princeton University Press, 1983), 334. There is a continuity between Anselm's search for rational articulation in the *Proslogion* and *Monologion* and later works, and his practice in his earlier prayers and meditations, in which he sought articulation in elegant and memorable phrases carefully patterned so that their form would mirror their content. Such articulation is aimed, inseparably, at both rhyme and reason.

To say that Anselm's *meditatio* is a practice of *articulation*, then, is to say that it provides the passage between reading and composition, between the texts of *lectio* and the articulated texts of the *Monologion*, the *Proslogion*, and the rest. And the tools of such *meditatio* are 'the rules of logic and grammar'.[47] They allow Anselm to ask of a difficult text, 'Why this word here?', and 'How does this go with that?' They provide a set of techniques and vocabularies of conceptual distinction and connection, by which the unruly, disorganized materials discovered by *lectio* can be categorized and strung into chains of connected argument.

Even the *Proslogion*, which stands, if anything, further from the coalface of *lectio* than does the *Monologion*, is ultimately driven by the same processes. On the one hand, there stands meditation on the text of Psalm 13:1: 'the Fool has said in his heart, there is no God' (and it is perfectly possible to read the *Proslogion* as one vastly extended gloss to that verse: why is the disbeliever said to be a *fool*, specifically?). On the other hand, there stands Anselm's continued restless desire to articulate further the results of his earlier meditation.

Reflecting that [the *Monologion*] was made up of a connected chain of many arguments, I began to wonder if perhaps it might be possible to find one single argument that for its proof required no other save itself... But as often as I diligently turned my thoughts to this, sometimes it seemed to me that I had almost reached what I was seeking, sometimes it eluded my acutest thinking completely, so that finally, in desperation, I was about to give up what I was looking for as something impossible to find. However, when I had decided to put aside this idea altogether, lest by uselessly occupying my mind it might prevent other ideas with which I could make some progress... it began to force itself upon me more and more pressingly.[48]

The remaining disorder of his earlier conclusions distressed him, and he sensed or hoped that a further articulation—a more articulate articulation—of the fruits of his earlier meditation might be possible. Its birth was not without its labour pains: a 'restless anxious mood' of the kind that Carruthers says 'was regarded in monastic circles as a common, even necessary preliminary to invention'—that is, to the drawing together of the materials sorted and stored by *memoria* into an articulated composition.[49] The driving force of the meditation that gives birth to the *Proslogion* is this restless desire for unity, for economy or elegance in articulation: 'one single argument'.

[47] Southern, *Saint Anselm*, 79.
[48] Anselm, *Proslogion*, Preface, tr. M. J. Charlesworth, in Anselm, *The Major Works*, 82–104: 82.
[49] Carruthers, *Craft*, 62. For the connection between reason and memory in scholasticism, see Paul J. Griffiths, 'Scholasticism: The Possible Recovery of an Intellectual Practice' in José Ignacio Cabezón, *Scholasticism: Cross-Cultural and Comparative Perspectives*, Toward a Comparative Theology of Religions (ed. Paul J. Griffiths and Lauri L. Patton) (Albany, NY: SUNY, 1998), 201–35: 214–16.

Finally, of course, the light dawns: 'So it was that one day when I was quite worn out with resisting its importunacy, there came to me, in the very conflict of my thoughts, what I had despaired of finding, so that I eagerly grasped the notion which in my distraction I had been rejecting.'[50] Anselm, as it were, *sees* a solution: he seems to grasp it all at once. His biographer Eadmer said of him that 'He put his whole mind to the task of seeing with the eye of reason those things which seemed to be hidden in the deepest obscurity', and emphasizes the visionary nature of this task by connecting it to a moment when, deep in meditation on a question about the prophets, 'giving all his energy to this question, eagerly seeking to understand it, and fixing his eyes on the walls around him . . . all at once he saw the various monks going about their tasks in different parts of the monastery as if they were in his presence'.[51] Just so, his whole mind fired with a desire to articulate further the findings of the *Monologion*, Anselm all at once saw how they hang together in a single chain, depending on nothing but itself.

Anselm's practice of reasoning—fundamentally a matter of *lectio*-driven *meditatio*—provides a vantage point from which to inspect the emergence of the university, not because he is a precursor of university reason, nor because he can stand as a 'representative' of earlier medieval practice, but simply because he provides a convenient comparison. Seen from this vantage point, two things become apparent about the emergence of the university. First, it is hard to sustain any version of the Rashdall myth of the emergence of reason *over against* tradition and devotion; second, it *is* possible to understand university reasoning as in part a new form of medieval devotional practice, or as a form of spiritual discipline.

As for the first of these: it should be clear enough by now that Anselm's own practice of reason does not lend itself to description in terms of an opposition between reason and tradition, if by 'tradition' we mean a collection of texts taken to be authorized routes to rightly ordered understanding. Even when the finished articulation is presented without the telltale citations of *lectio*, as in the *Monologion* or in the *remoto Christo* method of the *Cur Deus homo*, Anselm's reason is an aspect of his commitment to his tradition.[52]

Description in terms of such an opposition does not become any more appropriate if we turn to the rise of the *sic et non* method, absent from Anselm

[50] Anselm, *Proslogion*, Preface, in *The Major Works*, 82.
[51] Southern, *Saint Anselm*, 70–1.
[52] In the finished argument of the *Proslogion*, Anselm orbits the world effortlessly, with no apparent external support. Yet he only reached this orbit—could only conceivably have reached it—by relying on the gigantic launch vehicles of the Scriptures and the fathers. The reader who simply gazes admiringly on the orbiting craft from below need not know of the burning of meditational fuel that got Anselm there; the believer who wishes to join Anselm in orbit will certainly need to know it, and use it.

but so important to later scholasticism. After all, *sic et non* is simply one formal tool for use in the same kind of passage from *lectio* to *meditatio* that Anselm's work displays: it identifies those nubs of material that call for the work of *meditatio*. If one thinks of *lectio* as a matter of stocking one's mental treasury—a practice of that *memoria* which is always a matter of selecting and arranging, never simply a matter of stowing gathered material willy-nilly in a vast lumber room—*sic et non* is the creation on *lectio*'s to-do list of a list of snags requiring attention, matters on which *memoria*'s labour needs to be exercised. The *sic et non* method in itself does not require us to develop a narrative of progressive freedom from tradition.

Discussing *sic et non* brings us back, of course, to Abelard, even though he was by no means its first proponent.[53] His use of the method, and specifically the Prologue to his *Sic et non*, is often cited by those who see him as a champion of reason over against the obscurity of the past. Of course, some of the words of that Prologue would not have sounded strange on Anselm's lips:

When, in such a quantity of words, some of the writings of the saints seem not only to differ from, but even to contradict, each other, one should not rashly pass judgement concerning those by whom the world itself is to be judged . . . Who does not see how rash it is for one person to make a judgment concerning the sense and intelligence of another when our hearts and thoughts are revealed to God alone?[54]

At other times, Abelard's words suggest that, while his method differs in detail from Anselm's, the broad direction is the same. For instance, Abelard is doing no more than describing the role of *sic et non* as a hinge between *lectio* and *meditatio* when he says that

it seems right, as we have undertaken, to collect the diverse sayings of the Holy Fathers, which stand out in our memory to some extent due to their apparent disagreement as they focus on an issue; this may lure the weaker readers to the greatest exercise of seeking the truth, and may render them sharper readers because of the investigation. Indeed this first key of wisdom is defined, of course, as assiduous or frequent questioning.

---

[53] In the Christian West, it can be found in the work of legal scholars like Bernold of Constance (*c*.1054–1100) and Ivo of Chartres (*c*.1040–1116), and a little later Gratian (fl. *c*.1140); Makdisi traces Islamic analogues (the juristic practice of *al-khilāf*, the compilation of differing opinions), back to the eighth century (Makdisi, 'Scholastic Method', 644–9).

[54] Abelard, *Sic et non*, prologue, tr. W. J. Lewis; <www.fordham.edu/halsall/source/Abelard-SicetNon-Prologue.html> (accessed 2 Sept. 2009). It is easy to assume that these comments of Abelard's are a hypocritical attempt to make his radical approach palatable to a traditionalist readership. His actual practice as a theological writer does not, however, support such a view: he is clearly still a writer immersed in, and seeking articulation of, a tradition he regards as authoritative. See Colish, 'Abelard and Theology', *passim*.

There are, however, two aspects of the Prologue in which Abelard's distance from Anselm is apparent. In the first place, it describes a set of preliminary techniques for selecting and tidying the materials of *lectio*, techniques that may smooth the path of a *meditatio* seeking to reconcile apparent difficulties. One should be alert to the possibility of misattributed sources, or of scribal errors; one should take account of any retractions that an author may have produced, and note where an author is giving someone else's opinion rather than his own; and so on. This is a more explicit and refined repertoire of preliminary techniques for the passage from *lectio* to *meditatio* than anything to be found in Anselm, and does imply a certain kind of distancing from the texts of the tradition that one does not easily find in Anselm. And that sense of distancing is stronger in the second, more striking way in which Abelard's Prologue differs from Anselm. Abelard acknowledges that 'among such manifold writings of the Holy Fathers some things seem to be handed down or written *erroneously*', such that our task is not to articulate but to *correct*—a claim that would not necessarily have been impossible for Anselm, but to which he could hardly have given such prominence.

Yet Abelard's famous self-confidence is best understood precisely as a confidence in his power to discover and display the rational order of the doctrines of the faith. When in his *Historia calamitatum* he reports that his students asked him for a treatise on the Trinity, saying that 'nothing could be believed unless it was first understood, and that it was absurd for anyone to preach to others what neither he nor those he taught could grasp with the understanding',[55] he gives no hint that the truth of the doctrine is on trial—rather, it is his subtlety as a dialectician that is to be demonstrated over against the timidity of those who cannot or will not understand what they teach. He can declare himself 'ready to receive correction and make amends' if he has 'taught anything contrary to the Catholic faith',[56] not because he bows to the practical necessity of curbing his reason, but because he is supremely confident that his reason has been adequate to the task of explicating even the most recondite truths of the Catholic faith.

Identification of possible errors in the writings of the Fathers is a minor note in his practice of reason, dangerously close to an admission of defeat. To the extent that it does become necessary, it is possible only as a correction of the tradition for the sake of the clearer articulation of the tradition. It is a *reparative* move. What we see in Abelard's *Prologue*, therefore, is not a decisive step in a progressive journey away from tradition—an episode in the supposed 'secularization' of the twelfth-century renaissance—but a

---

[55] *Historia calamitatum* 9, in *Letters of Abelard and Heloise*, 20.
[56] *Historia calamitatum* 9, in *Letters of Abelard and Heloise*, 21.

modulation in the manner in which the tradition is inhabited.[57] For Abelard, no less than for his opponents, reason does not stand alone, as a self-contained and isolated procedure whose products stand over against the existing patterns of an already formed life. It is a practice undertaken within and upon such life, for the sake of the better ordering of such life.

When we turn directly to the ideology and practice of the emerging university, the implausibility of a narrative of progressive freedom from an authoritative tradition becomes even more apparent. The Moralists advocate more consistently and convincingly than did Abelard the need for scholarly life to be pervaded by humility, and it is clear that for them reason cut loose from authority can only be rootless and feckless, a matter of *curiositas* (the quality of a mind cast to and fro by gusts of disordered enthusiasm, rather than intent upon the journey towards truth) and *vanitas* (a concern with the demonstration of one's scholarly prowess more than with the truth and import of what one says).[58] It is true that they appear to be faced with scholars who do not take such humility seriously, and who are willing to use their dialectical and grammatical skills to undermine their teachers and the texts of their tradition, but the university shaped by the Moralists is, in part, a form of self-regulation designed to prevent rather than to encourage such excesses.

Finally, and most obviously, *lectio*, the careful reading of authoritative texts, in which understanding was formed by those texts precisely as the readers sought to form what they found into a coherent articulation, was *the* central practice of the emerging university.[59] It was, of course, a scholastic *lectio*, with a

---

[57] There is, of course, a more complex story to tell here. William of St Thierry, for instance, accused Abelard of regarding everything as a matter of opinion, open to disputation, so weakening authority by making acceptance of authoritative statement depend upon the outcome of reasoned disputation (Ferruolo, *Origins*, 73). This might make it sound as if we *are* dealing with a conflict between reason and authority, freedom and tradition—until we remember that this is a caricature produced by an opponent. To explore the modulation one finds in Abelard more fully, one would need to delve into the changes implied in the growth of a literate culture (see Stock, *Implications of Literacy*) and into changes in historical consciousness (see Marie-Dominique Chenu, *Nature, Man and Society in the Twelfth Century: Essays on New Theological Perspectives in the Latin West*, tr. Jerome Taylor and Lester K. Little, 2nd edn (Chicago: University of Chicago Press, 1968), ch. 5)—broad and complex cultural shifts already under way in Anselm's day, and visible well beyond the life of the schools.

[58] On humility, see Ferruolo, *Origins*, 223–6; on vanity, see 233–4; on curiosity, see 232–3 and Carruthers, *Craft*, 82–4. See also below, Ch. 5, n. 31.

[59] Philip de Harvengt (d. 1182), writing to a student in the Parisian schools, spoke of Paris as that 'happy city, in which the sacred tomes are pored over with much zeal and their involved mysteries resolved by the gift of the outpoured Spirit' (quoted in George H. Williams, *Wilderness and Paradise in Christian Thought: The Biblical Experience of the Desert in the History of Christianity and the Paradise Theme in the Theological Idea of the University*, The Menno Simons Lecture 1958 (New York: Harper and Bros, 1962), 164). See also the 1215 Statutes of the University of Paris, produced by the papal legate Robert Curzon (de Courçon), and the prominence of regulations on when one is allowed to lecture, and what the lecturer will read (and students hear): Henricus Denifle (ed.), *Chartularium Universitatis Parisiensis*, i. *1200–1286* (Paris: Delalain, 1889), 78–80; <www.archive.org/details/chartulariumuniv01univuoft>, tr. Dana

markedly different flavour from the monastic *lectio* in which Anselm was steeped: the story of the university's emergence is not the story of a straightforward affirmation of existing patterns of authority. Scholastic *lectio* inculcated and assumed a different relation to the materials of tradition, with a more pronounced historical consciousness, and a more explicit machinery of techniques and technologies available for *lectio* and the accompanying *meditation*—a relation more textual than oral, perhaps.[60] Nevertheless, the university was above all an institution for *lectio*, and so a vehicle for exploratory immersion in a tradition, relying upon such immersion as the high road to rightly ordered understanding.[61] The narrative of reason's emergence from traditional tutelage is simply mistaken.

REASON AS SPIRITUAL DISCIPLINE

Undermining Rashdall's narrative is not, in itself, a very interesting achievement, and I have dwelt on it simply because it provides a stepping stone to what, for my purposes, is a more interesting task: the reconceptualization of the nature of emergent university reasoning practices that becomes possible when they are seen not in opposition to the inescapably religious practices of reason of someone like Anselm, but in complex continuity. Specifically, my question is whether the scholastic *lectio–meditatio* that provided the medieval

Carleton Munro in *Translations and Reprints from the Original Sources of European History* 2 (Philadelphia, PA: University of Pennsylvania Press, 1896), 3.12–15; <www.archive.org/details/translationsrepr02univiala> (accessed 30 Sept. 2009).

[60] See Ivan Illich, *In the Vineyard of the Text: A Commentary to Hugh's Didascalion* (Chicago: University of Chicago Press, 1993); and Richard H. Rouse and Mary A. Rouse, '*Statim invenire*: Schools, Preachers, and New Attitudes to the Page', in Benson and Constable (eds), *Renaissance and Renewal*, 201–25.

[61] R. W. Southern, *Scholastic Humanism and the Unification of Europe*, i. *Foundations* (Oxford: Blackwell, 1995), 24. It is worth remembering that thirteenth-century debates about the relationship between faith and reason are *not* in any straightforward sense debates about the tension between authoritative texts and a reason that is free of them; they are debates about the relationships between differing sets of authoritative texts and the forms of articulation they call for, with 'reason' simply naming the traditions of the 'old logic' and the 'new'. 'For the old logic, the beginner's books, the *Isagoge* of Porphyry, Aristotle's *Categories* and the *De interpretatione*, were covered by Boethius' commentaries; Cicero's *Topics* and Boethius' commentary, together with Boethius' monograph *De differentiis topicis* were also known. Much of the new work of the twelfth century consisted in the writing of short manuals that were designed to turn Boethius' reflections into manageable handbooks for the schoolroom' (G. R. Evans, *Old Arts and New Theology: The Beginnings of Theology as an Academic Discipline* (Oxford: Clarendon Press, 1980), 22). The 'new logic' simply added extra texts: 'during the middle years of the century the *Sophistici Elenchi* appeared in the schools, and before 1200 the Aristotelian *Topics* and the *Prior* and *Posterior Analytics* were available' (Evans, *Old Arts*, 22–3). See also Makdisi's comments on the parallels with the Islamic practice of *jadal* (Makdisi, 'Scholastic Method', 649).

university with its backbone had, in the course of its evolution from earlier forms of *lectio*, lost its character as a spiritual discipline or devotional practice. In order to answer that question, we need to turn back briefly to Anselm.

The result of Anselm's *meditatio* (the finished, elegant articulation) is as much something discovered—or, better, something *given* to him—as it is something he makes. His *meditatio* is, therefore, properly thought of as a practice of contemplation, at once a process of invention (of deliberate composition) and a process of reception. *Meditatio* is an activity that yields receptivity: a serious constructive endeavour that teaches him obedience to a structure of thought that is not his to command.[62]

For Anselm, then, even though at times reasoning (that is, meditation) threatened to become a form of selfishness, drawing him away from more useful pursuits into self-absorption, it was more fundamentally a matter of his being taken out of himself, and out of disordered understanding towards ordered understanding. It was an ec-static practice. The struggle of his *meditatio* is precisely the struggle to find—or to be found by—the order that his understanding lacks: it is a discipline of attentiveness, and it requires that he learn to let go of alternative articulations, of attractive arrangements that nevertheless do not work; it is a work of purification, and so of continual compunction and penitence. There is a fundamental continuity here between the great meditations (the *Monologion* and *Proslogion*) and Anselm's earlier meditations, which sought to inculcate both knowledge of God and despair at the self's sin and incapacity.[63]

It should be no surprise, therefore, that the *Proslogion* can be written down as a prayer, and can finish with the petition:

I pray, O God, that I may know You and love You, so that I may rejoice in You. And if I cannot do so fully in this life may I progress gradually until it comes to fullness. Let the knowledge of You grow in me here, and there be made complete; let Your love grow in me here and there be made complete, so that here my joy may be great in hope, and there be complete in Your reality.[64]

---

[62] For Anselm's aesthetic reasoning, see David S. Hogg, *Anselm of Canterbury: The Beauty of Theology* (Aldershot: Ashgate, 2004). Cf. Southern, *Saint Anselm*, 74–5, 77, on the relation between rhyme and reason in Anselm's writing.

[63] It is in this context that we might rediscover a role for the martial rhetoric that often surrounds dialectic. Southern can say that the context for the *Monologion* and the *Proslogion* was one of 'nearly twenty years [of] monastic peace', and that the great meditations 'were the products of this new peace' and stand as a 'peaceful record of Anselm's thought' (Southern, *Saint Anselm*, 113), but the process of *meditatio* is a struggle, and it is one in which Anselm is regularly and necessarily wounded (see Carruthers, *Craft*, 101–7; Ward, 'Introduction', 53–6). The outcome may be a joyful moment of seeing, but on the way Anselm's meditation leaves him 'quite worn out with resisting', and the task 'force[s] itself upon' him. *Lectio–meditatio* is ordered towards the wounding or puncturing of the ego, and the reordering of its desire away from itself.

[64] Anselm, *Proslogion* 26, in *The Major Works*, 103–4.

The knowledge and joy that this meditation produces are aspects of Anselm's ascent towards fullness of knowledge and joy—and the process of meditation (with grammar and dialectic its tools) is one part of the process by which this ascent takes place. Dialectic in Anselm's hands may be reaching new heights, but it *belongs* in its monastic context; it is a discipline of contemplation and purification.

If we turn to the reasoning of the university, we find it driven by something similar to Anselm's rage for order: a 'drive towards unity of thought and behaviour': towards rightly ordered understanding and rightly ordered life.[65] It was driven by a desire to bring coherent and inclusive articulation to all the materials studied in *lectio*, especially those difficult materials identified by various forms of *sic et non*,[66] and in the process to be purified.

So, Walter Rüegg, in his summary of the 'academic ethic' that developed in the medieval universities, places at its head 'belief in a world order, created by God, rational, accessible to human reason', coupled with the recognition that human enquirers are fallen creatures, learning by means of 'modesty, reverence and self-criticism'.[67] For the Moralists, academic study is indeed a form of contemplation,[68] and, even if they see it as less deeply connected to prayer than monastic contemplation, it is still a matter of the pursuit of rightly ordered understanding, and so of rightly ordered life before God, private and public. In particular, it is a matter of the learner being so ordered that he might in turn, by word and example, lead others into order.

One of Peter Comestor's sermons as Parisian chancellor quotes some lines that had become a commonplace in twelfth-century discussions of learning. 'A humble mind, eagerness to inquire, a quiet life, | Silent scrutiny, poverty, a foreign soil.'[69] These are the keys to learning.[70] They are not extrinsic to

---

[65] Southern, *Scholastic Humanism*, 156. We should not for a moment think that a drive towards the right ordering of *thought* could have been seriously thought in the twelfth or thirteenth century independent of a drive towards rightly ordered life.

[66] According to Marcia Colish, the primary need of scholastic theologians in the twelfth century was for 'a syllabus offering a cogent and defensible rationale for its coverage and organization. And they needed to teach their students how to reason theologically, how to come to grips with the Christian tradition as they had inherited it . . . The repute and durability of a scholastic theologian in the first half of the twelfth century stood or fell on how successfully his work met these demands' (Marcia L. Colish, 'Systematic Theology and Theological Renewal in the Twelfth Century', *Journal of Medieval and Renaissance Studies*, 18/1 (1988), 135–56: 142; repr. in Colish, *Studies in Scholasticism*, §I).

[67] Rüegg, 'Themes', 32–3.

[68] See above, n. 29.

[69] *Mens humilis, studium quaerendi, vita quieta, scrutinium tacitum, paupertas, terra aliena* (Peter Comestor, *Qui non humiliaverit*, PL 198, 1730D, translated in Ferruolo, *Origins*, 223; see also John of Salisbury (*Policraticus* 7.13), and Hugh of St Victor, *Didascalion* 3.12). John of Salisbury attributes the lines to Bernard of Chartres (d. *c*.1124); see Ferruolo, *Origins*, 38, 138–9, 327 n. 39).

[70] The longer version of the quotation given by Hugh of St Victor and others continues: 'These, for many, unlock the hidden places of learning' (Ferruolo, *Origins*, 38).

learning, as if they were simply ways of preventing the gains of learning from undermining the moral and spiritual health of the learner, or the stability of his community. They are *intrinsic*: they are the conditions that allow learning to be most fully itself, for it to be capable of leading to rightly ordered understanding. The lines play with language appropriate to the cloister, and suggest that *something like* monasticism (though not monasticism itself—Peter was not seeking the conversion of his congregation to a religious life) is proper to reason. Learning is a devout discipline.[71]

That this account of the nature of learning bears some relation to the actual practice of the emergent university is suggested by the alliance that was eventually possible between university reason and the religious life, in men like Bonaventure and Aquinas. Despite the complexity and acrimony of relations between the secular masters and the mendicants,[72] the possibility of the alliance found in someone like Bonaventure suggests something fundamental about scholastic reason. When Antony of Padua asked Francis if he had his permission to teach the friars theology, Francis replied: 'I am pleased that you teach sacred theology to the brothers providing that, as is contained in the Rule, you "do not extinguish the Spirit of prayer and devotion" during study of this kind.'[73] For Bonaventure, however, a regent master of Theology at the University of Paris in the 1250s before becoming General of the Franciscan order, the relation between scholarship and devotion went beyond a simple absence of incompatibility: the two became parts of a united whole, a journey of purification and ascent, the right ordering of the soul.[74] Of course, Bonaventure and other friars involved in the university are to some extent a special case: their learning was bound up with continued monastic practice, and the secular masters' was not. Nevertheless, the scholastic reasoning of the friars was not in itself of a wholly different character from the reasoning of the secular masters; though it was for the secular masters a spiritual discipline set within a different context, it was still a spiritual discipline: a self-involving discipline devoted to the right order of rational, faithful life.

In other words, it was possible for at least some influential participants in early university life to portray the very practices of university reason as engines of purification and ascent. And such portrayals do not work by emphasizing aspects of those reasoning practices that have nothing to do with their

---

[71] Ferruolo, *Origins*, 218–26.

[72] Gordon Leff, *Paris and Oxford Universities in the Thirteenth and Fourteenth Centuries: An Institutional and Intellectual History* (New York: John Wiley & Sons, 1968), 34–47.

[73] Francis of Assisi, 'A Letter to Brother Anthony of Padua', in Francis of Assisi, *Early Documents*, (ed. Regis J. Armstrong, J. Wayne Hellman and William J. Short), i. *The Saint* (Hyde Park, NY: New City, 1999), 107.

[74] Kevin L. Hughes, 'Remember Bonaventure? (Onto)Theology and Ecstasy', *Modern Theology*, 19/4 (2003), 520–45; Christopher M. Cullen, *Bonaventure*, Great Medieval Thinkers, ed. Brian Davies (Oxford: Oxford University Press, 2006), 3–35.

rationality: they work by emphasizing those aspects that allow the reasoner intent upon coherent and detailed understanding to have his thoughts reshaped by the resistances to his existing articulations of the material he studies. For such portrayals, at least, reason and devotion go naturally together. Reason seriously practised is a means by which the reasoner is called out of himself; it waits humbly upon an articulation that it cannot simply invent, attending to an ordering in things that is understood as God's good gift.

The emergence of the university, then, can be seen as in part the emergence of a form of meditative spiritual discipline not tied to monastic life.[75] This development took place, moreover, precisely at a time when, as Marie-Dominique Chenu puts it, 'the monastery could no longer be considered "the city of God" to which one would lead society', and when the idea of non-monastic Christian vocation was gaining ground. Chenu quotes Gerhoh of Reichersberg (1093–1169):

Whoever has renounced at baptism the devil and all his trappings . . . even if that person never becomes a . . . monk, has nonetheless definitely renounced the world . . . Whether rich or poor, noble or serf, merchant or peasant, all who are committed to the Christian faith reject everything inimical to this name and embrace everything conformable to it. Every order and absolutely every profession in the Catholic faith and according to the apostolic teaching has a rule adapted to its character; and under this rule it is possible, by striving, to achieve the crown of glory.[76]

One of the storylines that weaves through the emergence of the University of Paris, therefore, is the story of the nurturing by some university practitioners of what they saw as a new form of spiritual discipline: a contemplative and purificatory *meditatio* outside the monasteries, ordered towards the establishment of well-ordered individual and public life before God. It can also be told as the story of a search for the proper form of corporate discipline, of polity, within which this new non-monastic spiritual discipline can be sustained.

MEDITATIO AND DISPUTATIO

The institutional development of the university was driven in part by the need to find a form of regulation, a form of corporate discipline, in a situation where the schools of Paris no longer fitted into existing patterns of regulated life. While this was partly a matter of the need to secure the rights and privileges of

---

[75] It was also a form of discipline taken on only for a period, en route to some other occupation.
[76] Gerhoh of Reichersberg, *Liber de aedificio Dei*, 43 (PL 194, 1302) in Chenu, *Nature, Man and Society*, 222.

scholastic clerics in a context where the available system of jurisdictions left them exposed, it was also a matter of finding an appropriate institutional or social form for the maintenance of the emerging form of devout life that I have been describing, a pattern of regulated life that could contain the excesses and ill-discipline that the relatively unregulated life of the twelfth-century schools had made possible, and that the competitive and disputatious life of scholasticism all too easily fostered.[77]

The twelfth-century schools have a martial reputation bordering on the anarchic in significant part because of the belligerence possible in *disputatio*, its dynamics of defence or defeat. Alongside *lectio*, staged public disputation was a core scholastic activity, and its textual representation in the *quaestio* (at various points on the spectrum from reportage to conventionalized fiction) was to become one of the staple forms of scholastic writing.[78] The emergence of the *universitas* of masters—a self-regulating guild of masters in turn responsible for the regulation of their students—is in part a matter of disciplining *disputatio*: reining in its excesses, curbing some of its tendency toward violence.

But *disputatio* should not be seen simply as a disruptive force to be reined in, or as a practice inherently opposed to peace; it is also an essential component of scholastic reason as spiritual discipline. Once again, the comparison with Anselm is instructive. Brian Stock can describe the formation of the *Monologion* as a matter of 'interior dialogue'; Anselm himself spoke of his *meditatio* as a matter of the 'silent reasoning within himself', as a 'conflict of [his] thoughts',[79] even as a *disputatio*.[80] Despite his communal monastic context, there is a sense in which Anselm's reasoning is fundamentally solitary, and the dialogue that drives it is a dialogue in his head. He places a very high value on friendship; he teaches and writes for a number of pupils; but (with the exception of the enigmatic Gaunilo[81]) Anselm's reasoning does not take place on the whole amid the give and take of intellectual peers. One need only look at the dialogue form of *Cur Deus homo* to see all too clearly a literary representation of this: the interlocutor Boso is the almost entirely passive

---

[77] Hugh Primas (*c*.1093–1160), a teacher in Orleans and Paris, wrote: 'In the schools of disputation they're discordant and diverse, aberrant and dispersed. What this man denies, this one affirms; this man's conquered, this one conquers: the Doctor contradicts all' (quoted in Catherine Brown, *Contrary Things: Exegesis, Dialectic, and the Poetics of Didacticism* (Stanford, CA: Stanford University Press, 1998), 37).

[78] Makdisi notes that the distinction between *disputatio* and *lectio* parallels the Islamic distinction between *munāzara* and *qirā'a*, a distinction he traces back to the tenth century; see Makdisi, 'Scholastic Method', 648, and cf. his *Humanism*, 210–12.

[79] Anselm, *Proslogion*, Preface, in *The Major Works*, 82.

[80] Anselm, Epistle 77, translated in Southern, *Saint Anselm*, 71.

[81] The dispute with Gaunilo of Marmoutiers is remarkable for its combination of friendly respect, delight, and serious criticism; see Gaunilo, *Pro insipiente* and Anselm, *Reply to Gaunilo*, tr. M. J. Charlesworth in *The Major Works*, 105–10 and 111–22.

recipient of Anselm's teaching, prompting its production by curious questioning, but lacking any solidity of his own that might have acted as a whetstone to Anselm's wits.[82] He is a student who would have fitted well into Jaeger's eleventh-century colloquies, but he never brings Anselm to a re-examination of his own mind.

If one wanted to chart the differences between Anselmian reason and the reason of the university, the most important would be that in the university we see the making corporate of what in Anselm is ultimately solitary: *disputatio*. The schools can, therefore, be seen as practising something like Anselmian reason made public: the internal processes by which he subjected his own thinking to scrutiny, challenged it, winkled out inconsistencies and exposed fudges, and drove it deeper (or higher), are now made external, corporate, and sociable.[83]

Such *disputatio* requires peace, not as its curb, holding it in check, but in order to become itself: in order for it to function fully as a means of reasoning. This is something that the Moralists seem at least partially to have grasped. It requires peace in which to hear and take seriously opposing arguments; peace in which to hunt for the articulations that will clarify, resolve, or decide disagreements; peace in which to undergo the self-examination and penitence that scholasticism as contemplation and ascent calls for. If the Moralists had had their way—and it is very hard to gauge the extent to which they did, but the evidence is that their success was at best mixed—the emergence of the university would be seen as an experiment in a certain kind of peaceable community: the attempt to build a reasoning community, not now held together by the bonds of deference praised in the cathedral schools of the eleventh century, but held together by the giving and testing of reasons, by mutual holding to account.[84] Their work enables us to see a distinction between, on the one hand, disagreement and argument, which are essential to university reason as a devotional practice, and violent disputatiousness, which is not—which is, indeed, inimical to it. In such a light, the violent direction marked out by the fractious Abelard would be a dead end: he would represent a temptation that had to be overcome in order for the disputatious university to be possible, and for university reason to flourish.

---

[82] Even the student in *De Veritate*, who has rather more to contribute than Boso, says: 'If I cannot do anything else, I will at least help by being a good listener' (*De Veritate* 1 in Anselm of Canterbury, *Truth, Freedom and Evil: Three Philosophical Dialogues*, ed. and tr. Jasper Hopkins and Herbert Richardson (New York: Harper & Row, 1967), 92).

[83] In his discussion of the medieval academic ethic, Walter Rüegg speaks of the importance of 'the subjection of one's own assertions to the generally valid rules of evidence, openness to all possible objections to one's own argument, and the public character of argument and discussion' (Rüegg, 'Themes', 33).

[84] For peace as a desideratum of the medieval university, see Williams, *Wilderness and Paradise*, 167.

The development of the scholarly *universitas* was an attempt to create a pattern of regulated life devoted to nurturing and sustaining scholastic life in its own right, rather than leaving it to find a space within institutions and patterns of regulation designed primarily with some other form of life in mind.[85] In the broadest sense of the word, taken to cover not simply the formal disputations but the whole life of scholarly conversation that is the form academic *meditatio* properly takes, the emergence of the scholarly *universitas* was the emergence of an institution designed for the maintenance of intensive *disputatio*.[86] The further development of the scholarly *universitas* as a a *studium generale*, capable in principle of training its students to teach in *any* school, was an attempt to give some formal recognition to the extensity of this conversation; it gave some formal recognition to the idea that there was an *international* fraternity of disputation—a conversation of scholars not simply limited to one school, one city, one university, a conversation on a scale unthinkable in Anselm's day.

CONCLUSION

So, what kind of characterization of the emergence of the university—what repaired myth of university origins—does this examination provide? On the one hand, I have argued that it does not make sense to describe the emergence

[85] One need only think of the fate of the school of St Victor, which flourished under masters like Hugh of St Victor, but which by 1173 was struggling in a context where the new prior, Walter of St Victor, was 'an uncompromising and outspoken opponent of the schools'. He eventually disbanded it completely. In the twelfth and thirteenth centuries, the perceived differences between scholastic and monastic discipline meant that a monastery was not necessarily a safe foundation for a school (Ferruolo, *Origins*, 43–4).

[86] The development of the college is significant here. The first colleges in Paris, such as the Collège des Dix-Huit, emerged at the end of the twelfth century as 'nothing more than modest pious foundations, serving to provide shelter for a handful of students, often in the midst of other "poor clerics"' (Verger, 'Patterns', 60; cf. Cobban, *Medieval English Universities*, 114), but they later grew in significance. The College of the Sorbonne, founded in 1257/1258 by Robert de Sorbon, chaplain to Louis IX, 'was to be essentially a community of scholars with like-minded interests who, in theory at any rate, were to live together in harmonious amity and in an environment of stimulating intellectual exchange; a Christian society embodying spiritual, moral and academic excellence' (Cobban, *Medieval English Universities*, 115). In Oxford, where colleges became an even more significant element of the academic landscape, the 38th chapter of the 1274 Statutes for Merton College by Walter de Merton urged that 'peace, unity, and the bond of charity be promoted with complete affectionate earnestness' (as translated by Astrik L. Gabriel, 'The Ideal Master of the Mediaeval University', *Catholic Historical Review*, 60/1 (1974), 1–40: 15; cf. Edward France Percival, *The Foundation Statutes of Merton College, Oxford* (London: William Pickering, 1847), 36). See also Gabriel, 'The College System in the Fourteenth-Century Universities', in Francis Lee Utley, *The Forward Movement of the Fourteenth Century* (Columbus, OH: Ohio State University Press, 1961), 79–124. For the relations between these Christian institutions and Islamic analogues, see Makdisi, *The Rise of Colleges*.

of the university as a triumph of reason over tradition, or of freedom over authority: such a narrative simply reads back much later ideologies into a twelfth- and thirteenth-century context.[87] On the other, I have argued that university reason can be understood as a spiritual discipline, or a form of devotion. I do not mean that university reason actually functioned that way all the time—or even much of the time. I claim rather that such a description establishes a set of coordinates against which the actual practice and progress of medieval university life could properly be plotted—and that, measured against such coordinates, it will become clear that the university's all-too-regular failures to be devout are also failures to be reasonable, and its all-too-regular failures to be reasonable are also failures to be devout.

Of course, *disputatio* could (and did) often become a matter of violent ambition, or it could (and did) often become a routine exercise in which nothing of value was at stake; meditative articulation could (and did) often become a matter of commodification, the chopping-up of material into manageable chunks that could be passed from teacher to student simply as stable possessions, or it could (and did) often become a matter of sheer pedantry, the dissection of materials safely isolated from their environment and from any possibility of making a difference to the right ordering of the world or of the knower.[88] Nevertheless, however imperfectly and confusedly the idea was realized in the actual shape that university life and development took, a portrayal of the emergence of the university can appropriately be framed by the ideal that the university practice of reason should be a spiritual discipline. That is at least an idea of the university that the twelfth-century Moralists enable us to imagine.

To put it another way, the kind of practice of reason that the establishment of the University of Paris was intended by at least some of its practitioners to secure was one that made sense in the context of a set of theological assumptions. It was assumed that the materials given for study—the texts of the tradition, but also the inner and outer world about which they spoke—were amenable to articulation: they had a God-given harmony or beauty about them, even if it was hidden to the untutored eye. It was assumed that to discover that harmonious ordering was not simply an intellectual game, but

---

[87] Of course, we have seen the handholds onto which a more 'secularizing' account can cling: the shift to a more reparative relation to tradition (which does imply a certain kind of critical distancing in the midst of immersion), and the development of this form of *meditatio* away from the monastic contexts where the language of purification, penitence and ascent—of specifically *spiritual* discipline—was most at home.

[88] One should beware reading back too glibly into the twelfth-century critiques of eighteenth-century university practice; see Theodore Ziolkowski, *German Romanticism and its Institutions* (Princeton: Princeton University Press, 1990), 220–8. As with the 'rise of the middle classes', the 'rise of the commodification of university studies' is a theme that can be pinned to almost any century from the twelfth to the twenty-first.

one of the means (or part of the means) for discovering the good ordering of human life before God, including the good ordering of social life. It was assumed, moreover, that this discovery of good order was possible only through a certain kind of conformity to it: the good ordering of the scholar's life in humility, piety, and peace—and this both as a prerequisite to learning, and as something deepened and established *through* learning.[89]

In this view, learning and virtue belonged together (learning required virtue, and learning taught virtue), and they belonged together in a double sense. In the first place, it was assumed that one could learn the good ordering of the materials at one's disposal only if, in humility and trust, one took the risk of being called to penitence and transformed understanding by them—called to right order before God by the God-given resistances (the *sic-et-nons*) of one's material, as one placed oneself at God's disposal. In the second place, one could learn the good ordering of one's materials only by participation in a certain kind of communal good: a community involved in the friendly exchange of calls to such penitence before God—a community of mutual compunction, if you like; a community of peaceable but serious disputation. It is on this ground—the ground of virtue and sociality orientated towards the good ordering of life before God—that I will be erecting my own theological account of university reason in the remainder of this book.

[89] For an overlapping account of the nature of medieval university study, see José Ignacio Cabezón, 'Introduction', in Cabezón, *Scholasticism*, 1–17.

2

Berlin

In the previous chapter, I presented a picture of medieval learning, and claimed that it was one way of construing what was going on in the emergent University of Paris. It was a picture of learning as devout: a matter of purification and ascent, and of peaceable disputation; a matter of knowing the good by becoming good, individually and socially. It was not my plan to claim that there was in the Paris of the thirteenth century any kind of golden age of the university when this picture of learning held unchallenged sway, nor to offer any history of its subsequent medieval successes or failures. I simply claimed that this picture was in play at a crucial point in university history (or at least that the fragments from which I built it were). It was one of the contesting ideologies from whose interaction the development of the university was woven—and its presence there is enough to undermine any account of the university that unthinkingly sets the university and reason over against Christian tradition and devotion.

Just as the story of the emergence of the University of Paris is sometimes presented as a story of the struggle away from Christian tradition and devotion, so the later history of the university is sometimes presented as a story of progressive secularization. In this chapter, I turn to the icon of such a story: the foundation of the University of Berlin in the early nineteenth century. Against any such simplistic narrative of secularization, I will argue that the rejection in Berlin of a Christian theological account of reason and of university life is by no means as straightforward as it might at first appear.

So, we now leave medieval Paris, travel forward several hundred years to the late eighteenth century, and hop over the linguistic border into German-speaking territory. This is a journey that takes us from a context in which the university was in the process of being born to one in which it was widely perceived as decaying and corrupt.[1]

---

[1] See Thomas Albert Howard, *Protestant Theology and the Making of the Modern German University* (Oxford: Oxford University Press, 2006), ch. 2, and Theodore Ziolkowski, *German Romanticism and its Institutions* (Princeton: Princeton University Press, 1990), 220–8, for good general accounts. The failures that I will describe were by no means exclusive to the German-

In part, the perceived failings were moral. The medieval view of the university called for a 'humble mind, eagerness to inquire, a quiet life'—and, whatever story is to be told about the proximity to that ideal of medieval student life, the typical story told of universities in the eighteenth-century German-speaking world was of arrogance, indolence, and above all rowdiness. University students were notorious for breaching the peace, a byword for fecklessness and disruption.[2]

In part, the perceived failings could be called metaphysical. That is, it appeared that the connections had been severed between learning and the good—those connections that in the medieval picture made learning *inherently* a matter of purification and ascent. It had become easier to imagine that university studies dealt with independent objects that were simply and only themselves, the focus of forms of expertise with no links to the investigator's moral or spiritual progress, nor that of his intellectual community, nor that of the society in and for which he wrote. Universities were perceived to be the home at best of dry erudition, more often of useless pedantry.[3]

In part, the perceived failings could be called political. Instead of an international fraternity of learning, imagined as coextensive with Christendom, universities were seen as locked into fragmented antagonism. After the Peace of Westphalia, and the settlement that allowed *cuius regio* to have *eius religio*, each *regio* also had its own university,[4] and those universities were by design 'centres for sending out educated clerics able to refute the religious opposition'.[5] Polemic and controversy, rather than peaceable disputation, were the watchwords of university life.[6]

---

speaking world (as the next chapter will demonstrate). Nevertheless, the response to those failings that this chapter will describe was, to begin with, a distinctively German matter, so it makes sense to focus on German understandings of the problems.

[2] See Ziolkowski, *German Romanticism*, 220, 227; R. Steven Turner, 'The Prussian Universities and the Concept of Research', *Internationales Archive für Sozialgeschichte der deutschen Literatur*, 5 (1980), 68–93: 70.

[3] Ziolkowski, *German Romanticism*, 220, 226.

[4] Michael J. Hofstetter, *The Romantic Idea of a University: England and Germany 1770–1850*, Romanticism in Perspective: Texts, Cultures, Histories, ed. Marilyn Gaull and Stephen Prickett (Basingstoke: Palgrave, 2001), 2. He draws on the account provided by Friedrich Paulsen of the 'territorial–confessional university' of the sixteenth and seventeenth centuries; see Paulsen, *Die deutschen Universitäten und das Universitätstudium* (Hildesheim: Georg Olms, 1966 [1902]), 40–52.

[5] Howard, *Protestant Theology*, 69.

[6] Martin Gierl, in '"The Triumph of Truth and Innocence": The Rules and Practice of Theological Polemics', tr. William Clark, in William Clark and Peter Becker (eds), *Little Tools of Knowledge: Historical Essays on Academic and Bureaucratic Practices* (Ann Arbor: University of Michigan Press, 2001), 35–66, describes the culture of polemic, as well as the process by which later academic life began to differentiate itself from that culture.

With this moral, metaphysical, and political breakdown, the core practices of university life, lectures and disputations, had subsided into a disreputable senility. Lectures were seen as little more than the dull repetition of the content of textbooks—a sorry and pointless substitute for private reading.[7] (Johann Gottlieb Fichte (1762–1814), writing in 1807, claimed that, while it made sense for lectures to be a form of dictation in the era before printing—a substitute for access to the books themselves—lectures in his day had become a pointless exercise in 'continuing the *emergency method* long after the emergency has ceased'.[8]) Disputations, too, were regarded as having become decadent: there was nothing genuinely dialogical about what had become rehearsed, formalistic, and disregarded performances, of interest only to those of very obscure theatrical taste.[9]

Beyond all this, universities were suffering from declining matriculation numbers, chronic financial mismanagement, and near-terminal curricular stagnation.[10] Calls for their abolition were by no means rare: they 'were seen as relics of a past monastic life and utterly unsuited for present realities'.[11]

In the myth of university origins, it is against this dingy backdrop that the foundation of the University of Berlin in the early years of the nineteenth century appears as a decisive step forward—a new moral, metaphysical, and political settlement for the university. It represented the inauguration of a new model of what an institution of higher education could be: the *research university*, embodying dedication to *Wissenschaft*—that is, to rigorous scholarly knowledge. It was a model that was to spread first around the German-speaking world, and then much further, especially to the United States, and eventually even to the United Kingdom.

---

[7] The University of Ingolstadt explicitly forbade dictation in lectures in its regulations in 1582, which suggests that it was perceived to be a real problem. See William Clark, *Academic Charisma and the Origins of the Research University* (Chicago: University of Chicago, 2006), 85.

[8] J. G. Fichte, 'Deduced Scheme for an Academy to be Established in Berlin (1807)', tr. G. H. Turnbull, in Turnbull, *The Educational Theory of J. G. Fichte: A Critical Account, Together with Translations* (Liverpool: University of Liverpool; London: Hodder and Stoughton, 1926), 170–259: 172. The German original, 'Deduzierter Plan einer in Berlin zu errichtenden höheren Lehranstalt', in Ernst Anrich (ed.), *Die Idee der deutschen Universität* (Darmstadt: Hermann Gentner Verlag, 1956), 125–217.

[9] Clark, *Academic Charisma*, 88; but see Kristine Louise Haugen, 'Academic Charisma and the Old Regime', *History of Universities*, 22/1 (2007), 199–228: 216–17; cf. Friedrich Schleiermacher, *Occasional Thoughts on Universities in the German Sense, with an Appendix Regarding a University Soon to Be Established (1808)*, tr. Terrence N. Tice with Edwina Lawler (Lewiston, NY: Edwin Mellen, 1991), 60; German original, 'Gelegentliche Gedanken über Universitäten im deutschen Sinn', in Anrich (ed.), *Die Idee der deutschen Universität*, 219–308.

[10] Howard, *Protestant Theology*, ch. 2.

[11] Ziolkowski, *German Romanticism*, 227.

THE FOUNDATION OF THE UNIVERSITY OF BERLIN

In October 1806, Napoleon's armies had won the battle of Jena–Auerstedt, and Prussia had fallen under French control.[12] Shortly afterwards, Napoleon suppressed the University of Halle (temporarily, as it turned out), and a delegation of dispossessed Halle professors headed by Theodor A. H. Schmalz (1760–1831) travelled to petition Friedrich Wilhelm III (1770–1840) to provide them with some replacement.[13] The king is said to have replied: 'That is right, that is commendable. What the state has lost in physical strength it must replace with intellectual strength.'[14] The drawing-up of plans for a Berlin institution of higher education began almost immediately.

Friedrich Wilhelm's response to this petition did not emerge from nowhere, however. It was one more step in a process of the reform of Prussian institutional, political, and educational life that, though accelerated by reaction to defeat, had been initiated well before. Eighteenth-century Prussia had seen the rise to power of reforming civil servants hoping 'to *rationalize* the social order as a means of enhancing the prosperity and power of the monarchical state'.[15] These civil servants were themselves the vanguard of the burgeoning *Bildungsbürgertum*: a Prussian middle class with a 'progressive, rationalizing, meritocratic, and statist social vision'.[16] For these reformers, defeat provided

a unique opportunity to enact far-reaching domestic social reforms, which were inspired partly by eighteenth-century philosophical ideals of universal freedom and equality. They anticipated that these new laws, by forging a cohesive and prosperous

[12] For this narrative, see Ziolkowski, *German Romanticism*, 286–308. Famously, Hegel is said to have completed *The Phenomenology of Spirit* in Jena as the battle raged outside.

[13] Edwina Lawler, 'Neohumanistic–Idealistic Concepts of a University: Schelling, Steffens, Fichte, Schleiermacher and von Humboldt', in Herbert Richardson (ed.), *Friedrich Schleiermacher and the Founding of the University of Berlin: The Study of Religion as a Scientific Discipline* (Lewiston, NY: Edwin Mellen, 1991), 1–44: 2.

[14] Lawler, 'Neohumanistic–Idealistic Concepts', 2, citing Rudolf Köpke, *Die Grundung der königlichen Friedrich-Wilhelms-Universität zu Berlin* (Berlin: Gustav Schade, 1860), 37. Cf. Heinrich Steffens, *The Idea of the University*, tr. Gordon Walmsley, *Copenhagen Review*, 2 (2008); <www.copenhagenreview.com/backissues1-5/two/the%20university.pdf> (accessed 27 Nov. 2009), 9: 'Certainly external power, the instigator of revolutions, belongs to a nation foreign to us. Yet an inner power, quietly germinating, preparing a significant future, belongs to us' (Walmsley's translation is of Lecture 1 of Steffens's *Vorlesungen über die Idee der Universitäten*; the original German of the full lecture series is reproduced in Anrich (ed.), *Die Idee der deutschen Universität*, 309–74.) Cf. J. G. Fichte, *Addresses to the German Nation*, ed. George Armstrong Kelly, tr. R. F. Jones and G. H. Turnbull (New York: Harper and Row, 1968), 2.

[15] Matthew Levinger, 'The Prussian Reform Movement and the Rise of Enlightened Nationalism', in Philip G. Dwyer, *The Rise of Prussia 1700–1830* (London: Longman, 2000), 259–77: 261. Levinger speaks of 'an ambitious cadre of reform-minded officials': Karl Freiherr vom und zum Stein (1757–1831), Karl August von Hardenberg (1750–1822), Karl von Stein zum Altenstein (1770–1840), Heinrich Theodor von Schön (1773–1856), and Wilhelm von Humboldt himself (259).

[16] Howard, *Protestant Theology*, 19.

society, would help mobilize the full energies of the Prussian populace in the service of the state.[17]

Karl Friedrich von Beyme (1765–1838), the king's chief of cabinet, was initially tasked with drawing up the plans for the new institution, and he commissioned statements from, among others, Schmalz, the philologist Friedrich August Wolf (1759–1824), and Fichte. He also received an unsolicited response from Friedrich Schleiermacher.[18] In 1808, there was a reshuffle, and Wilhelm von Humboldt (1767–1835) received the post of Secretary for Religion and Public Instruction, and with it the task of turning these plans into reality, which he adopted with enthusiasm and celerity. Progress was rapid: lectures began in 1809, and the university was formally opened in October 1810, though not before Humboldt himself had resigned, to be replaced in time by Friedrich von Schukmann (1755–1834)—a man with rather stricter ideas about the new university's accountability to government officials, and the need for government control of its finances.[19]

BILDUNG AND WISSENSCHAFT

The story of Berlin's emergence is normally read through the lens of a number of more-or-less Romantic theorists of higher education, from Schiller to Schleiermacher and beyond.[20] Those theorists mixed, in differing proportions,

---

[17] Levinger, 'Prussian Reform', 261. Cf. Brendan Simms, 'Political and Diplomatic Movements, 1800–1830: Napoleon, National Uprising, Restoration', in Jonathan Sperber (ed.), *Germany 1800–1871* (Oxford: Oxford University Press, 2004), 26–45.

[18] Clark, *Academic Charisma*, 196–7.

[19] Of course, the reforms in Berlin do not stand quite so isolated as this brief sketch implies. The University of Halle had itself been founded in 1694 as a new, more useful type of higher-education institution (Howard, *Protestant Theology*, 88–104); the eighteenth century had seen the foundation of various technical academies that had changed the academic landscape (Ziolkowski, *German Romanticism*, 227); there had been attempts at reform at Göttingen in the second half of the century (in the writings of J. D. Michaelis (1717–1791), for example, advocating a deeply utilitarian and profit-orientated future for the university; see Hofstetter, *Romantic Idea*, 5–7); the new Prussian legal code of 1794 had a section on universities designed to reform academic behaviour (Ziolkowski, *German Romanticism*, 226, citing the *Allgemeines Landrecht für die Preußischen Staaten* (*ALR*), II.12.67–129: 'Von Universitäten'; <www.smixx.de/ra/Links_F-R/PrALR/PrALR_II_12.pdf> (accessed 27 Nov. 2009)); Jena and then Halle had in the 1790s both been centres for reinvigorated academic practice (Ziolkowski, *German Romanticism*, 268–78); and there had been substantial reforms in Königsberg in 1808. Nevertheless, even at the time Berlin was presented as a dramatic new development, and its place at the centre of the myth of the modern university's emergence has proved resilient.

[20] There is a standard list of five texts that influenced the formation of the University of Berlin: Fichte's 'Deduced Scheme for an Academy to be Established in Berlin' (see n. 8 above), Humboldt's 'On the Spirit and the Organisational Framework of Intellectual Institutions in Berlin' (n. 28), Schelling's lectures *On University Studies* (n. 23), Schleiermacher's *Occasional*

a number of standard ingredients. They drew on Enlightenment appeals to reason (and their transformation in Kant); they drew on the anti-utilitarian neohumanism of Winckelmann (1717–68), Herder (1744–1803), and Goethe (1749–1832), with its focus on *Bildung* (the cultivation of human sensibility and nobility, 'the freer, fuller, and more harmonious development of human personality');[21] they drew on related ideas in the educational theories of Rousseau (1712–78) and Pestalozzi (1746–1827), advocating the cultivation of each individual to the fullness of his own creative and scholarly potential; and they drew on (or were the developers of) post-Kantian Idealism, with its talk of the organic, encyclopaedic unity of knowledge, and of each individual knower's participation in some kind of universal, absolute knowing.[22] Put together, these ingredients produced what has been called the *Wissenschafts-ideologie*—and it provided the intellectual soil in which the University of Berlin took root.

The main notes of this ideology were already audible when the poet and historian Friedrich Schiller gave his first lecture as Professor of History at the University of Jena, to a packed audience. He set before his students two ways to live. On the one hand, they could be bread-scholars (*Brotgelehrte*); on the other, they could be philosophically minded (*philosophische Köpfe*).[23] The scholar who feeds on bread alone is interested only in a job, or rather in the

---

Thoughts on Universities in the German Sense (n. 9), and Steffens's lectures on *The Idea of a University* (n. 14). The German text of all five is provided by Anrich (ed.), *Die Idee der deutschen Universität*; discussions of all five texts can be found in Howard, *Protestant Theology*, ch. 3, Lawler, 'Neohumanistic–Idealistic Concepts', and Elinor S. Shaffer, 'Romantic Philosophy and the Organization of the Disciplines: The Founding of the Humboldt University of Berlin', in Andrew Cunningham and Nicholas Jardine (eds), *Romanticism and the Sciences* (Cambridge: Cambridge University Press, 1990), 38–54: 39. I also draw on Schiller's lecture, 'What Is, and to What End do We Study, Universal History?' (see n. 23), and on Kant's *The Conflict of the Faculties* (n. 47). Turner, in 'Prussian Universities', 82–3, notes that alongside the original generation of Romantic theorists there are those bureaucrats who turned the theory into official policy—Humboldt himself, Johannes Schulze (1786–1869), Karl vom Stein zum Altenstein (1770–1840), and Johann Wilhelm Süvern (1775–1829)—and that there is a second generation of theorists who speak from within the institutions established by the earlier generation—e.g., August Boeckh (1785–1867), Friedrich Savigny (1779–1861), and Friedrich Thiersch (1784–1860).

[21] Howard, *Protestant Theology*, 138.

[22] Howard, *Protestant Theology*, 28–9.

[23] Friedrich Schiller, 'What Is, and to What End do We Study, Universal History?', tr. Caroline Stephan and Robert Trout, <www.schillerinstitute.org/transl/Schiller_essays/univer-sal_history.html> (accessed 27 Nov. 2009); German original 'Was heißt und zu welchem Ende studiert man Universalgeschichte', *Der Teutsche Merkur*, 4 (1789), 105–35; <de.wikisource.org/wiki/Was_heißt_und_zu_welchem_Ende_studiert_man_Universalgeschichte%3F> (accessed 27 Nov. 2009). F. W. J. Schelling, in *On University Studies*, tr. E. S. Morgan, ed. Norbert Guterman (Athens, OH: Ohio University Press, 1966), 35–6, makes the same comparison between 'bread studies' or the 'bread scholar (*Brotstudiums* or *Brotgelehrte*) and the 'true scholar'. The German original, 'Vorlesungen über die Methode des akademischen Studiums', is in Anrich (ed.), *Die Idee der deutschen Universität*, 1–124.

rewards of fame, money, and favour that a job might bring him. He therefore has an interest only in demonstrably useful knowledge. He sees knowledge as a commodity to be accumulated and then spent, to win those rewards and to see off material need. For such a scholar, any intellectual innovation, originality, or challenge is therefore a threat, likely to reduce the value of his existing hoard, and so he is constitutionally conservative and intransigent. He is also jealous: his learning has value only in competition with others, and so he 'fences himself in against all his neighbours' and lives in 'hostile solitude'. The bread scholar's learning is fragmentary, a heap rather than a whole, and he is on the side of egoism, barbarism, and war.

The philosophical student, on the other hand, is someone with a thirst for knowledge itself. He is a subject of the 'kingdom of knowledge' ('a kingdom of complete freedom'), and he experiences that kingdom as a realm not of fear but of delight; the meeting of this kingdom's demands is for him a matter of joyful courage. This student works diligently for ennoblement through understanding, and for 'the perfection of his knowledge'. He seeks the beautiful unity of all knowledge, a unity at once systematic (the harmony of all his knowledge in one coherent whole) and social (the harmony of his knowledge with the knowledge of others). He works towards the *systematic* unity of knowledge with a 'noble impatience [that] cannot rest until all of his conceptions have ordered themselves into an organic whole', but, as 'he has always loved truth more than his system', he will willingly accept and embrace challenge, innovation, or revolution, and his progress will involve him tearing down and rebuilding, time and again. In any case, he knows that the systematic perfection he seeks is really available only to 'the infinite understanding'. But he is also dedicated to *social* unity: 'All minds work for him', and he knows that 'among thinking minds an intimate community of all goods of the mind is in effect; what is obtained in the kingdom of truth by one is won for all'. The unity of knowledge is a unity of people, the pursuit of philosophy at the same time the pursuit of the common good—and so Schiller's vision has an expansive political aspect. He claims that, for the philosopher, 'all thinking minds are now bound together by the bond of world-citizenry', a bond that is increasingly visible in Europe, which is being bound together (with philosophy's help) as a family of states no longer tearing one another limb from limb—a poignant comment to have made in the middle of 1789.

Twenty years later, the proposal to create a university in Berlin was seen by many as an opportunity to create an institution precisely for the philosophically minded, and to the exclusion of bread scholarship—and the 'philosophically minded' learning that Schiller had marked out was now further specified as a matter of *Bildung* and *Wissenschaft*.[24]

---

[24] Turner, in 'Prussian Universities', 78, notes that the conversations surrounding the foundation of Berlin were full of 'lofty appeals to a visionary ideal of intellectual and personal

Wilhelm von Humboldt, who as Secretary for Religion and Public Instruction did more than any other to make the University of Berlin a reality, was a devotee of *Bildung*—of 'salvation through culture', as it has been called.[25] He envisaged learning as a process of 'weeding [one's] mental and emotional garden',[26] of growing in nobility, poise, judgement, and freedom. 'The true end of man', he wrote, 'or that which is prescribed by the eternal and immutable dictates of reason, and not suggested by vague and transient desires, is the highest and most harmonious development of his powers to a complete and consistent whole.'[27]

The University of Berlin was, he wrote, to be devoted to the 'moral culture [*moralische Kultur*]' of the nation, its 'spiritual and moral formation [*geistigen und sittlichen Bildung*]'.[28] But it was to be so precisely as an institution devoted to *Wissenschaft* 'in the deepest and widest sense of the word'. *Bildung* and *Wissenschaft* are, for him, almost identical.[29]

In other presentations, *Wissenschaft* itself is the dominant note. One of the reports that Humboldt had in front of him as he drew up his designs set the tone. Written for his predecessor, Beyme, it was by Fichte, and it described an academy (Fichte would not call it a university) that, building on the

---

development through study, through exposure to *Wissenschaft*, a development simultaneously intellectual, moral, and aesthetic'. I am downplaying the differences he identifies between the Idealists, Fichte, Schelling, and Steffens, and the Neohumanists, Wolf, Schleiermacher, and Humboldt. Andreas W. Daum, in '*Wissenschaft* and Knowledge', in Jonathan Sperber (ed.), *Germany 1800–1871*, 137–61: 144, argues that the Idealists (for him, Fichte and Schleiermacher) stress *unity*, where neo-Humanists such as Wolf and Humboldt stress *Bildung*. For the differences between versions of the *Wissenschaftsideologie* beholden to Kant and to Schelling, see Frederick Gregory, 'Kant, Schelling and the Administration of Science in the Romantic Era', *Osiris*, 2nd ser. 5 (1989), *Science in Germany*, 16–35.

[25] H. Bruford, *The German Tradition of Self-Cultivation: 'Bildung' from Humboldt to Thomas Mann* (Cambridge: Cambridge University Press, 1975), 13.

[26] Bruford, *German Tradition*, 14.

[27] Wilhelm von Humboldt, *The Sphere and Duties of Government (The Limits of State Action)*, tr. Joseph Coulthard (London: John Chapman, 1854), 11; <files.libertyfund.org/files/589/0053_Bk.pdf> (accessed 27 Nov. 2009); a different translation is provided in Bruford, *German Tradition*, 15. Timothy Bahti, in 'Histories of the University: Kant and Humboldt', *Modern Language Notes* (*MLN*), 102/3 (Apr. 1987), 437–60: 452, notes the deep Romantic pattern of Humboldt's plans: the university is 'the visible form of an *essentially* other, invisible "spirit", "idea", or "reason"—*Wissenschaft*'. The university is approximately a sacrament of reason (that is, reason's outward and visible sign).

[28] Wilhelm von Humboldt, 'On the Spirit and the Organisational Framework of Intellectual Institutions in Berlin', *Minerva*, 8 (1970), 242–50: 242; German original, 'Über die innere und äussere Organisation der höheren wissenschaftlichen Anstalten in Berlin', in Anrich (ed.), *Die Idee der deutschen Universitäten*, 375–86.

[29] Schelling strikes the same note when he says that the highest purpose is 'to ennoble one's mind through knowledge [*durch Wissenschaft veredelten Geistes*]' (*On University Studies*, 6).

foundation provided by the schools (in which the basic furnishings of the mind had already been installed),[30] was to be a home for *Wissenschaft*. It would cultivate above all 'the art of criticism, of sifting the true from the false, the useful from the useless, and the subordination of the less important to the more important'.[31] It was to be a 'school of the art of using the *wissenschaftlich* understanding'.[32]

In setting out this vision of *wissenschaftlich*, *Bildung*-orientated endeavour, men like Humboldt and Fichte envisaged altering the whole shape of the university as an institution. It could not be, they said, an institution devoted only to teaching. It had to be devoted to *research* as well. Students should now be apprentices in the service of *Wissenschaft*, and can therefore learn their art only by joining in with professors who are themselves active masters of it. As Andreas Daum says: 'Professors therefore had to be more than simply purveyors of knowledge. They were seen as moral models and agents of creativity, restlessly aiming at expanding the limits of knowledge, disregarding any utilitarian purpose or social constraints, and guided only by their free will.'[33] And Stephen Turner puts it this way:

No difference in personality or intellect can exist between the ideal teacher and the ideal scholar–discoverer, because the 'capacity for original thought' is prerequisite to teaching and judgment as well as to original research. From this reasoning the founders of the *Wissenschaftsideologie* concluded not only that the professor can and should be a creative scholar as well as a teacher; from it they drew also the much more radical, indigenously German idea that he must be both in order to be either.[34]

This *Wissenschaftsideologie* produces what Turner has called the 'uniquely German conviction that the university professor's responsibility is not only to

---

[30] These institutions are also clearly schools of *memoria*—see Fichte, 'Deduced Scheme', 181, on the role of the school in 'filling the well-known rooms in [the students'] ancestral abode with treasures'.

[31] Fichte, 'Deduced Scheme', 176.

[32] Fichte, 'Deduced Scheme', 165.

[33] Daum, '*Wissenschaft* and Knowledge', 145. Cf. Schelling, *On University Studies*, 26–7: 'A man who lives within his science as though on another's property, who is not himself in possession, who has never acquired a sure and living feeling for it, who is incapable of sitting down and reconstructing it for himself, is an unworthy teacher even when he attempts no more than to expound the ideas of others.'

[34] Turner, 'Prussian Universities', 82. Although he tends to separate formal research and teaching more thoroughly than the other theorists, Schleiermacher set out a vision of teaching that matches Daum's and Turner's comments well. He focuses specifically on lecturing, downplaying live dialogue as a central mode of teaching for practical reasons. The lecturer should, on the one hand, begin with his students' current patterns of understanding, and lead them on Socratically, dialectically, towards transformed understanding. But the lecturer should, on the other hand, be 'reproducing [his] own coming to know', 'so that the listeners are not constantly gathering more information but are directly perceiving the activity of reason in bringing forth knowledge and are perspicaciously continuing that activity' ('Occasional Thoughts', 29). Lecturing is a means by which students are caught up in an activity that is real for the lecturer, not a means of transmitting the *results* of that activity.

transmit academic learning but to expand it, through research and publication',[35] and what Charles McClelland calls the 'graft of searching intellect . . .
onto the pruned and rejuvenated trunk of the essentially teaching-oriented
university'.[36] In other words: the *Wissenschaftsideologie* underwrote the creation of a new kind of institution: the *research university*.[37]

We might well ask, however, what exactly is new about this way of thinking
about learning. What more is there to it than an attempt to overturn specific
abuses and return to the ideal of devout learning familiar from the previous
chapter? After all, for all differences in detail, the way in which learning is
described in this *Wissenschaftsideologie* is, far from being shockingly new,
immediately recognizable.[38] The idea, for instance, that students were apprentices in an activity modelled for them by their teachers (an activity that was
more than simply the transmission of content) is as appropriate to Paris as to
Berlin. And even the insistence upon research is not necessarily a mark of
fundamental discontinuity. Though the regimes of knowledge differ enough to
make the analogy a loose one, there is a parallel between the searching intellect
beloved of the *Wissenschaft* ideologues and what in the prevous chapter
I described as the Parisian desire for articulation.

Fichte was probably the *Wissenschaft* theorist most sharply aware of his
distance from the Christian theological tradition.[39] As one commentator has

---

[35] Turner, 'Prussian Universities', 68.

[36] Charles E. McClelland, '"To Live for Science": Ideals and Realities at the University of
Berlin', in Thomas Bender (ed.), *The University and the City: From Medieval Origins to the
Present* (New York: Oxford University Press, 1988), 181–97: 181.

[37] Such institutes as the philology seminars established at Halle in 1786 by Friedrich August
Wolf had helped make this transition imaginable. See Turner, 'Prussian Universities', 83, 86–9;
cf. Clark, *Academic Charisma*, ch. 5.

[38] Schleiermacher explicitly set his proposals for Berlin in the context of an existing tradition:
his task, as he saw it, was to reconstrue that tradition so as to determine 'what was essential or
accidental in what existed before' (Schleiermacher, 'Occasional Thoughts', 2). His example is not
insignificant: 'Schleiermacher deserves to be regarded with von Humboldt as the co-founder of
the University of Berlin' according to Terrence N. Tice in his 'Dedicatory Preface' to Friedrich
Schleiermacher, *Occasional Thoughts on Universities in the German Sense, with an Appendix
Regarding a University Soon to Be Established (1808)*, tr. Terrence N. Tice with Edwina Lawler
(Lewiston, NY: Edwin Mellen, 1991), pp. i–iv: ii. After all, 'it was Schleiermacher who crafted and
most eminently sustained the articulated vision that in large part underlay the University's
design. That vision, in turn, has made a significant impact on subsequent definitions of the
modern university, in both theory and practice' (p. ii).

[39] In the other direction, of the five authors of the classic university texts, it is not Schleiermacher but Steffens who makes the *strongest* connections between his proposals and specifically
Christian faith. His seventh lecture (*Vorlesungen über die Idee der Universitäten*, 368–74) makes
it clear that the unity sought and experienced in the university is the unity of the 'communion of
saints' (p. 369), and that the *Mittelpunkt* that *Wissenschaft* seeks and anticipates is present in
Jesus Christ (pp. 371–2): the ascent and purification he describes are explicitly theological,
Christological, and ecclesial. As one might expect, given the genre, theological notes also
sound very loudly in Clemens Brentano's *Universitati Litterariae: Kantate auf den 15ten October
1810* (Berlin: Julius Eduard Hitzig, 1910); facsimile available online at <www.archive.org/details/
5471646> (accessed 3 Dec. 2009), which opens with a Chorus of Trustees singing that the

said, however, his vision of the ideal institution for higher education 'strongly resembles a monastic institution in which a community of scholars, both masters and apprentices, would live together isolated from the rest of the world'.[40] And the continuities are not entirely superficial: the degree to which Fichte appropriated explicitly theological categories to elaborate the workings of his proposal is striking.[41] He talks of the end of Wissenschaft being 'help and salvation . . . for poor mankind' and the consequent need for 'holy earnestness and reverence' in one's discussions of it.[42] Of the absolute unity of knowledge that Wissenschaft seeks, he says in another writing that 'the whole world exists solely in order that the supernatural, the Godhead, may be displayed in it'[43]—and, since the university is dedicated to this unity, 'all separation between the supernatural and the worldly is ended in the University, and the University is the visible representation of the unity of the World as the manifestation of God, and God himself'.[44]

More generally, Fichte's academy of *Wissenschaft* is clearly a context for purification and ascent. The learning that is to take place there is a matter of being caught up in a providential process and being remade by it, taken out of limited, incurved perspective to participation in a vision deeper and wider than any that one could have reached on one's own. It is a process of elevation, and the language Fichte needs to describe it is inescapably moral, in the broadest sense: there is a deep connection between this learning and the good of the individual, of the learning society, and of the whole world. One could see Fichte's account of the university as an attempt to overcome precisely the metaphysical and moral unravelling that had marked the disintegration of the Parisian ideal, and so as the re-establishment of a form of learning inherently devout.[45]

---

university's teachers are imitating Christ, and a Chorus of Teachers insisting that the content of their learning and teaching is nothing other than the divine essence (pp. 3–4).

[40] Lawler, 'Neohumanistic–Idealistic Concepts', 17; cf. Fichte, 'Deduced Scheme', 208, 216.

[41] For Celia Applegate, in 'Culture and the Arts', in Sperber (ed.), *Germany 1800–1871*, 115–36, the whole tradition of thinking about Bildung is 'a secular theology', its advocacy a matter of the 'transference of religious terminology' (118); Bruford calls *Bildung* religion without personification (18), and a matter of 'the salvation of the soul' (*German Tradition*, 27).

[42] Fichte, *Deduced Scheme*, 187.

[43] J. G. Fichte, 'Concerning the Only Possible Disturbance of Academic Freedom' (Fichte's inaugural lecture as Rector of the University of Berlin in 1811), extracts in Turnbull, *The Educational Theory of J. G. Fichte*, 263–5: 263.

[44] Fichte, 'Only Possible Disturbance', 264. Cf. Schelling, *On University Studies*, 11–12: 'all knowledge is a striving for communion with the divine essence, for participation in the primordial knowledge of which the visible universe is the image and whose source is the fountainhead of eternal power'.

[45] Schelling retains the pre-eminent place for the theology faculty—albeit one in which theology has now has its true essence realized as Idealist philosophy (*On University Studies*, 82–102).

Nevertheless, the vast distance from Paris is also clear. Fichte's proposal is marked by an explicit rejection of 'what is old and traditional', and of positive Christian theology specifically,[46] and such an opposition structures many of the other proposals as well, albeit less visibly. After all, the scene for all the *Wissenschaft* ideologues, even to an extent Schleiermacher, was set by Immanuel Kant's *Conflict of the Faculties*, with its opposition between the biblical and the rational, the ecclesiastical and the *purely* religious, and its refusal to allow the positive, historical content of Christian theology any constitutive role in determining the shape that reason will give to life.[47]

In order to understand the discontinuity as well as the continuity between Paris and Berlin, therefore, we need to dig a little deeper. For my purposes, it is not so much in the metaphysical or the moral spheres that the difference between Paris and Berlin can best be approached, though there are certainly telling differences between the forms of purification and ascent envisaged in both contexts: it is in the social or political sphere. In other words, the crucial theme is the *sociality of reason*,[48] reason's conversational and public nature. That is the point at which the proponents of *Wissenschaftsideologie* draw most deeply and creatively on the Christian theological tradition that they had inherited, and also the point at which they thought they had identified the central inadequacy or contradiction of that tradition, and had set about its reconstruction.

THE SOCIALITY OF REASON

At the end of the previous chapter, I suggested that the University of Paris could be seen as an experiment in the formation of a certain kind of moral community, a community of reasoning intended to have peaceable *disputatio* at its heart. The thinking of the *Wissenschaft* ideologues surrounding the emergence of the University of Berlin is, in part, a reinvention of precisely this wheel. That is, even though they were very conscious of the collapse of *disputatio*, and even though they show no signs of regarding themselves as elaborating a medieval model of corporate reasoning (quite the reverse!), they end up developing an account of the social nature of reason, and of the kind of reasoning communities that can properly sustain it, that parallels the Parisian ideas I have described, and that draws explicitly (and pervasively) on some of

---

[46] Fichte, 'Only Possible', 264.

[47] Immanuel Kant, *The Conflict of the Faculties* in *Religion and Rational Theology*, ed. Allen W. Wood and George di Giovanni (Cambridge: Cambridge University Press, 1996), 233–327; see especially the appendix on 'The Conflict between the Theology and Philosophy Faculties', 262–4.

[48] This phrase is borrowed from Terry Pinkard, *Hegel's Phenomenology: The Sociality of Reason* (Cambridge: Cambridge University Press, 1994).

the same theological language that can be used to describe those Parisian ideas. Of course, the wheel that the modern authors invent is not simply identical to the medieval wheel: it uses new materials, and is constructed in new ways. Nevertheless the continuities are striking.

This witting or unwitting reinvention emerges from a very specific practical context: the realm of enlightened public conversation in the 'Republic of Letters'—the sphere of 'reciprocal exchange based on a model of friendship that contrasted markedly with the absolutist state, corporative society, and the family'.[49] That is, the rediscovery of the sociality of reason in the *Wissenschaft-sideologie* was in part nurtured in the conversations of the cultured eighteenth-century salon, and in the wider exchange of letters, periodicals, and papers that surrounded those conversations. More specifically, the *Wissenschaftsideologie* emerged from certain late-eighteenth- and early nineteenth-century salons in which the enlightened culture of the Republic of Letters had been given a decidedly Romantic inflection.

Two particular contexts within the broader Republic of Letters were directly generative for several of the key players in the establishment of the University of Berlin: Jena in the 1790s, a decade after Schelling's inaugural lecture there, and Berlin's own salon culture in the early 1800s.[50] The first of these, eighteenth-century Jena, is not at first glance an obvious place to look for inspiration when considering the sociality of reason. It had a 'notoriously appalling' reputation for student rowdiness, and was a byword for cultural coarseness.[51] In the mid-1780s, however, Carl August, duke of Weimar, set up a commission chaired by Goethe tasked with proposing reforms. For various reasons, the reforms took a while to bite, but by the mid-1790s a real change was beginning to show. For a time—in part, perhaps, because its relative poverty meant it could afford only junior appointments to the faculty, in part because it existed in a situation of some jurisdictional complexity that allowed those faculty members a fair degree of academic freedom,[52] in part because of the kind of men who were attracted by the presence of Goethe and Schiller—Jena became *the* context for the development of Romanticism. What might otherwise have taken place outside formal institutional walls in

---

[49] Dena Goodman, *The Republic of Letters: A Cultural History of the French Enlightenment* (Ithaca, NY: Cornell University Press, 1994), 2. See also Peter Burke, *The Art of Conversation* (Ithaca, NY: Cornell University Press, 1993), ch. 4: 'The Art of Conversation in Early Modern Europe'. Goodman's discussion of the Republic of Letters could be extended backwards to the Scientific Revolution, which can itself be read in large part as a revolution grounded in the development of certain kinds of reasoned communication—see Lisa Jardine, *Ingenious Pursuits: Building the Scientific Revolution* (London: Abacus, 2000), and the opening of Chapter 8 below.

[50] See Ziolkowski, *German Romanticism*, 218–19.

[51] Ziolkowski, *German Romanticism*, 228, 230. 'It seems unlikely...that a movement as intellectual as German Romanticism should have been associated with any university, much less with Jena' (p. 233).

[52] It belonged to Weimar, Coburg, Gotha, and Meiningen.

a salon took place under the auspices of a university: the meeting of the Schlegels, Fichte, Schelling, Novalis, Brentano, and others in what Friedrich Schlegel called 'a symphony of professors'.[53] Heinrich Steffens, himself one of the theorists of the Romantic university, reflected in his autobiography that during those years in Jena 'all of us believed ... that we were carrying out a common task, and there arose a covenant of spirits that had a profoundly significant effect'.[54] The poet Ludwig Tieck said that 'these spirits and their ... aspirations for life, poetry and philosophy, constituted almost uninterruptedly a festival of wit, esprit and philosophy'.[55] The experience and memory of Jena were formative for the ideas and ideals surrounding the establishment of the University of Berlin.

The other formative context lay in Berlin itself in the salon of Henriette Herz, a Jewish hostess whose house 'was for many years the centre of a sociable and intellectual circle, which ... embraced all that was most celebrated in literature and science in Berlin',[56] and which included the Humboldt brothers, and the Friedrichs Schlegel and Schleiermacher.[57] Schleiermacher's friendship

---

[53] Ziolkowski, *German Romanticism*, 261, citing Friedrich Schlegel's 'Ideen zu Gedichten', vi. 46, in *Kritische Friedrich-Schlegel-Ausgabe*, 16, ed. Hans Eichner (Munich: Schöningh, 1891), 198.

[54] Heinrich Steffens, *Was ich erlebte*, ed. Willi A. Koch (Munich: Winkler, 1956 [1840–1844]), 92, cited in Ziolkowski, *German Romanticism*, 218.

[55] Ludwig Tieck, *Schriften*, 5 (Berlin: G. Reimer, 1828), dedication to A. W. Schlegel; cited in Ziolkowski, *German Romanticism*, 219.

[56] Frederica Rowan (ed. and tr.), *The Life of Schleiermacher as Unfolded in his Autobiography and Letters* (London: Smith, Elder and Co, 1860), i. 135. The quotation is from one of Rowan's additions to the German editors' notes.

[57] See Deborah Hertz, 'Salonières and Literary Women in Late Eighteenth-Century Berlin', *New German Critique*, 14 (1978), 97–108, and Roswitha Burwicke, 'From Aesthetic Teas to the World of Noble Reformers: The Berlin Salonière (1780–1848)', *Pacific Coast Philology*, 2/.2 (1994), 129–42. The received image of these salons is that they were 'tolerant, informal, unceremonious, and supposedly free of ideologies' (Burwick, 'Aesthetic Teas', 129), but 'the idyllic image of an open society cannot stand up to scrutiny' (Barbara Hahn, *The Jewish Pallas Athena: This Too a Theory of Modernity*, tr. James McFarland (Princeton: Princeton University Press, 2005), 52). Hahn argues that the inclusion of Jewish women came at the price of a pressure 'not merely to acculturate but also to leave behind their distinctive history, culture, and faith' (Barbara Hahn, 'A Dream of Living Together: Jewish Women in Berlin around 1800', in Emily D. Bilski and Emily Braun (eds), *Jewish Women and their Salons: The Power of Conversation* (Yale: Yale University Press, 2005), 149–58: 150) and she notes that Henriette Herz's salon met on Friday evenings—the Sabbath (152). William Rasch, in 'Ideal Sociability: Friedrich Schleiermacher and the Ambivalence of Extrasocial Spaces', in Ulrike Gleixner and Marion W. Gray (eds), *Gender in Transition: Discourse and Practice in German-Speaking Europe 1750–1830* (Ann Arbor: University of Michigan Press, 2006), 319–39: 320, argues that the salons did not really shake the gender constraints of the time, and Ulrike Weckel, in 'A Lost Paradise of Female Culture? Some Critical Questions Regarding the Scholarship on Late Eighteenth- and Early Nineteenth-Century German Salons', tr. Pamela E. Selwyn, *German History*,18/3 (2000), 310–36: 326, argues that the salons simply served purposes of 'group formation and self-reassurance of a new cultural elite'. The term 'salon' is itself anachronistic—see Weckel, 'Lost Paradise', 318–19, and Hahn, 'Dream of Living Together', 151. For the Berlin context in general, see Graham Ward, 'The Emergence of Schleiermacher's Theology and the City of Berlin', in Mike Higton, Jeremy

with Herz, and his experience of the intellectual and cultural community that she gathered around her, fed into a 1799 essay for the *Berliner Archiv der Zeit und des Geshmacks*: 'Toward a Theory of Sociable Conduct'.[58] In the words of Jeffrey Hoover, Schleiermacher's essay provides a theory of 'the arena of privately-motivated associations and gatherings that primarily serve the purpose of cultivating the individuality of persons through society with others. This domain of social interaction is conceived in opposition to the institutionally organized areas of social life such as church, school and politics.'[59] William Rasch writes that

Schleiermacher imagined an extrasocial space in which the fragmented, functionalized citizen could be formed into the well-rounded human being . . . [an] ideal form of human intercourse—in which occupational differences among men and the purportedly essential differences between men and women could be bracketed. He sought a common discursive ground based on non-specialized knowledge accessible to all educated people who gather together for no other purpose than the self-enrichment that comes from the mutual exercise of the human being's intellectual and spiritual capacities.[60]

Schleiermacher's theory, or what we have of it (he intended to write a continuation, but was distracted by work on the *Speeches on Religion*), is focused on the purity of the reciprocity that should characterize such sociality. Between 'the cares of domestic life and the affairs of public [*bürgerliche*] life' stands 'free sociality [*freie Geselligkeit*]',[61] 'the free association of rational and mutually-cultivating persons' (p. 21) in which 'many persons are to act upon each other and . . . this action cannot be unilateral in any way' (p. 24). Free sociality involves 'a reciprocal action that is interwoven among all the participants but one that is also fully determined and made complete by them' (p. 24). The purpose of such sociality 'is not at all to be conceived as lying outside it. The action of each individual should be aimed at the activity of the others, and the activity of individuals should be their influence on the others' (p. 24). It should be a sociality into which each can bring all that is distinctively

Law, and Christopher Rowland (eds), *Theology and Human Flourishing: Essays in Honour of Timothy J. Gorringe* (Eugene, OR: Wipf and Stock, 2011), 108–26.

[58] For the origin of the essay in Schleiermacher's friendship with Herz, see Rasch, 'Ideal Sociability', 322.

[59] Jeffrey Hoover, 'Introduction to "Toward a Theory of Sociable Conduct"', in Ruth Drucilla Richardson (ed.), *Friedrich Schleiermacher's* Toward a Theory of Sociable Conduct *and Essays on its Intellectual–Cultural Context*, New Athenaeum/Neues Athenaeum 4 (Lewiston, NY: Edwin Mellen, 1995), 9–19: 10. 'The general aim of free sociality is exhausted by the intent to stimulate and encourage the development of individuals simply for the sake of stimulating them and developing them' (p. 15).

[60] Rasch, 'Ideal Sociability', 320.

[61] F. D. E. Schleiermacher, 'Towards a Theory of Sociable Conduct', in Richardson (ed.), *Friedrich Schleiermacher's* Toward a Theory of Sociable Conduct, 20–39: 21; subsequent page references in text.

his or her own, for the benefit of all: 'All are to be stimulated to a free play of thought through the communication of what is mine', and, reciprocally, I can receive from each of the others. 'All is to be reciprocal action' (p. 25).

The context is unmistakably the refined drawing room—and Hoover can aptly say that Schleiermacher's ideal requires one 'to have a wide range of topics of conversation with which you are comfortable, to be able to expand or constrict your focus according to the objects of discussion, and to be able to leave a mark of your characteristic style on the content of sociality'.[62] According to Schleiermacher, however, such sociality will inherit the world. As he put it elsewhere: 'What I hold worthy of the name of world is only the eternal fellowship of minds, their mutual influence, their reciprocal formation of each other, the noble harmony of freedom.'[63]

Much of the attention of the Romantic theorists of the university (including Schleiermacher himself) is focused precisely on this same quality of intimate, reciprocal sociality that they had experienced in Jena or in the house of Henrietta Herz, or in other similar contexts, and which they believed should characterize institutions of true *Bildung* through *Wissenschaft*. Humboldt could speak of 'a contest of personalities for moral and intellectual influence in which it is as blessed to receive as to give . . . By being oneself one enriches the world as it presents itself to others, who, in turn, perform the same service for oneself.'[64]

According to Fichte, a class of students should 'remain in continual communication and *wissenschaftlich* relations with one another, in which each shows to all his individual view of science', and the relation between teacher and student should be no less reciprocal.

Not only the teacher but also the pupil must continually express himself and communicate his thoughts, so that their mutual relationship in learning is a continuous conversation, in which each speech by the teacher is the answer to some question asked by the pupil concerning what immediately preceded, and the putting of some new question by the teacher, which the pupil answers in his next statement.

The life of *Wissenschaft* should be the life of a 'Socratic school', and be held together by love.[65]

It is against this background that we should read more formal descriptions of *Wissenschaft*, like that provided by Schleiermacher in his lectures on *Dialectic* in 1811—a course of lectures offered from the second year onwards

---

[62] Hoover, 'Introduction', 17.

[63] Schleiermacher, *Monologen*, ch. 1, translated in Bruford, *German Tradition*, 70.

[64] Quoted in Bruford, *German Tradition*, 16. We have not moved very far from that sentiment in Humboldt's definition of an academy: 'a society constituted for the purpose of subjecting the work of each member to the assessment of all the others' ('On the Spirit', 248).

[65] Fichte, 'Deduced Scheme', 177.

of the University of Berlin's existence, and intended by Schleiermacher quite explicitly as an introduction to the reasoning processes that should constitute the university as a whole.[66] Dialectic as it were sets out the grammar of knowledge in all the sciences (pp. 1–3);[67] Schleiermacher can describe it as 'the principles of the art of doing philosophy' (p. 3) or, more significantly, as 'the art of accomplishing a philosophical construction *together with another person*' (6; emphasis added), noting that for the Socratic schools 'the principles for dialogue and for construction of knowledge overall were the same' (p. 7).[68] 'The interest of dialectic arises because each person strives to join the particular that he or she has found by his or her particular talent to what is general' (p. 7). More abstractly, 'The knowing of one person must be able to cohere with the knowledge of every other person, and what is on the one hand the unity of reason is on the other hand the sum total of sense perception' (p. 21).[69]

In his own proposal for the formation of the University of Berlin, *Occasional Thoughts on Universities in the German Sense*, Schleiermacher insists that

Wissenschaft is by no means a business for the individual as such . . . it cannot be brought to fruition and fully possessed by one person alone but must be a communal effort to which each contributes a share, so that for its purposes each is dependent on all the rest and can by him- or herself possess only an isolated fragment and that very incompletely.[70]

---

[66] Friedrich Schleiermacher, *Dialectic or, The Art of Doing Philosophy: A Study Edition of the 1811 Notes*, tr. Terrence N. Tice, American Academy of Religion Texts and Translations, ed. Terry Goodlove, 11 (Atlanta, GA: Scholars Press, 1996), translations slightly altered; subsequent page references in text.

[67] Fichte had lectured on the theory of *Wissenschaft* in the same slot in the first semester, and some of Schleiermacher's comments appear to be directed against him—so, here, he insists that dialectic cannot form any kind of distinct system prior to the various sciences, but only exists in relation to them.

[68] Schleiermacher, *Dialectic*, 7. See also Manfred Frank, 'Metaphysical Foundations: A Look at Schleiermacher's *Dialectic*', tr. Jacqueline Mariña in Mariña (ed.), *The Cambridge Companion to Friedrich Schleiermacher* (Cambridge: Cambridge University Press, 2005), 15–34: dialectic is 'the art of conversation', the 'cooperative search for truth' (p. 15). Away with Fichte's 'dialogical forgetfulness' (p. 16)!

[69] Cf. Humboldt, 'On the Spirit', 243. This sense of the conversational, communal nature of knowing, and the drive towards inclusivity in the community of knowing is inseparable from—indeed, is the flip side of—a drive towards the unity of knowledge/reason, a unity that we assume in all our acts of knowing: 'We . . . presuppose it as existing already . . . it exists in all our knowing' (Schleiermacher, *Occasional Thoughts*, 9); it is at once a supreme coincidence of being and knowing, and the unity of all knowing.

[70] Schleiermacher, 'Occasional Thoughts', 2, translation slightly altered; subsequent page numbers in text. For Schleiermacher, the primary task of the university is to set all individual, fragmented practices and habits of knowing within this broader context—to awaken them to the awareness of their ingredience in this quest for social unity. 'The business of the university, then, is this: to awaken the idea of science in the more noble youths, who are already supplied [at school] with many kinds of information, to aid the idea's holding sway over them in the area of knowledge to which each chooses to be especially devoted, so that it will become second nature

That science can be such a communal effort, a harmonious sharing rather than a battle between incompatible perspectives, is grounded for Schleiermacher in the fact that the world is one—so that 'every particular admits of thorough inspection only in combination with all the rest' (p. 2). There is an ideal whole in which each act of knowing participates and which each act of knowing anticipates, in 'an ever advancing approximation' (p. 18). 'All scientific endeavours pull together, tending towards oneness' (p. 3). That whole is at once, as it were, the perfect unity of God's-eye vision—the 'encyclopaedic perspective' (p. 17), in which knowledge and reality coincide fully and reality is fully known—and a perfect *social* unity in which all knowers are united with each other in perfect harmony. Therefore Schleiermacher can say that 'communication is the primary law governing every effort to attain knowledge' (p. 3).

So, for the theorists of the *Wissenschaftsideologie*, reason is inherently social, and reasoning is practised in, and as, a certain kind of community of peaceable, loving exchange—a free flow of giving and receiving in which differing perspectives and understandings become gifts rather than challenges, and in which it is as blessed to receive as to give. In fact, one might say that *Wissenschaft* simply *is* this sociality, and this sociality *is* *Wissenschaft*. The rules that govern *Wissenschaft*—that make it truly philosophical rather than a matter of bread scholarship—are precisely the rules of free exchange that constitute this sociality: Schleiermacher's rules of sociable conduct *are* the rules of reason. That which resists or distorts *Wissenschaft* is precisely that which restricts or distorts the full freedom of giving or the full freedom of reception in the community of scholars. Such social unity is grounded in, and a mirror of, the unity of the truth that the various individual reasoners pursue; they now see the unity of that knowledge partially and dimly, but in their knowing and in their conversation they anticipate the fuller, universal, or absolute vision that is God's alone.

for them to contemplate everything from the viewpoint of science, to perceive nothing for itself alone but only in terms of the scientific connections most relevant to it, and in a broad, cohesive manner bringing it into a continual relation to the unity and totality of knowledge, so that they may learn to become conscious of the basic laws of science in every thought process and precisely in this way gradually to develop in themselves the capacity to investigate, to contrive and to give account' (p. 16). (Cf. my comments in Ch. 6, p. 177, on Lynn Holt's description of excellent apprehension.) Schleiermacher admits that his vision will not hold for all university students; some will be capable only of advanced technical schooling—they will not have the philosophic bent. Therefore the university must *also* have the character of 'advanced schools for specialists' (p. 26).

PUBLIC REASON

So far, it would be possible to present all this material as an attempt to elucidate, deepen, and extend—albeit in a new intellectual key—all that I said about the peaceable community of knowing in the last chapter, and the theological language in which so much of it is couched would be evidence that, in casting around for a way to articulate their sense of the peaceable sociality of knowledge, the theorists of *Wissenschaft* had hit upon precisely the remnants of the theological tradition that underpinned Paris, and had drawn them back into use.[71]

Nevertheless, there is another side of the story that pulls strongly in a rather different direction. To put it simplistically: however church-shaped the sociality of reason described by the Romantic theorists might be, they insist upon the separation of reason from any actual church—and its connection, instead, to the state. In order to understand this aspect of the ideology surrounding the formation of the University of Berlin, we need to turn to a text that, while not itself a Romantic theory of the university, deeply influenced the Romantic theorists: Immanuel Kant's *The Conflict of the Faculties*.

In early 1792, Kant sent the first of a planned quartet of essays on religion to the *Berlinische Monatsschrift* for publication. The Prussian authorities under Friedrich Wilhelm II had recently tightened the practices of censorship in Prussia, but the *Monatsschrift* had moved its publication base to Jena, beyond the reach of those practices, but whence books and journals could be imported to Prussia with no difficulty.[72] Nevertheless, Kant insisted that his essays should be submitted for Prussian scrutiny. The censor approved the first for publication, on the grounds that it was 'only intended for, and of appeal to, the thoughtful scholar, adept to enquiry and distinctions—not any reader in general', and so unlikely to disturb the equilibrium of the state.[73] The second essay, submitted later in the year, was, however, refused by the censor: it contained material on the Bible, which in the eyes of the censor made it a theological text—and the theological advice that the censor received was decidedly unfavourable. Kant therefore decided to try another route. University publications were not subjected to direct state censorship in the same way,

---

[71] I am not forgetting that Henriette Herz was Jewish rather than Christian. Nevertheless, the theorizing of her salon's free sociality in the hands of men like Schleiermacher was recognizably Christian—and, as I have already noted, a downplaying of her Judaism seems to have been a price that Herz paid for fuller participation in Berlin society (see n. 57 above).

[72] On the Königsberg context, see Riccardo Pozzo, 'Kant's *Streit der Fakultäten* and Conditions in Königsberg', *History of Universities*, 16/2 (2000), 96–128. Pozzo argues that Kant is actually promoting a return to the conditions that existed under Frederick the Great (1712–86) and his minister Karl Abraham von Zedlitz und Leipe (1731–93) until 1786, against Friedrich Wilhelm II (1744–97) and his minister Johann Christoph von Wöllner (1732–1800).

[73] George di Giovanni, 'Translator's Introduction' [to *Religion within the Boundaries of Mere Reason*], in Kant, *Religion and Rational Theology*, 41–54: 41–2.

but could be regulated by the universities themselves (presumably in part because university publications were deemed to be inherently material only for 'the thoughtful scholar, adept to enquiry and distinctions'). So Kant first checked with the Königsberg theology faculty that they regarded his four essays as primarily philosophical, and then sent the essays for approval to the philosophy faculty at the University of Jena. In 1793, *Religion within the Boundaries of Mere Reason* was published.

Kant was at work on an essay prompted by this affair, explaining the relationship between the theology and philosophy faculties, when a letter of reproof arrived from Johann Christoph von Wöllner, writing on behalf of the king. It reprimanded Kant for abusing his role as a public teacher, and publishing material of an inflammatory nature. Kant replied, defending himself, insisting that the book was 'not at all suitable for the public' and not likely to be read by them,[74] but agreeing that, as a loyal subject of the king, he would publish no more on religious topics. In late 1797, however, Friedrich Wilhelm II died, and Kant chose to regard himself as freed from his promise (he was, after all, no longer a loyal subject of *that* king). He set in train publication of his essay on the theology and philosophy faculties, with the letter of reproof from Wöllner and his reply as a Preface, and essays on the law and medicine faculties as a supplement. It was published in 1798 under the title *The Conflict of the Faculties*.[75]

Kant's work is built around the contrast between the 'higher faculties' (theology, law, and medicine) and the 'lower faculty' of philosophy. The business of the higher faculties, according to Kant, is to teach what they are commanded to teach by the appropriate authority—ultimately the authority of the state.[76] Their content is given to them by 'statute', that is, by the decision of some authority external to them, and it will, therefore, be drawn from some authoritative textual corpus rather than invented or derived by the faculties themselves. The higher faculties teach state officials (church ministers, lawyers, and medical doctors) who will head out into the wider world beyond the university to instruct, guide, and help the populace in the ways that the state desires.

On the other side stands the lower, philosophy faculty. Raising the status of the philosophy faculty, and making the case for its centrality to the whole project of the university, is the central abiding achievement of Kant's text—

---

[74] Kant, *Conflict*, 241.

[75] Jacques Derrida, in 'Mochlos; or, The Conflict of the Faculties', tr. Richard Rand and Amy Wygant, in Richard Rand (ed.), *Logomachia: The Conflict of the Faculties* (Lincoln, NE; London: University of Nebraska Press, 1992), 1–34: 6, notes the irony that Kant's whole discussion of autonomy in *The Conflict of the Faculties* is prompted because the state has accused him of irresponsibility (of being *unverantwortlich*) and has asked him for a response (*Verantwortung*): his whole discourse represents an exercise in negotiating his heteronomy.

[76] Kant, *Conflict*, 250–1; subsequent page references in text.

and the point on which he was most influential on (or most in tune with) the Romantic theorists. The philosophy faculty does not take as its basis any statute, nor any authoritative text, but only reason. It is able to take any content treated by the other faculties, or any other concrete proposal of the state, and test it to see if it accords with reason—whether it has the *universality* that reason demands. The philosophy faculty therefore plays a critical role: it determines the rational legitimacy of the principles employed by the state and by the other faculties (pp. 255–6)—a role entirely distinct from that of the higher faculties. 'The higher faculties must . . . take great care not to enter into a misalliance with the lower faculty, but must keep it at a respectful distance, so that the dignity of their statutes will not be damaged by the free play of reason' (p. 251).[77]

Kant refers to the higher faculties' role as *private*, the lower faculty's as *public*,[78] and, at first sight, this is a strange choice of words. The 'private' work of the higher faculties is devoted, as we have seen, to the instruction of state officials, and through them to the instruction of the general populace. It has as its addressees the whole of the population of this particular state. The public work of the lower faculty, on the other hand, is addressed only to the intelligentsia—and we have seen that, in context, it was important to Kant that he could insist upon this restriction. His offending work in *Religion within the Boundaries of Mere Reason* was, he says, not intended for general consumption, nor were the general populace capable of consuming it (p. 241).[79] It was intended only for the intellectual elite, those capable of assessing it *as* a contribution to a rational, scholarly conversation, and of understanding the proper limits and role of such conversation in relation to state power. *Religion within the Boundaries of Mere Reason* was, in other words, intended for the consumption of the Republic of Letters.

Kant's insistence nevertheless on describing his writing in and for this context as 'public' points to one of the Republic of Letters' central paradoxes: it was both universal and elitist. The Republic was, in the understanding of its citizens, open and universal, excluding no one. Many of the contexts in which its discourse was conducted minimized distinctions of rank and inherited wealth. Yet in practice it was a sphere constituted by an educated elite: it

[77] Cf. Schleiermacher, 'Occasional Thoughts', 34–5: theology, law, and medicine 'have arisen individually by virtue of the need to provide a sure foundation for absolutely essential practice through theory, through the passing on of information'; 'the single faculty of philosophy, therefore, alone represents what the scientific union by itself would have established as a university'.

[78] Cf. Immanuel Kant, 'An Answer to the Question: What is Enlightenment?', in Kant, *Practical Philosophy*, ed. Mary J. Gregor and Allen W. Wood (Cambridge: Cambridge Univerity Press, 1996), 11–22.

[79] Kant says that *Religion within the Bounds* was 'not at all suitable for the public'—i.e., it was not an act of general teaching of ordinary people, and so properly subject to state censorship: rather, it was part of that conversation of the intelligentsia that the state needs to be free.

was the playground of the intelligentsia, the clerisy. (Thomas Broman puts it well: 'In principle, they excluded no one, even if in practice they excluded nearly everyone.'[80])

The Conflict of the Faculties presents the philosophy faculty itself, or philosophy faculties in general, as perhaps the focal embodiment of this intellectual elite.[81] Nevertheless, the conversation in which this faculty engages, a conversation all but confined to the community of such faculties (and so considerably more restricted than the communication of the other faculties, intended for dissemination to the whole population), is still, for Kant, public. The higher faculties' work is private precisely because it is carried out under a specific external authority: it is carried out by faculty members only in so far as they stand under the relevant authority, and it is addressed only to those who stand under the same authority.[82] The work of the philosophy faculty, on the other hand, is carried out by members of the faculty thinking and writing in their own persons, under the dictates of their own autonomous reason, and it presents arguments and draws on criteria of relevance to any other autonomous user of reason—it addresses them qua scholars, rather than as members of this or that specific jurisdiction.

The work of the philosophy faculty is, therefore, inherently free from entanglement with the church, according to Kant. That is, it is necessarily free from any kind of ecclesial authority that could require a member of the philosophy faculty, when speaking *as* a member of that faculty, to affirm or defend a principle simply because ecclesial authority said so, and regardless of what his reason might otherwise have had him say. The philosophy faculty can only speak philosophically—and so speak 'publicly', in Kant's sense—to the extent that its members are free to speak and to interact with one another in their own right, and so on the basis of the reason that is the organ of their own autonomy, rather than speaking *as* members of some particular, positive community or system of authority that is not universal. 'Public' reason is in principle the conversation of the whole, universal human community; 'private'

---

[80] Thomas Broman, 'The Habermasian Public Sphere and "Science *in* the Enlightenment"', *History of Science*, 36 (1998), 123–49: 127.

[81] Shaffer, 'Romantic Philosophy', 39, describes Kant's philosophy faculty both as his version of the clerisy, and as a permanent opposition party. Broman, in 'The Habermasian Public Sphere', 138, notes that, 'while anyone potentially could represent universal humanity in the public sphere, only the young men educated in the universities and especially those who were called to higher scholarship had had the opportunity to cultivate those natural gifts, and therefore only they could be counted on to speak from the position of representing universal reason'.

[82] Jonathan Peterson, 'Enlightenment and Freedom', *Journal of the History of Philosophy*, 46/2 (2008), 223–44, 228, sees the public–private distinction as falling between action on another's authority and action in one's own person; Onora O'Neill, 'The Public Use of Reason', *Political Theory*,14/4 (1986), 523–51: 530–1, defines it more in terms of *audience*.

reason the conversation of some positive (and to that extent arbitrary) subset of that universal community.

The Romantic theorists, however different their understanding of the nature of the faculties,[83] largely inherited the structure of Kant's thought on this point. *Wissenschaft* is the free exchange of the community of scholars as scholars, swayed only by the reasons they are able to offer one another, not by their heteronomous deferral to external authorities. The Romantic theorists, as we have seen, convey more of a sense than did Kant that the *individuality* of the contributors to this conversation will matter, such that *Wissenschaft* will involve a weaving-together of all those individualities into a whole greater than the sum of its parts—but what the conversation partners properly bring is strictly rooted in the autonomous spirit of each. And the differing ways in which the theorists separate the university, or at least the philosophy faculty, from the church are grounded in the assumption that the authority of the church, or of the historical Christian tradition precisely in its positivity, cannot but be a restriction on the freedom and proper flourishing of this intensive, serious exchange. Each participant in free sociality is supposed to wear his difference as a gift, not as a way of being separated from his interlocutors—and in a context where theological traditions were seen to be both inherently oppositional, and to be conversations of inherently limited extent (open only for the involvement of those who accepted the relevant positive authorities), a conversation seeking to be freely and openly sociable *could not* be ecclesial. In other words, the Romantic theorists turn away from the church (the institution, guardian of an authoritative, positive tradition, standing outside the boundaries of mere reason) for the sake of the 'church' (a re-thought Body of Christ stripped of its particularity; the community of free giving and receiving, of participation in and anticipation of the absolute or universal community of knowing). If in their descriptions of the sociality of reason the theorists of *Wissenschaft* drew implicitly or explicitly on ecclesial or monastic models, in their advocacy of fully public conversation they saw themselves as raising that theological inheritance to a new level, freed from particularism and conflict. And, because they can no longer accept the church as the primary context for the ascent and purification of reason, nor as the guarantor of their freedoms and privileges as scholars, they turn instead to the state.[84]

---

[83] See, e.g., Schelling, *On University Studies*, chs 6, 9, 10, and 11.

[84] This claim is, of course, complicated by the changing relationship between the church and the state in nineteenth-century Prussia. Howard (*Protestant Theology*, 22) describes the 'process whereby the churches were virtually annexed to the modernizing state'—particularly as expressed by the *Department of Ecclesiastical Affairs and Public Education: Die Sektion des Kultus und des öffentlichen Unterrichts* (the so-called *Kultusministerium*). He describes the attenuation of any sense of the church as mediating institution between state and individual, at least in so far as that entailed being a concrete, historical, traditioned force: 'Religion was spiritualized, made

THE UNIVERSITY AND THE STATE

The subject matter of the philosophy faculty is not restricted to its own internal business, but covers in principle any and every topic, including the practices and policies by which the social life that surrounds it is shaped. The philosophy faculty cannot, therefore, avoid substantive relationship to the government of that social life: the state. In part, this is simply because it is capable of subjecting the principles and proposals of the state to rational scrutiny, and to pronouncing them in accord with, or contrary to, reason. As such, like the eighteenth-century Republic of Letters, it might be thought of as standing over against the state as critic, a kind of permanent opposition party.[85] However, in the context of a state that is seeking to promote enlightenment, this critical role becomes the state's own *self*-criticism.[86] Rather than standing over against the state as opponent, the philosophy faculty becomes for Kant, and for the Romantic theorists, an agency *of* the state, by which the enlightened state seeks to become more fully itself.

The enlightened state needs reason because it regards unreason as feckless, anarchic, immoderate, and unsustainable. In order to have a means by which its own principles and practices can be subjected to properly rational testing, it therefore needs the philosophy faculty to function in a fully rational, fully *wissenschaftlich* manner—and that means, given what Kant has said about the nature of reason in the philosophy faculty, that the state needs the philosophy

---

immanent in the general experience of humanity, divorced from the necessity of particularist, ecclesiastical manifestations' (p. 22). 'The result was a theology truly remarkable in the history of Christian thought for its detachment from creedal and ecclesial interests, for its many-layered connections to a modern state, and for its critical rigour and scientific aspirations' (p. 27).

[85] Summarizing Jürgen Habermas, Broman, in 'The Habermasian Public Sphere', 125, says of the public sphere that it is 'the cultural and political expression of the self-consciousness of members of civil society'. Civil society in turn emerges, in the context of the developing modern distinction between the private (or the domestic) and the public (or the proper realm of direct state action): it is 'the public side of the private sphere': the sphere of exchanges between citizens, which the state retains certain powers to regulate. 'There arises in opposition to the state's intervention a self-consciousness among the members of civil society of themselves *as* the public' (p. 126)—a self-consciousness grown in coffee houses, salons, and Masonic lodges, and communicated in newspapers and periodicals, 'vehicles for the expression of what could be called "public opinion"' (p. 127), and that is concerned, above all, with the assessment and critique of the public claims of the state (and the church). 'More than anything else, it is criticism that characterizes the life of the public sphere' (p. 129). Dena Goodman (*Republic of Letters*, 2) is speaking of the same reality when she says, of the Republic of Letters, that, 'since the eighteenth century, those who participate in it have tried to work out a way of maintaining citizenship in the political and geographical states that define their nationality without compromising their primary allegiance to the values of the Republic... The transformative impulse, the desire to change the world to conform to the Republic of Letters, its values and practices, is the constructive result of this critical position. It is the project of Enlightenment.'

[86] Kant, *Conflict of the Faculties*, 239: 'An enlightened government... is releasing the human spirit from its chains and deserves all the more willing obedience because of the freedom of thought it allows.'

faculty to be 'public', and in some regards autonomous. Such a state should therefore establish and maintain philosophy faculties that are free from direct rule by the state.[87] 'The philosophy faculty, because it must answer for the truth of the teachings it is to adopt or even allow, must be conceived as free and subject only to laws given by reason, not by the government.'[88] That does not mean, however, that such faculties will need freedom to pick their own questions, nor that they will need freedom to do with their answers what they will[89]—but it does mean that, when the state poses them a question, the state (for the state's own reasons) cannot determine in advance what answer the philosophy faculties will give.[90] Academic freedom, in this context, is the freedom to answer, on behalf of the state, the questions that the state sets, but to do so without regard to the answers that the state prefers.[91]

Romantic theories of the state went some way beyond Kant. They saw the state as an 'ideally harmonious and unified political community',[92] and Friedrich Ludwig Jahn (1778–1852) was speaking for many of them when he voiced the ideal that 'the citizen will feel, think and act *with* the State, *through* it, *for* it, and *in* it. He will become one with it, and with the *Volk*, in life, passion, and love.'[93] Heinrich Steffens, in his lectures on *The Idea of the University*, having announced that part of the problem of the modern world is that the citizen has become 'something separate from the state',[94] goes on in his third and fourth lectures to provide just such a rapturous account of the organic unity possible

---

[87] Kant, *Conflict of the Faculties*, 83.

[88] Kant, *Conflict of the Faculties*, 255. The government needs this help, because it is not competent in its own right to decide on questions of *truth* (only of expediency and efficiency) (p. 248). The philosophy faculty is a kind of permanent opposition party, tasked 'to see that *everything* put forward in public as a principle is true' (p. 259). In Ciaran Cronin's reading of Kant's 'What is Enlightenment?', in 'Kant's Politics of Enlightenment', *Journal of the History of Philosophy*, 41/1 (2003), 51–80: 58–9, she argues that 'it is ultimately the contractually based political authority of the sovereign . . . that secures legitimate domains of privacy and ensures their compatibility with enlightenment by regulating the boundary between private and public uses of reason'. Public reason circulates beyond all this, forming public opinion, and so leading to proposals for the revision of the existing system of contracts, which the sovereign enacts according to his sense of the public benefit. According to Peterson, 'Enlightenment and Freedom', 224, 'public reason is something that the state has to both respect and protect'.

[89] So, for instance, Kant acknowledges that the state is 'entitled not only to permit but even to require the faculties to let the government know, by their writings, everything they consider beneficial to a public religion of the land' (*Conflict of the Faculties*, 241).

[90] 'Only scholars can pass judgment on scholars as such' (*Conflict of the Faculties*, 247).

[91] Jacques Derrida, in 'The Principle of Reason: The University in the Eyes of its Pupils', tr. Catherine Porter and Edward P. Morris, *Diacritics*, 13/3 (Autumn 1983), 3–20: 3, notes that Kant's essay points to the fateful involvement of state in university life, and argues that the subordination of the university to needs of state has made for universities that are considerably more tightly controlled and censored than in Kant's day.

[92] Matthew Levinger, *Enlightened Nationalism: The Transformation of Prussian Political Culture 1806–1848* (Oxford: Oxford University Press, 2000), 99.

[93] Friedrich Ludwig Jahn, *Deutsches Volkstum* (Berlin: Aufbau-Verlag, 1991 [1810]), 187, quoted in Levinger, *Enlightened Nationalism*, 109.

[94] Steffens, *Idea of the University*, 4.

(by means of *Wissenschaft*) for the state. It is possible to imagine and work for a state 'where each one seeks his own blessedness' and yet 'recognizes his higher nature as that of the whole', and where the state in turn 'perceives its inner essence in the development proper to each citizen'.[95] Steffens's fifth lecture introduces the university primarily as a (or *the*) means by which the wisdom of this organically unified state is to be developed and maintained.[96]

Fichte, in his 'Deduced Scheme for an Academy to be Established in Berlin', explained that its students would need freedom from anxiety (especially anxiety about funding) in order that 'there should be quite firmly rooted in the State, and especially in its highest officials, the disposition, not to serve the community in order to be able to live, but to live solely in order to be able to serve the community'. His monastic academy is to be a means by which the state procures a certain kind of devotee, a certain kind of unity between itself and its citizens. 'The State, with all its compulsory measures, must regard itself as an educational institution for making compulsion unnecessary.'[97]

The sociality of reason is thus not simply the proper characteristic of an institution devoted to *Wissenschaft*, for Fichte. It is a microcosm of the ideal state:

Our Academy, considered in and for itself, shows in the realization indicated by us the picture of a perfect State; honest interaction of the different powers which are welded together to organic unity and completeness for the sake of a common purpose. In it the real statesman sees ever present and existing that form which he endeavours to give his material too, and accustoms to it his eye, which is henceforward to be satisfied by nothing else.[98]

It is only in that context—the context of an intimate connection between state and academy, macrocosm and microcosm—that we should understand Fichte's call for a somewhat fuller academic freedom than that advocated by Kant. 'No limit . . . should be set to the teacher's instruction, nor should any subject be indicated to him as an exception, on which he is not to be free to think and to communicate his independent thought with the same freedom

---

[95] Steffens, *Idee der Universität*, 335.

[96] Steffens, *Idee der Universität*, 346.

[97] Fichte, 'The Theory of the State', extracts translated in Turnbull, *Fichte's Educational Theory*, 265–83: 281. Ziolkowski, *German Romanticism*, 245, says that for Fichte 'the scholar . . . has essentially a social responsibility: *more than any other class* he exists through and for society' (emphasis added). Turner, in James Albisetti, Charles E. McClelland, R. Steven Turner, 'Science in Germany', in *Science in Germany: The Intersection of Institutional and Intellectual Issues*, Osiris 2nd ser. 5 (1989), 285–304: 298, notes rather more critically that this *Wissenschaftsideologie* 'promoted the potentially dangerous identification of German intellectuals with the state and its interests'.

[98] Fichte, 'Deduced Scheme', 258. The state is, or is becoming, the kingdom of reason: Fichte, 'Theory of the State', 266.

from limitation.'[99] This freedom, no less than Kant's, is a freedom *from* the state *for the sake of* the state: it is the freedom that the state needs to nurture in order to become a more perfect state.

Humboldt, even though he was writing as a minister of the state, makes the links between the university and the state somewhat less insistently: there is more sense in his notes 'On the Spirit and the Organisational Framework of Intellectual Institutions in Berlin' that the university has an independent purpose (that is, the pursuit of *Bildung*), albeit one that will *cohere* with the purposes of the state. It is, after all, in the state's interest, in so far as it desires 'moral culture', to promote academic freedom: to 'sustain a continuously self-renewing, wholly uncoerced and disinterested collaboration'.[100] But the state 'must always remain conscious of the fact that it never has and in principle never can, by its own action, bring about the fruitfulness of intellectual activity', because Wissenschaft is 'ungovernable' (p. 244). 'The state', he says, 'must in general... demand nothing from [the universities] simply for the satisfaction of its own needs'. Nevertheless, he continues: 'It should instead adhere to a deep conviction that if the universities attain their highest ends, they will *also realise the state's ends too*, and these on a far higher plane' (p. 246; emphasis added).[101]

It is Schleiermacher who, of all the *Wissenschaft* ideologues, allows most distance between the state and the university. He shares the Romantic theory of the state as an organic union of its citizens,[102] but he conveys a stronger sense of the limitations of current state life, given that the truly organic state is only in the process of emerging, and given the tendency of present, incomplete states to curtail the freedoms necessary to that emergence. Nevertheless, Schleiermacher insists, in the first place, that *Wissenschaft* needs the state. True, *Wissenschaft* arises naturally wherever people seek a way beyond the unordered accumulation of information, beyond custom, beyond instinct, beyond unexamined authority.[103] But, given the unavoidably communal nature of reason, this arising of *Wissenschaft* takes the form of a community of

---

[99] Fichte, 'Only Possible Disturbance', 264–5.

[100] Humboldt, 'On the Spirit', 243; subsequent page references in text.

[101] The state's interest in the university will, however, extend at least as far as control over faculty appointments (p. 249).

[102] Theodore Vial, 'Schleiermacher and the State', in Mariña (ed.), *Cambridge Companion to Friedrich Schleiermacher*, 269–85. 'A state, for Schleiermacher, is a healthy development of a social organism that occurs when that organism establishes laws that sanction and express its customs. It furthers the end of that organism and helps express that organism's individual personality' (p. 272); it 'represents the completion of human life and the maximum of the good' (p. 273). 'For Schleiermacher the principle that leads to the formation of healthy and strong nations is the freedom of individuals to cultivate their talents and interact with each other in a way that allows the formation of a common life from the bottom up. This freedom entails a responsibility, too. Citizens must act not selfishly but for the good of the whole, and further they must exercise their political maturity through active participation' (p. 278).

[103] Schleiermacher, 'Occasional Thoughts', 2; subsequent page references in text.

those with a passion to understand (p. 3), and, even if such a community is initially informal, the state enters the picture as soon as it develops further, and reaches a stage where it needs institutional forms and legal protections in order to continue its work (p. 4).

It is therefore natural for *Wissenschaft* to require the state, for Schleiermacher; and it is equally the case that any state that hopes to develop in the direction of ideal organic unity will need *Wissenschaft*. It will be 'manifest that information and the sciences are something salutary and highly important' (p. 5). And, if the state recognizes this, it will recognize that it needs *Wissenschaft* to be itself: that is, it will recognize that it needs more than a 'meagre empiricism' (p. 9), which on its own is nothing but 'an unsteady groping about' (p. 10)—and it will provide the practitioners of *Wissenschaft* with those freedoms that they need in order to form the kind of community of free exchange that constitutes true reason.[104]

But states do not always recognize these things. One must remember that 'the state works only for itself' and that it is 'self-seeking through and through; thus it tends not to offer support to *Wissenschaft* except on its own terms, within its own boundaries' (p. 6). It is by no means a foregone conclusion that the state in a given place and time will recognize where its real, long-term self-interest lies. In particular, as well as the more banal failure to recognize that it needs *Wissenschaft* for more than the discovery of efficient means to present ends, there is a more complex way in which the state may fail to recognize the freedom proper to *Wissenschaft*. The form that the public conversations of *Wissenschaft* take is, for Schleiermacher, necessarily linguistic—we might say encultured (p. 4)—and the natural form that association in pursuit of knowledge takes is therefore first of all a community coextensive with a language group, and only then a multi-linguistic community of communities. So, if the state needs *Wissenschaft* to be fully itself, it must allow *Wissenschaft* to participate freely in exchange within the whole of a linguistic region, rather than confining it within the boundaries of some territorial subset of that region. And that means that Schleiermacher's *Wissenschaft*, if it is free to be *Wissenschaft*, will be at the vanguard of a movement towards the unity between all the states that share a common language. 'Actually,' he says, 'nothing can be more odd, or further from what the common weal requires, than for a German state to be confined with respect to its *wissenschaftliche* cultural institutions. Rather the community within which such states must

---

[104] 'We who are sworn devotees not only of freedom but also of the distinctiveness of each person, we who have never set store by a general form and norm of knowing or faith nor by a single infallible method for attaining it for all: How can we do other than assume that in each person this higher spirit of gaining knowledge breaks forth in its own way? How can we do other than assume—and act accordingly through the arrangements we make—that this process cannot be managed in any mechanical fashion whatsoever but in all aspects must bear within it an entirely opposite character, namely that of freedom?' (p. 51).

exist should nowhere be expressed more fervently than in *wissenschaftliche* matters' (p. 7).

Wissenschaft serves the state, yes, but if it is (as it must be) free *Wissenschaft* it will serve the state not by upholding its narrow interests, but by leading the state beyond them.[105] *Wissenschaft* 'upholds good judgment, is untainted by special interest, and gradually roots out petty passions and prejudices', says Schleiermacher (p. 7)—and in context that is clearly as much a political claim as a moral one.

So, for Schleiermacher, the university (the institution devoted to *Wissenschaft*) needs the state and the state needs the university—but the relationship might be an uneasy one: the state may not appreciate the freedoms that the university needs, and the university will be seeking to lead the state in a direction that it might not want to travel. In Schleiermacher's view the university is an institution that can, and must, work upon, and even protest against, the state in its present form. Schleiermacher therefore insists, more directly than the other Romantic theorists, upon the qualified independence of the university: 'should it not be advisable that the state leave the sciences to themselves, place all internal management entirely in the hands of the scholars as such, and reserve for itself only economic administration, police supervision and oversight regarding the direct influence of these institutions on civil service?' (p. 22). And

In all that belongs to its own domain the university has to be independent and free to form its own domestic law [*Hausrecht*] and to be able to alter that law as circumstances dictate. In such matters the state can assume no direction; it can demand only that it be privy to information and exercise oversight so that the university does not overstep its bounds. (p. 48)[106]

Nevertheless, even for Schleiermacher, the research university is inherently, and from the start, an institution locked into relationship with the state. It is an agency of the state, by which the state is reminded of, and enabled to pursue, its proper goal of becoming more enlightened, more cultured, more philosophical, and more rational. The university is for Schleiermacher too a microcosm of the state—showing in the organic sociality of *Wissenschaft* a model and anticipation of the organic unity, the pan-German unity, to

---

[105] Compare this with what Turner describes as the 'academic mercantilism' of the eighteenth-century universities (Turner, 'Prussian Universities', 69): the state's university trains its own jurists, bureaucrats, clergy, doctors; it thereby keeps them in the state; it also attracts by its prestige those from other states; publishing by staff is a matter of attracting those students to the university—so is an important but auxiliary duty, and one that must not become so specialized ('monkish, dogmatic, and pedantic') as to be unattractive.

[106] For instance 'the true spirit of the university is that of allowing the greatest freedom possible to prevail within every faculty as well. It is folly to prescribe sequences that lectures must follow or to divide up the whole domain of scholarship into precise individual parts' (p. 39).

which the state itself aspires (or to which it should be persuaded to aspire).[107] And it is precisely because it has *that* role—of service to and critical guidance of the state—that it has to be allowed the freedom to deliberate apart from the state's direction. For Schleiermacher, as for the other Romantic theorists, true service of the state is the *raison d'être* of the university, *and* the *raison d'être* of academic freedom.[108]

THE UNIVERSITY AND BUREAUCRACY

Once the relation between the university and the state is in view, the question of bureaucracy cannot be far behind. It is possible to tell the story of the actual emergence of the University of Berlin as the triumph of bureaucratic reality over Romantic ideals, or even as the progress of an already established rationalizing bureaucracy without any regard for Romantic theorization.[109] Such ways of formulating the narrative are mistaken, however: Romantic theory and bureaucratic reality in fact go hand in hand.[110]

Schelling, for instance, in his discussion of the proper purpose and organization of the university, declares in fine Romantic–Idealist style that 'universities can have only an absolute purpose—beyond that they can have none'.[111] That is, universities serve the perfection of *Wissenschaft*, disinterested, pure, and unconstrained. In the very next sentence, however, Schelling continues: 'To accomplish its aims the state must impose divisions—not such as arise out of inequalities of rank, but far more essential—by isolating and setting in opposition individual talents, by repressing many individualities and directing energies into various channels where they will serve more effectively.' The state, in other words, is tasked with clearing the way for the *Wissenschaft* it needs: reforming and reinvigorating institutions that are all too often decidedly *unwissenschaftlich*. 'Talent needs no special protection *so long as its opposite is not fostered*; intellectual capacity naturally creates for itself the highest and most decided influence. This is the only policy we need in order to make institutions of knowledge flourish, to give them all possible dignity

---

[107] Eventually, 'the government may find the freedom of the philosophy faculty, and the insight gained from this freedom, a better means for achieving its ends than its own absolute authority' (p. 261).

[108] Ziolkowski, *German Romanticism*, 299: the University of Berlin was from the start 'an institution by, of, and for the state'. Martin Heidegger's rectorial address, 'The Self-Assertion of the German University [1933]' (tr. Karsten Harries, *Review of Metaphysics*, 38/3 (1985), 470–80) can be read—to somewhat chilling effect—in this light.

[109] Clark, *Academic Charisma*, tends in this direction.

[110] Recognized by Levinger, *Enlightened Nationalism*, 123.

[111] Schelling, *On University Studies*, 29; subsequent page references in text.

within their walls and earn them respect outside' (p. 30; emphasis added). The state may not be able to dictate the results of *Wissenschaft*'s enquiries—but it can, according to Schelling, foster it and protect its advance, and it will do this by creating something like an internal market of intellectual talent, a meritocratic and competitive system of advancement that will drive the development of *Wissenschaft* within the university, and drive up the prestige of the university in the eyes of others.

This is, it turns out, exactly what happened. As William Clark puts it at the start of his magisterial account of the bureaucratic reform of German universities: 'German ministers of state and avatars of the market worked, as they saw it, to reform and modernize benighted academics. As a consequence of their efforts, a joint bureaucratization and commodification of academic practices took place, from which the research university emerged.'[112] He describes how the state worked, by intensive bureaucratic interventions, and the creation of a vast machinery of monitoring and regulation, to create and maintain just the market in academic prowess that Schelling envisaged. And the Romantic cult of academic personality, charisma, and originality was not the enemy of this process, but the entrepreneurial energy on which the market fed.[113]

As Schelling's phrase about the state 'repressing many individualities' suggests, the process of bureaucratization and commodification involved, first of all, taking control of hiring and firing. As Schelling said: 'Whoever [among the teaching staff] cannot prove his diligence and readiness to work should be expelled' (p. 29). The control was real, and direct. When Karl vom Stein zum Altenstein was Minister of Cultural, Religious, and Educational affairs, he overrode the theology faculties' own suggestions for new appointments in a third of cases between 1817 and 1840. In part, this was a matter of guarding against the appointment of disruptive and disreputable candidates, but more often it was because he could supposedly be trusted to operate a more truly meritocratic system of appointment and advancement than the still-too-nepotistic and collegial academics themselves.[114]

---

[112] Clark, *Academic Charisma*, 3.

[113] Clark, *Academic Charisma*, 12–14. Clark argues that this involved the creation of a strange kind of persona for the academic, neither fully public nor fully private. 'Let us call the "public" self that which is supposed to inhabit the office, striving for objectivity, impartiality, impersonality, and the public good, and distancing itself from private interests. Call the "private" self that which inhabits the home, thus able to cultivate private, personal, intimate interests. Given such definitions, the market induced a private–public self, a sort of third man or body mercantile, fraught with oxymoronic and odd qualities, as well as much charisma' (p. 14).

[114] Daum, '*Wissenschaft* and Knowledge', 146. Cf. Clark, *Academic Charisma*, ch. 7. Clark describes this as part of a turn away from an old, collegial juridico-ecclesiastical model in which nepotism was not simply acceptable but normal, towards a rationalized politico-economic and cameralistic system (p. 8).

Bureaucratization also involved the creation and operation of vast regimes of paperwork (the 'essence of police power'[115]) designed to monitor every aspect of the work of scholars. There were reports on who was lecturing what to how many students,[116] dossiers documenting the research productivity and prestige of members of the faculty, reports on teaching quality, on curriculum design, on public utility, and so on, and on, and on. A twenty-first-century academic reading about these developments will realize that the machinery of scrutiny and measurement within which he or she is caught is not a recent aberration on the part of governments that have forgotten the true nature of the research university. All these forms of reporting, monitoring, and control are essential features of the research university from the very start of its life, and they developed hand in hand with Romantic theorization of the dignity of *Wissenschaft*.

The modern research universities were, from the very beginning, inherently a function of the state, and that function was one that the state believed itself capable of understanding (it believed itself capable, that is, of grasping the *process*, even if any determining of the results was beyond its remit). It inevitably followed that the state was engaged in the business of monitoring and regulating the life of these institutions, in order to facilitate and sustain those processes to make sure they served their proper function as fully as possible. And it followed just as surely that such monitoring and control were presented as a means to the freedom proper to *Wissenschaft* rather than as a curb upon it, and as a means of saving the university from its own worst, *unwissenschaftliche* tendencies. Negotiating its relationship to the state that it serves, and negotiating the boundary between those forms of monitoring and regulation that truly serve *Wissenschaft* and those that in fact constrain it, are ongoing and complex tasks inherent in the constitution of the research university—and they have been there from the very beginning.

FRAGMENTATION

Despite the wishes of both the Romantic theorists and the bureaucrats, educational reform in Berlin and elsewhere in Prussia was in fact slow, fitful, and underfunded.[117] And, just as there is a question about whether and to what degree the Parisian ideal was ever embodied, so there are questions about the Berlin ideal. Later critics certainly believed that the ideal had not been fully

---

[115] Clark, *Academic Charisma*, 47.
[116] Clark, *Academic Charisma*, 49. Wonderfully, Clark reproduces a termly report on teaching from Andreas Osiander in 1607 (p. 51).
[117] Turner, 'Science in Germany', 298.

realized. In particular, they pointed to the breakdown of three forms of unity upon which the Romantic theorists had insisted: the unity of *Bildung* and *Wissenschaft*; the metaphysical unity of all knowledge; and the social unity that was inseparable from that metaphysical unity. The first of these accusations need not occupy us here; suffice it so say that the Berlin model was fairly soon subjected to a familiar range of criticisms: that teaching was coming a poor second to research, that the ethical formation of students was all but invisible, and that the ethical formation of faculty was not much more obvious.[118]

More importantly for my purposes, however, the growth of *Wissenschaft*, far from leading in the direction of a realization of the unity of knowledge, in fact led to a proliferation and fragmentation of newly professional discrete disciplines.[119] The emergence of such disciplines had already started before the University of Berlin was founded (with classical philology the most obvious example), but it was driven further and faster by the research productivity that Berlin model required and fostered. These newly professional disciplines evolved a series of practices and institutions that created a division between respectable academic work and amateurism. There were academic journals, whose editors acted as gatekeepers, promoting certain styles of academic writing as respectable and making certain kinds of footnoted conversation with existing philological literature inescapable.[120] There were semi-independent seminars created around top-flight academics such as Friedrich August Wolf or August Boeckh, and acting as very powerful organs for socializing the cream of philological students into the practices and discourses of their teachers, and contexts for the build-up of intergenerational academic momentum.[121] More and more disciplines emerged as intensive, particular conversations with carefully policed boundaries, and well-understood criteria for what counted as an acceptable contribution.[122] As a result, 'countless numbers of disciplines effectively began to withdraw large regions of scientific knowledge from the public sphere almost as soon as it formed and to establish

---

[118] 'Humboldtian ideals of research came to contradict equally Humboldtian ideals of *Bildung*' (Anthony Grafton, 'Polyhistor into *Philolog*: Notes on the Transformation of German Classical Scholarship, 1780–1859', *History of Universities*, 3 (1983), 159–92: 169).

[119] Turner, 'Prussian Universities', 75–6; Howard, *Protestant Theology*, 273–303; McClelland, 'To Live for Science', 187.

[120] Turner, 'Prussian universities', 87.

[121] See also R. Steven Turner, 'The Great Transition and the Social Patterns of German Science', *Minerva*, 25 (1987), 56–76: 62. The emerging professions (not just academics) 'all tried to enhance their status by requiring formal education, introducing state licensing, defining bodies of required theoretical knowledge, working out legitimatory arguments, and maintaining specialised periodicals'. Cf. McClelland, 'To Live for Science', 189.

[122] Turner, 'Prussian Universities', 86. Other disciplines followed suit—with history, for example, being increasingly professionalized from about 1820 on, and the natural sciences from about 1830.

problem domains largely defined and regulated by themselves alone'.[123] And 'the vision of the unity of the disciplines faltered in the march toward scientific specialization, a positivist hierarchy of the sciences challenged the philosophic order of idealism and the very numbers who flocked to the universities swamped the Socratic dialogue between scholar and student'.[124]

Nevertheless, the Romantic vision was not simply washed away by this development: it adapted to cope. August Boeckh, writing at a time when disciplinary specialization had already advanced some considerable distance, could still say that 'the goal of learning will be consummated in the totality of the scholarly state just as the goal of the civil state is consummated in its members collectively'—but the sense that this goal can never actually be reached, and in particular that it is a unity that can never be realized in an individual mind, is strong: 'In its full significance it is realized only ideally, in the totality of its followers; into innumerable intellects diversely divided and more or less completely represented, and yet in all who are called to it ever the same.'[125]

CONCLUSION

The description of the university propounded by the theorists who inspired the foundation of Berlin has remained a powerful one, a point of reference for those working in the institutional *Wirkungsgeschichte* of Berlin. To some extent, it is a vision that coheres with, and in places extends, the Parisian vision explored in my first chapter—even though in other respects it stands adamantly against it.

In the first place, the vision of learning that the Romantic theorists presented is no less than the Parisian picture a matter of purification and ascent. Learning and virtue, learning and the formation of rightly ordered life, learning and ever deeper participation in truth, goodness, and beauty, are inseparable. It is not, for the Romantic theorists, that *Bildung* provides a broader goal for university life than *Wissenschaft* alone, nor even simply

---

[123] Broman 'Habermasian Public Sphere', 141–2; cf. Daum, '*Wissenschaft* and Knowledge', 149: the *Wissenschaftsideologie* was still around in 1870, but disciplinary differentiation, the loss of the integrative role of philosophy, a more thoroughgoing alliance with state, and the rise of positivism had altered its character.

[124] Shaffer, 'Romantic Philosophy', 52.

[125] August Boeckh, 'Festrede gehalten auf der Universität zu Berlin am 15. October 1855', in *Gesammelte Kleine Schriften*, ii. *Reden* (Leipzig: B. G. Teubner, 1859), 115–31: 128, translated in Turner, 'Prussian Universities', 85. Turner comments: 'Only the scholarly community as a whole, conceived as an ideal unity, can comprehend knowledge as a whole. Even this collective vision is postponed into the infinite future, for *Wissenschaft* will never be completed.'

that *Wissenschaft* provides a means to *Bildung* as an end: rather *Bildung* and *Wissenschaft* are identical: the right ordering involved in the self-cultivation that is *Bildung* is the right-ordering provided by reason. To be cultivated and to be *wissenschaftlich* are, for the Romantic theorists, effectively the same thing.

In the second place, and more centrally, the vision of learning in Berlin was a vision of the inherent sociality of reason. I have explored this point rather more thoroughly, because it seems to me that the Berlin theorists here present an important development and extension of the ideas about peaceable *disputatio* that I was only able to touch on in the previous chapter. For the Romantic theorists, the pursuit of reason simply has to mean the pursuit of certain kinds of exchange with those investigating the same reality from a different perspective, and such exchange is only truly *wissenschaftlich* to the extent that the participants are able to speak in it in their own voices (rather than as the mouthpieces of some heteronomous authority) and to address themselves to others who are similarly free to respond for themselves. The freedom of *Wissenschaft* is a freedom for the flourishing of a sociality of unimpeded gift and reception. The rules that govern *Wissenschaft* are precisely the rules of sociable conduct; that which resists or distorts reason is precisely that which restricts or distorts the sociality of the community of scholars.

However, in the third place, the Berlin vision also takes us in a different direction from any I pursued in my sketch of Paris. Inherent in the constitution of the research university is an orientation to the state; such universities are by definition caught up in a relationship between their existence as agencies of the state and their academic freedom. This orientation towards the state is an element of the repair that the Romantic theorists sought to carry out on the medieval tradition of the ecclesial university. I have said that those theorists turned away from the church (the institution, guardian of an authoritative, positive tradition, standing outside the boundaries of mere reason) for the sake of the 'church' (a re-thought Body of Christ, the community of free giving and receiving, of participation in and anticipation of the absolute or universal community of knowing). They took the ideal of free sociality from the theological tradition they had inherited, and used it to pass judgement on the fractious and cacophonous ecclesiastical form in which that tradition came to them. The state became for them a reinvented church: a church without the divisions of particular denomination from particular denomination; a church in which each citizen would be able to speak on his own behalf to every other citizen, rather than allowing the conversations of the state to be locked within denominational silos.

In later chapters, I will attempt a repair of this repair. That is, I will seek to overcome the obvious flaw in the Romantic theorists' plans: the fact that the university that they envisage does *not* actually allow each citizen to speak on his own behalf if he is not allowed to speak as the member of the particular, positive religious and secular traditions that have shaped him. The very stricture that the Romantic theorists erect in order to preserve free sociality is one that makes it impossible. In line with much other recent work in political theology, however, I will argue for the possibility of a free intellectual sociality (and a commitment to the common good of a secular and religiously plural society) in which religious difference is acknowledged rather than repressed— and I will argue that the repair of the university that the Romantic theorists set in motion can therefore be completed (not undone) by a return of religiously particular voices. My own attempt to write a Christian theology of higher education is therefore not a rejection of the Berlin revolution, but its continuation.

3

Oxford and Dublin

In the first chapter, I argued that the emergence of the medieval University of Paris presents us with a picture of reason as a corporate spiritual discipline and a form of Christian devotion. In the second chapter, I argued that the secularization of university reason promoted by the Romantic theorists could be seen as an attempted repair from within of such a theologically freighted understanding of reason. I suggested that in a religiously plural and secular society their repaired account of university reasoning can itself be seen to be in need of repair—in need, specifically, of the acknowledgement that participants in public reason must be free to speak in their own tradition-formed voices if reason is truly to be constituted by free sociality.

In this chapter, therefore, I turn to the most famous Christian theological voice to speak about the nature of university life in modernity: John Henry Newman (1801–90). I explore some of the ways in which his account of the place of virtue and sociality in university life parallels and amplifies the claims I have made about Berlin and Paris, but finish by suggesting that his account does not finally allow the repair of the Berlin settlement that I am seeking. Most obviously, this is because *The Idea of a University* was always intended as an account of a specifically Catholic university, secured *over against* other secular or religiously plural accounts, and it thus demonstrates precisely the kind of religious exclusivity that the *Wissenschaft* theorists sought to over-come. More subtly, it is because his account is structured by a distinction between nature and grace that leaves his description of intellectual formation itself largely untheological, such that his Catholic faith is left to be an external curb and guard on that formation. Later chapters will make it clear that Newman's problem, from my point of view, is that he does not explicitly recognize, in this context, the deep theological patterns already shaping his account of intellectual formation. Once those patterns are acknowledged, it becomes far less clear that faith appears primarily as support and supplement. In other words, it will turn out that the problem with Newman's account is not that it is too theological, but that it is not theological enough.

BACKGROUND

In the English-speaking world, it was above all Newman who 'transformed the inherited legalistic description of a university as a corporate body possessing endowments and privileges pertaining to learning into a thrilling, emotion-laden, higher-order conception of education'.[1] *The Idea of a University*, the work in which this transformation is performed, is certainly the most famous, and the most influential (or at least most cited) English-language analysis of the nature and goal of university education. Yet the book was not written as a treatise for a general readership, nor as an abstract proposal about the future of universities in general, but as a set of addresses to a specific audience, the educated and professional Catholics of Dublin, with a view to persuading them on a specific point: the need to establish an avowedly and exclusively Catholic university in their city.[2]

As we shall see, Newman provides an account of the university as a school of intellectual virtue, forming its students as human beings, citizens, and professionals—and an account of why such an institution requires the support of Catholic teaching for its full, undistorted flourishing. Yet the strange thing about his account is that all of it, including the insistence on the exclusively Catholic nature of the university, was shaped by his career in Protestant Oxford.

Newman arrived in Oxford in 1817, as an undergraduate at Trinity College; from 1822 he stayed on as a Fellow of Oriel. By the time he left, following his conversion to Catholicism in 1845, he had been in Oxford for nearly thirty years. The Oxford he knew has aptly been described as first of all 'an ecclesiastical institution tied seemingly inextricably to the Church of England. It aimed in this capacity at inculcating sound religion.' Second, it was 'a politically conservative and socially exclusive institution . . . a closed society. As a socio-political institution it formed a finishing school for gentry, aristocracy and clergy.' Finally, whatever might have been said about its eighteenth-century form, early nineteenth-century Oxford was also an educational institution, focused on the teaching of classical literature first, mathematics second, and other subjects a distant third.[3] And it was an educational institution

---

[1] Sheldon Rothblatt, *The Modern University and its Discontents: The Fate of Newman's Legacies in Britain and America* (Cambridge: Cambridge University Press, 1997), 7. 'Since Newman the belief that universities possess a core idea or have an historical undertaking or a special responsibility and trust beyond the moment . . . has remained a constant part of the process of institutional self-evaluation and internal debate' (p. 12).

[2] It was also, of course, written by a new convert to Catholicism, and one who was seeking to make Catholic sense of his university experience in Protestant Oxford.

[3] Peter Slee, 'The Oxford Idea of a Liberal Education 1800–1860: The Invention of Tradition and the Manufacture of Practice', *History of Universities*, 7 (1988), 61–87: 62. On the first point, P. B. Nockles notes that the university had recently undergone reforms that 'actually reinforced the religious and establishmentarian emphasis of the university' and were 'designed to render the

shaped by recent reforms, forced by controversy to reflect on and articulate the view of education that was implied in its reformed practice, and engaged in a series of debates about their further refinements or expansions.

Newman's ideas about education were to a significant extent ideas shaped in this context; it can fairly (though not without qualification) be said that 'in conception, purpose, structure and tone, Newman's idea of a university is both English and Oxford'[4]—and, specifically, that it was an idea born in the common room of Oriel, the college in which he held his Fellowship. At the time when Newman joined it, Oriel was home to the so-called Noetics, who were at the forefront of the attempt to articulate and secure the Oxford vision of a robust liberal education, training student minds by immersion in difficult, stringently rule-bound subject matter.[5]

Newman was not, however, simply a passive recipient of this emerging Oxford idea, but an active participant in the debates about its proper form who had strong ideas about the particular direction in which it needed to be taken. At the end of the 1820s, he tried, with some of his friends in Oriel, to institute a reform of the tutorial system. They had a more active, intensive, and religious view of the tutorial office than was the norm, and wanted tutors to play a more intimate role in shaping the religious, moral, and intellectual lives at least of those of their students who showed an interest in taking their time in Oxford seriously.[6] The new tutorial practice eventually brought Newman into dispute with the then provost, Edward Hawkins (1789–1882), and was discontinued, in part because of Newman's disagreement with him on other matters—but,

---

Anglican confessional nature of Oxford more of a living reality' (in 'An Academic Counter-Revolution: Newman and Tractarian Oxford's Idea of a University', *History of Universities*, 10 (1991), 137–97: 138).

[4] Sheldon Rothblatt, 'An Oxonian "Idea" of a University: J. H. Newman and "Well-Being"', in M. G. Brock and M. C. Curthoys (eds), *The History of the University of Oxford*, vi. *Nineteenth-Century Oxford*, Part 1 (Oxford: Clarendon Press, 1997), 287–304: 290.

[5] 'It was in the Oriel common room, with its daily collision of mind with mind, that he found embodied the very idea of a university' according to A. Dwight Culler, *The Imperial Intellect: A Study of Cardinal Newman's Educational Ideal* (New Haven: Yale University Press, 1955), 45; cf. Rothblatt, 'Oxonian "Idea"', 291. William James Copleston, in his 'Memoir of Edward Copleston, DD Bishop of Llandaff, *Christian Remembrancer*, 23 (1852), 1–29: 18, says that both Tractarian and liberal parties in Oxford were 'the development of private discussions and every-day conversations within the walls of Oriel common-room'. The Provost of Oriel, Edward Copleston (1776–1849), 'the first to formulate' the Noetic, Oxford idea of a university education, was its most compelling embodiment when Newman's career began (Culler, *Imperial Intellect*, 38), and he 'was later to single out Newman as the outstanding justification of the college's policy of discouraging the kind of technical expertise encouraged by more conventional examinations in favour of real intellectual distinction and originality' (Ian Ker, *John Henry Newman: A Biography* (Oxford: Oxford University Press, 1988), 19). For more on Oriel, see K. C. Turpin, 'The Ascendancy of Oriel', in Brock and Curthoys (eds), *History*, 183–92.

[6] Only in this way did the link between a Fellowship and ordination make sense to Newman. He held that 'there were various modes of fulfilling the vow of ordination, of which a college tutorship was one' (Ker, *Newman*, 28, quoting Newman, *Autobiographical Writings*, ed. Henry Tristram (London: Sheed and Ward, 1956), 87).

however short-lived, the experiment indicated quite clearly the tight covenant between religion and education that Newman saw as proper to university life.

In 1829, Sir Robert Peel, the university's representative in parliament, stood for re-election because the university was firmly against Catholic emancipation, and Peel's Tory government had changed to a pro-emancipation policy. This dispute galvanized Newman: as he saw it, the university (and the church that it represented in the intellectual sphere) was being asked to swing to the winds of expediency, adjusting its views to suit the political weather.[7] Any such changeableness could only be possible to the extent that the university had lost its moorings, allowing its intellect to become unsteady: it needed, in Newman's eyes, to be called back to religious seriousness before it squandered its moral authority. This was the germ of the Oxford Movement, and there is no need to retell here the whole story of the way in which that Movement grew out of Newman's efforts in this campaign (and out of his earlier disappointment at Oriel),[8] nor of the trajectory towards Catholicism on which it set Newman himself. What matters for our purposes is that the Movement was dedicated both to re-establishing the traditional roots and consequent stable authority of the church, *and* to securing the religious stability and authority of the university as the church's intellectual powerhouse and guardian. A key part of the Movement's activities was, therefore, the fight to keep Oxford's religious exclusiveness intact, by preserving the requirement that matriculating students affirm the Thirty-Nine Articles.[9] As we shall see, the Newman of the *Idea of a University* is very much still recognizable as the Newman of these battles.

The context in which Newman was to deliver the lectures that became *The Idea of a University* was not, however, Oxford, nor the Oxford Movement; it was Dublin, and the Catholic Church. The 1793 Catholic Relief Act had permitted Catholics to take degrees and hold offices in any college of the University of Dublin except Trinity College. As there was at that time no college in the university except Trinity, this was not seen as a generous concession, and the situation was only partially ameliorated when a Royal Letter of 1794 allowed interim admittance of Catholics so long as they were allowed neither scholarships nor positions of responsibility.[10] A more serious remedy was proposed in 1844: the establishment in Belfast, Cork, and either Limerick or Galway of 'Queen's Colleges', components of a new Irish university, open without constraint to Catholic and Protestant students and staff. After a debate in which they acquired the adhesive nickname 'Godless

---

[7] Culler, *Imperial Intellect*, 69–70; Ker, *Newman*, 32–5.
[8] For the relation of the Oxford Movement to educational reform in Oxford, see Nockles, 'Counter-Revolution'.
[9] Ker, *Newman*, 101–2, 111, 116–17, 123.
[10] Culler, *Imperial Intellect*, 124.

Colleges' (on account of the deliberate omission from the plans of any provision for official religious instruction), a bill to this effect was passed in 1845.[11]

The Irish Catholic bishops were divided on the question of whether they should support the 'mixed education' proposed for the Colleges. Before the passing of the bill, they had asked for various concessions and revisions; when it was passed largely unmodified, they voted to reject it, by a divided vote of 17 to 8. In November of that year, still divided, they referred the matter to Rome.[12] The reply was a long time coming, but in October 1847, a 'Rescript from the Sacred Congregation of Propaganda' pronounced against the Queen's Colleges, and urged the establishment instead of a distinct Catholic university.[13] The message was repeated in a second Rescript in 1848, and (after the opening of the Queen's Colleges in Belfast, Cork, and Galway) a third was sent in April 1850 forbidding clergy from holding any office in the Colleges.[14] In August of that year, therefore, the bishops met in synod at Thurles, reiterated the papal condemnation of the Godless Colleges, and set up a Catholic University Committee to pursue the Pope's recommended alternative.[15]

The Irish Bishops were still not united, however, and negotiations surrounding the proposed Catholic university were shaped by at least three broad tendencies. The dominant group was represented by Paul Cullen (1803–78), previously the Rector of the Irish College in Rome, who was appointed Archbishop of Armagh in 1848 and of Dublin in 1852. He was a determined opponent of mixed education, and became the driving force of the Committee, insisting above all things that the university must be thoroughly Catholic.[16] Another group was represented by John MacHale (1791–1881), who, wearied by heroic efforts to offer relief from the Irish Potato Famine that had been raging since 1845, insisted that the university must be above all things Irish, and must serve Ireland.[17] Finally, there was a group represented by Daniel Murray (1768–1852), Archbishop of Dublin. Murray had always

---

[11] Fergal McGrath, *Newman's University: Idea and Reality* (London: Longmans, 1951), 9–10, 43–4.

[12] McGrath, *Newman's University*, 45–6, 60–2.

[13] McGrath, *Newman's University*, 63–4.

[14] McGrath, *Newman's University*, 67, 73.

[15] McGrath, *Newman's University*, 73–4.

[16] Ian Ker, 'Editor's Introduction', in John Henry Newman, *The Idea of a University Defined and Illustrated*, ed. Ian Ker (Oxford: Clarendon Press, 1976), pp. xi–lxxv: xxxii.

[17] Ker, 'Introduction', p. xxxii. Newman clearly believed that the university was intended for all English-speaking Catholics, but commentators disagree on whether this matched the view from Rome, or from the Irish bishops. See Ker, 'Introduction', p. xxiv, and n. 5; McGrath, *Newman's University*, 148—and, making the case that Newman was mistaken, Vincent Alan McClelland, *English Roman Catholics and Higher Education 1830–1903* (Oxford: Clarendon Press, 1973), 85–172.

thought that the planned mixed education of the Queen's Colleges was, if not ideal, the only practicable solution—and he kept alive in the debate questions about the practicality and desirability of a Catholic university.[18]

In April 1851, Robert Whitty (Vicar-General of Nicholas Wiseman, Cardinal Archbishop of Westminster) wrote to Cullen, to suggest that he should invite Newman to Dublin to advise on the establishment of the university, and to provide some lectures on university education. Cullen, who knew Newman from the latter's stay in Rome in the late 1840s, agreed, and wrote to Newman.[19] A few months later he visited him twice at the Birmingham Oratory (Newman's new home and the focus of his energies) and, after a short courtship, offered him the post of Rector, and asked him for a series of lectures.[20] Newman agreed to both proposals.

In August, the Catholic University Committee (on which Newman, despite his new role, did not sit) asked him to work with two others, Patrick Leahy (Vicar-General of Cashel) and Myles O'Reilly (a layman with educational interests), to prepare a proposal for the structure of the university.[21] Once it was approved at a meeting in mid-November, Newman began work on the requested lectures—though his efforts were interrupted and delayed by preparations for his trial for libel, which rumbled on until June 1852 (or until 1853, if you include his fruitless attempt to secure a retrial).[22] It was not until early May 1852 that Newman left for Dublin, ready to deliver the first of the lectures. In the event he delivered five, one a week from 10 May to 8 June,[23] before travelling back to England to see to his trial and to problems at the Oratory. He prepared the next five lectures for print rather than delivery, between July and November of that year.[24]

The story of Newman's involvement with the university from that point on is not a happy one, and not one we need dwell on. The university struggled from the start to find students (although the medical school was a success). It did not receive a royal charter for conferring degrees; it faced continued

---

[18] Ker, 'Introduction', p. xxxii; *Newman*, 383.

[19] McGrath, *Newman's University*, 103–5.

[20] Ker, 'Introduction', p. xii; McGrath, *Newman's University*, 103–7.

[21] McGrath, *Newman's University*, 109–12. The proposal took for its model of institutional structure the University of Louvain, but with the addition of colleges and tutors for social and religious formation (Ker, 'Introduction', p. xxiii). Louvain had been founded in 1835, and was regarded as a successful model by the Catholic hierarchy (see McGrath, *Newman's University*, 89).

[22] This was the Achilli affair. Newman had repeated in print others' charges against an ex-Catholic who was travelling the country speaking against Rome. Newman was found guilty on 24 June 1852 in what was widely regarded as a miscarriage of justice—but the infliction of a very small fine was seen as a species of moral victory. Some of the funds that Newman was able to draw on in the early years of the Catholic University were left over from the large defence fund donated to help with the costs of this trial. See Ker, *Newman*, 372–5, 381, 397–9.

[23] Ker, 'Introduction', p. xvi.

[24] Ker, 'Introduction', p. xvii.

suspicion; it was partially hobbled by national and ecclesiastical politics.[25] Newman, formally installed as Rector in 1854, resigned his post in 1859. The university he had shaped survived until 1882, when it was merged with the new Royal University of Ireland,[26] but Newman's 'campaign in Ireland' can hardly be considered a triumph.[27]

Newman's lectures, on the other hand, though quietly received at first, went on to have a more impressive career. Initially published as individual pamphlets, they were collected together for publication in 1853 as *Discourses on the Scope and Nature of University Education: Addresses to the Catholics of Dublin*, and then gathered together with various other addresses and articles Newman had written during his time as Rector[28] for republication in 1873 as *The Idea of a University Defined and Illustrated*.[29] Its effect on English-language discussion of university education, well beyond the Irish Catholic context in which it was born, has lasted much longer than the troubled institution to which it was initially devoted.

INTELLECTUAL FORMATION

The Idea of a University opens with the words: 'The view taken of a University in these Discourses is the following:—That it is a place of *teaching* universal knowledge' (p. 5 [p. ix]).[30] It seems a straightforward enough start, but already

[25] As Newman himself had said, the Catholic University of Ireland 'finds its most formidable obstacles, not in anything inherent in the undertaking itself, but in the circumambient atmosphere of misapprehension and prejudice into which it is received', especially 'reluctant or perplexed public opinion' (*The Office and Work of Universities* (London: Longman, Brown, Green and Longman, 1856), 3 = *Historical Sketches*, iii. *Rise and Progress of Universities* (London: Longman, Green, 1909), 2).

[26] Ker, 'Introduction', pp. xxvii–xxviii.

[27] Newman suggested this phrase as a title for his collection of papers relating to the university (according to W. Neville in Newman, *My Campaign in Ireland*, ed. W. Neville, i. *Catholic University Reports and Other Papers* (Aberdeen: A. King, 1896), p. xxxv). See the final section of McGrath, *Newman's University*, for an account of the successes and failures of the campaign.

[28] Several of which had appeared in Newman's *Catholic University Gazette*, and which had been published together in 1858 as *Lectures and Essays on University Subjects*.

[29] In 1859, Newman published a shortened and revised version of the Discourses as *The Scope and Nature of University Education; or University Teaching Considered in its Abstract Scope and Nature*. Discourses I and II were combined, and Discourse V omitted. In the 1873 version, Discourses I and II were separated again, but Discourse V was not reinstated. The book went through several editions, the ninth in 1889, the year before Newman's death, and a tenth posthumously in 1891.

[30] Ker's critical edition gives the 1889 text. I follow his text, giving his edition's page number first, followed by the 1889 page number in square brackets. The present quotation gives the final version of the opening words of the preface, originally added in 1852 when the Discourses were being prepared for publication as a book, and then slightly revised in 1859 and 1873. Newman

one needs to take care not to miss Newman's meaning. He makes it clear later (p. 94 [p. 99]) that university education can be considered from the point of view either of its studies (that is, its content) or of its students. The opening quotation seems to focus on the latter: 'universal *knowledge*' sounds like a description of the comprehensive content with which a university should concern itself. Newman's real emphasis, however, falls more strongly on the student, and the word 'knowledge', for him, primarily denotes a shaping of the student's intellect. It would not be too misleading (though it would certainly be clumsy) to paraphrase his definition to read 'a University . . . is a place for well-rounded intellectual formation',[31] an interpretation confirmed when he goes on in the remainder of the preface to speak of 'cultivation of mind',[32] 'mental culture', and the 'discipline and refinement of intellect' (pp. 9–10 [pp. xv–xvi]). To teach universal knowledge is to shape the intellect 'to reason well in all matters, to reach out toward truth, and to grasp it' (p. 114 [p. 126]).

In a specific sense, then, Newman's university is in the business of the formation of persons. Intellect is one (though only one) of the fundamental aspects of human being; we were made for knowledge, and become more fully ourselves to the extent that our knowing is properly shaped;[33] university education is meant to *perfect* human beings in this respect.[34] Newman therefore calls what is gained in university education a 'habit' (p. 6 [p. xi])—by which he means 'a state of mind which is always upon us, as a sort of ordinary dress or inseparable garment of the soul';[35] it is the acquisition of a second nature, completing and activating our first.

---

was drawing on familiar ideas; Edward Tatham (1749–1834), for instance, called the university 'a seat of *Universal Learning* . . . the place of *Universal Teaching*' in an address to convocation in 1807 (quoted in Rothblatt, 'Oxford "Idea" ', 292).

[31] Eric Ashby was nearly right to say of Newman's account that 'the touchstone of a university education was not to teach great truths, but to teach truth in a great way' (Ashby, 'The Future of the Nineteenth Century Idea of a University', *Minerva*, 6 (1967), 3–17: 13). It would be more accurate to say that the touchstone was not *only* to teach great truths, but to teach those great truths in a great way. A properly formed intellect is, for Newman, one so shaped as to take into due account great truths, and organize its mental landscape around them.

[32] See also the unused preface prepared for the first printed version of what was then Discourse VI, provided in Ker, 'Introduction', pp. xxxii–xxxiii, n. 5; see point 5 in particular.

[33] Cf. H. Francis Davis, 'Our Idea of a University', in H. J. Parkinson (ed.), *Some Centenary Addresses on Newman's Idea of a University* (London: Newman Association, 1953), 1–17: 4.

[34] When Newman says 'perfect' or speaks of 'perfecting', the meaning normally seems to be 'complete'—and to indicate something fully rounded, with all its parts connected and in due proportion. So when he said of *Idea* that it was 'one of his two most perfect works, artistically' (*The Letters and Diaries of John Henry Newman*, xv. *The Achilli Trial*, ed. Charles Stephen Dessain and Vincent Ferrer Blehl (London: Thomas Nelson, 1964), 226) he was not quite saying that it was the most nearly unblemished or that it could hardly have been improved; rather that he had got close to properly articulating a comprehensive view of his subject.

[35] Newman, 'Sermon 15: Mental Prayer', in *Parochial and Plain Sermons* (London: Longmans, Green and Co, 1908), vii. 204–16: 205.

The business of university education is, then, a training in intellectual virtue,[36] and the discourses are littered with generalized descriptions of the ideal intellectual character. If the university does its job, Newman says, a 'habit of mind is formed which lasts through life, of which the attributes are, freedom, equitableness, calmness, moderation, and wisdom' (p. 96 [p. 101]) and 'good sense, sobriety of thought, reasonableness, candour, self-command, and steadiness of view' (p. 11 [p. xviii]). He speaks of 'the force, the steadiness, the comprehensiveness and the versatility of intellect, the command over our own power, the instinctive just estimate of things as they pass before us' (p. 10 [p. xvi]) of such a mind. It

cannot be partial, cannot be exclusive, cannot be impetuous, cannot be at a loss, cannot but be patient, collected and majestically calm, because it discerns the end in every beginning, the origin in every end, the law in every interruption, the limit in each delay; because it ever knows where it stands, and how its path lies from one point to another. (p. 124 [p. 138])[37]

Newman clearly expects a lot from university education. Yet it is important to realize that he does not expect a student to pick up these virtues as it were accidentally. The university is to be a school that *aims directly at* the inculcation of intellectual virtues. It is to be quite directly a training in intellectual patience, in intellectual balance, in intellectual sociality.

The formation that a university should provide is, in its way, counter-cultural—albeit in a deeply conservative sense.[38] Newman explains what he has in mind by drawing a contrast between *viewing* and *viewiness*, where a well-formed mind is a mind with views, and the ill-formed alternative can possess only an ersatz and insubstantial viewiness.[39] One can get some idea of what he meant by reading some of his earlier uses of the term 'view'. In September 1834, for instance, he had dinner with the Dean of Chester in Tunbridge Wells, and 'was disgusted to find that the Dean "has no *views*, and

---

[36] Newman tends to reserve the word 'virtue' for specifically moral and religious formation; nevertheless, in its broader sense—as a counter in the language game that includes 'character', 'formation', and 'habit'—it is appropriate here.

[37] Douglas Adams might have said that such a student 'really knows where his towel is' (*The Hitch Hiker's Guide to the Galaxy* (London: Pan, 1979), 25).

[38] For instance, Newman speaks of the need for 'a wisdom, safe from the excesses and vagaries of individuals, embodied in institutions which have stood the trial and received the sanction of ages, and administered by men who . . . [are] supported by their consistency with their predecessors and with each other' (p. 15 [p. xxii]).

[39] Stephen Colbert, in the episode of *The Colbert Report* that aired on 17 October 2005, coined the word 'truthiness' to describe opinions put forward with great sincerity and fervour, and all the appearance of truth, but without regard to fact or argument. Newman, by coining 'viewiness', had got there before him. For more on viewiness and views, see Arthur L. Kennedy, 'The University as a Constituting Agent of Culture', in Gregory J. Walters (ed.), *The Tasks of Truth: Essays on Karl Jaspers's Idea of the University* (Frankfurt am Main: Peter Lang, 1996), 97–115: 99–105.

in consequence is like a ship without a rudder"'.[40] In his novel *Loss and Gain*, he said of such people that 'their lines of argument diverge; nothing comes to a point; there is no one centre in which their mind sits, on which their judgment of men and things proceeds'.[41] Such viewiness is the tone of mind actively promoted in a world beset by the 'never-intermitting issue of periodicals, tracts, pamphlets, works in series, and light literature'[42]—a world in which 'our seats are strewed, our pavements are powdered, with swarms of little tracts; and the very bricks of our city walls preach wisdom, by informing us by their placards where we can at once cheaply purchase it'.[43] Such a culture, which demands 'reckless originality' (p. 14 [p. xxi]), is a world of opinions got up for the occasion. The university is to be a context in which people are trained in *resistance* to this culture.

Newman illustrates in passing what a real 'view' might look like when, in his first Discourse, he provides an apology for the fact that he will be drawing deeply on his Oxford (and so Protestant) past in what follows. Precisely because he does this, his audience can know that they are hearing his 'tried and sustained conviction' (p. 21 [p. 3]), of which he is the 'cordial and deliberate maintainer and witness'; they will hear 'views' that are 'grown into my whole system of thought, and are, as it were, part of myself' (p. 21 [p. 4]).

'View' was 'part of the jargon of Newman's group at Oxford'—probably originating with Newman's dear friend Richard Hurrell Froude (1803–36).[44] It suggested the opinion of someone who refused to take intellectual short cuts, or to rest content with the surface of things. Newman's practice as tutor had been aimed precisely at the formation of such convictions in his students. He

wanted [the student] really to understand what he was reading, and in order to do this the student must draw out the implications of the work and discover its underlying assumptions. He must compare and systematize, challenge and contradict; he must reduce the argument to its logical form and test it by historical examples; and then, if he could reproduce it in his own words or apply the method to a present occasion or imitate its style upon another topic, he would know that he had really entered into the book in the manner that Newman desired.[45]

---

[40] Ker, *Newman*, 108, citing *The Letters and Diaries of John Henry Newman*, iv. *The Oxford Movement*, ed. Ian Ker and Thomas Gornall (Oxford: Clarendon Press, 1980), 337.

[41] Newman, *Loss and Gain: The Story of a Convert* (London: Longmans, 1906), 18.

[42] Newman, *Office and Work*, 10 = *Rise and Progress*, 7.

[43] Newman, *Rise and Progress*, 8; revised from *Office and Work*, 11.

[44] Culler, *Imperial Intellect*, 195.

[45] Culler, *Imperial Intellect*, 76. Compare Newman's description of university entrance examinations in 'Elementary Studies'—a collage of various articles Newman had written for the *Catholic University Gazette*, published as the fourth of the Occasional Lectures and Essays in *Idea* (pp. 274–308 [pp. 333–80]). Edward Copleston had said that the need 'to *exercise* the mind of the student is the business of education, rather than to pour in knowledge. Hence, *things made easy* appear to me to defeat the end of education' (William James Copleston (ed.), *Memoir of*

Such a student will be becoming the kind of person who can read a newspaper report and be wary of the hasty formation of a reactive opinion, swayed by the rhetoric of the report, by mood, and by superficial resemblances to other matters about which he has more settled opinions. He will instead be trained to dig down into his emerging opinion, and into the subject matter it refers to. What is really going on? What is at stake? On what principles is he basing this opinion? Are they consistent with his other principles? Do they truly apply to this instance? What more would he need to know about this instance in order for that application to be secure? What other disciplines or people might he need to consult?

The formation of such views takes time. One could almost say, in fact, that the point of Newman's form of university education is to teach one to pause on the way to opinion—pausing long enough for a 'process of intellectual digestion' to take place.[46] It is a training in patient questioning.

The formation that Newman looks for in a university is also training in the formation of an evolving, comprehensive vision that will provide the imaginative context for one's deportment and one's action. One of the recurring metaphors that Newman uses to explain what it is to have a view is that of a person's ability to arrange what his eyes see into a coherent landscape. Newman describes the process that begins 'when the eyes of the infant first open upon the world' to see 'a medley of colours and shadows', and that proceeds as the child 'gradually converts a calidoscope into a picture' (p. 272 [p. 331]). Just so,

when . . . men for the first time look upon the world of politics or religion, all that they find there meets their mind's eye as a landscape addresses itself for the first time to a person who has just gained his bodily sight. One thing is as far off as another; there is no perspective. The connection of fact with fact, truth with truth, the bearing of fact upon truth and truth upon fact, what leads to what, what are points primary and what secondary—all this they have yet to learn. It is all a new science to them, and they do not even know their ignorance of it.[47]

What is needed instead is 'enlargement of mind', where 'enlargement consists, not merely in the passive reception into the mind of a number of ideas hitherto unknown to it, but in the mind's energetic and simultaneous action upon and towards and among those new ideas' (p. 120 [p. 134]).[48]

Edward Copleston (London: John W. Parker and Son, 1851), 38, quoting a letter to J. Penrose of 1808).

[46] From the original 1852 Discourse V, given by Ker in Newman, *Idea*, 423. For more on time-taking, waiting, and patience, see p. 120 [p. 134], p. 75 [p. 75]; cf. Ker, 'Introduction', p. lxiii.

[47] Newman, *Loss and Gain*, 16.

[48] Newman describes what happens when one encounters something really new, and is forced to see things in a new perspective (as when one leaves one's village for the town for the first time, or is introduced to astronomy, or intently watches creatures whose lives are simply other than

The person who attains to such enlargement, who arranges what he has received into a coherent perspective, and who patiently builds up a more comprehensive vision of the landscape, will be someone who has an imaginative context to inhabit—a construal of the world *as* a world—and who therefore has the possibility of living a coherent life. The piecing-together of fragments of vision into a view is at the same time the piecing-together of fragments of experience and action into a life.

Newman's idea of a university education is therefore a formation in counter-cultural intellectual virtue: in patient questioning and the pursuit of coherence or integrity. It also aims, however, at a certain kind of intellectual *objectivity*. Newman repeatedly draws on a contrast between 'reality' and 'unreality'. One's vision of the world is 'unreal' to the extent that one sees things from one angle only, or in one set of relations only. To grasp the 'reality' of things involves seeing them from multiple coordinated perspectives and learning how to combine them—so that what at first appeared only flat will emerge as a fully three-dimensional object.[49]

This idea of a unity between multiple perspectives is central to Newman's presentation. 'Truth means facts and their relations', he says, and these form 'one large system or complex fact' (p. 52 [p. 45]); 'all knowledge forms one whole, because its subject-matter is one' (p. 57 [p. 50]), 'one integral subject for contemplation' (p. 52 [p. 45]). To form a view is, as one commentator puts it, to learn to 'see things whole';[50] comprehension therefore requires 'method, order, principle, and system' (p. 12 [p. xix]). 'A philosophic comprehensiveness, an orderly expansiveness, an elastic constructiveness, men have lost them, and cannot make out why. This is why: because they have lost the idea of unity...'[51] 'Knowledge without system is not philosophy'[52] but 'a mere fortuitous heap of acquisitions and accomplishments'.[53]

Individual intellectual disciplines (or 'sciences') can each provide only a partial view. If one is to 'see things whole', to be objective, such partial views will require cross-fertilization, supplementation, and qualification. The cultivated mind will, therefore, be one adept at 'the comprehension of the bearings of one science on another, and the use of each to each, and the location and limitation and adjustment and due appreciation of them all, one

---

our own). Such experiences 'throw us out of ourselves' (p. 118 [p. 131]), and can lead either to the enlargement of tumult (p. 120 [p. 133]) in which one is simply tossed about and can make nothing coherent of all this information, or this enlargement of peace.

[49] See (p. 54 [p. 48]); for Newman's best discussion of 'reality', see 'Sermon 3, Unreal Words' in *Parochial and Plain Sermons* (London: Longmans, Green and Co., 1907), v. 29–45.

[50] Culler, *Imperial Intellect*, 180.

[51] Original 1852 Discourse V, given by Ker in Newman, *Idea*, 423.

[52] 'Sermon 14. Wisdom, as Contrasted with Faith and with Bigotry', in *Oxford University Sermons* (London: Longmans, Green and Co., 1909), 278–311: 289.

[53] Original 1852 Discourse V, given by Ker in Newman, *Idea*, 422.

with another' (p. 57 [p. 51]). It is no surprise, therefore, to find that Newman's plans for Dublin included a much broader range of subjects than the classical literature and mathematics that dominated Oxford. 'It is a great point then', he said, 'to enlarge the range of studies which a University professes' (p. 95 [p. 101]). The *Report on the Organization of the Catholic University of Ireland*, which he, Leahy, and O'Reilly presented to the Catholic University Committee just before Newman began work on the lectures, lists (amongst other subjects): Latin, Greek, Semitic and Modern Languages, History Ancient and Modern, Archaeology, English Literature and Criticism, Logic, Metaphysics, Ethics (including Economy and Politics), Philosophy of Religion, Mathematics, Natural Philosophy, Chemistry, Natural History, Mineralogy, Geology, Medicine, Law, and Theology.[54]

Yet 'nowhere does he write as if this argument entailed an encyclopaedic curriculum for every undergraduate'.[55] Rather, he envisages students living in the midst of a circle of those representing different sciences (p. 95 [p. 101]). What he seeks to produce is not walking encyclopaedias, but students accustomed to participation in intensive, multidisciplinary *conversation*. After all, a university is formed when

an assemblage of learned men, zealous for their own sciences, and rivals of each other, are brought, by familiar intercourse and for the sake of intellectual peace, to adjust together the claims and relations of their respective subjects of investigation. They learn to respect, to consult, to aid each other. Thus is created a pure and clear atmosphere of thought. (p. 95 [p. 101])[56]

A university is therefore 'in its essence, a place for the communication and circulation of thought, by means of personal intercourse'.[57] It is 'a place where inquiry is pushed forward, and discoveries verified and perfected, and rashness rendered innocuous, and error exposed, by the collision of mind with mind, and knowledge with knowledge'.[58] As well as being a context for formation in

---

[54] Newman, *Campaign*, 77–81, §II.
[55] A. C. F. Beales, 'The Modern University in the Light of Newman's Idea', in Parkinson (ed.), *Centenary Addresses*, 34–51: 37.
[56] At one point, he asserts that a better education would emerge from a university with no teachers than from one in which students were crammed with a disordered accumulation of information—provided only that the students were pressed into constant conversation with one another. 'For the pupils or students come from very different places, and with widely different notions, and there is much to generalize, much to adjust, much to eliminate, there are interrelations to be defined' (p. 130 [p. 146]). For Newman's comparison of this sociality to a political empire, see 'Christianity and Scientific Investigation' (p. 370 [p. 458]). For a comparison to his ecclesiology, see Ker, 'Introduction', p. lxxv.
[57] Newman, *Office and Work*, 9 = *Rise and Progress*, 6.
[58] Newman, *Office and Work*, 24 = *Rise and Progress*, 16. While still at Oriel, Newman had been captivated by the medieval establishment of the college as a quasi-monastic community of scholars (without undergraduates) committed to a disciplined communal life of time-taking study individually and together. See Culler, *Imperial Intellect*, 89–91; cf. Nockles, 'Academic

intellectual seriousness, in patient questioning and attentiveness, in the pursuit of coherence and integrity, and in multidisciplinary objectivity, it is a context for formation in a disciplined, conversational sociality.

A note on research

In the definition that opens *The Idea of a University*, Newman insists that the university is not *in its essence* a context for research: 'its object is...the diffusion and extension of knowledge rather than the advancement' (p. 5 [p. ix]). In practice, research was certainly part of the picture he painted of the university, and part of the Catholic University of Ireland in its actual functioning.[59] Newman even founded the university's journal *Atlantis* in 1858 as a context for the publication of its research.[60] It is not simply, however, that the focus of his account of the university lay elsewhere—on formation rather than discovery and advance, *Bildung* rather than *Wissenschaft*. Rather, it is precisely because he sees the goal of the university as being well-rounded intellectual formation that research *must* be kept in a subordinate place. Research is inherently immoderate; it involves 'exclusive devotion to science' (p. 7 [p. xii]).[61] Newman speaks of 'men of great intellect, who have long and intently and exclusively given themselves to the study or investigation of some one particular branch of secular knowledge, whose mental life is concentrated and hidden in their chosen pursuit, and who have neither eyes nor ears for any thing which does not immediately bear upon it' (p. 51 [p. 43]). Research, by its very nature, is hostile to the step back, the broader view—and to the proper sociability of the well-formed mind. It is a pursuit for those who have already been formed in the intellectual virtues that will help them keep their immoderate pursuit in its place, and prevent its intensity becoming a contraction of their minds.[62]

Counter-Revolution', 143, and 167: 'the pre-Reformation college statutes offer[ed] a counter-revolutionary model of university reform'.

[59] Ian Ker, 'Editor's Notes', in Newman, *Idea*, 574–669: 575, n. 5.6.

[60] Ker, 'Introduction', p. xxvi.

[61] In Newton's case it involved 'an intense severity of meditation which almost shook his reason' (p. 8 [pp. xiii–xiv]). The language Newman uses about research is similar to that he uses of the 'immoderate and extravagant' forms of knowledge enjoyed by young boys (p. 10 [p. xvi]).

[62] Alasdair MacIntyre, in 'The Very Idea of a University: Aristotle, Newman and Us', *New Blackfriars*, 91/1031 (2010), 4–19: 5, rightly says that 'we might exaggerate somewhat if we formulated Newman's view in contemporary terms by saying that the possession of a PhD or a DPhil is too often the mark of a miseducated mind, but we would come close enough to make it clear why Newman must seem not just irrelevant, but offensive [to the inhabitants of the modern research university]'. Rothblatt notes that, in Newman's England, 'the research function had not been raised to the level of an ideology. There was no strong culture of research that put a premium on originality and stressed the importance of discovery and a division of intellectual labour' (Rothblatt, *Modern University*, 16).

UTILITY

The educational world of Newman's day was divided on the question of the utility of a university education. The Oxford (and Cambridge) practice of liberal education had long been opposed by those who wanted universities to do more to prepare their students directly for the professions on which they were due to embark, and those utilitarian principles had recently received institutional form in the foundation of the University of London.[63] When he fought against the 'Godless colleges' of Ireland, Newman was seeing the shade of London looming behind Belfast, Cork, and Galway: all had abandoned the principles of a well-rounded intellectual formation for the sake of a limited expediency.

Newman's own position on utility, however, is complex. He holds together several somewhat different claims—not in tension or in contradiction, as has sometimes been argued,[64] but in a strict hierarchy. At the top of the hierarchy lies the principle that knowledge—sound intellectual formation—is an end in itself, and a 'very tangible, real and sufficient end' (p. 97 [p. 103]) at that. It needs no other utility in order to be a good worth pursuing; irrespective of whether it leads to individual happiness, to social harmony, to the spread of justice, to practical aplomb, or to intellectual influence; irrespective of 'physical comfort and enjoyment . . . of health, of the conjugal and family union, of the social tie and civil security' (p. 98 [p. 105]), it is simply and straightforwardly good to have a mind that is capable of sorting truth from falsehood—a mind that can see past delusions and shallow opinions, ask critical questions, and get closer to the reality of things. 'To open the mind, to correct it, to refine it, to enable it to know, and to digest, master, rule and use its knowledge, to give it power over its own faculties' (p. 112 [p. 122]) is a good worth pursuing simply and purely for its own sake, and a good that needs to be valued for its own sake if it is to be attained.

That further advantages accrue to us and redound to others by its possession, over and above what it is in itself, I am very far indeed from denying, but independent of these, we are satisfying a direct need of our nature in its very acquisition . . . Knowledge . . . is valuable for what its very presence in us does for us after the manner of a habit, even though it be turned to no further account, nor subserve any direct end. (pp. 97–8 [p. 104])

---

[63] Renamed University College London after the foundation of King's College London. See P. A. Dale, 'Newman's "The Idea of a University": The Dangers of a University Education', *Victorian Studies*, 16/1 (1972), 5–36: 7. For more on the foundation of the University of London, see F. M. G. Wilson, *Our Minerva: The Men and Politics of the University of London 1836–1858* (London: Athlone, 1995).

[64] See, e.g., Culler, *Imperial Intellect*, 173–270, and Martha McMackin Garland, 'Newman in his own Day', in Frank M. Turner's edition of Newman's *Idea of a University* (New Haven: Yale University Press, 1996), 265–81.

Newman thinks that this claim is, once stated clearly, simply indisputable.[65]

Yet, as Fergal McGrath says, 'there is no question whatever of the mind wrapping itself in a cocoon of knowledge and going into a fruitless sleep'.[66] Newman used Cicero as an example of one who championed knowledge for its own sake, in opposition to all forms of utility, but, in the appendix added to the published discourses in 1852, he warned that Cicero was in danger of making philosophy a matter of 'intellectual amusement' and 'mental recreation', a 'refinement in the arts of social enjoyment' and nothing more.[67] Newman insists in contrast that, 'though the useful is not always good, the good is always useful' (pp. 143–4 [p. 164]).

In the first place, that is simply because 'good is prolific . . . it communicates itself' (p. 144 [p. 164]); it has an 'intrinsic fecundity' (p. 103 [p. 111]). In other words, this good, precisely because it is truly a good in itself, is contagious.

> If then the intellect is so excellent a portion of us, and its cultivation so excellent, it is not only beautiful, perfect, admirable, and noble in itself, but in a true and high sense it must be useful to the possessor and to all around him; not useful in any low, mechanical, mercantile sense, but as diffusing good, or as a blessing, or a gift, or power, or a treasure, first to the owner, then through him to the world. (p. 144 [p. 164])

These considerations do not yet take us beyond knowledge (well-rounded intellectual formation) as an end in itself. To seek the diffusion of knowledge is still, after all, to seek for more of the good that knowledge is. Of course, knowledge is, for Newman, a good irrespective of whether it spreads—but a complete lack of any power or tendency to spread might make one question whether the knowledge one has gained is as sound as one had thought. That does not mean, however, that a facility in intellectual persuasion and influence should become one's *direct* goal, nor the criterion one uses to judge the worth of one's education; to aim directly at persuasion and influence will make one a sophist before it will make one a scholar, an advertiser rather than a philosopher. Yet to aim at sound knowledge will certainly (according to Newman) tend towards giving one persuasion and influence. True knowledge is a treasure with a power of diffusion, and one may seek it secure in the knowledge that it has that power, and that by seeking it one is not, barring accidents, seeking something that will remain entirely one's own possession.

---

[65] In 1873, the same year in which *The Idea of a University* was first published, a then obscure German philologist wrote 'On Truth and Lying in a Non-Moral Sense'. Newman, unsurprisingly, did not see Nietzsche coming.

[66] Fergal McGrath, *The Consecration of Learning: Lectures on Newman's* Idea of a University (Dublin: Gill and Son, 1962), 123.

[67] Original appendix to 1852 edition, given by Ker in Newman, *Idea*, 463–5. The original material on Cicero is *Idea*, 98–9 [104–6].

Newman's fullest description of the social value of university education is that 'it aims at raising the intellectual tone of society, at cultivating the public mind, at purifying the national taste, at supplying true principles to popular enthusiasm and fixed aims to popular aspiration, at giving enlargement and sobriety to the ideas of the age, at facilitating the exercise of political power, and refining the discourse of private life' (p. 154 [pp. 177–8]). All of these, except one, are simply descriptions of the spread of knowledge—of the growth of a society towards views instead of viewiness; they do not necessarily involve any step away from knowledge as an end in itself. The list includes, however, the goal of 'facilitating the exercise of political power', and that certainly sounds like a goal external to knowledge itself—and a somewhat troubling one at that. Yet Newman's account of the good of knowledge fairly regularly includes items like this, at least one step away from the spread and deepening of knowledge itself. He clearly holds that a life securely rooted in the appre-hension of truth is (all else being equal) a more stable, more peaceful, more harmonious life than one that is not—and that this will be true both for individuals and for society.[68] To pursue the sound formation of the mind is, therefore, *ipso facto* to contribute to well-ordered individual and social life more generally—and the university therefore can properly be expected to turn out students who will further this good order. As Newman says: 'If then a practical end must be assigned to a University course, I say it is that of training good members of society. Its art is the art of social life, and its end is fitness for the world' (p. 154 [p. 177]). Note Newman's wording, however: '*If . . .* a practical end must be assigned'. This practical end—the stable and peaceable ordering of society—must be kept firmly in its place. Once again, to aim directly at the effect (stable ordering) rather than at its cause (rootedness in the truth) would be a betrayal of the idea of the university. The truth must come first, because the other benefits that Newman sees university education producing are benefits *of* the truth—and are subordinate goods relative to truth itself as the primary good. That means that in the planning of a university—its curriculum, its patterns of education—one must first focus on sound intellectual formation in and of itself, and on the structures, prac-tices, and disciplines that the institution needs for that pursuit, and only then

---

[68] Newman sketched an optimistic vision of the future of the Catholic University of Ireland in *Office and Work*, 47–8 = *Rise and Progress*, 32. He pictures students from across the world flocking to Dublin, and then returning to carry over all the earth 'peace to men of good will'. He assured a room full of new evening class students that, 'in your advancement, Ireland is advanced;—in your advancement in what is good and what is true, in knowledge, in learning, in cultivation of mind, in enlightened attachment to your religion, in good name and respect-ability and social influence, I am contemplating the honour and renown, the literary and scientific aggrandizement, the increase of political power of the Island of the Saints' (p. 388 [p. 482]).

ask how the further benefits that this knowledge brings with it can be secured and advanced.

So: Newman first insists that intellectual formation is an end in itself, regardless of its utility. He second describes the natural diffusiveness of that good—not introducing some end other than intellectual formation, but giving that end a social aspect. He third discusses the higher utility that flows from this good: its tendency to aid in the formation of stable social and individual life. But there is also a fourth aspect to Newman's discussion of utility, because he does at times claim for intellectual formation a lower utility (where 'lower utility' concerns 'that which conduces directly either to the pursuit of particular professional ends'[69]).

Newman believes that a liberally educated man 'will be placed in that state of intellect in which he can take up any one of the sciences or callings I have referred to, or any other for which he has a taste or special talent, with an ease, a grace, a versatility, *and a success* to which another is stranger' (p. 145 [p. 166]; emphasis added).[70] It will teach students to 'fill any post with credit' (p. 154 [p. 178]), 'to fill their respective posts in life better' (p. 7 [p. xii]), and provide them with 'a faculty of . . . taking up with aptitude any science or profession' (p. 11 [p. xviii]).

Duke Maskell and Ian Robinson detect a serious mis-step in Newman's argument here. Newman, they suggest, 'convinced Victorian England that education as an end in itself was the best means to the end of Utility, and thus paved the way for the defeat of his own party'. They expose 'Newman's fraudulent promise, which the university went on making to practical men (and taxpayers) for almost 150 years': 'that if it is left free to pursue the good, it will provide them also with the useful, that cultivating disinterestedness is the way to many self-interested ends, that an education which treats knowledge as its own remuneration will be very remunerative'.[71]

There is some truth in this charge, but Newman is trading on two distinct but related assumptions that Maskell and Robinson do not sufficiently address. In the first place, he assumes that the learned professions do truly require intellectual virtues—those virtues that are essential to our ability to sort truth from delusion, and to ask questions about how individual truths add up to a coherent whole. He therefore assumes that these professions do indeed need people who are trained directly in those intellectual virtues that pertain to truth. And Newman regards a narrowly utilitarian education as simply

---

[69] Dale, 'Newman's "Idea"', 28. I have chopped off the remainder of Dale's definition: 'the advance of knowledge and of society's general material and political well-being', because it smears the boundary between higher and lower utility.

[70] Cf. McGrath, *Consecration*, 15.

[71] Duke Maskell and Ian Robinson, *The New Idea of a University* (London: Haven, 2001), 27, 31.

incapable of delivering those intellectual virtues with anything like the same depth and security. For the student, 'if his reading is confined simply to one subject, however such division of labour may favour the advancement of a particular pursuit . . . certainly it has a tendency to contract his mind' (p. 95 [p. 100]).[72] The problem of narrowly professional studies might be said to be the same as the problem of research, for Newman: they require an exclusive focus on one particular discipline, and so yield a development that cannot but be unbalanced. That is why Newman begins his discussion of utility by going back to rehearse his insistence that no science can stand alone (p. 94 [pp. 99–100]), and expands on the dangers of intellect 'sacrificed to some particular or accidental purpose' (p. 135 [p. 152]).[73] The learned professions, if they do indeed have a stake in well-formed intellects shaped to seek out truth, need something broader than a purely professional training. Maskell and Robinson's argument implies not so much that Newman had mis-described the university, as that he had misunderstood the professions: those professions do not, Maskell and Robinson imply, need that kind of truth-seeking intellectual formation from their students, or at least they (and the governments that oversee them) do not *know* that they need it.

Newman's argument as a whole also suggests a second, slightly different response to Maskell and Robinson, however. Rather than simply seeing the intellectual virtues as part of the proper *content* of professional education, Newman's argument also presents them as part of the proper 'context'. True intellectual formation shapes students who will be able to keep their professions in their place. Education serves a direct need of human nature, according to Newman, and one might say that the student he envisages is a human being first, and a (prospective) professional only second. They are truly the latter, and so most students will quite rightly have one eye on their professional future[74]—but they are truly the former as well. The education Newman suggests therefore forms them first as human beings, and second as

---

[72] In Discourse VII, Newman draws on Edward Copleston's response to the *Edinburgh Review*'s criticisms of Oxford. Copleston held that, in a society marked by the division of labour, education had been replaced by narrow expertise. 'In proportion as his sphere of action is narrowed his mental powers and habits become contracted, and he resembles a subordinate part of some powerful machinery, useful in its place, but insignificant and worthless out of it' (p. 147 [p. 168]).

[73] When Newman says that 'the highest [pursuits] lose it' (i.e., their liberal character) 'when they minister to something beyond them', it sounds as if any connection to utility is injurious; when he says that he is opposing concentration on 'the learned professions, *considered merely as professions*', it becomes clear that it is seeing education *primarily from the point of view* of utility is the problem, not utility *per se* (p. 99 [p. 106]).

[74] 'Professors will ordinarily lecture, and students ordinarily attend them, with a view, in some shape or other, to secular advantage. Certainly; few persons pursue knowledge simply for its own sake' (Newman, *Office and Work*, 73 = *Rise and Progress*, 49).

professionals—or, better, first as human beings, second as citizens, and third as professionals. The plans he set out for the Catholic university begin with two years of liberal education from 16 to 18, aimed at the human being and the citizen, which can then be followed by two years of professional training from 18 to 20.[75] Liberal education provides the context—and the framework—for professional training, and the compromise implied between the liberal and the professional is no more than the institutional reflection of the 'compromise' that people make by engaging in professional work in the first place—by being at once human and professionals.

NATURE AND GRACE

Despite its length, all that I have said so far is radically incomplete. In fact, if I stopped here, I could be said to have missed the whole point of Newman's discourses. After all, the central purpose of *The Idea of a University* is to define the idea of a *Catholic* university. To leave out of account the relationship between the university and the Catholic Church is to leave out the keystone of Newman's argument.[76] One might say that Newman's *Idea of a University* treats universities both in relation to nature *and* in relation to grace, and that what I have said so far has been almost entirely related to nature.[77] That is, what I have discussed so far is, according to Newman, 'founded on truths in the natural order' (p. 22 [p. 5]); it is 'dictated by human prudence and wisdom' and 'recognized by common sense' (p. 22 [p. 4]). What of grace?

The relationship between nature and grace is twofold, for Newman. On the one hand, grace supports nature: it steadies and secures the achievement of

---

[75] See *Report to their Lordships, the Archbishops and Bishops of Ireland, 1854–55*, in Newman, *Campaign*, 3–56: 31–2.

[76] This is a misinterpretation that Newman is keen to see off right at the start of the book. He acknowledges in the preface that much that he is going to say will resemble earlier (Protestant) discourses on university education (such that, for instance, he could include long extracts from the work of Edward Copleston and John Davison, apologists for Oxford's patterns of liberal education, in Discourse VII). But readers should not think he can 'be interpreted by the objects or sentiments' of those from whom he 'happened in the first instance' to learn these truths—and specifically should not be thought to be upholding this account of education 'to the disparagement of that Knowledge [i.e., of the Catholic faith] which I profess to be so strenuously upholding' (p. 5 [p. x]).

[77] Newman characteristically talks not in terms of 'nature' and 'grace', but in terms of 'essence' and 'integrity'. To describe the 'essence' of the university is to describe it in and of itself, as a natural institution, without reference to the work of grace upon it and through it. To describe its 'integrity' is to describe 'a gift superadded to its nature without which that nature is indeed complete, and can act, and fulfil its end, but does not find itself, if I may use the expression, in easy circumstances' (*Office and Work*, 271 = *Rise and Progress*, 180).

natural ends. On the other, grace goes beyond nature: it takes one further than one's natural capacity could, however completely it fulfilled its innate potential.

In the first place, then, Newman argues that grace steadies nature. Starting with what he takes to be a purely natural definition of the university, a definition in terms of natural capacities, Newman proceeds to show how those natural capacities cannot be fully engaged without the assistance of Catholic faith, even if they can be recognized and described more ecumenically. He first shows this at the level of subject matter. After all, no education can call itself well rounded, no university can claim to teach 'universal knowledge', no view can claim to have been shaped by conversation with all the most important disciplinary perspectives that can be brought to bear, if the discipline of theology is deliberately excluded—even if that exclusion is (as in the case of the Queen's Colleges) undertaken for the sake of preserving the intellectual peace between denominations. 'Religious doctrine is knowledge, in as full a sense as Newton's doctrine is knowledge. University Teaching without Theology is simply unphilosophical. Theology has at least as good a right to claim a place there as astronomy' (p. 50 [p. 42]).[78] And it is not simply the case that, without theology, one science would be left out. Every science would be impoverished by the lack of the proper impact upon it of robust conversation with theology. To include theology makes all the disciplines taught in a university 'not only more Christian, but more philosophical in their construction and larger and deeper in their provisions' (p. 34 [p. 21]). The sciences

say what is true, *exceptis excipiendis*; what is true, but requires guarding; true, but must not be ridden too hard, or made what is called a *hobby*; true, but not the measure of all things; true, but if thus inordinately, extravagantly, ruinously carried out, in spite of other sciences, in spite of Theology, sure to become but a great bubble, and to burst. (p. 89 [p. 94])

Of course, the same could perhaps be said of the omission of any significant science; it would be true of a university without political economy, perhaps, or without history. But it is most especially true of theology. After all, 'admit a God, and you introduce among the subjects of your knowledge, a fact encompassing, closing in upon, absorbing, every other fact conceivable' (p. 38 [p. 26]).

To include theology, therefore, is not simply to plug a curricular gap. It is to 'form and fix the Sciences in a circle and a system, and give them a centre and

---

[78] Newman is addressing an audience of Catholics, just as in earlier disputes he was addressing an audience very largely of Anglicans. He is not faced with having to take seriously the views on university constitution of those who are avowedly atheist.

an aim'.[79] Catholic teaching, according to Newman, therefore helps orient the intellectual landscape within which the mind works: it provides authoritative 'landmarks' (p. 82 [p. 84]) around which the landscape can be construed *truly*.[80] Without such aid, the mind's attempt to resolve the data of its senses into a coherent landscape might succumb to some optical illusion: it might take some feature of the landscape to be near and small when in fact it is far and large, and proceed to construe the entire landscape around that error, coherently but falsely. As Newman sees it, the church thus provides a home for, rather than a curb on, enquiry; it is 'a kind and watchful teacher and guide, encouraging us forward in the path of truth amid the perils which beset it'.[81] Such guidance, he insists, will not 'interfere with the real freedom of any secular science in its own particular department'[82]—though it is important to note that the 'real' freedom a science has 'in its own particular department' is precisely the freedom it has within the broader landscape orientated by Catholic teaching.

This is not simply a matter of content, however. If we look at the formation of the student rather than the curriculum, we can see that in the absence of theology his mind might well be trained in the forming of views, and so formed in the natural intellectual virtues; it might well therefore benefit from some of the stability and robustness that those virtues produce—but only to an extent. Without theology, it would be a mind kept from the full development even of its natural virtues. It would be patient to a degree—but impatient of theology; enlarged to a degree—but narrowed by the religious truth ignored; sociable to a degree—but constricted by its refusal to participate in the fuller catholicity of the church. The 'steadying' that the church provides to the university is an aid to the proper and full development of those natural intellectual virtues that are the university's *raison d'être*.

So, whereas in my earlier discussion the highpoint of the development of intellectual virtue seemed to lie in the art of conversation, the mutual

---

[79] Original 1852 Discourse V, given by Ker in Newman, *Idea*, 423.

[80] He does not go into detail about the kind of landmark that Catholic teaching will provide. It is clear that it can include extra, supernatural data: 'Thus, in the science of history, the preservation of our race in Noah's ark is an historical fact, which history never would arrive at without Revelation' (p. 73 [p. 73]). Newman provides a more interesting example when discussing the founding of the university. The idea of a Catholic university is a good one in the abstract, he says—but is it practicable and expedient? After all, it is not always the case that practice must follow what is abstractly true (except in the case of those sacred truths that yield imperative rules of conduct). But the pope has, by asking the bishops to found such a university here and now, declared authoritatively that, here and now, the foundation is both possible and practicable. 'If ever there was a power on earth who had an eye for the times, who has confined himself to the practicable... such is... the Vicar of Christ' (p. 28 [p. 13]). Church teaching has answered a question that unguided debate might have left opaque.

[81] This is the text from the 1852 version, not the 1873; Ker gives it in Newman, *Idea*, 502.

[82] Original 1852 Discourse V, given by Ker in Newman, *Idea*, 428.

adjustment and combination of the various different perspectives that one might find in the conversations of the Oriel common room, what we are now seeing is a deeper truth. If Catholic teaching provides the most comprehensive backdrop against which it is possible to position and adjust the individual sciences properly, and most fully develops the intellectual virtues necessary to grasp their truth, what is needed is rather a theologically informed, religiously shaped version of the art of conversation. The 'science of sciences' (p. 57 [p. 51]) is, for Newman, the kind of conversation one might find in an Oriel common room now raised to a higher order—or perhaps an Oriel returned to its devoutly Catholic medieval foundation.

The Church does more, however, than simply steady the university in the pursuit of its essential intellectual goal. However high the natural goal pursued by the university, it is not by itself enough. For sure, Newman can say that 'the intellect, which has been disciplined to the perfection of its [natural] powers', is

almost prophetic from its knowledge of history; it is almost heart-searching from its knowledge of human nature; it has almost supernatural charity from its freedom from littleness and prejudice; it has almost the repose of faith, because nothing can startle it; it has almost the beauty and harmony of heavenly contemplation, so intimate is it with the eternal order of things and the music of the spheres. (p. 124 [p. 139])

But that repeated 'almost' is a serious qualification. 'The radical difference indeed of this mental refinement from genuine religion, in spite of its seeming relationship, is the very cardinal point on which my present discussion turns' (p. 164 [p. 190]). And 'we shall please [God] best . . . when we use what we have by nature to the utmost, at the same time that we look out for what is beyond nature in the confidence of faith and hope' (p. 22 [p. 6]).[83] We will see the university in its proper place in the hierarchy of goods only when we see its pursuit of the (real, irreducible) good of the intellect put into service in pursuit of a still higher good—a 'supernatural' good that the university is simply incapable of approaching on its own.

Newman had long held that the human mind 'may be regarded from two principal points of view'—intellectual and moral.[84] The perfection of the intellectual aspect of human life is that cultivation of the mind that I have been discussing so far in this chapter. The perfection of the moral aspect of

---

[83] Newman's 'sustained eulogy of a liberal education is systematically qualified by reminders of its limitations' (Ker, *Newman*, 385; cf. Ker 'Introduction', p. xlviii).

[84] Newman, 'Sermon 1: Intellect, the Instrument of Religious Training', in *Sermons Preached on Various Occasions* (London: Longmans, Green and Co., 1908), 1–14: 5. This is one of 'Eight Sermons Preached before the Catholic University of Ireland in 1856, 1857, being the first year of the opening of its Church'.

the mind is found in religion—and the religious perfection of humanity is incomparably higher and greater than its intellectual perfection.[85] No amount of intellectual development and perfection can produce religion: knowledge does not break the power of temptation; it does not mend the human heart. 'Knowledge is one thing, virtue is another; good sense is not conscience, refinement is not humility, nor is largeness and justness of view faith' (p. 110 [p. 120]). Intellectual cultivation 'does not supply religious motives; it is not the cause or proper antecedent of any thing supernatural; it is not meritorious of heavenly aid or reward' (p. 161 [pp. 185–6]). 'Quarry the granite rock with razors, or moor the vessel with a thread of silk; then may you hope with such keen and delicate instruments as human knowledge and human reason to contend against those giants, the passion and the pride of man' (p. 111 [p. 121]). Religion, on the other hand, can exist without intellectual refinement.[86]

Yet knowledge and religion are not entirely independent. Knowledge can impinge on religion either positively or negatively. 'Under the shadow indeed of the Church, and in its due development, Philosophy does service to the cause of morality; but, when it is strong enough to have a will of its own . . . then it does but abet evils to which at first it seemed instinctively opposed' (p. 174 [p. 202]). In other words, properly steadied by the church, university education can be a service to it, and the pursuit of that knowledge, which is a good in itself, can become a component in the formation of human beings who have been perfected harmoniously both in that intellectual aspect of their being, and in the still more important moral aspect of their being. Unsteadied by the church, however, intellectual development can become positively injurious to religion. Just as one science, if not held in proper concert with other sciences, can run amok and render both itself and the other science less scientific, so intellectual excellence, if not held in its proper position—a position of inherent but limited dignity—can run amok and damage both its own intellectual sphere and the religious sphere that should be its proper context.

---

[85] William Sewell (1804–1874) wrote of himself and his fellow Tractarians that 'we . . . do not consider the communication of knowledge as the chief design of our post, or the grand end of education . . . We are . . . entrusted with the care of the young . . . and our consideration is to form and fashion and bring them to that model of human nature, which in our conscience we think is perfection. This model . . . we do not find, and therefore we will not place in the intellect of man. And this is the first grand point in which we differ, wholly and irreconcilably differ, from the maxims of the present day' (*Thoughts on the Admission of Dissenters to the University of Oxford: and on the Establishment of a State Religion* (Oxford: D. A. Talboys, 1834), 7). Cf. Nockles, 'Academic Counter-Revolution', 147.

[86] People 'may be religious without Knowledge', Newman said in the unused preface prepared for the first printed version of what was then Discourse VI, provided in Ker, 'Introduction', pp. xxxii–xxxiii, n. 5, point 7.

Newman is thus deeply ambivalent about the idea of a 'gentleman', which is the word he uses to name the product of a university considered purely from a natural point of view.[87] On the one hand, he can include in the term 'gentleman' all the undoubted intellectual virtues, and their genuine social fruit, that I have been discussing; he can admit that a natural university education will 'manifest itself in . . . courtesy, propriety, and polish of word and action' (p. 10 [p. xvi]). But to be a gentleman is not the same as being genuinely religious, and if gentlemanliness is all that a university aims at—if it is limited to the natural—then the gentlemanly ideal can become positively injurious to religion. For the good of each, intellectual and religious formation *must* go hand in hand; the university needs to aim at producing not the gentleman but the Catholic.[88]

Newman's argument is, through and through, an argument for an explicitly and exclusively Catholic university.[89] It is an argument for the necessity of 'a direct and active jurisdiction of the Church over [the university] and in it' (p. 184 [p. 215]).[90] In a passage in the 1852 Discourses that was not preserved

---

[87] Newman (p. 6 [p. x]) cites Victor Huber, who wrote that 'a "liberal education", such as could scarcely be obtained, but at the Universities, was, at all events, requisite for a perfect Gentleman: not to the exclusion, however, of other requisites, such as birth, wealth, and position . . . The cultivation of the faculties was more thought of than the amount of knowledge required' (Victor Aimé Huber, *The English Universities*, ed. and tr. Francis W. Newman, vol. II, pt 1 (London: William Pickering; Manchester: Simms and Dinham, 1843), 321–2).

[88] Paul Cullen wrote, in a September 1850 *Address to the People of Ireland* from the Catholic University Committee, that 'the Catholic Church . . . looks upon the work of education as only half done unless diligent moral culture and practical piety proceed *pari passu* with intellectual improvement' (quoted in McGrath, *Newman's University*, 101). This relation between religion and intellect is reflected in the constitution Newman proposed for the Catholic University. Following the model of Louvain (rather than of Oxford), he proposed a university where the professoriate was in charge of intellectual excellence: they had charge, as it were, of the *essence* of the university, and ordered its intellectual affairs. But he supplemented that professorial model with a collegiate system in which the responsibility for religious and moral formation would be concentrated: the students, who would gain their intellectual sustenance at the hands of the professors, would be organized into small residential communities in the hands of tutors, modelling, as closely as Newman could arrange in the conditions of modern Dublin, both his own earlier tutorial practice in Oriel, and his more recent vision of the quasi-monastic medieval college community (see Ker, 'Introduction', p. xxiii, and Rothblatt 'Oxonian "Idea"', 293). To that extent, Roy Jenkins is right to say that 'Newman wanted an idealized version of collegiate life under the dreaming spires, undefiled by the Reformation, trans-shipped to Leinster' (Jenkins, 'Newman and the Idea of a University', in David Brown (ed.), *Newman: A Man for Our Time—Centenary Essays* (London: SPCK, 1990), 141–58: 148). 'I admire the Professor,' Newman said, but 'I venerate the College. The Professorial system fulfils the strict idea of a University; and is sufficient for its being, but it is not sufficient for its well-being. Colleges constitute the integrity of a University' (*Office and Work*, 274 = *Rise and Progress*, 182).

[89] 'He wanted, above all, to create an intellectual élite, a cultivated Catholic laity, who could defend their faith and convert or compete with their educated Protestant confreres' (Sheridan Gilley, 'What has Athens to do with Jerusalem? Newman, Wisdom and the *Idea of a University*', in Stephen C. Barton (ed.), *Where Shall Wisdom Be Found? Wisdom in the Bible, the Church and the Contemporary World* (Edinburgh: T&T Clark, 1999), 155–68: 162).

[90] Cf. Dale, 'Newman's "Idea"', *passim*.

in the 1873 edition, Newman says clearly enough that 'the main principle on which I shall have to proceed is this—that Education must not be disjoined from Religion, or that Mixed [i.e., non-denominational] Schools... are constructed on a false idea'.[91]

He has argued that theology must be included in the curriculum and that, once included, theology cannot help but substantively shape the whole tenor of the education provided, and that the education provided by a university therefore cannot but consist in *religious* intellectual formation. And, since there is no such thing as theology or religion in general, only the theology and religion of specific ecclesial communions, a university that is worthy of the name cannot avoid being an institution substantially shaped by the theology of a particular denomination, and providing an education shaped by that denomination's teaching. A university can only properly be religiously exclusive.

Similarly, Newman has argued that a university education provides some kind of training of character, perfecting the intellect of man. But it can do this steadily, fully, and without distortion only if it works with the aid of religion, and in any case the intellectual training it provides needs to be supplemented by religious training if the formation that it provides is not to become positively irreligious and dangerous to true morality.

A university education must be intimately united to proper moral and religious formation, or it must fail on both intellectual and moral grounds,[92] and, for a Catholic speaking to an audience of Catholics, that can only mean that a university education must be intimately united to the Catholic faith. Newman was simply summarizing the whole drift of his argument when, on the final night of the original run of lectures in Dublin, he closed by saying that 'a University... which refuses to profess the Catholic Creed, is... hostile both to the Church and to Philosophy'.[93]

---

[91] This is the text from the 1852 version, not the 1873; Ker gives it in Newman, *Idea*, 498. Newman wrote: 'Curious it will be if Oxford is imported into Ireland, not in its members only, but in its principles, methods, ways, and arguments' (*The Letters and Diaries of John Henry Newman*, xiv. *Papal Aggression*, ed. Charles Stephen Dessain and Vincent Ferrer Blehl (Oxford: Clarendon Press, 1963), 389–90; see Ker, *Newman*, 377), but Dale is right: 'The Oxford that Newman says in this letter he wants to import to Dublin is not, then, the Oxford of liberal education, as many seem to suppose. It is the Oxford that he and the Tractarians had fought to preserve from mixed education' (Dale, 'Newman's "Idea"', 11).

[92] Compare the openings of Discourses I and II: Discourse I states that the two central topics are utility and religious exclusiveness; Discourse II refers back to this, but quietly rephrases the latter so that the question is 'whether it is consistent with the idea of a University to exclude Theology from a place among the sciences which it embraces' (p. 33 [p. 19]). See also the original 1852 opening of the lecture, given by Ker in Newman, *Idea*, 506–8; it is considerably clearer in its insistence on Catholic exclusivity.

[93] This is the conclusion to the original 1852 Discourse V, given by Ker in Newman, *Idea*, 434. It is just what Cullen has asked Newman to do (see Dale, 'Newman's "Idea"', 9). Ker insists, however, that Newman wrote as much against 'the narrow dogmatism of a defensive clerical Catholicism' as against 'Utilitarian criticism of liberal education' (*Newman*, 383).

CONCLUSION

Newman intended his *Idea of a University* as the idea of an exclusively Catholic university, yet he drew in its formulation upon the educational practices and discourses that he had encountered—and been steeped in—in Protestant Oxford. Newman held these two impulses together by means of a distinction between nature and grace, construed as a distinction between a purely educational ideal pertaining to the intellectual aspect of human nature, and a religious ideal pertaining to the moral aspect of human nature. Protestant Oxford could speak only to the former; only the Catholic Church could speak truly to the latter. And the latter is incomparably the higher; a human being whose moral nature is secured and established by the Catholic faith without a matching intellectual development lacks nothing of ultimate importance; one who is intellectually advanced without knowing the true faith lacks everything, and even his intellectual advancement will be impaired.

There is a limit, therefore, to the help that Newman can offer, if I am pursuing a theological account of secular and religiously plural universities. His account of intellectual virtue, and of the assured path that it enables its possessors to take through the marshes of a media-saturated environment, is a powerful one, but his nature–grace framework ensures that Christian faith is presented largely as a set of guy ropes holding down (and holding in shape) a tent whose fabric is not itself theological.

I am able to develop a theology of higher education, and to speak theologically about secular and religiously plural universities, because I tread a different path. Strange thought it may seem, I am able to speak more positively than Newman can about secular and religiously plural universities precisely because I do not carve out a realm of educational nature separate from the realm of religious grace. My account of intellectual virtue and practice is theological all the way down—or all the way up: I will argue that there are no natural ends to education, but that the only proper end for all education is (in a specific sense) supernatural. That means, however, that, when I consider positively the education available in a secular or religiously plural university, whatever I may need to say about its incompleteness (that is, about its penultimate nature), I am not giving value to a practice that simply stands apart from, or over against, faith. Chapters 6 to 9 below will argue that, for a Christian practitioner, the educational pursuit of intellectual virtue in a secular and religiously plural university can already itself be an aspect of faithful discipleship—and that for the non-Christian practitioner too such an education is properly understood when it is seen to lie alongside such discipleship.

To advance to those positions, however, it is necessary to leave behind Newman's insistence on a sharp distinction between intellect and religion, and to abandon his supposedly non-theological account of natural intellectual formation. As I said in the Introduction: it will turn out that the problem with Newman's account is not that it is too theological, but that it is not theological enough.

4

Contemporary Theological Voices

In the first three chapters of this book, I have explored episodes from the history of higher education in the West that have had a compelling imaginative hold on many who seek to make sense of universities in the present. In the chapter after this, I will begin my own attempt at such sense-making—an attempt to speak about the present life of universities in the shadow of Paris, Berlin, Oxford, and Dublin. I have made no secret of the fact that I will be making that attempt as a Christian theologian, even if I have not yet made clear what kind of contribution to contemporary debates I think a Christian theologian can properly have. That I think such a contribution can be made should certainly be clear (flick through the remaining pages of the book: there are a lot of them, and not many are blank), but the questions of its plausibility and content still remain—especially given my avowed intention to write predominantly about the life of *secular* universities. After all, one could plausibly define a secular university as one in which most of those who shape policy and practice would greet an attempt at theological intervention with surprise, bafflement, incredulity, or distaste.

I am, of course, very far from being the only recent writer to think that a Christian theological contribution can and should be made. In fact, there is (at least in North America, and to a certain extent elsewhere) a flourishing industry of theological commentary upon higher education, predominantly in the guise of commentary upon the possibility of Christian scholarship or the responsibilities of Christian colleges. As a bridge between my historical investigations and my own constructive proposals, therefore, I will spend this fourth chapter exploring that recent literature, asking why the authors think that a Christian theological voice might have something useful to say about higher education, and how (if at all) they expect such a theological voice to make a difference. We will find ourselves moving from territory not all that dissimilar from Newman's, in which faith comes in to steady and to supplement the natural but fallible workings of intellectual formation, to territory on which a directly theological account of that intellectual formation begins to come into view.

SPEAKING IN A CRISIS

A good deal of the extensive recent literature on Christian faith and higher education has been written by Christian academics for a context in which, as they see it, Christian contributions to debates about the nature of higher education are widely regarded as either irrelevant or unwelcome—even in institutions with historic Christian identities, present links to churches, or formal constitutions that supposedly commit them in some way to Christian principles.

There are numerous analyses in the literature of how a higher-education sector once connected so closely to the churches and to Christian formation came to such a pass.[1] To select only the broadest of brushes from the set provided by these accounts, the change is attributed to the spread of a broadly Kantian construal of public reason, and an account of universities as homes for such public reason—and the story presented is therefore to some extent the continuation of the story I told about Berlin in Chapter 2. In such a construal, properly public reasoning takes place when a person, acting as a citizen rather than as a member of some specific sub-community, offers arguments designed to carry weight with any other rational citizen, regardless of the different sub-communities to which he or she might belong. Whatever role private religious communities and commitments might properly have on the periphery of universities, they will necessarily be irrelevant to the public business of promoting and pursuing such public reason.

Such a trend is but one strand of the broader cultural trends identified in the literature. George Marsden, for instance, refers to 'the larger process of the disestablishment of Protestantism as the semi-official religion in America', a process that gave rise to the assumption that '*no* explicitly religious viewpoint could be privileged without discriminating against the views of other religions', and that in turn led to the growth in academic culture (as elsewhere in public life) of 'the tendency to view religious perspectives as being in bad taste'.[2] The end result was that, 'no matter what the subject, our dominant academic culture trains scholars to keep quiet about their faith as the price of full acceptance' in the academic community.[3]

According to Marsden and to many of the other contributors to recent debate, it is not only explicitly Christian discourse that has been leached from

[1] The two most famous narratives of the de-Christianization of US academic life are provided by George M. Marsden, *The Soul of the American University: From Protestant Establishment to Established Nonbelief* (New York: Oxford University Press, 1994), and James Burtchaell, *The Dying of the Light: The Disengagement of Colleges and Universities from the Christian Churches* (Grand Rapids, MI: Eerdmans, 1998).

[2] George M. Marsden, *The Outrageous Idea of Christian Scholarship* (New York: Oxford University Press, 1997), 23.

[3] Marsden, *Outrageous Idea*, 7.

university life by this process. The attempt to build a public life from which the contentious commitments of particular communities have been excluded is seen to have contributed to a drastic thinning of the shared moral discourses that hold society together—and that can properly be admitted in debates about society's education. Relegated to the 'private' realm beyond reach of public reason, those commitments can feature in public life only as unaccountable preferences, options in a marketplace of values, or the coin-in-trade of political pressure groups: they cannot be the subject matter of publicly reasoned argument, including reasoned argument about the nature of public reason itself, and of the institutions that support it. Instead, debates about the goals, conduct, and principles of higher education have to focus on the only topic on which agreement can properly be secured: the pragmatic, value-free administration of a marketplace of diverse and incompatible values.[4]

In the absence of other shared measures of value, the easiest available alternative measure is money. Gavin D'Costa addresses his book on higher education to 'those who believe that the university might be other than the intellectual production line in the industrial halls of late postmodern capitalist society',[5] bemoaning the fact that 'finance is the chief criterion, without any organic vision of the relation of the different disciplines, without any shared values regarding the good of men and women, or concerning what truth might possibly be'.[6] Bound only by such an abstract measure of 'value', 'fragmentation, competitive professionalism, and utilitarianism in the universities have no check'.[7] Money, the publicly exchangeable substance par excellence, takes the place left vacant by the impossibility of publicly exchangeable arguments about 'values'. As John Milbank puts it, 'utter incoherence and lack of ability to withstand the critical trials of reason does not matter so long as one can come up with cash and customers'.[8]

---

[4] As Stanley Hauerwas notes, 'you do not need to be able to provide a coherent account of the activity that should characterize what universities are about as long as the university can be "administered"' (*The State of the University: Academic Knowledges and the Knowledge of God* (Oxford: Blackwell, 2007), 21 n. 20).

[5] Gavin D'Costa, *Theology in the Public Square: Church, Academy and Nation* (Oxford: Blackwell, 2005), p. ix. I should perhaps take this opportunity to explain why D'Costa's book—one of the most important theological works on higher education to be published recently in the UK—does not feature any more prominently in this chapter. D'Costa's book answers two main questions: Is there any place for theology in the modern secular university?, and (given that his answer to the first question is negative) What would a renewed Catholic university look like? However important they are, these are, as should by now be clear, not my questions—and I have therefore looked elsewhere for my main interlocutors.

[6] D'Costa, *Public Square*, 2.

[7] D'Costa, *Public Square*, 19.

[8] John Milbank, 'The Conflict of the Faculties: Theology and the Economy of the Sciences', in John Milbank, *The Future of Love: Essays in Political Theology* (London: SCM, 2009), 301–15: 302.

A similar move from substance to form can be found in the rise of 'Quality Assurance' in British universities. One of the clearest analyses of this is provided by Bruce Charlton. 'Quality Assurance', he says, 'is a technical managerial term for that type of auditing which is concentrated upon *systems and processes* rather than outcomes.' Such forms of monitoring are attractive because

> educational debate has shifted away from the contested territory of outcome measures towards obtaining agreement on a standard *system* of practice—and this must be a fully explicit Quality Assurance system in which all essential elements can be planned, documented, monitored and audited. Such a deft act of redefinition has the effect of rendering teaching *at last* amenable to quasi-objective quantitative measurement, to external monitoring, and to external control.[9]

In the words of George Marsden, 'contemporary university culture is hollow at its core'.[10]

This 'moral indeterminism'[11] and exclusion of substantive religious voices is seen as deeply injurious to the university's wider social mission. In *The Decline of the Secular University*, John Sommerville writes that 'the secular university is increasingly marginal to American society, and . . . this is a *result* of its secularism. In effect, I mean that questions that might be central to the university's mission are too religious for it to deal with.'[12] It is incapable of promoting real debate about its own purpose, about the nature of the human good it pursues, about the way forward in a situation where conceptions of the human good clash—and so incapable of leading, or even contributing to, a wider public debate about the common good.[13] All that it can supply to public discourse is fragmented 'expertise', fuel for a society that has forgotten how to think about its own values and ends.[14] Where values and ends are

---

[9] Bruce Charlton, 'Audit, Accountability and All That: The Growth of Managerial Technologies in UK Universities', in Stephen Prickett and Patricia Erskine-Hill, *Education! Education! Education! Managerial Ethics and the Law of Unintended Consequences* (Thorverton: Imprint Academic/Higher Education Foundation, 2002), 13–28: 20, 21.

[10] Marsden, *Outrageous Idea*, 3. Such comments abound in the literature. For instance, Richard B. Hays warns that the university is becoming 'intellectually incoherent and therefore captive to market forces that threaten to distort its mission beyond all recognition' ('The Palpable Word as Ground of *Koinonia*', in Douglas V. Henry and Michael D. Beaty (eds), *Christianity and the Soul of the University: Faith as a Foundation for Intellectual Community* (Grand Rapids, MI: Baker Academic, 2006), 19–36: 20).

[11] Marsden, *Outrageous Idea*, 111.

[12] Sommerville, *The Decline of the Secular University* (Oxford: Oxford University Press, 2006), 4.

[13] Sommerville notes, for instance (*Decline*, 8) that, however good universities might be at increasing one's earning power, one might well ask 'where in the university . . . would you go to learn how to spend your money intelligently?' ('Wisely' might have been a better word.)

[14] See also Nathan O. Hatch on 'the erosion of public trust in colleges and universities' in 'Christian Thinking in a Time of Academic Turmoil', in Douglas V. Henry and Bob R. Agee

fundamentally private, and so insulated from public discourse, there is noth-ing for the university to do but to discover ever more efficient means of meeting existing desires.

Any commitment by the university to something like the disinterested pursuit of truth, and to the dissemination of such a pursuit and its fruit across society more widely, is therefore itself under threat. Christian writers look at the university and see 'a bewildering jumble of competing and conflicting arguments, which appear to admit no finally valid claims to truth',[15] or a generalized 'lack of confidence in the truth'.[16] Dallas Willard puts it more strongly: 'The ideal of the intellectual, artistic and academic life as the pursuit of truth . . . is far beyond being in "deep trouble" in the university today, and in many places is approximating the status of a "lost cause".'[17] And Murray Rae writes that 'the intention to pursue the *truth* [is not] taken without question to be constitutive of the university's existence, and . . . figure[s] hardly at all in the mandatory "aims and outcomes" of university education'.[18] Fragmented ex-pertise is the coin of such a university, not truth. Any strong version of a commitment to truth—strong enough, that is, to guide the university past the lure of problematic funding sources, to drive it beyond fragmentation, to offset the temptations of the purely pragmatic and utilitarian—turns out, according to these authors, to flounder when removed from the water of robust concep-tions of the human good, and so to be among those things bound eventually to become extinct in the realm of attenuated public reason. Universities can (and do) pay lip service to the commitment to truth, but this has become nothing more than an ideological smokescreen: they no longer know how to discuss truth, nor how to make clear judgements about the implications that pursuing it would have for their life.[19]

Various of these authors bemoan the fact that supposedly Christian colleges provide no haven in this storm. There, too, 'confusion, fragmentation, and

(eds), *Faithful Learning and the Christian Scholarly Vocation* (Grand Rapids, MI: Eerdmans, 2003), 87–100: 87.

[15] Robert Royal, 'Introduction', in Alice Ramos and Marie I. George (eds), *Faith, Scholarship and Culture in the 21st Century* (Washington: American Maritain Association/Catholic Univer-sity of America, 2002), 1–10: 1.

[16] Gavin T. Colvert, 'The Spirit of Medieval Philosophy in a Postmodern World', in Ramos and George (eds), *Faith, Scholarship and Culture*, 32–56: 33.

[17] Dallas Willard, 'How Reason can Survive the Modern University: The Moral Foundations of Rationality', in Ramos and George (eds), *Faith, Scholarship and Culture*, 181–91: 181.

[18] Murray Rae, 'Learning the Truth in a Christian University: Advice from Søren Kierke-gaard', in Jeff Astley, Leslie Francis, John Sullivan, and Andrew Walker (eds), *The Idea of a Christian University: Essays on Theology and Higher Education* (Bletchley/Waynesborough, GA: Paternoster, 2004), 98–112: 98.

[19] Cf. Alfred J. Freddoso, '*Fides et Ratio*: A "Radical" Vision of Intellectual Inquiry', in Ramos and George (eds), *Faith, Scholarship and Culture*, 13–31: 13–14, and Colvert, 'Spirit of Medieval Philosophy', 33.

ideological strife' reign.[20] 'Disappointingly, at precisely the point where church-related colleges and universities ought to display a countercultural communitarian impulse, they generally mirror the radically individualistic tendencies of the rest of American culture.'[21] Church-related colleges have, these authors say, by and large, taken the same path as secular universities. In fact, given my definition of a 'secular university' as 'one in which most of those who shape policy and practice would greet an attempt at theological intervention with surprise, bafflement, incredulity, or distaste', the church-related colleges are as secular as any—and where they are not it is because they are so far from the academic mainstream as to be peripheral to any serious discussion of the health of higher education in general.

Yet Christian voices—or, more generally, religious voices—are precisely what is needed, according to nearly all the recent literature on Christian higher education. John Sommerville speaks for many when he writes that 'there are many terms that even the secular university cannot do without, like "truth", "freedom", "sanity", "responsibility", and "purpose", that are more comfortable within various religious discourses'.[22] These authors insist that only a frank, open, multi-traditional conversation that deliberately and explicitly includes religious voices and arguments will, therefore, allow such concepts, so central to the mission of the university and its contribution to society, to return to centre stage. Only such a frank, open, multi-traditional conversation can save public reason.

A POSTMODERN OPPORTUNITY?

Over much of the recent writing about faith and higher education, then, a general sense of crisis looms,[23] but for some authors at least this is combined

---

[20] Douglas V. Henry and Michael D. Beaty, 'Introduction', in Henry and Beaty (eds), *Soul of the University*, 9–15: 9.

[21] Henry and Beaty, 'Introduction', 10.

[22] Sommerville, *Decline*, 35.

[23] Of course, this is neither new nor universal. That it is not new should be clear from anyone who has read the earlier chapter on Newman; a more recent example (chosen at random) is provided by David M. Paton's *Blind Guides? A Student Looks at the University* (London: SCM, 1939). Higher education is, he says, beset by confusion—and that confusion is symptomatic of 'the essential and radical decay of the foundations of our society' (p. 7). That it is not universal is indicated by various contributors to the current debate who deliberately step back from the doom-laden tone of their conversation partners. For instance, Andrea Sterk insists that hers is not simply 'yet another book about... the perilous plight of the American university' in a context of many books on 'secularization, de-Christianization, postmodernism, identity crisis, and a host of other ills allegedly afflicting the modern academy' (Andrea Sterk, 'Preface', in Andrea Sterk (ed.), *Religion, Scholarship and Higher Education: Perspectives, Models and Future Prospects. Essays form the Lilly Seminar on Religion and Higher Education* (Notre Dame, IN:

with a belief that the contemporary situation also presents a significant, if ambiguous, opportunity. With the shift to what tends to get called a 'post-modern' culture, and a postmodern structure to the higher-education sector, the possibility exists again, such authors say, for a distinctive Christian voice to sound within the university (alongside many other particular voices, religious and non-religious), or for Christian institutions of higher education to redis-cover their corporate distinctiveness (alongside many other particular institu-tions, religious and non-religious). Public reason may have thinned until it is little more than the administrator of a marketplace of ideas and values—but precisely that situation allows Christians to set up their stall boldly and unashamedly, and to make a case in public for a different way of working.

For George Marsden, this can be described as a shift from a situation ruled by John Dewey to one ruled by William James. He sees Dewey as representing a university in which the rules of a public reason from which particular religious commitments have been excluded are regarded as absolute. Dewey's liberalism forms a new 'common faith' governing all that may properly be said.[24] Marsden sees James, on the other hand, as representing a form of liberal pragmatism much friendlier to particular commitments. He quotes James's famous image of a hotel corridor:

Innumerable chambers open out of it. In one you may find a man writing an atheistic volume; in the next someone on his knees praying for faith and strength; in the third a chemist investigating a body's properties. In a fourth a system of idealistic metaphysics is being excogitated; in a fifth the impossibility of metaphysics is being shown. But they all own the corridor, and all must pass through it if they want a practicable way of getting into or out of their respective rooms.[25]

Marsden comments that the pragmatic rules of neutral public discourse provide 'the modus operandi for the contemporary academy', but provide 'no basic reason why the intellectual implications of particular religious beliefs may not be explicitly brought into public discourse'—provided that, once those ideas are out in the corridor, their religious bearers agree to abide by the rules that govern corridor traffic (p. 46).[26] Just as Christians will abide by

---

University of Notre Dame Press , 2002), pp. xiii–xviii: p. xiii). More directly, Martin E. Marty tells all concerned to stop their constant whining ('The Church and Christian Higher Education in the New Millennium', in Henry and Agee (eds), *Faithful Learning*, 50–61, and 'Foreword', in Douglas Jacobsen and Rhonda Hustedt Jacobsen (eds), *Scholarship and Christian Faith: Enlar-ging the Conversation* (Oxford: Oxford University Press, 2004), pp. vii–ix).

[24] Marsden, *Outrageous Idea*, 46, citing the title of John Dewey's *A Common Faith* (New Haven: Yale University Press, 1934); subsequent page references to Marsden in text.

[25] William James, *Pragmatism and the Meaning of Truth* (Cambridge, MA: Harvard Univer-sity Press, 1978), 32; cited in Marsden, *Outrageous Idea*, 46.

[26] Note that, for Ian Markham, a hotel is exactly what a Christian university can avoid being—see 'The Idea of a Christian University', in Astley et al. (eds), *Idea*, 3–13: 5. Marsden would not necessarily disagree.

the rules of the game when playing chess, so (unless those rules conflict directly with their Christian commitments) they will be happy to play by the rules of the academic hotel while they are its guests.[27]

Such accommodation to the rules of the game is likely to be largely unproblematic, since 'outside of theology itself... distinctive Christian teachings seldom dictate scholarship that is distinctive in the sense that a non-Christian might not say more or less the same thing on a given topic' (p. 69). 'The fact is that explicitly Christian convictions do not very often have substantial impact on the techniques used in academic detective work, which makes up the bulk of the technical, scientific side of academic inquiry' (p. 47). Just as it makes little sense to think that there is such a thing as a distinctively Christian rulebook for chess, it makes little sense to think that a Christian theologian might have much to say directly about the rules of academic life—according to Marsden.[28] Rather, the distinctiveness of the Christian scholarly voice will be found more in the acknowledgement of the deepest sources of motivation that guide its choice of topics and its operative hunches, its insistent interest in the wider implications of any given academic discipline ('questions of larger meaning' (p. 22) and 'the larger questions of life' (p. 28)),[29] its sense of the proper limits of each discipline, and the generous scholarly 'ethos' that it seeks to embody (p. 7).[30]

Nicholas Wolterstorff's presentation of similar ideas about Christian scholarship contains a somewhat more robust account of the kind of insights and challenges that might make it into the academic corridor from the privacy of the various rooms. He writes that 'our postmodern situation is that Christians

[27] Marsden, *Outrageous Idea*, 56: 'When religious people play by the rules of the various games of society—the rules of law, the pragmatic rules of the United States Constitution, the rules of the market, or the rules of mainstream academia—they are not necessarily violating Christian principles by temporarily accommodating themselves to those rules.'

[28] I will not be following Marsden here, though it is true that I will have little to say about the rules of Christian chess.

[29] Cf. Rae, 'Learning the Truth', 109: 'So, while there may be nothing in particular to say theologically about the turning of litmus paper red... the interrelatedness of such knowledge with other things that go on in the universe and its application to our wider human projects will soon give rise to discussions in which the fact that this is God's world and that it is directed towards the fulfilment of his purposes becomes of the utmost importance.' See also C. Stephen Evans, 'The Calling of the Christian Scholar-Teacher', in Henry and Agee (eds), *Faithful Learning*, 26–49: 40. Evans argues that mathematics will be least affected by distinctively Christian scholarship, closely followed by the natural sciences, then the human sciences, history, literature, and arts, and finally philosophy and theology, where the distinctiveness of Christian scholarship will be most clearly on display.

[30] Cf. Evans, 'Calling', 34: 'Christian scholarship is scholarship that is done to further the kingdom of God. It is scholarship carried out as part of a calling by citizens of that kingdom whose character, attitudes, emotions, and convictions reflect their citizenship, and whose work as scholars is shaped by their Christian convictions, emotions and character.'

are entitled to enter the conversation of science [by which he means academic scholarship in general] *as Christians'*.[31]

For we have learned that the practice of science is not some purely and generically human enterprise, nor some autonomous self-governing and self-sustaining enterprise; but an eminently concrete social-historical enterprise incorporating goals and standards and intuitions and values that people bring to it and that emerge from their interaction with each other after their induction into the practice... We do not shed all our ordinary convictions and commitments at the door of the conversation room of science and enter as nakedly human... We enter as who we are; and we begin conversing on whatever is the topic in hand. When some disagreement turns up, we deal with that. We do not make sure that we have forestalled it in advance. Often we learn from our disagreements. (p. 127)

After all, 'we human beings *see* things differently, without that fact itself being the sign of irrationality on anyone's part' (p. 45). 'Our narrative identities lead us to notice things and believe things that otherwise would almost certainly go unnoticed and unbelieved'—they provide 'privileged cognitive access' (p. 237). It is on this basis that 'the Christian as Christian enters the ongoing practice of science and there interacts with the other participants, sometimes in agreement, sometimes in disagreement, but either way, interacting' (p. 128). To the extent that this is a possibility in the postmodern academy, 'what choice does the Christian have but to engage in that complex dialectic of cooperating with one's fellow scholars in the *human* task of pursuing meaning while yet working out a *Christian* interpretation of experience and of meaning?' (p. 104).[32]

There is more of a sense in Wolterstorff than in Marsden that the nature of public reason can be productively rethought in the postmodern context. Indeed, for him, the vocation of the Christian scholar seems to include a witness to the possibility of a different kind of public reason: a multi-voiced but still properly conversational science, in which the particularity of each

---

[31] Nicholas Wolterstorff, *Educating for Shalom: Essays on Christian Higher Education*, ed. Clarence W. Joldersma and Gloria Goris Stronks (Grand Rapids, MI: Eerdmans, 2004), 127; subsequent page references in text.

[32] Marsden and Wolterstorff have a common background in the Dutch Reformed tradition that has shaped their sense of the possibilities here. See Wolterstorff, *Shalom*, 64–86. Richard T. Hughes, in 'Christian Faith and the Life of the Mind', in Henry and Agee (eds), *Faithful Learning*, 3–25: 5–7, describes this Reformed perspective as emphasizing the possibility of a distinctive Christian world view, within which 'all learning should be integrated into a coherent understanding of reality, informed by explicitly Christian convictions' (p. 6). See also Douglas Jacobsen and Rhonda Husted Jacobsen, 'More than the "Integration" of Faith and Learning', in Douglas Jacobsen and Rhonda Husted Jacobsen (eds), *Scholarship and Christian Faith*, 15–31, and Daryl B. Hart, 'Christian Scholars, Secular Universities, and the Problem with the Antithesis', *Christian Scholar's Review*, 30/4 (2001), 383–402. For an account of the Christian University that places a Christian 'world view' centre stage, see D. A. Carson, 'Can There Be a Christian University?', *Southern Baptist Journal of Theology*, 1/3 (1997), 20–38.

scientist is acknowledged and even welcomed.[33] It is, by contrast, not clear in Marsden's presentation whether the particular voices speaking into the corridor from their respective rooms can be heard, and discussed, as anything other than private preferences. It is not clear, in other words, whether Marsden's Christian scholar has any way to challenge the incapability of modern public reason to sustain the reasoned discussion about differing conceptions of the human good (or, we might say, about differing world views).[34] However, along with many other participants in the debate about Christian higher education, Marsden does allow that it might be possible to contribute on theological grounds to renovating and protecting the basic rules of academic life. Noting that 'there seems to be an inverse relationship between scholarly production and spiritual virtues' (p. 107), Marsden nevertheless insists that 'much of scholarly research and writing can be means of relating to others, communicating to others, and attempting to serve others by discovering or saying something worthwhile' (p. 197), and that a Christian scholar should therefore be dedicated to pursuing his or her academic vocation in such a way as to overcome 'isolation, self-absorption, and self-promotion' (p. 108). There might, therefore, be a distinctive *ethos* to Christian scholarship, and that ethos might have some strong connection to the quality of the basic practices by which academic life progresses—but Marsden does not pursue this idea far enough to see what it might mean for a renewal or transformation of academic or public reason per se.

CHRISTIAN COLLEGES AND UNIVERSITIES

The witness that an individual Christian scholar can provide to the possibility of a different practice of reason is, of course, limited by the fact that reasoning is a social activity. Beyond a focus on the work of the Christian scholar, therefore, much of the recent discussion of faith and higher education has focused on Christian institutions: Christian colleges and universities.[35] The same postmodern culture that is held to present an opportunity for the

---

[33] See also below, p. 120, for other ways in which Wolterstorff gives a theological account of the nature of public reason.

[34] Marsden acknowledges that the opportunity provided by the postmodern situation is an ambiguous one, and he insists that 'Christians and other believers who reject the dominant naturalistic biases in the academy would be foolish to do so in the name of postmodern relativism' (Marsden, *Outrageous Idea*, 30). It is not clear, however, given his belief that he has nothing distinctive to say as Christian about the rules of the academic game, whether he has anything to offer except such relativism.

[35] Marsden speaks of the need to form Christian sub-communities, networks, and institutes—but in his presentation they are needed primarily to sustain individual Christian scholars in their work (*Outrageous Idea*, 101–7).

individual Christian scholar to regain a voice is often held to present an opportunity for such Christian institutions to regain their distinctiveness.[36] For instance, the authors of a recent collection of essays on the future of church-related colleges in the USA, *Professing in the Postmodern Academy*, write that the postmodern situation 'opens up the possibility of rethinking the idea and rationale of the church-related college',[37] as it is 'more favourable to "reprivileging" the Christian tradition' in such colleges.[38] Nathan Hatch writes that Christians 'have an unusual opportunity to articulate what may be the only coherent educational philosophy in the marketplace'—they have 'a clear opportunity to assert their distinctives'.[39]

Prescriptions for such reassertion vary quite widely. For some, it is a matter of preserving (or developing) an ethos and sense of purpose that, though grounded in Christianity, can be expressed in quite general terms. Arthur Holmes, for instance, writes that 'the heart and soul of the Christian academy' will consist in a commitment to '(1) The usefulness of liberal arts as preparation for service to both church and society; (2) The unity of truth; (3) Contemplative (or doxological) learning; (4) The care of the soul (what we call moral and spiritual formation.'[40] All this will be orientated to the pursuit of wisdom, or 'good judgment that embodies fundamental values inherent in the overall meaning and purpose of life'.[41]

For others, a church-related college will provide an education that is more explicitly an induction into a particular intellectual tradition. For Ian Markham, a Christian university is one that (1) is intellectually honest, recognizing the tradition-constituted nature of its work (unlike the secular university with its pretence at neutrality); (2) acknowledges that it is attempting to inculcate certain 'faith-based' values; (3) includes the 'philosophy of each subject' in the

---

[36] For a survey of recent writings about church-related colleges, see Stephen R. Haynes, 'A Review of Research on Church-Related Higher Education', in Stephen R. Haynes (ed.), *Professing in the Postmodern Academy: Faculty and the Future of Church-Related Colleges* (Waco, TX: Baylor University Press, 2002), 1–30.

[37] William J. Cahoy, 'A Sense of Place and the Place of Sense', in Haynes (ed.), *Professing*, 73–111: 75. For a fairly typical account of 'our "postmodern" moment in history', see Paul Lakeland, 'The Habit of Empathy: Postmodernity and the Future of the Church-Related College', in Haynes (ed.), *Professing*, 33–48: 34.

[38] Margaret Falls-Corbitt, 'Prolegomena to Any Postmodern Hope for the Church-Related College', in Haynes (ed.), *Professing*, 49–71: 49.

[39] Hatch, 'Academic Turmoil', 89; cf. Joel A. Carpenter, 'The Mission of Christian Scholarship in the New Millennium', and Arthur F. Holmes, 'The Closing of the American Mind and the Opening of the Christian Mind: Liberal Learning, Great Texts, and the Christian College', in Henry and Agee (eds), *Faithful Learning*, 62–74: 101–22.

[40] Arthur F. Holmes, *Building the Christian Academy* (Grand Rapids, MI: Eerdmans, 2001), 2. The book provides a quick history of the emergence of this model of Christian learning, and Holmes's model harks back at least to Clement's Alexandria: 'In the Alexandrian school moral and spiritual formation and the usefulness of liberal learning joined the unity of truth in an all-encompassing doxology to the God of creation' (p. 20).

[41] Holmes, *Building*, 5–6.

curriculum; and (4) is committed to a 'celebration of "rationality" and "conversation" in the quest for truth'.[42] For Andrew Walker and Andrew Wright, a Christian university or college will be 'the training ground for the reclamation of Christian tradition',[43] and it will 'treat teaching and research not as ends in themselves but as instrumental to the health of the student community, and through them for the church and society as a whole'.[44] Its life will begin and end in worship (p. 69). For David S. Dockery, Christian higher education is on a mission to teach its students to think Christianly.[45]

Nicholas Wolterstorff

Alongside his account of the nature of individual Christian scholarship, discussed above, Nicholas Wolterstorff provides one of the most careful articulations of the nature of Christian higher education at the institutional level. He sets his proposals in the context of a specific moment in the history of relations between the churches and the wider culture in the United States. There exists in the USA, as in any country, something we can call public piety: the 'cluster of beliefs, goals, rituals, symbols, and objects of veneration' that shape national life.[46] Hitherto in US life, many people have seen 'no significant tension, let alone contradiction, between the Christian religion and the American public piety'—unsurprisingly, given that, 'on the one hand, the public piety has been shaped (in part) by the churches, and on the other hand, the churches have at the same time accommodated themselves to public piety' (p. 5). Yet, for Wolterstorff, 'our American attempt to treat and see the various Christian denominations, indeed, the various religions, as nothing more than specific versions of the public piety that unites us all—that is a deep illusion' (p. 7).

The opportunity for Christian institutions of higher education is, paradoxically, created precisely by the fact that US public piety has shifted further and further in the direction of an 'anti-religious, libertarian, self-centered sensualism' and that 'a much deeper sense of overagainstness with respect to

---

[42] Markham, 'Idea of a Christian University', 10, 11.

[43] Andrew Walker and Andrew Wright, 'A Christian University Imagined: Recovering Paideia in a Broken World', in Astley et al. (eds), *Idea*, 56–74: 57.

[44] Walker and Wright, 'Christian University', 69.

[45] David S. Dockery, *Renewing Minds: Serving Church and Society through Christian Higher Education* (Nashville, TN: B&H Academic, 2007). For Denton Lotz, 'it is . . . the task of Christian higher education to prepare the groundwork for the conversion of this neo-pagan society' ('Christian Higher Education and the Conversion of the West', in Henry and Agee (eds), *Faithful Learning*, 123–38: 128). For Joel Carpenter, 'what we are called to do as intellectuals is missionary work' ('The Mission of Christian Scholarship in the New Millennium', in Henry and Agee (eds), *Faithful Learning*, 62–74: 72).

[46] Wolterstorff, *Shalom*, 5; subsequent page references in text.

American culture than was ever present before' has begun to emerge in many American churches (p. 6). This will require a change in those institutions whose agenda is significantly shaped by those churches. 'The implication . . . is that the cozy notion that we could base our teaching on what everybody in our society holds in common, adding to that our own sectarian peculiarities, seems less and less plausible' (p. 6). In the context of this renewed 'overagainstness', Christian higher education can be freed to be a distinctive witness,[47] and 'the most fundamental thing to say about the Christian college is that it is an arm of the body of Christ in the world. It is of and by and for the church' (p. 33).

Such institutions will, therefore, educate for the peaceable kingdom of God; they will educate for *shalom*, where 'to dwell in shalom is to find delight in living rightly before God, to find delight in living rightly in one's physical surroundings, to find delight in living rightly with one's fellow human beings, to find delight even in living rightly with oneself' (p. 23). Such institutions will 'cultivate in students the disposition to work and pray for shalom, savoring its presence and mourning its absence' (p. 144). They will do so by elaborating and conveying a Christian social ethic, and patterns of Christian ethical reasoning (p. 146); they will do so by educating students in critical attentiveness to the contemporary world in which they live (p. 147). They will go further than that, however: they will seek to provide a discipline (complete with forms of 'praise and . . . dis-praise') designed to shape what students find praiseworthy (pp. 149–50); they will provide ongoing encounters with real and fictional individuals who actively *model* the patterns of life and thought that the college is seeking to convey (p. 150); and they will place a strong emphasis on serious engagement with examples of suffering, in which the development of empathy is specifically encouraged (p. 150).

Over against institutions of higher education that claim to inculcate no particular tradition, no particular set of values (other than those necessary for participation in a public sphere where all traditions and values are allowed, provided they can be kept from violence towards each other or towards the public sphere itself), Wolterstorff's vision is unashamedly particular: it is of an education that inducts students quite deliberately into one specific tradition of thought and action. And he believes that we *need* such particularity, if we are to form students to respond to the 'wounds of humanity' (pp. 22, 88, 164). Higher education otherwise provides no such response; it is a matter of chance if it turns out students likely to respond to those wounds.

Though it is not a central emphasis for him, Wolterstorff provides one intriguing glimpse of what reasoning will look like in such an institution—a

---

[47] Cf. Anthony Campolo, 'The Challenge of Radical Christianity for the Christian College', in Henry and Agee (eds), *Faithful Learning*, 139–57: 139: 'Radical Christian colleges are characterized by a counterculturalism . . . that finds its ground in a rich and enriching commitment to biblical Christianity.'

glimpse that takes us a step beyond the picture I discussed earlier, of scientific dialogue between scholars with different perspectives and differing 'traditions of privileged cognitive access' (p. 237). He acknowledges that such a dialogue is inherently fragile, threatened as it is by the resentments that spring from histories of violence and of suffering. A genuine conversation, in which members of different traditions are able to learn from one another truly, will require 'forgiveness', 'repentance', even 'suffering owned redemptively' (p. 238).

> What is needed if the academy is to survive in the face of injury and suffering are those fundamental acts of the soul taught us by Christ for walking in his Way . . . And beyond those acts of the soul, what is needed . . . is the embrace of the conviction, fundamental to Christianity, Judaism, and Islam alike, that there is more to human beings than the merely particular. There is shared narrative. (p. 239)

Christian institutions of higher education, precisely in so far as they are formed by such practices and convictions, precisely in so far as they possess a lived vocabulary of forgiveness and redemption, and a lived vocabulary of the human, are in a position to *model* reasoning for a fragmented postmodern world.

Wolterstorff is by no means alone in this conviction. One of the staples of the recent discussion of faith and higher education has been an emphasis on the properly intellectual virtues in which the Christian tradition can or should provide a training. The literature is filled with discussions of the importance of self-transcending friendship (Alfred J. Freddoso), open-mindedness, openness to criticism, and reverence for truth (Dallas Willard); empathy and hospitality (Paul Lakeland); a willingness to listen, a willingness to articulate our own claims, and the courage to give them up when they are seriously called into question (Richard J. Bernstein); patience (Denis Robinson); responsibility to the truth (Murray Rae); humility and precision (Chris Anderson); genuine conversation and critical discernment (Richard T. Hughes); intellectual honesty (C. Stephan Evans); and truth-seeking, honesty, wisdom, faith, hope, humility, open-mindedness, a self-critical attitude, a lack of defensiveness, ardour, vigilance, and fortitude (J. P. Moreland).[48] Seen like this, scholarship is

---

[48] Freddoso, '*Fides et Ratio*', 17; Willard, 'How Reason can Survive', 185, 187; Lakeland, 'Habit of Empathy'; Richard J. Bernstein, 'Religious Concerns in Scholarship: Engaged Fallibilism in Practice', in Sterk (ed.), *Religion, Scholarship*, 150–8; Denis Robinson, '*Sedes Sapientiae*: Newman, Truth and the Christian University', in Astley et al. (eds), *Idea*, 75–97: 81; Rae, 'Learning the Truth', 108; Chris Anderson, *Teaching as Believing: Faith in the University* (Waco, TX: Baylor University Press, 2004), 133; Hughes, 'Christian Faith', 4; Evans, 'Calling', 36; J. P. Moreland, *Love God with All Your Mind: The Role of Reason in the Life of the Soul*, NavPress Spiritual Formation, ed. Dallas Willard (Colorado Springs, CO: NavPress, 1997), 106–11.

'a spiritual discipline'[49] with theological roots, and reasoning properly takes place at the foot of the cross.[50]

Steve Holmes

My friend and colleague Steve Holmes has explored one way in which a Christian university might be capable of sustaining reason more fully than its secular counterparts, in a paper that originally had the typically demure title 'Awesome Hospitality, or, How to Run a Baptist University if Liberty of Conscience, Doctrinal Standards, and Academic Freedom are All Bad Ideas'.[51] He examines the familiar question of whether a Christian university that is committed to some set of doctrinal standards can claim nevertheless to protect academic freedom, and ends up by claiming that it might be capable of sustaining such freedom *more* robustly than secular institutions.[52] Holmes takes 'doctrinal standards' to be 'stated or unstated commitments that operate to define what may be taught, published, and even thought by members of the university community' (insisting that 'control over teaching and publication is control over thought', given that 'at least in the case of a Christian University, hypocrisy or mendacity is unlikely to be encouraged'). The kind of academic freedom that he is concerned with is freedom in research: 'a scholar's right to pursue the truth in her research agenda regardless of where that pursuit might take her'. The concepts 'research' and 'academic freedom' are, he argues, correlative, since, 'if you know what the outcome is before undertaking the project, you aren't doing research': to research is to head into the wide blue

---

[49] Moreland, *Love God*, 111.

[50] Cahoy, 'Sense of Place', 105.

[51] I have quoted from a pre-publication draft of this paper; it is due to appear as Stephen R. Holmes, 'Awesome Hospitality: On the Absurd Idea of a Baptist University', in Stephen R. Todd (ed.), *The Baptist University* (Waco, TX: Baylor University Press, forthcoming). A single, as-yet-unpublished paper may not seem to deserve the space I devote to it here, but my reasons for this attention are twofold. In the first place, Holmes does something surprisingly rare in the literature I have been exploring: he shows how thinking through one of the commitments central to the secular idea of the university (academic freedom) from within a very specific theological tradition (Holmes's Baptist tradition) allows one to support, extend, and refine that commitment—and he therefore provides a model for some of the work I want to do in the second half of the book. In the second place, I set out this material here in preparation for Chapter 9, where I use an imagined conversation between Holmes and me as an example of how cross-traditional conversation can work—deliberately using as an example someone with whom I have indeed had such conversations.

[52] Discussions of the question abound. Wolterstorff, for instance, argues that abridgements of academic freedom can be acceptable in 'a religiously pluralistic society with a liberal democratic polity' where multiple colleges with differing commitments abound (*Shalom*, 246). See also Elmer John Thiessen, 'Objections to the Idea of a Christian University', in Astley et al. (eds), *Idea*, 35–55, for the familiar argument that *all* institutions in fact abridge academic freedom in some way—so there is no special violation of academic life when Christian colleges do so.

yonder without knowing quite where you are going to end up. With these definitions in hand, Holmes insists that 'a university committed to doctrinal standards is demanding that no research be done by its staff or students'. After all, 'the most apparently innocuous examination of achievements in mathematics among 10-year-olds might conceivably set in motion a train of thought that leads to a questioning of the doctrines of grace. If you can be certain it won't, then by definition you are not doing research.'

Holmes is, of course, not willing to rest there. In order to get beyond this apparent *impasse* he delves more deeply into the kind of stance towards doctrinal standards that a specifically Baptist university ought to take. He discusses the Baptist notion of 'liberty of conscience', according to which 'human beings cannot be compelled to change or hold religious beliefs'; he discusses the nature of a doctrinal statement as a *norma normata*, a 'normed norm', itself subject (at least in principle) to correction by the *norma normans*, the 'norming norm' of Scripture; he discusses the nature of the church in Baptist ecclesiology as *ecclesia reformanda et semper reformans*; and so on. In such a theological context, he argues, no doctrinal standards, no current ecclesial structure, no churchly or worldly authority, no existing reading of Scripture, can stand in the place of Christ for the believer; all must be held relative to Christ's lordship. And, as 'every light that shines is only a partial and broken reflection of the Light that shines still in the darkness and will one day illuminate the Holy City', someone seriously pursuing truth in *any* department of life, with 'humility, teachableness and prayer', cannot regard any worldly or ecclesial authority as absolute. 'If no Bishop may command my theological opinions, no provost may command my scientific ones,' Holmes says. In other words, for a Baptist believer, freedom of enquiry is not a right asserted over against his or her Baptist identity, but a consequence and demand *of* that identity. A commitment to freedom of enquiry can therefore appropriately be 'the last and crowning statement of a rich and careful exposition of Baptist doctrine' and 'a Baptist university might see its administration's role, and its trustees' duty, as the protection of the God-given freedom to pursue truth of its faculty and students. This would specifically include defending the academic freedom of any whose convictions or research results were at variance with the doctrinal standards of the institution, because that is the Baptist way.' In this light, academic freedom is a form of Christian hospitality. Holmes qualifies it carefully: it is freedom in regard to the conclusions reached by academic research, not the freedom to teach opinions unrelated to research, nor freedom to promote results reached by means of research that was clearly intellectually lacking. Within those bounds, however, the freedom is radical. Holmes argues that Christians have good reason to extend this hospitality even to those whose research leads to conclusions deeply unacceptable to the church or to the wider society, provided that they can assure themselves of the academic rigour of the work—even though it might be necessary for the institution 'to publicly distance itself from the research, even to sponsor further work in the hope and confidence (deriving precisely from its doctrinal standards) that the earlier conclusions will be comprehensively disproved'.

It is at this point that the doctrinal foundation of this account of academic freedom becomes most important: 'the Baptist university, in contrast to its secular counterpart, can provide hospitality to ideas with confidence that they are wrong... A Baptist university will... trust the Lord of History for its preservation, and indeed for the final triumph of truth.'

In other words, precisely at the point where many critics would regard Christian commitments as problematic for the full exercise of reason, Holmes has argued (drawing on the patterns of theological thinking in one specific Christian tradition) that a Christian university has the capacity to be *more* reasonable than its secular counterparts: it has the capacity for a better grounded, less anxious, and so more capacious respect for freedom of enquiry, and a greater ability to articulate the nature of its hospitality even to the most offensive results of such freedom.[53] It begins to become clearer that, *pace* Marsden, a Christian theologian might well have quite a lot to say about the basic rules of academic life.

BETWEEN THE CHURCH AND THE SECULAR
UNIVERSITY: STANLEY HAUERWAS

Marsden and others presented a call to individual Christian scholars to participate in a higher-education sector in crisis, and to model in their work and by their interactions with other scholars a more sustainable version of the public reasoning that characterizes universities at their best. This call to individual scholars is matched, in recent literature, by a call to shape Christian institutions—institutions that, among other things, model renewed reason corporately. The vision presented, in differing ways by different authors, is of enclaves of rescued reason that are not only clearer about the overall purpose of their studies, but also capable of being *more* reasonable than their secular counterparts because of their Christian nature, not less—because they can be more serious about the formation of intellectual virtue, and (for some authors at least) because they can give a deeper and more nuanced

---

[53] It is not relevant to my purposes here to engage in any critique of Holmes' argument—but see my comments in Ch. 9, pp. 247–9. See also Richard Hughes, 'Christian Faith', 16–22, for a differing Baptist model of Christian higher education, and Aurelie A. Hagstrom, 'Christian Hospitality in the Intellectual Community', in Henry and Beaty (eds), *Soul of the University*, 119–31, for more on hospitality as a Christian intellectual virtue.

account of the nature of intellectual life itself, on theological grounds. No less than Marsden's individual Christian scholars, such Christian institutions are called to become witnesses to the possibility of reason in a higher-education sector, and a wider public world, in which reason is under threat.

The work of Stanley Hauerwas places the nature of such witness into the spotlight, by relentlessly asking how such witness can be sustained, and what it is a witness *against*. His answer to these questions in *The State of the University*[54] is shaped by a double conviction: first, that universities are inherently and unavoidably moral institutions; second, that they are not and cannot be *primary* moral institutions. As for the first, 'all education, whether acknowledged or not, is moral formation' because 'any knowledge worth having cannot help but shape who we are and accordingly our understanding of the world' (p. 46). As for the second, universities unavoidably stand in relation to some community that they serve. That community forms its young people in certain moral habits or virtues, and it supports the university in taking those already formed young people and developing them in the direction of some end that the community knows how to value. The community, both by providing the initial formation, and by knowing how to value the kind of person that the university forms, is the primary moral context; the university is secondary.

Hauerwas, however, regards the moral formation provided by universities today as in significant part a mis-formation, perpetrated on behalf of a morally mis-formed community: the liberal state. One of the characteristics of the liberal state—a characteristic that we have already seen in the failure of the Berlin theorists to acknowledge the tradition-specificity of their claims—is its constitutional inability to recognize that it promotes a particular, contestable moral settlement. The universities' consequent failure as institutions is in the first place their failure to recognize the moral nature of the reasoning process in which they are involved. The training in virtue that is necessarily involved in liberal educational practice 'cannot be acknowledged, because the neutrality that allegedly is required for education to be for anyone makes it impossible to make candid that any education is a moral education' (p. 56). What has been obscured is precisely the connection of the university to the primary moral institutions that it serves and sustains, and the moral *particularity* of the formation provided by those institutions in such a context. The university perpetuates 'the illusion we all speak the same language—meaning either that [we] will agree with the government or be quiet, as in communist or fascist states, or that [we] will politely ignore [our] disagreements or disagree "provisionally" as in American universities. Real language, real discourse, are destroyed' (p. 96). Hiding behind this illusion, 'the university is the great

---

[54] Hauerwas, *State of the University*; page references in text.

institution of legitimation in modernity whose task is to convince us that the way things are is the way things have to be' (p. 6).

The moral particularity of the liberal settlement can be seen most clearly when it is set against the church. It is seen, for instance, when students emerge from college 'formed by knowledges that seem to make it impossible for them to think that what Christians believe could be true' (p. 47), as when they are shaped by deep assumptions about the private nature of religious commitment. Hauerwas repeatedly argues that 'there is a link between the politics that would relegate the church to the private and the knowledges of the university that legitimate the subordination of the church to the state in the name of peace' (p. 4).

The moral failure of the university is seen in the most surprising places. Hauerwas detects it, for instance, in mantras about knowledge for knowledge's sake. In order to explain what he means, he contrasts an Aristotelian vision of virtue with a Stoic. For the former, virtue is not its own reward, but the reflecting back to the wider community of that which is 'assumed to be the good life' (p. 88); in other words, it is virtue that makes sense in the context of a *polis* that values this virtue as the proper means of its own continuation and perfection. Stoic virtue, on the other hand, 'had to become its own reward because there no longer existed any politics necessary to name as well as make intelligible a virtuous life' (p. 88). Stoic virtue is well suited to a liberal order in which it is assumed 'that a social order should be constituted by procedural arrangements that require no account of goods held in common' (p. 88). 'Knowledge as an end in itself' is a slogan that reinforces the capacity of the university to deceive itself about the interests, the moral communities, or the traditions that it serves, by suggesting that it can exist without serving any.

Similarly, Hauerwas criticizes generalized appeals to 'critical thinking'. He cites an address by Richard Levin to the incoming class of 1993 at Yale, in which Levin assured the students that they were entering upon a course of studies designed 'to develop the freedom to think critically and independently, to cultivate one's mind to its fullest potential, to liberate oneself from prejudice, superstition, and dogma'.[55] Such an account, says Hauerwas, makes out that the critical mind is a neutral tribunal, capable of scrutinizing all claims from a position unshaped by any particular form of belonging. Such 'reason' is seen as reasonable only to the extent that it is set over against the formation that the student receives in any particular moral tradition—and to proclaim such critical thinking the goal of a university education is to obscure the real dependence that all university education has upon the particular communities and moral formations that sustain and direct it. Hauerwas argues that 'the attempt to make truth qua truth the purpose of the university results in the

---

[55] Richard Levin, 'The Capacity for Independent Thought', cited in Hauerwas, *State of the University*, 14.

failure of those at universities dedicated to the "search for truth" to acknowledge whose truths they serve because they think they serve no one's truth in
particular' (p. 134).[56]

In part, the problem is that the university, for all its talk of critical thinking,
lacks a sufficiently critical grasp of the conditions—especially the financial
conditions—of its own existence. Hauerwas again and again pushes the
question 'Who does the university serve?', and again and again suggests that
we follow the money—since 'money is but a name for people the university is
meant to serve' (p. 87).

But suspicion on its own is not enough. A university that does indeed value
truth and pursue critical thinking (including critical thinking about the truth
of its own dependence) can flourish only if it lives in symbiotic relationship
with what Hauerwas, borrowing from Alastair MacIntyre, calls a 'learned
public' (p. 97), by which he means a wider community capable of supporting
and giving direction to the university, valuing and being served by the kind of
education that the university provides, and forming people ready for participation in it.[57] A university can be honestly committed to truth only if it serves
a 'learned public' that values and practices real truthfulness (and is willing to
spend money on it). 'A university able to resist the mystifications legitimated
by the abstractions of our social order will depend on a people shaped by
fundamental practices necessary for truthful speech' (p. 104).

In other words, the existence of a truthful, critical university depends upon
the existence beyond it of a community that 'in the everyday habits of life'
(p. 51) exhibits a care for truth.[58] And this is the service that the church can, in

---

[56] Elsewhere, Hauerwas runs a skewer through the standard defences of specifically Christian
higher education. They are justified as providing a genuinely liberal education, 'yet we know that
the liberal arts curriculum does not make one liberal—even if we knew what being liberal meant
or we could show that to be such was an inherently good thing'. A liberal education can all too
easily mean a training in forgetting on whose behalf one is educated. Christian higher education
is justified as addressing the 'whole student' (which means, Hauerwas says, little more than that
the college has a 'good counseling service' and provides 'the opportunity to get to know the
professors outside the classroom'—and that all too often such provisions 'only act as a way to
delay the student's growth out of adolescence'). Christian higher education is defended as
teaching values, yet we know for certain that 'the teaching of [goodness or virtue] is a much
more subtle process than the simple expediency of taking an ethics or values course', and in any
case we are 'not sure what values we want'. Furthermore, 'for universities to teach values—or to
help students clarify values—only reinforces the ideas that the moral life is but another form of
consumer choice' (Stanley Hauerwas, *Christian Existence Today: Essays on Church, World and
Living in Between* (Durham, NC: Labyrinth Press, 1988), 222–3, 242).

[57] A university sustained by a 'learned public' will have a proper parochiality to it: it will
recognize that it is not a learning institution that speaks to and from 'humanity in general', but
one that speaks to and from a specific community.

[58] James K. A. Smith has written that, 'too often, the rhetoric of "integrating faith and
learning" trades on a very thin notion of "faith" and tends to generate a very individualistic
(and modernist) paradigm: I, the lone ranger Christian scholar, am trying to integrate *my*
particular faith commitments into my scholarly work' (*The Devil Reads Derrida, and Other
Essays on the University, the Church, Politics and the Arts* (Grand Rapids, MI: Eerdmans,

principle, provide for the university: 'by developing a people capable of bearing the burden of honor and truthfulness, a people without which the university (and, interestingly, democracy), as I conceive its task, cannot exist'.[59] Only if it serves, and is sustained and directed by, such a community can the university properly preserve or restore the moral shape of its own life, in which 'those who occupy the hierarchy of the university are there because they are distinguished by their willingness to expose themselves to the truth by developing the skills of critical intelligence'.[60]

Such a church and such a university feed one another:

the church must charge the university to do what it can—namely to develop people of critical intelligence—for it is just such a people the church requires for its purpose. But the church must also support the university by providing the resources necessary for the university to contribute its work in a world that generally only wants truth on the world's own terms.[61]

None of this, however (and despite the claims of many of Hauerwas's detractors) is meant to detract from the universities' commitment to, and participation in, properly public discourse. It is simply a delusion to think that honest public discourse is possible only when the communities from and for which we speak are ignored. After all, 'dialogue is impossible if we think we must begin by compromising our convictions in order to reach a common understanding' (p. 54). In that case, instead of argument, we get the clash of preferences believed to be utterly autonomous, and so utterly irrational. There can be no 'because' to my values or to yours (no dependency on a tradition, on a community, on deep reasonings, on patterns of speech and argument and persuasion) and so nothing to be said when our values clash. Hauerwas's stance, on the other hand, makes public dialogue—or, perhaps better, public *argument*—possible. He can, he thinks, 'provide a more defensible account of democracy than that based on the rationalism of modernity' (p. 56).

So, Hauerwas's vision for the university is of an institution that can be properly committed to truth and to critical thinking only if it is sustained by a community that truly (and generously) values such things, and that has already begun to form its people in the habits of life and mind that such commitments require. Such habits are not, and cannot be, the habits of no

---

2009), 51). Rather, what matters is the connection between the university and the worshipping life of the church.

[59] *Christian Existence Today*, 223. The killer question for Hauerwas is, of course, 'Do we have a church that is distinctive enough that it can set priorities and purposes for its universities?'

[60] *Christian Existence Today*, 228. Hauerwas (briefly) analyses the virtues that such a university will inculcate: integrity, honesty, justice, humility, humour, and kindness (pp. 230–1).

[61] *Christian Existence Today*, 232. Hauerwas therefore says, 'for me a university is Christian if it receives its financial and moral support from the church' (p. 223).

particular people, committed to no particular story, no particular ritual, no particular common life: they can only be, one way or another, the habits of a particular people—or perhaps we should say the habits of a peculiar people.[62] Yet such a particular formation does not, as Hauerwas sees it, pull a university so supported out of the public realm and into the private, for he has rejected the whole public/private schema on which such a claim can be built. Rather, it makes it possible for people to participate in public reason *as themselves*.

There is, however, a final poignancy to Hauerwas's account. He notes that 'the university has been more my home than the church' (p. 93). He insists that he certainly 'does not want Christians to abandon the secular university', which in any case is 'not secular through and through' (p. 8). 'I assume . . . [that] if a "secular" university is open to the challenge Christians should represent then no Christian should turn down that opportunity. Indeed I assume we are in an in-between time in which secular universities may be more hospitable to Christian knowledges than many universities that are allegedly Christian' (p. 8). Perhaps uncharacteristically, Hauerwas finally leaves open the question of how the ecclesial formation that he deems necessary can shape the kind of secular (or mostly secular) university within which he himself works—aware, perhaps, that 'any attempt to justify Christian participation in the university as we know it is an invitation to self-deception' (p. 106), but unwilling to turn away. After all, he believes that 'the university can be and sometimes is one of the institutions of God's time. As Christians who have the privilege of being called to do the work of the university, we must do our work with the confidence and joy that comes from having good work to do' (p. 136).

EXPERIMENTS IN SECULAR UNIVERSITY LIFE

My survey of contemporary voices is going to finish with a set of authors who, whatever the marked differences between the content and approach of their contributions, share two things. First, each writes primarily about English universities, and does so as an Anglican theologian. Second, all—albeit in differing ways—ask what it means for Christians to work for the good of the secular, public universities that dominate the English higher-education sector. That is, they do not primarily ask what Christian scholarship or a Christian university would look like, but rather ask what Christians might have to contribute to the good of scholarship and of universities per se.[63]

---

[62] 1 Peter 2:9, King James Version.

[63] I do not want to overplay the difference between these writers and the authors I examined earlier. There are many points of overlap, as when Stephen Evans, for instance, says that,

Dan Hardy

In 1991, Dan Hardy delivered a lecture to a gathering of university chaplains.[64] Characteristically, he approached the question of their role in the university by asking first about the place of the university in God's ways with the world. God is at work, Hardy said, forming social life, by drawing existing patterns of social life beyond themselves and towards Godself. God's work is found wherever social life is becoming truly itself. It is, therefore, found in the contexts in which, and processes by which, societies take true account of themselves, of the configurations of their social practice, of the visions of the common goods that bind them together—and labour rightly to repair and extend their life.[65] This labour takes multiple forms (pp. 208–9): labour to know the world more truly (to test their existing patterns of life and thought against the resistance of the world, and to discover in the world new possibilities for action); labour to understand and imagine directly their own ways of acting (construing their social life in such a way as to identify its fractures and to see ways in which it might be healed); labour to recognize and to replenish the language they speak (a constantly evolving inheritance of metaphors and similes, of idioms and grammatical habits that make possible whatever conversation a society can sustain); labour to comprehend and to shape their culture (a constantly proliferating collection of stories and representations, in many media, that carry the identity of the society).

In this context, universities can be understood as institutions whose job is to concern themselves explicitly with a society's means of reproduction, repair, and extension; they are, or *should* be, engines that drive the processes by which societies become more social—and therefore they are, or *should* be, forms of participation in the work of God in the world. Hardy assumes that his audience of Christian chaplains are among those who can acknowledge and name this fact; they are, indeed, involved in the characteristic form that this acknowledgement and naming takes: worship.[66] But he makes it clear that it is

---

'without trying to play God or think that the kingdom of God can be achieved on earth through human means, we Christians must not withdraw from our common human cultural endeavors, but must strive to engage with those areas of cultural action and transform them' (Evans, 'Calling', 29).

[64] Dan Hardy, 'The Public Nature of Theology', in *God's Ways with the World: Thinking and Practising Christian Faith* (Edinburgh: T&T Clark, 1996), 206–16. I also refer to one other piece from the book: 'Created and Redeemed Sociality' (188–205); subsequent page references in text.

[65] Hardy speaks of the relationship of this work to God in a variety of ways: the activities by which a society becomes more fully social '*exemplify* God's activity in the world' (p. 215); this activity '*perpetuates* God's work' (p. 214); it can be identified '*as* God's work' (p. 215). 'God works *through* the ways in which society fashions itself' (p. 216). All emphases added.

[66] Cf. the words of Robert Runcie, in 'Theology, the University and the Modern World', in Paul A. B. Clarke and Andrew Linzey (eds), *Theology, the University and the Modern World* (London: Lester Crook Academic Publishing, 1988), 13–28: 16, who says that those moments of

neither the case that *only* those who worship can contribute to proper formation of social life (and so participate in God's work), nor the case that those who worship simply add an extrinsic, decorative gloss to a labour of social formation and transcendence that can function perfectly well without them. Indeed, he counsels the chaplains against two temptations. On the one hand stands the temptation to think that the Christian, especially the ordained chaplain, has power, such that he or she is capable of simply *producing* proper sociality, either in a Christian enclave or as a mover and shaker in the wider world. The action of the Christian is always a participation in a prior activity of God. On the other hand stands the temptation to think that Christians have no responsibility, no gift to give, no vocation that has anything to offer to the work of those who labour on public sociality—but simply a blessing from a distance on what God is doing there already.

Between these two temptations lies the work of witness. Though they have their proper role in God's work in the world, 'society and its institutions lack a rationale by which to proceed on firm pathways; and lacking this they are prey to shifting policies or to the manœuvres of the powerful' (p. 188). Christians, precisely because they are people who worship the triune and incarnate God, have the means by which to identify the true end of society, and therefore to name some of society's pathological deviations (p. 189). The church as worshipping society therefore witnesses 'to the possibility of a true society in the wider society around it' (p. 189), and by this witness calls other institutions (such as universities) to their proper form.

The role of Christians in higher education is, in part, to hold all those who labour in universities (including themselves) open to the deepest vision of what is going on. Penultimately, their role is to remind people that they are about the formation of a sociality that is whole, that is one; it is to keep alive rumour of a common good. Ultimately, it is to draw those labourers into worship of the triune and incarnate God—into the acknowledgement, that is, of the 'highest ground' of their work. Yet Christians can pursue their penultimate task even where the ultimate, the deepest spring of their vision—the God acknowledged in worship—is not, or is not *yet*, recognized by the social labourers they seek to help. Their role is certainly to speak, as Hardy puts it, '*from* the deepest awareness of the truth of God's work in human life' (p. 206; emphasis added), but not all such speech will be speech explicitly about God. The Christian task, as Hardy describes it, is to assist at the emergence of social vision from within the contexts and processes by which a society already takes account of itself and works on itself, working out moment by moment, context

---

illumination that animate good teaching and good research alike are 'like a blessing' and 'a reason for gratitude'. 'It is one of the theologian's functions in a university to bear witness to this graciousness. And more than that, to celebrate it, to draw out the appropriate response of gratitude.'

by context, how to speak and act towards that vision.[67] A chaplain's job—and, he might have added, a theologian's job—is to 'help the universities identify themselves and their future' (p. 212) and 'to hold up for the university the vision of the society it exists to serve' (p. 214). In other words, the chaplain's job is both to remind the university of its own proper orientation towards the common good, and to remind it of the nature of the common good to which it is orientated. In and through that (and, perhaps, *only* in and through that) the chaplain's job is to call the university to worship.

David Ford

Hardy's comments are brief, and not always entirely clear; it is not, perhaps, obvious what the issuing of this call might look like in practice. The work of David Ford, however, provides more detailed suggestions about the kind of call that Christians can issue to the university. That call will emerge from Christians' corporate, worshipping life: 'At the heart of our contribution to the university is our participation in conversations in ways shaped by worship, scripture and our own conversations with each other and our traditions.'[68] The most characteristic call that they will bring from that life to the university is the call to recognize that, whether it likes it or not, the university is inextricably bound up with questions of *wisdom*—questions about the good of human life together, about human flourishing. In the first place, then, the Christian call will be manifest simply in the insistent asking of questions 'about the integrity of truth, the uses of knowledge in relation to power, the ethics and politics of learning, teaching and researching (including account-ability), the shaping of institutions, responsibilities to "stakeholders" and to those with little power or "stake", and so on'.[69] Christians should not allow the university to get away with any claim that these matters are secondary, or any claim that its business is properly abstracted from such concerns, or neutral with regard to them. Ford therefore reminds his audiences that, however

---

[67] Here it matters that Hardy's audience was a gathering of Christian university chaplains in England. The church in England (and not just the Church *of* England) is, Hardy claimed, well placed to carry out the kind of task he has been sketching, because, unlike the American churches, the English church is 'immersed in social life' (p. 208). 'Church life in this country', he says, 'is deeply immersed in the means by which English sociality occurs', in 'the means by which the public is a public', in 'the devices and means by which the public sustains itself'. The church works 'right within the places by which English society continues' (p. 210). Such a church is well placed to be sociality's midwife. University chaplains are one example of the way in which this immersion works: they work right in the heart of the universities by which English society is itself.

[68] David F. Ford, 'God and the University: What Can We Communicate?', paper delivered at the National Convention on Christian Ministry in Higher Education, no date.

[69] Ford, 'God and the University'.

much temptation there might be to regard universities as factories producing certain kinds of information, or certain kinds of employability, or certain kinds of efficiency, they are also 'the principal places of socialisation into key roles and decision-making responsibilities in [the] economy and culture'[70] and therefore 'a prime resource for society's interpretation of itself to itself'.[71] Universities work 'in the interests of the long-term ethical and intellectual ecology of our civilisation' and therefore cannot avoid being tangled up with our 'frameworks of overall meaning and . . . our convictions about what it means to be human, about justice, peace, and the nature of a good society'.[72] In the first place, then—and just as for Hardy—Ford insists that Christians are called to remind the university that it has to do with the good.

The issuing of this call cannot, for Ford, be a matter of proclamation from the sidelines. It is, rather, issued by means of navigating a way forward within 'a negotiable and negotiating university'.[73] So, the majority of Ford's writings on this theme, however widely they set the scene, are animated by an attempt to make sense of what is possible in one specific university: Cambridge.[74] They are marked by an attention both to the history of that university and to the particular institutional possibilities and constraints in its present. Furthermore, his writings are directed quite deliberately to specific audiences in and around that university, and seek not to provide an overview from a distance, but to draw each specific audience into enthusiasm for a 'richer and broader understanding' of the university's life.[75]

Where the audience is not a specifically Christian or theological one, Ford tends to begin with descriptions of the possibilities and responsibilities of university life that are not framed in any explicitly theological way—presenting them, rhetorically, as descriptions that his secular audience will be likely to recognize, at least in part. He then provides some account of how those recognizable possibilities and responsibilities can be fitted together into a coherent and attractive vision of university life—noting as he does so that he is drawing on the resources of Christian wisdom to help him develop such a picture. His arguments therefore serve both to advocate a certain vision of the

---

[70] Ford, 'God and the University'.

[71] David F. Ford, *The Future of Cambridge University*, Lady Margaret's Sermon, Commemoration of Benefactors (Cambridge: Cambridge University Press, 2001), 2.

[72] David F. Ford, 'Knowledge, Meaning, and the World's Great Challenges' (The Gomes Lecture, 2003), *Scottish Journal of Theology*, 57/2 (2004), 181–202: 193, 200.

[73] David F. Ford, *Christian Wisdom: Desiring God and Learning in Love* (Cambridge: Cambridge University Press, 2007), 336. See below, Ch. 9.

[74] In conversation, Ford has made it clear that he is committed both to the idea that wisdom about higher education is developed and refined as one seeks to make sense of, and make a difference in, a specific university context, and to the idea that the wisdom so gained is not restricted to that one context but is a contribution to the process of making sense and making a difference in other specific contexts.

[75] Ford, *Future*, 2.

good university life, and to promote the idea that the university can appropriately continue to be shaped by patterns of Christian wisdom, just as it has been at times in the past.

Ford's claim is not, however, that the university is, or should become, simply Christian. He thinks that Christian wisdom can and does contribute to the proper shaping of Cambridge University, but that it does not and should not do so alone. The university is already, and should continue to be, a 'religious and secular' institution: one that is, and can appropriately continue to be, recognizably shaped by multiple religious and secular traditions of wisdom.[76] In a move reminiscent of some discussed earlier in this chapter, Ford insists that the university cannot flourish by denying that its life is shaped by such deep and various religious and secular commitments, and differing visions of the human good; rather, 'the university needs to provide what one might call "mutual ground" for the engagement of wisdom traditions, both religious and secular, with each other'.[77]

The heart of Ford's positive vision for university life lies in the intensification and extension of face-to-face conversation.[78] The life of the individual reasoner is one of internalized conversation; the life of a department or discipline is one of intensive conversation; the life of the university as a whole should be one of pervasive conversation on multiple scales. 'Limited interdisciplinarity or short-term projects are not enough. The scale of the challenge requires a whole culture of intensive conversation sustained year after year.'[79]

The long-term flourishing of such conversation is particularly important to Ford: the university can do its job well only if it sustains 'extraordinarily long-term ideals and practices', which means sustaining them 'across generations'.[80] Ford therefore writes about the building of conversational lineages: teachers who form students for participation in the teachers' own research conversations, so training at least some of them to become teachers in their turn—perpetuating local traditions of scholarship over decades, even centuries.[81] This, above all, is what universities have to contribute to public life: the

---

[76] David F. Ford, 'Faith, Universities and Wisdom in a Religious and Secular World: A View from Cambridge', lecture at the University of Lund, 2004. Ford therefore argues that universities need to be institutions 'where religion is taken seriously in intelligent and responsible ways' (*Future*, 14).

[77] Ford, 'Faith, Universities and Wisdom', 14.

[78] The theological roots of the convictions Ford explores here can be found most fully in his *Self and Salvation: Being Transformed* (Cambridge: Cambridge University Press, 1999).

[79] Ford, *Future*, 7; cf. *Christian Wisdom*, 320–3. Ford writes at length about the opportunities represented for such an ecology by Cambridge's collegiate structure; see, e.g., Ford, 'Knowledge, Meaning', 197.

[80] Ford, 'Knowledge, Meaning', 187.

[81] Ford, 'Knowledge, Meaning', 189.

sustaining of such time-taking, intensive, multidisciplinary conversation in pursuit of wisdom.[82]

Rowan Williams

In the context of lectures and papers that, like Ford's, address both Christian and secular audiences within the university, Rowan Williams suggests ways in which Christians can call the university to a deeper vision of reason both as an exercise in trusting vulnerability, and as a multi-voiced conversation about the common good.

In the Prologue to *On Christian Doctrine*, Williams described his work as involving celebratory, communicative, and critical moments, and it is the celebratory and communicative modes that are clearest in his writings on universities. Celebratory theology attempts 'to draw out and display connections of thought and image so as to exhibit the fullest possible range of significance in the language used' by a Christian community; communicative theology, on the other hand, is 'theology experimenting with the rhetoric of its uncommitted environment'.[83] So, in Williams's writings on the university, we find some 'celebratory' work, when he discusses in explicitly Christian theological terms the nature of learning. More often, however, we find him in communicative mode, experimenting with apparently untheological discourses about education, seeking to expose the possibilities they contain of being extended or intensified in the direction that his celebratory work has suggested. In other words, he works with an apparent confidence that discourses concerning higher education recognizable to a non-Christian audience still, despite appearances, contain the possibility of being opened up in the direction of theology.

In some ways, of course, appearances are strongly against such a possibility. Williams agrees that 'it isn't clear what the university's paymasters think the university is there for; they only know that they want it to give value for money' (and the only value they really understand is wealth creation); he agrees that the university is beset by destructive language about efficiency and by broken forms of accountability.[84] And he acknowledges that, at a deeper

---

[82] Ford is well aware that this raises the question about who will pay for the sustaining of such conversation. His answer (in his lectures, and also in his own practice) has focused on the raising of endowment, especially endowment specifically dedicated to the creation of permanent niches for long-term conversation, relatively free from the short-term patterns of control implied in most other forms of funding. See, e.g., 'Knowledge, Meaning', 186, and *Christian Wisdom*, 336.

[83] Rowan Williams, *On Christian Theology* (Oxford: Blackwell, 2000), p. xiv.

[84] Rowan Williams, 'Faith in the University', in Simon Robinson and Clement Katulushi (eds), *Values in Higher Education* (St Bride's Major: Aureus/University of Leeds, 2005), 24–35: 24.

level, faith and university life may seem to be utterly inimical. After all, 'a university looks, in many ways, as if it were deliberately designed to intensify faithlessness': its commitment to competitive entry, and its inculcation of the constant need to prove oneself in order to progress, seem to stand directly against the knowledge of faith 'that your being there and your being who you are, are not under threat'.[85]

Williams is, however, convinced that, at least for those not wholly won over by managerial discourses, it is possible to find territory where a directly theological account of education (the 'celebratory' discourse) and the theologian's experimentation with recognizable contemporary discourses about higher education (the 'communicative' discourse) can meet. He points to two such territories in particular: the first in accounts of the life of reason within the university itself; the second in accounts of the university's contribution to the life of public reason more generally.

The first opening in secular discourse about education can be found in the very acknowledgement that the competitive nature of university life 'colludes very readily' with the temptation on the part of the learner to put himself beyond real risk: to secure and defend his position, and to refuse to allow himself genuinely to be at stake in his learning or research.[86] Yet true learning, true research, requires that one is freed from this—freed from the need to know in advance, to remain in control; freed for genuine 'surprises'.[87] Christian faith provides precisely such an assurance that one's real worth and standing cannot be affected by the outcomes of one's research, or by the discovery that one has been mistaken. It enables one to see exposure to the truth as 'an entry into a reality which affirms and holds together all our explorations'.[88] In other words, Williams trades on the hunch that a secular university audience will recognize the inherent vulnerability of learning, and the strange trust that is required from anyone who throws himself or herself into the process; he trades on the hunch that such an audience can, therefore, see the connection between their leaning and an account of human life that is not reducible to competitive self-assertion. Such recognitions, if indeed they take place, provide doorways through which a Christian may speak about the good of university life as Christian faith understands it.

The second context in which secular and Christian discourses about higher education meet is in the realm of the public purpose of university life. Williams looks back to medieval Oxford, and notes that, far from pursuing any vision of knowledge for its own sake, medieval Oxford

---

[85] Williams, 'Faith in the University', 25–6.
[86] Williams, 'Faith in the University', 26.
[87] Williams, 'Faith in the University', 33, 29. See below, Ch. 6, p. 162.
[88] Williams, 'Faith in the University', 33.

was in large part an institution designed to give a professional formation to the clergy who would shape the policy of a kingdom; and that formation assumed that to govern a kingdom you needed to know how language worked, what the difference was between good and bad arguments, and how you might persuade people to morally defensible courses of action.[89]

Such an account of the purpose of higher education has become unfamiliar, and we do not any longer 'think of education as a formation in the kind of reasonable argument and decision that will make someone a sure guide to others'.[90] Yet, 'if you're going to be a decision-making citizen, you need to know how to make sense and how to recognize when somebody else is making sense. You need to know what arguments are communicable to other people and what aren't. You need to know how to share forms of argumentation.'[91] Understood in this way, a university exists to form people who 'are committed not only to reasoned argument...but to a responsibility to the ideal of rational government and rational public discourse'; it exists to form 'a sense of the importance and the vulnerability of reasoned conversation for a just common life'.[92] Such a common life will be 'one in which we know how to talk with each other, how to negotiate, to challenge, to argue coherently about what is good for human beings as such'. It will not require any 'method for discovering by abstract argument what is best for everyone'; rather, it will flourish when 'differences can be talked about without being abolished'.[93]

The university serves such a reasonable society not only by forming individual students in habits of reason, but by *modelling* such sociable reason itself. 'A truly functioning university will also, through the encounters of diverse disciplines, model ways in which cultural traditions, religious loyalties and ethnic identities can co-exist, not in mutual indifference, but in a climate of mutual and honest questioning, in which the various commitments are not automatically opposed but can enrich one another.'[94]

If this is a recognizable account of the responsibility of academic life for a secular audience, it provides Williams with another doorway through which he may speak of the good of that life as Christian faith understands it. Williams claims that university life so understood can itself best be understood in the light of church life—in the light of Christian teaching, certainly, but more substantially in the light of Christian practice.

[89] Rowan Williams, Oxford University Commemoration Day Sermon, 2004; <www.arch-bishopofcanterbury.org/1205> (accessed 17 Mar. 2010).
[90] Williams, Commemoration Day Sermon.
[91] Rowan Williams, 'Faith, Reason and Quality Assurance: Having Faith in Academic Life', 2008; <www.archbishopofcanterbury.org/1644> (accessed 17 Mar. 2010).
[92] Williams, Commemoration Day Sermon.
[93] Williams, Commemoration Day Sermon.
[94] Rowan Williams, 'What is a University?', 2006; <www.archbishopofcanterbury.org/698> (accessed 17 Mar. 2010).

Christians believe . . . that true public life, life in which humans exercise their innate power and responsibility in consulting and acting together, is most fully realised in the Body of Christ, where the guilt and burden of rivalry, the uprising of person against person which so damages and obscures the image of God, are taken away by the work of Christ, so that the Spirit may make each one a gift to every other.

'This', Williams says, 'is where the presence of theology, and specifically of theology grounded in living religious communities, becomes significant for the entire university.'[95] The church, by being the church (and only to the extent that it *is* the church) calls the university to be its reasonable self, and the university, by being its reasonable self (and only to the extent that it *is* its reasonable self) calls the wider social world to reason. The witness that the church provides to the university is one that—at least according to Williams's communicative experimentation—the university can hear; it is a witness (he trusts) that can enable the secular university to make good sense of itself, even in the midst of the current deep confusion about its nature and purpose. And it is a witness that calls the university to the renewal of its own life for the sake of public reason.

Timothy Jenkins

My final author, Timothy Jenkins, provides a more detailed account of the way in which something like Williams' communication and witness might function in the practical life of a university. Writing, like Daniel Hardy, for university chaplains, Jenkins is not addressing 'Christian scholars' or Christian theologians as such, yet his reflections on the chaplain's role do, like Hardy's, suggest ways of understanding the task of all Christians concerned to shape the life of the university.

He begins by asking, 'Why does a university have a chaplain?'[96] The standard answers he hears are given in terms of tradition (we have always had one), moderation (it is a good way to keep religion on campus sane), and kindness (they are there to provide support to the weak and weak-minded). All these, Jenkins says, are true enough ('I am very pleased that chaplains are supposed to stand for them and to exemplify them'), but 'chaplains stand for something more' (p. 5). Addressing the wider university, he insists that chaplains 'are also there, in an obscure and symbolic way, for you to *think*

---

[95] Williams, Commemoration Day Sermon.
[96] Timothy Jenkins, *An Experiment in Providence: How Faith Engages with the World* (London: SPCK, 2006), 5. I am drawing on the first two pieces in the book: 'Tradition, Moderation, Kindness and Chaplaincy' (pp. 5–6) and 'An Anglican Vocation: Chaplaincy as an Experiment in Providence' (pp. 7–13); subsequent page references in text.

with . . . for you to remind yourselves of the central concerns of the university amid the material constraints that the world imposes' (p. 6). They are there, in particular, to help people in the university think about the fact that 'matter and history . . . are full of surprises: you cannot know what you are going to find out in advance' (p. 6). And they are there to help people think about the fact that 'there can be cross-fertilization between disciplines . . . despite the endless fragmentation inherent in being research-led', indeed, that 'at some level things begin to add up, or point to some kind of patterning' (p. 6). That is, they are there to help people think about the ways in which their vocations of learning call them out of themselves, and call them together.[97]

When Jenkins says that chaplains are there to 'think with', he does not necessarily mean that they are there as explicit conversation partners. Rather, their presence and activity can act as a reminder, as an irritant, as a witness; they can pose questions. Jenkins therefore describes finding himself in a situation in which 'people of all sorts begin to use the chaplain to think with, in order to articulate or precipitate questions that are present within their institutional lives' (p. 10). As he sees it, 'success' for the chaplain does not therefore consist in 'masterminding well-attended events, but in finding oneself put to work in hitherto inaccessible places' (p. 8).

Jenkins describes the process by which this 'becoming available' takes place. The chaplain needs to make common cause with the Christian faith already there in the university, for 'only by being part of the body of believers that exists, by being clearly involved and clearly believing something, is it possible to raise the questions that faith poses in the institution' (p. 9). The chaplain does not become available for thinking with primarily by being an interesting individual, but by being one who worships, prays, and witnesses with others.

Sustained, formed, and guided by this participation, the chaplain will pursue his or her first duty in the wider university to pay patient attention, to find out what is going on.[98] As far as possible, the chaplain should go everywhere, so as 'to be in touch with the concerns and pleasures of the place . . . to discover its realities' (p. 7), especially its 'patterns of worth, recognition and success' (p. 8), and the ways in which questions of meaning, value, and purpose arise in it (p. 10).

Depending upon all this, 'there is a second stage, beyond the initial stage of paying attention, when people of all sorts begin to use the chaplain to think with, in order to articulate or precipitate questions that are present within their institutional lives' (p. 10). This is where the process described above begins to take place; the chaplain's presence and activity begin to enable the

---

[97] The connection to Williams's two themes should be clear.

[98] Jenkins's understanding of the nature of attention is shaped by his training as a social anthropologist, and is best illustrated by his *Religion in English Everyday Life: An Ethnographic Approach* (Oxford and New York: Berghahn, 1999).

asking of questions about 'whether things cohere and make sense, and how to do things better rather than worse within the bounds of the possible' (p. 10). This happens in part because of *who* the chaplain is—the life that he represents, the scent of worship and concern that he brings with him; and it happens in part because of *where* he is: he is someone who is to be found everywhere that the life of the university is going on.

Finally, and only on the basis of the understanding of the life of the university that his attention has yielded, and the awareness of the questioning that his presence and activity have already helped to catalyse, 'it becomes possible to initiate certain matters and to raise questions on one's own behalf or initiative' (p. 10).

The university cannot be described or engaged with from a distance. Attempts to set out an idea of the good of university life in general, abstracted from the patterns of social and individual life that the vocations of real university practitioners form, are bound to be of limited help. To engage faithfully with the university cannot be a matter simply of implementing a well-formed plan in a well-understood context: it can only be what Jenkins calls 'an experiment in providence' (p. 8): a making available of oneself for the unforeseen work of God, putting oneself in its way, and listening carefully for the rumour of its coming.

CONCLUSION

This chapter began with authors like George Marsden, who were concerned with the need for Christians to speak confidently in their own voice within a higher-education sector foundering for lack of a moral compass—speaking either as Christian scholars within secular universities or as participants in specifically Christian institutions. In such a view, Christians can participate in the ordinary practices of secular academic reason, but should do so with a set of distinctive motivations, a special concern with both the wider implications and the proper limits of their studies, and with a recognizably Christian ethos.

The chapter has tracked slowly towards theological visions of university life in which the 'ordinary practices of secular academic reason' themselves come into the spotlight—whether that be the suspicious (though not despairing) attention of Hauerwas, who sees the way in which those practices serve the moral dysfunctionality of the liberal state, or the writings of Hardy, Ford, Williams, and Jenkins, more concerned to discover ways in which those practices are already shaped towards God's purposes, and might be opened more deeply to those purposes.

In other words, the chapter has moved from positions analogous to Newman's, in which the basic armoury of intellectual formation is natural, and faith comes in to steady and to supplement it, to a position that Newman's analysis could not reach, in which that basic armoury is itself understood theologically. The possibility of a theological account, both negative and positive, of the practice and policy of secular and religiously plural contemporary universities has finally come into view—even if, so far, only in a rather fragmentary and inconclusive way—and it is that possibility that I will be exploring more thoroughly in Part II of this book.

Part II

5

An Anglican Theology of Learning

In this second part of the book, I provide a theological account, both negative and positive, of the practice and policy of secular and religiously plural universities. I begin, in this chapter, by arguing that my Christian theological tradition makes claims about the nature and good of *all* learning. In the chapters that follow, I will ask what sense, if any, this way of thinking about learning allows me to make of secular and religiously plural universities, and what possibilities there might be for such a theological voice to contribute to the ongoing arguments by which secular and religiously plural universities are formed. In this chapter, therefore, the university itself will not be directly in view. Indeed, it may by the end of the chapter be hard to see how it is going to come into view, and what connection there might be between the theological account of learning I have presented and the life and work of modern secular universities. Yet that is precisely the question that I believe faces me when I ask whether I, as a Christian theologian, can say of a modern secular university that the learning it pursues is really or potentially good, or that it has something of the good about it. It is, in other words, the question that faces me when I ask whether I, as a Christian theologian, can pursue learning in such a modern secular university as part of my Christian vocation.

In this chapter, then, I will be writing about learning from within a specific tradition. That does not mean that I am adopting the position of a spokesperson for that tradition; rather, it means that I draw upon resources and pursue forms of argument that I expect to be recognizable to an identifiable community of practice and discourse. I implicitly address myself to that community, and speak as someone who has, by dint of various forms of apprenticeship, become acclimatized to its patterns of conversation. Yet what I offer is not a repetition of what has already been said in those conversations but, at least in intention, a contribution to that community's ongoing thinking. In other words, I am not simply expounding the supposed 'world view' of this community, but attempting to participate in the always unfinished, always fragmentary processes by which something like a world view is being built (and rebuilt) from the swirl of practices and ideas and discussions that constitute this community's life.[1]

The title of the chapter also gives away the specific tradition I have in mind. I am conscious of writing *Anglican* theology—indeed (and this is not a tautology) *English* Anglican theology.[2] But that does not mean that I simply occupy this one, discrete circle, one of the mutually exclusive circles that exhaustively tile the intellectual landscape. I write in and for a complex nest of circles, not even neatly enough arranged to be concentric, and I hope that what I say will count as partially, even largely, recognizable to all sorts of people involved in conversations rather differently identified. These things are always, in practice, rather messy.

Nevertheless, though those circles might (if I am fortunate) turn out to spread quite widely, what I have written is not directly addressed to everyone; I have not pretended to write for 'all right-thinking people'. True, I am writing in a secular university context, and hoping to contribute to public conversations about the nature and good of such a university—but I am doing so precisely by articulating as clearly as I can the traditioned nature of my own thinking. I hope, of course, that this book might be read by those who have little or nothing to do with the English Anglican tradition, or the broader Christian tradition for that matter, but for such readers this chapter can be only an indirect address: an articulation of unfamiliar patterns of thought addressed to readers other than them, which nevertheless allows them to overhear, and make some sense of, one side of someone else's conversation.[3]

I take the liturgy of a *Common Worship* Eucharist service as the loose frame within which to construct my answer, drawing along the way on some of the other prayers that might be said in that context. That is not because that

---

[1] I am also trading on the fact that the very act of my offering such a construal is recognizable by the relevant community—that is, that I am engaged in a recognizable *kind of activity* (rather than standing like Nietzsche's madman in a bewildered marketplace). The community I am writing for is possessed of a polity that includes groups of theologians discussing various matters in the usual academic media, who interact (or overlap) in some contexts with church leaders, and who sometimes play a part in the training of ordinands, produce teaching resources that are used by the church, and so on. I speak a recognizable language, even if I use it to say distinctive things, and occupy a recognizable place, even if I do something different in it.

[2] It would be nice, in some ways, to be utterly local about this, and say that I write first and foremost as a member of All Saints Church, Okehampton. It is true that in the past few years, that has been the main community where I have worshipped, and so has (I hope) been a context where I have been formed in ways that will have shaped what I write. Nevertheless, the practices in which I am engaged (writing an academic book, giving associated seminars, discussing the contents with colleagues) simply are not organized at that level—and the conversations to which I am most directly seeking to contribute circulate across a wider swathe of territory, at least geographically.

[3] I have, therefore, quite deliberately spoken about what 'we' do, and about what happens to 'us', in what follows, adopting the stance not of an observer addressing other observers but of a participant addressing other participants. Chapter 9 will explain how I think such a stance can serve rather than sever wider conversation.

liturgy is the authoritative basis on which theological formulations must be based in my tradition, and I do not use it as a means by which to demonstrate the truth or faithfulness of the formulations that I offer. Were I seeking to demonstrate the account I expound here in any detail, I would need to write a whole book: I would need to dwell at much greater length on the Scriptures, read with the help of the Catholic creeds; I would need to engage in extensive interactions with the tradition, especially the patristic era; I would need to set out in detail the contemporary conversations with theologians Anglican and non-Anglican who have shaped my thinking; I would need to triangulate what I say against earlier Anglican pronouncements on higher education; and I would need to pay attention to earlier Anglican liturgical texts that have a rather more authoritative place in my tradition. That is not, however, the task I have set myself in this chapter. Here, I am simply writing as someone who participates in a particular modern Anglican liturgy Sunday by Sunday, and who has been trying to understand (with the help of some of the kinds of investigation and conversation just mentioned) what sense it makes to move from that church context to sit in my university office from Monday to Friday—and to do so as someone who believes that the liturgy in which he participates on Sundays dramatizes the deepest context within which his university life is carried on. I offer in this chapter not a description of the path by which I have arrived at my answer to that question, but a presentation of the answer on which I have, for now, settled: a theological construal of learning that I think coheres with and enables me to make sense of that liturgical experience *and* (as subsequent chapters will show) to make sense of my academic vocation.

I will argue that, for someone standing in this liturgical context, learning—*all* learning worthy of the name—is a matter of being invited as disciples to know God and the fulfilment that God has for God's creatures; that it unavoidably involves being crucified and raised with Christ; that it requires the bringing-together of learners in the Body of Christ; that the knowledge to which it leads takes the form of wisdom and delight; that it is part of the work of the Spirit making us holy; and that it nevertheless takes place both in and beyond the church, and sometimes more truly beyond the church than in it. And I will not yet begin to answer the obvious question, as to whether what takes place in modern secular universities *is* worthy of the name of learning, on this account.[4]

---

[4] There are not many footnotes in this chapter, because I have concentrated on articulating my own understanding, rather than engaging in explicit argument with others. But, as well as being informed by the conversations engaged in earlier in the book, this chapter has been shaped by engagement with many other authors, especially David F. Ford and Daniel W. Hardy, *Jubilate: Theology in Praise* (London: DLT, 1984) = *Praising and Knowing God* (Philadelphia: Westminster, 1985); Charles Mathewes, *A Theology of Public Life* (Cambridge: Cambridge University Press, 2007); John Milbank and Catherine Pickstock, *Truth in Aquinas* (London

KNOWING GOD AND THE WORLD

Towards the beginning of the *Common Worship* Eucharistic liturgy, the congregation say the Prayer of Preparation, which includes the petition: 'cleanse the thoughts of our hearts by the inspiration of your Holy Spirit, that we may perfectly love you, and worthily magnify your holy name'.[5] Those words could stand as a motto for the liturgy as a whole, or at least for a constant aspect of the whole: training in love and praise. As I shall explain below, the liturgy can be seen as a school in which the mind is educated towards its proper end: to know God in love and worship.

The *Common Worship* Eucharist service has four main sections: the Gathering, the Liturgy of the Word, the Liturgy of the Sacrament, and the Dismissal. In the Gathering, the congregation are welcomed, led through prayers of penitence, and invited to join in saying or singing the Gloria, in which they give voice to the knowledge that the liturgy as a whole is teaching them: knowledge of God's glory and mercy as Father, Son, and Holy Spirit, and knowledge of themselves as worshippers who give thanks and praise as recipients of God's mercy.

In the Liturgy of the Word, the Scriptures are read, the creed is said, and prayers of intercession are offered. The Collect for the Last Sunday after Trinity says that God 'caused all holy Scriptures to be written for our learning', and, as read in the context of the liturgy and orientated by the saying of the creed, the Scriptures are understood to be the most fundamental means by which the congregation are taught about God and God's ways with the world—about creation and God's covenants with creatures, about the formation of God's people in the midst of the world, about the end that God has for all things, and about the centrality to all of this of Jesus of Nazareth. The knowledge to which the congregation are invited in the liturgy is knowledge of 'all that is, seen and unseen': knowledge of all things in relation to God, and

---

and New York: Routledge, 2001); Susannah Ticciati, *Job and the Disruption of Identity: Reading beyond Barth* (London: Continuum, 2005); Oliver Davies, *The Creativity of God: World, Eucharist, Reason* (Cambridge: Cambridge University Press, 2004); Paul J. Griffiths, *Intellectual Appetite: A Theological Grammar* (Washington: Catholic University of America Press, 2009); Richard B. Hays, 'The Palpable Word as Ground of *Koinonia*', in Douglas V. Henry and Michael D. Beaty (eds), *Christianity and the Soul of the University: Faith as a Foundation for Intellectual Community* (Grand Rapids, MI: Baker Academic, 2006), 19–36; David H. Kelsey, *Eccentric Existence: A Theological Anthropology* (Louisville, KY: WJK, 2009); Bruce D. Marshall, *Trinity and Truth* (Cambridge: Cambridge University Press, 2000); and Andrew McFarlane, 'The Human Person as an Epistemic Agent: The Contours of Creaturely Cognition in Karl Barth's Church Dogmatics', unpublished Ph.D. Thesis, University of Edinburgh, 2008.

[5] I am drawing on 'The Order for the Celebration of Holy Communion also called The Eucharist and The Lord's Supper', Order One, from *Common Worship: Services and Prayers for the Church of England* (London: Church House Publishing, 2000), 166–205; all emphases added.

God in relation to all things.[6] The Liturgy of the Word therefore appropriately culminates in the Prayers of Intercession, in which the congregation hold before God's mercy the church, their local community, their society, and the whole creation. In the intercessions, the worshippers seek to look upon all things as God looks upon them, seeing them in love and in longing for their fulfilment; and they call upon God to bring that fulfilment about.

The Liturgy of the Word is followed by the Liturgy of the Sacrament. I shall have more to say about the Eucharist itself in the next section, but in some ways the sacramental liturgy simply recapitulates the lesson of the earlier parts, teaching the congregation to understand themselves as standing in God's merciful love, and to see the world around them as the object of that merciful love. That learning is repeated, however, in a new key: the worshippers learn to see themselves as recipients, along with the disciples, of Christ's gift of himself made at the meal on the night before he died and in the passion that the meal prefigured. Once again, however, the knowledge taught here extends to include the mercy of God shown in Christ to all things. One version of the Prayer after Communion ends: 'Keep us firm in the hope you have set before us, so we and all your children shall be free, and the whole earth live to praise your name; through Christ our Lord.'[7]

Finally, the service finishes with the Dismissal, during which the congregation are sent out into the world with a prayer that includes the words: 'The peace of God, which passes all understanding, keep your hearts and minds in the knowledge and love of God, and of his Son Jesus Christ our Lord.' The liturgy is a school, and the knowledge that is taught in it is of all things in relation to God, and God in relation to all things.

KNOWING TRULY

I have said that, in one sense, the Liturgy of the Sacrament simply recapitulates the lesson of the Liturgy of the Word, but the *way* in which this teaching takes place, through a drama enacted with broken bread and cups of wine, suggests something peculiar about the nature of the knowledge gained. I have said that the knowledge at which the liturgy aims is of all things 'in relation to God', but this knowledge should not be thought of as knowledge of one aspect of

---

[6] The Collect for the Second Sunday before Lent makes this scope clear: 'Almighty God, you have created the heavens and the earth and made us in your image: teach us to discern your hands in *all* your works and your likeness in *all* your children; through Jesus Christ your Son our Lord, who with you and the Holy Spirit reigns supreme over all things, now and for ever.'

[7] In the words of the Post Communion Prayer for Third Sunday of Easter: 'Living God, your Son made himself known to his disciples in the breaking of bread: open the eyes of our faith, that we may see him in *all* his redeeming work; who is alive and reigns, now and for ever.'

things—the religious aspect, perhaps—that might provide a pious supplement to other, supposedly more basic forms of knowing. The Post Communion Prayer for the Twentieth Sunday after Trinity asks God to 'let these holy mysteries open the eyes of our understanding', and the forms of reflection on the Eucharist with which I am most familiar do not encourage me to think that we might know things perfectly well by secular means, and then add to that knowledge a dispensable theological gloss.[8]

This might be made clearer by means of a contrast. Consider the idea that 'real' knowledge, knowledge at its most intense and acute, is arrived at by a process of scientific reduction. This would be the view of knowledge that would have me, when I see an object in front of me and know that it is a cricket ball, take that knowledge to be of a secondary, clumsy, and myopic variety compared to the more acute knowledge that sees the ball to be a symphony of unimaginably large swarms of subatomic particles. For such more acute knowing, to say that the ball is 'hard' or 'solid' is not to state primary facts about it, but to give inadequate names to vastly complex patterns of attraction and repulsion between the ranks of wave-like particles that constitute both my fingers and the ball. I might say, for instance, that the ball *looks* solid, but that it is *really* composed of tiny surges of energy circulating in empty space. To know the quantum ballet is *real* knowledge, in comparison to which knowing the ball just as a ball is a naive substitute.

Rejecting such reductionism, one might turn instead to a form of pragmatism. Knowledge does not naturally arrange itself into such a reductionist hierarchy, one might say. Within the practice of a certain kind of science, certainly, the salient objects are the particles and forces of the subatomic world, and within that practice knowing the ball can mean only knowing how its gross features emerge from interactions at the subatomic level. Yet within a different practice—the practice of the game of cricket, for instance—different stretches of the world are picked out as the fundamental objects. Within the practice called cricket, the ball is truly and simply a cricket ball—and the forms of knowledge that grasp it most fundamentally are of the role it plays in bowling and batting, of the regulations that govern ball-tampering, of the play-shaping differences in behaviour between a new ball and a ball scuffed and dulled by play, and so on. Knowledge is relative to practice, and to ask how the knowledge appropriate to one practice stands in relation to the knowledge appropriate to another is to ask how those practices go together in the complex patterns of life of a society.[9]

---

[8] The English Anglican tradition is, of course, shaped by diverse forms of Eucharistic theology. The most I can claim for my reflections here is that they are one recognizable voice within that diversity.

[9] Cf. Lynn Holt, *Apprehension: Reason in the Absence of Rules* (Aldershot: Ashgate, 2002), 30, on baseballs rather than cricket balls. One can, of course, say all that I have said in this paragraph while remaining just as insistent a realist about scientific knowledge as one wants.

One can, I think, grasp the nature of the learning called for in the liturgy if one takes a further step, beyond this pragmatic rejection of reductionism. The liturgy, creeds, and Scriptures, after all, teach us that there is a shape to the weave of practices that constitute our lives—and that the call to turn to God in worship, and the call to anticipate the kingdom of heaven in love of God and neighbour, are calls to the most fundamental practices that can and should hold all our other practices together. The knowledge of things that makes sense within the practices of worship and discipleship is, therefore, not the knowledge of a secondary aspect of things, but the deepest form of knowledge that there is.[10] It is the knowledge that has most right to be called knowledge of reality, knowledge of the objective truth of things. To know something— anything—truly is to know it as coming from and returning to God, to know it as a creature held by God's loving mercy on its way to the fulfilment that God has for it, and to know the forms of corruption and distortion that fight against that fulfilment. All other forms of knowledge, forms of knowledge that make sense within the other practices that constitute our lives, are knowledge of aspects of the realities that are known most truly in this way.

The celebration of the Eucharist makes this claim in a peculiarly intense way. The bread and wine are everyday, mundane realities—components of the weave of practices by which ordinary life is shaped. Yet these utterly ordinary objects are received in the Eucharist as truly and objectively gifts given back to us by Christ as forms of his self-presentation, means by which he makes himself present to us in his absence. In the context of worship and discipleship, it makes sense to say that the bread and the wine simply *are* Christ's gifts of himself—and, given the priority of this context, it therefore makes sense to say that this is the deepest truth, the fullest reality of the consecrated elements, the most perceptive thing that can be said about them.[11] All other practices of enquiry within which we might investigate these elements—the practice, for instance, of chemical analysis, which will reveal them to be through and through ordinary bread and ordinary wine—are secondary: knowledge of secondary aspects (of the 'accidents', we might say) of these realities properly known as Christ's gifts.[12]

To put it this way, however, might take us off in a distracting direction. My claim is not so much that, in my tradition, the claim that the bread and wine are Christ's gifts of himself to us is *more* objective or *more* truthful than, say,

---

[10] This is the deeper reason for the liturgical form of this chapter: to dramatize the claim that worship is the proper context for learning.

[11] Such a claim is, I think, compatible with various different positions in traditional arguments about the nature of the Eucharist.

[12] The non-availability of the consecrated elements for such enquiries—the fact that it would be regarded as deeply inappropriate to take the consecrated elements and subject them to such chemical tests, or indeed insert them into any practice that ignored the claim about them made in the Eucharist—witnesses to this.

the claim that they are still recognizably made of grain and grape, as if objectivity or truth were scales, and these two forms of knowing could be measured against those scales. It is rather that there is a practice within which the claim that the bread and wine are Christ's gifts of himself to us is basic and wholly objective, and that practice is more fundamental to Christian life than the practice within which the claim that the bread and wine are made of grain and grape is basic and wholly objective.[13] The practice of the liturgy, or more broadly the practice of worshipping discipleship of which it is a focal element, is the encompassing practice of our lives, and, if we are to understand the proper nature and place of any other practices—including the practices of scientific enquiry, or even the practices of ordinary speech about objects that lie to hand—it will be by understanding the place that they can have within the more fundamental practice of worship and discipleship. The meanings that objectivity, truth, enquiry, and knowledge take on in this most encompassing practice therefore gives us the clue to what they mean—what they *should* mean, what they *can* mean—in general.

This claim about the priority of learning in the context of worship and discipleship requires careful handling, however, if it is not to collapse into myopic arrogance. Closer attention to the Eucharistic liturgy can suggest a great deal about the forms of learning that are called for in worship and discipleship, and about their relations to other practices of enquiry and so to other enquirers. It turns out that the picture of learning suggested is not one of competitive achievement, where the knowledge that Christians secure stands over against, and trumps, the knowledge secured by others. It is not one in which it makes sense for a Christian to lord his or her knowledge over others, or to delight in the demonstration that their learning is nothing and that only Christian learning grasps the truth. It is, rather, a form of learning understood as the reception of a gift; it is a form of learning that involves travelling humbly the way of the cross; and it is a form of learning that inherently involves participation in a certain kind of gracious and open community.

KNOWING AND BEING KNOWN

The first of these claims, that the liturgy presents learning not as an achievement but as the humble reception of a gift, is an appropriate place to begin.

---

[13] This claim is further complicated both by the fact that the Eucharistic practice is one in which it continues to matter that the bread and the wine are ordinary products of grain and grape, and by the fact that the meaning of 'objective' differs from practice to practice. On the latter point, see Lorraine Daston and Peter Galison's richly detailed discussion of the changing nature of scientific objectivity in *Objectivity* (New York: Zone Books, 2007).

The first explicit mention of knowledge in the Eucharistic liturgy does not, after all, speak of human knowing, but of God's.[14] Having been greeted, the congregation join in the 'Prayer of Preparation', already quoted in part above.

Almighty God, to whom all hearts are open, all desires known, and from whom no secrets are hidden: cleanse the thoughts of our hearts by the inspiration of your Holy Spirit, that we may perfectly love you, and worthily magnify your holy name; through Christ our Lord.

God's knowing of our hearts, our desires, and our secrets is the context for the cleansing of our thoughts. When the liturgy goes on to the Prayers of Penitence (which follow directly on this Preparation), the knowing implicitly expected of the worshipper when the priest says to the congregation 'Let us confess our sins in penitence and faith' is a sharing in this divine knowledge, and the liturgy functions as a school by inviting the worshippers to this sharing.

Of course, these words on their own could suggest a rather unwelcome gift, as if the worshipper were invited to the realization that she is living in a panopticon, under constant surveillance. But the Prayer of Preparation follows directly on a greeting in which the president has welcomed the congregation with the words 'The Lord be with you', spoken as a blessing rather than a curse,[15] and the call to confess follows directly upon a declaration of God's love for the world. More than that, the words describing God's knowledge echo a familiar theme from Scripture and from other prayers: the idea that the knowledge God has of us, even if it includes the knowledge of the ways in which we have sinned, is most fundamentally the knowledge of a maker delighting in what he has made.[16] One of the most familiar Psalms in the Bible is Psalm 139, which includes the words

> O Lord, you have searched me out and known me;
> you know my sitting down and my rising up;
> you discern my thoughts from afar...

> If I climb up to the heaven, you are there;
> if I make the grave my bed, you are there also...

---

[14] I am not including the 'Prayers of Preparation': I have never been a member of a congregation where they were a visible part of the proceedings, or a widespread expectation for individual preparation.

[15] A longer form of greeting is sometimes used: 'Grace, mercy and peace from God our Father and the Lord Jesus Christ be with you.'

[16] The collect for Ash Wednesday, the beginning of the penitential season, begins: 'Almighty and everlasting God, you hate nothing that you have made...'.

For you yourself created my inmost parts;
You knit me together in my mother's womb. (vv. 1, 7, 12)[17]

Those words are normally read as matter of intimacy rather than of threat. The liturgical call to self-knowledge is, therefore, properly understood as a call to share in the loving knowledge that our maker already has of us, in which our origin in God is known, in which the present state of our lives in relation to God and one another is seen unflinchingly, but in which our present lives are seen against the backdrop of the perfect loving intimacy with God and neighbour into which we are being drawn. In other familiar words, the end point imagined for our learning is the perfection of such intimacy: 'For now we see in a mirror, dimly, but then we will see face to face. Now I know only in part; then I will know fully, even as I have been fully known' (1 Corinthians 13:12). We are called to know the one who knows us perfectly, and so to know ourselves as those who are known. One might say that the knowledge we are invited to share is knowledge of God and of the intimate fellowship that God has for us, and that this knowledge is itself an element of that intimacy.

We can understand this underlying structure of Christian learning more fully if we look at it from another vantage point. As I write, it is the Easter season. On Sundays from Easter Day to Pentecost, the normal liturgical greeting is replaced with the acclamation from the president, 'Alleluia. Christ is risen', to which the people respond, 'He is risen indeed. Alleluia.' In this and other ways, it is made clear that the story that the liturgy tells, of our being known, of our being drawn into knowledge of God, of our being drawn to share the knowledge that our maker has of us, and of our being drawn thereby into loving intimacy with one another and with God, is first and foremost the story of the worshipper's encounter with Christ—with Jesus of Nazareth, crucified and risen.

To understand this Christian knowing more deeply, therefore, it makes sense to attend to the narratives of encounter with Christ in the Gospels. In the Gospel of Mark, for instance, we read:

As Jesus passed along the Sea of Galilee, he saw Simon and his brother Andrew casting a net into the sea—for they were fishermen. And Jesus said to them, 'Follow me, and I will make you fish for people.' And immediately, they left their nets and followed him. As he went a little farther, he saw James son of Zebedee and his brother John, who

---

[17] From the *Common Worship* Psalter. The Psalmist declares: 'Such knowledge is too wonderful for me, so high that I cannot attain it' (v. 5) and later exclaims, 'How deep are your counsels to me, O God!' (v. 17); nevertheless, he finishes by calling on God to 'know my heart; try me and examine my thoughts' (v. 23) in the hope or expectation that God will find his thoughts pure and fitted for life with God (v. 24).

were in their boat mending the nets. Immediately he called them; and they left their father Zebedee in the boat with the hired men, and followed him. (Mark 1:16–20)[18]

Note that Jesus *sees* Simon and Andrew, James and John, and having seen, calls them. He calls Simon and Andrew to a strange fulfilment of what they are: he sees that they *are* fishermen, and calls them to *become* fishermen. On the other hand, he calls James and John *away* from what they are: they are mending their father's nets, but he calls them away. He is presented as seeing what these men are, and what they can and will be—and as seeing each of these in the light of the other. That seeing provides the context for his call to them to follow him, to start on a life of discipleship—just as God's knowledge of us is presented in the liturgy as the context for our call to repentance and the cleansing of the thoughts of our hearts. The learning to which worship and discipleship draw us, then, is not a lonely venture into the unknown. It is an invitation to share in a knowledge held open for us already, and it begins with the knowledge that we are ourselves already known in love.

Of course, Simon, Andrew, James, and John do actively respond to Jesus' call. Once he has seen them, he meets and calls them, and they see him and hear him, and then follow. Their following begins because they are in some way captivated.[19] That is, their path towards knowledge—towards knowing and being known in love—begins by their being given some kind of initial apprehension that awakens and orientates their desire. As the story goes on, it will become clear that this initial knowing is a mixture of apprehension and misapprehension (apprehension and misapprehension of who God is, who Christ is, and who they themselves are), but they nevertheless do in part see and hear truly even now—and they have seen and heard something attractive, indeed something truly *beautiful*, however much it may have been true to use Isaiah's words of Jesus and say that he 'had no form or majesty that we should look at him' (Isaiah 53:2). These fishermen are attracted by something glimpsed, something they think they hear—and their action springs from that attraction. Later in Mark, the people in the synagogue will recognize in Jesus' activity an 'authority', a power and presence; in Luke, one can think of the disciples on the road to Emmaus, whose hearts burnt within them as the risen Jesus showed them more of the picture they had not yet fully

---

[18] Attending to the story of the calling of the disciples seems particularly appropriate, given that the Greek text uses the word *mathetes* for disciples—which could equally well be translated 'learners'.

[19] In John's Gospel, Nathaniel is captivated precisely by hearing that he has been seen: 'Jesus answered, "I saw you under the fig tree before Philip called you." Nathanael replied, "Rabbi, you are the Son of God! You are the King of Israel!" Jesus answered, "Do you believe because I told you that I saw you under the fig tree? You will see greater things than these" (John 1:48–50). Think also of Jesus' encounter with the Samaritan women, who tells others what she has discovered in the words, 'Come and see a man who told me everything I have ever done!' (John 4:29).

apprehended. The disciples are invited and compelled by the glory of God in the face of Christ to share in God's knowledge of the fulfilment in Christ that God has for them.

The joint between divine and human knowing, or between Christ's knowledge (of the Father, of himself, of the disciples, and of the world) and the awakening of his followers to active sharing in that knowing, is made by beauty and promise—by a glimpse given to them in encounter with Christ of the fulfilment that God knows for them and for the world, a glimpse sufficient to awaken and redirect desire. It is no accident, then, that the liturgy of the Eucharist often begins in the midst of architectural and musical beauty, nor that its words and actions aim at beauty, gesturing towards the beauty of God's kingdom, however muddled, fragmentary, and inconsistent that gesture may be. Christian learning begins with a foretaste of the eschatological feast that, in Jesus' characteristic picture of the kingdom, God has prepared for the world (and for which the world was made): a taste of something that quickens the appetite. As we shall see, the knowledge of the world to which Christians are called is fundamentally a knowledge of how everything might be made ready for this feast.

Christian learning is a matter, therefore, of being given, by the awakening and reorientating of one's desire, and by the provision of the relationship within which this desire may be pursued, the very activity by which one learns, at the hands of God.[20] Whatever language of discipline, of risk, of strenuous pursuit I go on to use in my description of knowledge, this knowledge remains a matter of being lovingly known, and of being lured into receiving from the hand of God a share in God's knowledge of the beautiful fulfilment that God has for the world.

PENITENT LEARNING

Christian learning, then, is received—and it is received on the path of discipleship. The Prayer of Preparation that I quoted above leads on, however, into the Prayers of Penitence. Having learnt that we are loved and have been invited to a feast, we learn both that we are unprepared for it and that the means of preparation have been provided.

The Prayers of Penitence begin with a reminder of the great love commandments: the command to love God 'with all your heart, with all your soul, with

---

[20] The Post Communion Prayer for Palm Sunday therefore rightly petitions God to 'give us the mind to follow you', and the Collect for the Fifth Sunday after Easter asks that God 'grant that, as by your grace going before us you put into our minds good desires, so by your continual help we may bring them to good effect; through Jesus Christ our risen Lord'.

all your mind, and with all your strength' and to 'love your neighbour as yourself'; they continue with a reminder of God's love for the world, and then call us to confess our sins as a mark of our resolve 'to live in love and peace with all'. In the newer form of the Confession that follows, the congregation declare that 'We have not loved you with our whole heart' and 'We have not loved our neighbours as ourselves'; the Absolution spoken by the president assures the penitents of God's mercy, pardon, and deliverance, and prays for God to 'confirm and strengthen you in all goodness'. The path of learning along which the liturgy invites us is, in the words of Chapter 1, a journey of purification and ascent: a cleansing of the 'thoughts of our hearts' that consists in the setting right of minds that are not rightly ordered in love.

Penitence is at the heart of the nature of Christian learning, such that one could almost say that penitence is the characteristic form that learning takes. This might become clearer if we once again attend to Mark's Gospel, though we need to take a step or two back in order to place the penitential knowing in its proper context. There are many stories in the gospel in which we see the disciples being taught. Most often, the word 'disciples' appears in Mark when he is simply mentioning that they were *with* Jesus, accompanying him on his journeys (e.g., 2:15, 3:7, 6:1). Having responded to the call, they became apprentices, learning from their master by watching what he did, by partici-pating from time to time in what he did, and by obeying his instructions (e.g., 3:9, 6:45); we see Jesus teaching them in more direct ways from time to time: talking to them, explaining things to them, responding to their questions (e.g., 4:34, 7:17, 9:31, 10:10). In other words, even if Jesus' teaching practice is at times a little unconventional, and even if he does not go out of his way to make everything clear for the disciples, there is within Mark's Gospel a fairly conventional picture of a teacher surrounded by his disciples, teaching them by precept and example. And, sure enough, we do see the disciples learning. At a point fairly early on in his ministry, Jesus sends the disciples out two by two, and we are told that 'they went out and proclaimed that all should repent. They cast out many demons, and anointed with oil many who were sick and healed them' (6:12–13). They have clearly learnt something from their ap-prenticeship: they have learnt to behave in many ways like their master, to do the things that he does, to say the things that he says. And it is interesting to note that this description of their work is immediately followed in Mark by the comment: 'King Herod heard of it [i.e., presumably the disciples' ministry]; for *Jesus'* name had become known' (6:14). That is, the disciples' activity is taken by Herod (and by Mark) as an extension of the activity of Jesus, as part of the dangerous spreading of Jesus' name and influence; the disciples have clearly learnt something, and what they have learnt has enabled them to become agents of their master, acting so as to have his action working through them. The disciples as learners do not simply become recipients of what their teacher hands out—they become participants in, ministers of, the great movement of healing, renewal, and transformation to which he is devoted. They learn, not by accumulating their own hoards of extra knowledge and ability, but by becoming those who can give away what they have learnt.

However, despite all this rather positive material, there is at least as strong a strand in Mark about how the disciples fail to learn (e.g., 5:31, 6:52, 8:4, 9:18, 10:13, 14:37). For instance, no sooner have they returned to Jesus from the successful ministry trip I just mentioned, no sooner have they described all that they have done, than they once again show their incomprehension: they have no faith that Jesus can feed the crowd of five thousand who come to hear him and end up staying past their mealtime; and they are terrified a little later when they see Jesus walking across the lake. 'They were', Mark says at that point, 'utterly astounded, for they did not understand about the loaves, and their hearts were hardened' (6:51–2).

There are other similar examples of incomprehension and stony-hearted-ness, but the most important one comes a little later. Mark's narrative of Jesus' ministry has reached a turning point; the atmosphere begins to change, and the reader's attention is directed increasingly towards the clouds gathering over Jerusalem. Peter, who in Mark is presented as the paradigmatic disciple, their spokesman and leader, has just—for the first time—declared to Jesus, 'You are the Messiah.' That is, he has shown how much he now understands of the vision that captivated him at the beginning and propelled him into discipleship. That understanding, however, provides the context for further learning. Straight away, according to Mark,

Jesus began to teach them that the Son of man must undergo great suffering, and be rejected by the elders, the chief priests, and the scribes, and be killed, and after three days rise again. He said all this quite openly. And Peter took him aside and began to rebuke him. But turning and looking at his disciples, Jesus rebuked Peter and said, 'Get behind me, Satan! For you are setting your mind not on divine things but on human things.' (8:31–3)

And this harsh statement brings us to the most important aspect of the disciples' learning in Mark. It is learning that takes place *on the way of the cross.* The passage I have been quoting continues:

He called the crowd with his disciples, and said to them, 'If any want to become my followers, let them deny themselves and take up their cross and follow me. For those who want to save their life will lose it; and those who lose their life for my sake, and for the sake of the gospel, will save it.' (8:34–5)

Although the disciples have learnt many things, what they have gained is engulfed by a greater ignorance: they do not yet know the way of the cross. They cannot yet understand the one crucial point—the point that Jesus regards as the key to understanding him and his ministry—that he must suffer and die, and that his followers must be prepared to lose everything.

A few chapters later, Jesus has been arrested. And the same Peter, who has learnt from Jesus if any of the disciples have, who has even declared himself ready to die for Jesus' sake, discovers the depth of his ignorance. He finds that his expectations and understanding—expectations of a messiah who will overthrow his enemies and reign victoriously—still prevent him from seeing the reality of Jesus' task and fate. And then Mark tells us that Peter, accused of being a follower of the now imprisoned Jesus, 'began to curse, and he swore an oath, "I do not know this man you are talking about." At that moment the cock crowed for the second time. Then Peter remembered that Jesus had said to him, "Before the cock crows twice, you will deny me three times." And he broke down and wept' (14:71–2). The problem is not, of course, that Peter is lying. The problem is that he is speaking quite truthfully when he says, 'I do not know this man.' Even at this point, when he has seen and heard and— yes—learnt so much, he has as yet failed to grasp the shape into which all the pieces of his new knowledge fit. He only begins to learn, truly to learn, in the moment when he breaks down and weeps. When he *is broken* down, we might say: when the arrest and trial and impending death of his Master begin to crucify him too—and finally to break apart the mistaken shape that was governing his understanding.

Peter and the other disciples learn only under the shadow of Calvary; they learn only when, instead of accumulating information and skills, they are unmade and remade, crucified and resurrected—when the structure of their thinking and acting is undermined by a strange passage of events that contradicts their expectations, when the structure of their thinking and acting collapses about their ears—and when they begin to find their thinking and acting reconstructed by the strange course of events. The expectations that crumble are not idle fantasies, for these disciples: they have staked everything on them, have given up everything to follow Jesus in expectation of a certain kind of future. They have identified themselves with these hopes. But they only truly *learn* to the extent that they lose all that—to the extent that, as Jesus would put it, they lose their lives. The call to be a disciple, to be a learner, is in this gospel a call to a kind of death.

It is, of course, important to remember that such crucifixion is not the whole story. The rebuffs that the disciples receive, they receive once they have already been called and welcomed; the stark rebuke of Peter occurs in context of Jesus' welcome of Peter's recognition of Jesus' true identity. Peter's denial of Jesus during the passion itself occurs in the context—most clearly articulated in John[21]—of a drama in which Peter's following of Christ, and his repetition in his own life of Christ's ministry to his sheep and of Christ's death, are eventually confirmed. In other words, the disciples' share in the crucifixion of

---

[21] I am grateful for discussion of the Johannine material with David Holyan.

Christ is not a matter of their being broken down as an entry condition to learning, nor a matter of their being left broken. The entry condition is God's unconditionally welcoming love—an open-eyed love that welcomes them as the people they already are, that delights in the knowledge they display, and that sets them on the road to their fulfilment. The call to be a Christian learner is fundamentally a call to life; death is a secondary reality, and, if one is called to crucifixion, it is only because one is already welcomed to resurrection.

Nevertheless, crucifixion is an unavoidable part of what it means to be drawn by God to share in God's own knowledge. Rather than being handed a fixed and completed deposit of truth, one is drawn by God's welcoming and trustworthy mercy to active participation in Christ's crucifixion and resurrection—to an ongoing process of the breaking and remaking of the learner by means of the breaking and remaking of the sense that she has made of herself, her world, and her God. Learning is not a process from which the learner can stand aloof, remaining fundamentally unchanged as the possessor of her knowledge. Rather, learning—if it is true learning—is a process in which the learner's present understanding, her present configuration of desire, her present way of being in the world, are at stake. It is a process in which the learner's relation to the object of her knowledge, and so everything that she has invested in the present form of that relationship, are placed at risk. Yet the Gospel proclaims both that the learner must take such a risk with herself, and also that she is safe enough to take it. Held by God's lavish mercy, the learner is freed to take the risk of an ongoing *kenosis* that is the form of her journey deeper into God's own knowledge, and the proper form of learning.

KNOWING IN THE BODY OF CHRIST

Peter was, of course, not a lone apprentice; he was a member of a community of disciples. Similarly, the Eucharistic liturgy is misunderstood if it is seen simply as a context for individual discipleship, as if the corporate activity of worship simply provided a backdrop to private devotion. The liturgy culminates in a shared meal: it is a community-forming activity.

The kind of learning I have been describing is, therefore, not a pathway towards static and isolated completion, but is ineradicably communal. It is helpful, in order to understand why this is so, to distinguish various different forms that the incompleteness of human knowledge takes. In part, human learning is incomplete because human beings are sinful, and so see in distorted, deluded ways—hence the need for crucifixion on the way to truth. It makes sense to work against this form of inadequacy, and to hope for its eschatological eradication—for the cleansing of 'the thoughts of our hearts' that leads to perfect love and worthy praise. In part, human knowledge is partial because human beings are creatures in time, and at present situated *on the way* towards the eschatological feast that God is preparing for the world—and so we do not yet know ourselves or other creatures as we and they will be when redeemed. It makes sense to long, not for the end of our temporality, but for the end of our location in this time between the times, in the time before redemption, and so to hope for the arrival of redeemed knowledge, the 'life of the world to come'.

But human knowledge is also partial simply because human beings are creatures, and so properly finite—and the Christian hope is for redemption *as* creatures, not redemption *from* creatureliness. My place in the fellowship that God is preparing for the world is not somehow to know the whole, but to be one of the learners in a community of learning, which in its ongoing corporate life of learning participates ever more deeply in God's knowledge of the world, and in God's knowledge of Godself, which is the life of the Trinity. My role as a participant in that community is not to realize some overview, but to know truly from the place that I have been given to stand in, and to share that particular knowing with the body, in fellowship with others who know things truly from the different places that they have been given. In other words, I am called to participate as a creature in the Creator's knowledge, but the distinction between Creator and creature is not overcome by that participation.

The individual crucifixion and resurrection that I have been speaking of are, therefore, part of a larger picture. They are the form that the Spirit's work takes as the Spirit gives disciples together a share in Christ's life, uniting them to Christ's death and resurrection, and by those means draws them deeper into the life of the Body of Christ.[22] The unity of the Body of Christ takes a particular form, however. After all, the Christ to whom disciples are being united is a particular person, not a principle, and Christlikeness can no more be a characteristic that floats above the particularities of a disciple's life than it can be a characteristic that floats above Jesus' own particularities. Jesus does not show *in general* what it means to know God and the world truly, in a way that could simply be repeated identically by anyone; he shows how God is known by living his own particular life before God, in his own specific time and place.[23] If the Spirit, therefore, draws others to share Christ's life, it can only be by sharing it *differently*, in their own places and times. The Spirit teaches them what it means to live in conformity to Christ in that place and

---

[22] The Post Communion Prayer for the weekdays after the Day of Pentecost runs as follows: 'Gracious God, lover of all, in this sacrament we are one family in Christ your Son, one in the sharing of his body and blood and one in the communion of his Spirit: help us to grow in love for one another and come to the full maturity of the Body of Christ. We make our prayer through your Son our Saviour.'

[23] My thinking on this point has been shaped by conversations with Frances Clemson.

time, and enables their lives to show in that place and time what they have learnt.

The Spirit's drawing-together of the Body of Christ does not, therefore, consist in the spreading of an identical knowledge among the many members of the Body, nor in the drawing of disciples into uniformity. Rather, the Spirit draws all these differing disciples into what we might call, in the light of Chapter 2's discussion of Schleiermacher, the 'free sociality' of the Body of Christ: drawing them into deeper learning precisely by drawing them into fellowship with one another. It is precisely because of the endless particularity of the Spirit's work in forming disciples that each member of the Spirit-gathered Body needs, and can expect, to *learn* from the other members, and to *go on* learning from them. And that means that to be drawn by the Spirit into deeper fellowship in the Body means being called to a life of attentiveness to those other members whose lived understandings are never finally absorbed into our ways of making sense of them. The Spirit's work, in forming the differentiated Body of Christ, is to make each member's particular learning a gift to those around them, and to make each member receptive to the endless gifts presented by those around them—and the process of crucifixion and resurrection into which each disciple is drawn is nothing other than the process of being made more fully both gift and recipient.

The *form* that Christian learning takes, therefore, is inherently that of an ongoing corporate life. Christ is known, and therefore God and the world are known in relation to one another, precisely to the extent that they are seen truly from a multitude of different, constantly developing, viewpoints, and precisely to the extent that the knowledge gained from each viewpoint is set into circulation. Each person is, as it were, entrusted with what he is shown in his particular place, but also called to seek peace with those who have been given different gifts in trust. The end point imagined is not uniformity, but precisely an ongoing corporate life, in which these different lives of perception are able to function harmoniously together—and if such an end can be described as the possession together of the mind of Christ (1 Corinthians 2:16) that is not because that mind is a content somehow identically present in each member's mind, but because they function together as a differentiated network that as a whole constitutes a living understanding. The fulfilment of learning towards which the Spirit's work leads is, therefore, not the static individual possession of perfect understanding, but an ongoing circulation in the body in which each is attending to every other, challenging every other, learning from every other, and displaying in her own particular way, in her own particular location, what he or she goes on learning. Christian learning takes the form of an unending economy of giving and receiving, co-extensive with what the liturgy calls 'the whole company of Christ'.

The *content* of Christian learning is also corporate, however. Another way to specify what it is that Christians are called to know is to say that they are called to know how to live together as a body, and how to build up that body.[24] According to 1 Corinthians 14, therefore, the paradigmatic gift that people give to each other in the Body of Christ is prophecy. That is, the gift they give is some compelling construal of the life of the community, of the nature of its past and present, and of the possibilities and demands of its future, a construal into which that person has been drawn by the Spirit's work (that is, precisely by being united to Christ's crucifixion and resurrection, by being taught to see things as coming from and returning to God, by being formed by grace as a faithful member of this community). The prophet, granted an apprehension of his or her community's life, speaks from that apprehension (finds himself or herself *compelled* to speak, perhaps), and offers that construal as a challenge and a comfort to the Body. And such prophecy is met by discernment. The prophet by offering his or her construal also obediently submits it to testing by the body of prophets—and so opens himself or herself to judgement. Prophecy and discernment *together* are the form that the learning life of the Body of Christ takes, and their primary content is the wisdom needed in order to live together in love and peace before God.

The knowing to which the members of the body are called in Christ is not a knowing that stands outside the redemption that God is preparing for them, as if it involved inspecting that redemption and gaining an overview of it. Rather, the knowing that they are given is one *ingredient* of the redeemed life, both because it is one of the forms of circulation that bind that fellowship together, and because it is fundamentally a knowledge of how to live the redeemed life together. If the eschaton is imagined as a context in which prophecy ceases, that is not because the circulation that prophecy and discernment represent ceases, but because it is fulfilled in unimpeded living exchange, in which each participant is fulfilled in his or her ongoing knowing and knowability. *This* is the unity that is assumed and anticipated in all true knowing: the unity of the eschatological Body of Christ. All true learning now must take the form of a sociality that anticipates the economy of unrestricted gift and reception that will characterize that Body.

WISDOM AND DELIGHT

If learning takes the form that I have been describing, then to learn to know any creature truly is to know how the Body of Christ may live in relation to that creature before God—how that creature may be included in the fellowship

---

[24] This is not to deny that they are called to know all things in relation to God, and God in relation to all things. They are, after all, called to learn to live as a body in the world and before God.

being gathered by the Spirit. But it is equally true that, if learning takes the form that I have been describing, then learning to know any creature truly cannot be a matter of arriving at the one, static account by which that creature should be known. Rather, to learn to know is to go on discovering all the unexpected ways in which our life can properly respond to and so be shaped by that creature, and all the ways in which that unique creaturely particularity can contribute to the whole reconciled and redeemed fellowship of creatures with God.

We might, therefore, say that we know any creature properly to the extent that we know it as participating in God's generosity and infinity. That is, we know it to the extent that we know it as contributing its specificity (as invitation, as challenge, as surprise) to the life of the Body of Christ, and to the extent that we know that it is not ever exhausted by what we have so far received of it. And what the creature gives in this unending generosity is its own unsubstitutable contribution to the shared life of the Body that *is* our knowledge of God. We know that creature, therefore, to the extent that we know it *as* a creature: as created by God, a gift to the world at the hand of God, calling us to knowledge of God's glory in its own particular way.

What, though, does learning to share in such knowledge of creatures look like, for creatures such as us? As knowledge 'through a glass darkly' (because it is at present the knowledge of sinners, and knowledge not yet fulfilled, and because it is in any case the knowledge of creatures), it is learning caught in a tension between wisdom and delight. That is, it consists in the first place of fallible and partial glimpses of how we and the things that we know belong in a reconciled and redeemed community together—of how we and the things we know can live a peaceable and flourishing Christ-like life together. In this regard, knowledge is most deeply a form of practical wisdom. In the second place, however, it consists in registering the inadequacy of our glimpses, by registering the ways in which the things that we know have so much more to them than we know what to do with. In this regard, knowledge is most deeply a form of astonished *delight*: delight in the reality of things that we cannot yet see as ingredient in a common good, but simply as the beautiful unfolding of a life other than our own.[25] To participate in God's knowledge means to be caught in this tension between wisdom and delight.

---

[25] The Post Communion Prayer for the Third Sunday after Trinity says: 'O God, whose beauty is beyond our imagining and whose power we cannot comprehend: show us your glory as far as we can grasp it, and shield us from knowing more than we can bear until we may look upon you without fear; through Jesus Christ our Saviour.' The knowledge greater than we can bear might be understood as the overwhelming knowledge of the sheer particularity of things: a knowledge in which all patterns and strategies and ways of coping would disappear in a vision flooded with the sheer intensity of the difference of each thing in its own place, praising God with its own unique voice. Think, for example, of Funes the Memorious, in Borges' story: 'It was not only difficult for him to understand that the generic term dog embraced so many unlike

The knowledge that belongs to wisdom is the knowledge asked for in the Collect for the Weekdays after Pentecost: 'O Lord, from whom all good things come: grant to us your humble servants, that by your holy inspiration we may think those things that are good, and by your merciful guiding may perform the same.' This is the knowledge that shows itself in doing justice, loving mercy, and walking humbly with our God.[26] Such wisdom is not simply knowledge of how things may be manipulated; it is not the kind of knowhow that makes for success in our practical endeavours regardless of their character. It is knowledge ordered towards the common good: a form of cohabitation in the world with the reality that we know, characterized by obedience to Christ's proclamation of love and justice. It is, one might say, knowledge that allows one to live graciously with reality—knowledge that may involve all sorts of expertise, and may involve a grasp of the possibilities that skill, technique, and insight can wring from the world, but that nevertheless shows itself most directly and fully in habits of flourishing bodily life and in styles of sustainable social living in the world.[27]

Yet this practical wisdom needs, as I have said, constantly to be held in tension with the kind of delight displayed repeatedly in the Psalms, in the hymnody of the church, in worship songs and canticles. The Benedicite (a feature of the liturgy for Morning Prayer rather than the Eucharist) is perhaps the paradigmatic example. It begins

> Bless the Lord all you works of the Lord:
> sing his praise and exalt him for ever.
> Bless the Lord you heavens:
> sing his praise and exalt him for ever.
> Bless the Lord you angels of the Lord:
> bless the Lord all you his hosts;
> bless the Lord you waters above the heavens:
> sing his praise and exalt him for ever.

And so it goes on. And on. And on. The sun and moon, the stars of heaven, rain and dew, all winds that blow, fire and heat, scorching wind and bitter cold,

---

specimens of differing sizes and different forms; he was disturbed by the fact that a dog at three-fourteen (seen in profile) should have the same name as the dog at three-fifteen (seen from the front). His own face in the mirror, his own hands, surprised him on every occasion . . . To think is to forget a difference, to generalize, to abstract. In the overly replete world of Funes there were nothing but details, almost contiguous details' (Jorge Luis Borges, *Ficciones*, ed. Anthony Kerrigan, tr. Emecé Editores (New York: Grove Press, 1964), 114–15).

[26] Micah 6:8, quoted in the Prayers of Penitence.

[27] Knowledge is not so much an *adequatio intellectus ad rem* as an adequation of the life of the ecclesial community to the thing known. Properly speaking, therefore, there is no such thing as knowing how to kill, or knowing how to betray, or knowing how to manipulate. 'Knowing' in such cases is at best a parodic, distorted version of the real thing, surviving only as a parasite upon true forms of knowledge.

dews and falling snows, light and darkness, frost and cold, lightnings and clouds, mountains and hills, all that grows in the ground, springs, whales and all that swim in the waters, all birds of the air, beasts and cattle, all people on earth, the people of God, priests of the Lord, servants of the Lord, all you of upright spirit, you that are holy and humble in heart—all are called to bless the Lord, to sing his praise and exalt him for ever.

I must admit that I do not find the Benedicite a great joy to sing or read, despite the fascination of the early verses with the weather, which ought to make it a perfect contribution to an English liturgy. On the one hand, it is simply so *long*; on the other, it is sometimes hard to summon enthusiasm for calling scorching wind and bitter cold, or lightnings and clouds, to join our praise. That, however, is part of the point of singing the Benedicite: it sets the praise of the people of God in the context of a vast panoply of praise that is not arranged for our benefit or convenience—it is itself, in all its magnificence and variety. It is beyond us.[28] Knowledge as delight shows itself in willingness to be fascinated by the strangeness of the world, and be drawn by such fascination out of a myopically exclusive concern with our own place in that world.[29]

Knowledge, then, is properly both wisdom and delight. In a world like ours, however, both wisdom and delight come in a second form, when our learning is directed towards what one might call the shadow-side of creation. Wisdom, for instance, involves learning how to respond to all the ways in which the world is damaged—all the constrictions and distortions of the world's life that at present make sustainable fellowship impossible. As such, it is learning that shows itself in wise labour for the repair of broken situations. It is a learning that is directed not so much to understanding the world as to changing it.

---

[28] My attempt to think through these matters has been greatly helped by conversations with Dominic Coad, whose thesis 'Creation's Praise of God: An Ecological Theology of Non-Human and Human Being' (unpublished Ph.D. thesis, University of Exeter, 2010) demonstrates the place that this kind of delight can have in Christian responses to environmental crisis.

[29] Compare with this my discussion of Barth's 'secular sensibility' in 'The Fulfilment of History in Barth, Frei, Auerbach and Dante', in Mike Higton and John C. McDowell (eds), *Conversing with Barth* (Aldershot and Burlington, VT: Ashgate, 2004), 120–41. Cf. also Gerard Loughlin's account of 'wonder' in 'The Wonder of Newman's Education', *New Blackfriars*, 92/1038 (2011), 224–42. One of the only sermons that I heard as a teenager that I can remember with full clarity was, I believe, a short sermon for a Christmas midnight communion. The preacher—my father—was speaking about the fact that the one who became incarnate and was born of the Virgin Mary was none other than the Creator of heaven and earth, of all that is, seen and unseen. Instead of wrapping the point in more words than a midnight congregation would be able to take in, he simply showed us a series of overhead projector transparencies covered with speckles and blobs of grey and black. We stared at them, bemused, until he explained that they were negatives of star fields, photographs taken with powerful telescopes: the speckles and blobs were stars, galaxies, and clusters of galaxies spread out over distances too vast to grasp. The attempt to imagine such immensity could have been annihilating, but the dominant note that he struck—infectiously, despite the patent inadequacy of the transparencies—was delight. Alongside wisdom, such delight—and the contemplation that it calls forth—is the proper form of learning.

Delight too has its counterpart, in lament—in contemplation of the ways in which things are prevented from flourishing, in so far as that contemplation does not (or not immediately) lead to attempts at repair, but simply to a mourning without answers and without plans.[30]

From the point of view of a participant in Christian worship and discipleship, I suggest, any form of knowledge whatsoever—if we are to recognize it as knowledge at all—will take one or more of these forms. All other practices of enquiry have a place within the practice of Christian learning, and can claim to be practices that the Christian learner may recognize as tending towards truth, only to the extent that they serve wisdom or repair, delight or lament. I do not see how anything else can count as learning.[31]

RECOGNIZING THE WORK OF THE SPIRIT

When, during the Gathering section of the Eucharistic liturgy, the people have confessed their sins, the priest prays for God to pardon and deliver them from all their sins, and to confirm and strengthen them *in all goodness*. The whole liturgy can be understood as being directed towards the purification of the worshippers, cleansing them from what is not holy, and binding them to what is. If this liturgy is a school of learning, it is not because it allows worshippers to accumulate information or understanding, but because it reshapes worshippers' lives—providing the context within which certain foundational characteristics of holy living can flourish.

True learning is inseparable from growth in what Galatians 5:22 calls the fruit of the Spirit: love, joy, peace, patience, kindness, generosity, faithfulness, gentleness, and self-control. In the context of learning, love is that attentiveness to the object of one's knowledge that, with patience, allows the object to be itself, and accommodates the knower to the object's way of being; self-control holds back from too quickly imposing existing categories and patterns of understanding onto the object; joy delights in the discovery of the object as a gift that we could not have given to ourselves; peace looks for the ways of living a shared life with the object in all its difference from us; faithfulness trusts in God who promises such a shared life to us; and generosity is hospitable to

---

[30] I have been influenced here by discussions with Molly James of Christian understandings of grief.

[31] Any other form of enquiry, we might say, will take the form of *curiositas*, in the sense that word has in earlier Christian critiques of malformed learning. See John Webster, 'Curiosity', and Stanley Hauerwas, 'More, or a Taxonomy of Greed', both in Mike Higton, Jeremy Law, and Christopher Rowland (eds), *Theology and Human Flourishing: Essays in Honour of Timothy J. Gorringe* (Eugene, OR: Wipf and Stock, 2011, 199–223), and Griffiths, *Intellectual Appetite*.

those who know the object differently, welcoming them in the knowledge that they are themselves one form that God's generosity takes.

Such a description threatens to fall into pious generalizations precisely because the stuff of which true learning is made is the stuff of ordinary piety. Learning, as I have been describing it, is a spiritual discipline, and to grow in learning is to become more transparent to the working of the Spirit, who conforms people to Christ on the way to the Father. Learning is a form of piety.

The paragon of learning for Christians, then, is not the sole genius, but the saint in the communion of saints: someone who embodies and displays these fruits of the Spirit in the life that he or she shares with the Body of Christ. The Collect for All Saints' Day asks God rather to 'grant us grace so to follow your blessed saints in all virtuous and godly living'. People can be identified as learners to the extent that they resemble such saints, and to the extent that the learning communities of which they are part resemble the communion of saints. There is no other kind of knowing worthy of the name; learning and holiness are inseparable.

We might be tempted, therefore, to think that learning is a possession of the church. For instance, one form of the Prayer after Communion finishes with the words:

May we who share Christ's body live his risen life; we who drink his cup bring life to others; we whom the Spirit lights give light to the world. Keep us firm in the hope you have set before us, so we and all your children shall be free, and the whole earth live to praise your name; through Christ our Lord.

The service then finishes with the Dismissal, by which the congregation are sent back out into the world to bring life and give light. The impression might be given that the congregation are therefore in a position simply to distribute the knowledge that they have gained to those outside the church—who, being outside, can be assumed to lack it. Of course, Christians will not be able to think of themselves as those who teach from a position of stable mastery, since they will have been taught to think of themselves as on the path towards knowledge on the way of the cross; nevertheless, they might think of the church as the one true context in which knowledge is learnt and the way of the cross pursued.

The school of the liturgy can be thought of another way, however. If it is a school of training in discipleship and in the sociality of the Body of Christ, it is also a school of training in the *recognition* of Christ-like individual and corporate life wherever it is being formed. One of the forms of humility that those who are being so trained might need to learn is precisely the recognition of the puzzling dual fact that in the church, where one might expect to find it, Christ-like life is so often lacking, and that the same Christ-like life can so often be recognized flourishing outside the church.

In other words, Christian learners will find good learning already taking place in the world beyond the church. Christians will find learning that pursues what we think of as wisdom or repair, delight or lament; and we will find patterns of learning community that embody something of the economy of gift and reception that we expect of the Body of Christ. Indeed, Christian learners will often, not least because we are members of a sinful church of sinners, find *truer* learning in the world beyond the church than in the church or in our own lives. And, wherever we recognize this life growing in the world, we will acknowledge the work of the Spirit, not as a claim about the kind of efficient causality that must be invoked in order to explain so strange an occurrence, but as a claim about the recognizability of the life we have found. The Spirit is the one who forms Christ-like life in the world, wherever (and to whatever degree) it is to be found.[32]

To the extent that we recognize such life being formed in the world, however, we will recognize it not as something complete, but as an anticipation of the eschatological fulfilment of knowledge to which all true learning points, and we will recognize ourselves as called into fellowship with it. In particular, however firmly we recognize a Christ-like life of corporate and individual learning being formed already in the world beyond the church, we will also recognize that there is something fragile about such learning to the extent that it is disconnected from a life in which God is explicitly acknowledged in worship and discipleship.

It is in this sense that, even when faced by those who by the grace of God truly know more than we do, we are called to welcome others to share in the life of Christian learning into which we have already been welcomed. To be made learners by Christ is unavoidably to be made into fishers of people. To the extent that the learning to which we have been called is a matter of delight, the call to others is its overflow in joy, incapable of keeping its delight to itself. To the extent that this learning is a matter of wisdom, the call to others is the call to learn how they with their true knowledge and we with ours might live peaceably together in Christ, by the Spirit.

Moreover, if true knowledge is the knowledge of the whole body of Christ united in fellowship, and if *all* are called to membership of that body, and if each member or prospective member of that body is a unique gift to the body in his or her unsubstitutable particularity, then Christian learners can expect gifts even from strangers and from those who acknowledge no call to membership. Christians are called to a practice of hospitality, to welcoming the stranger not as an exercise of our own generosity but as a recognition of God's generosity in giving the stranger to us, and the stranger's generosity in

---

[32] I am construing the relationship between grace and nature rather differently from Newman. I claim that *all* knowledge takes this form, and so is in one sense 'supernatural', but that more of the natural participates in this supernatural than one might have expected.

allowing himself to be welcomed. We can expect to learn (and to go on learning) from any stranger, precisely to the extent that the stranger is one of God's creatures—and so, whether the stranger knows it or not, a participant in the infinite generosity of God.[33]

CONCLUSION

A systematic theology of learning like this operates at a fairly high level of generality. Standing back from the practice of worship and pausing for reflection, it sketches what it takes to be the broadest contours of its subject. Such a pause for reflection, however, exists for the sake of the transformed practice to which it leads, and the movement of abstraction and reflection is completed by the return to specific contexts of lived practice, to ask what ways of negotiating one's way through those contexts are suggested and supported by these theological reflections.

In the remainder of this book, I turn back to the specific context of the contemporary secular and religiously plural university, to ask what if anything of the good of learning I can recognize there, and whether it might be possible to call such universities deeper into the good, and to be called deeper into it by them in turn. I can well understand that, at this point in the argument, it may seem implausible that I will have much of a positive answer to give to this question. One thing is clear already, however. I am not allowed by the theology of learning that I have been exploring to say that because learning is the possession of church there can be no true learning in the university; nor am I allowed simply to affirm the university as an institution devoted to the independent secular good called knowledge, and leave it at that. It is possible in the light of the theology that I have been sketching to recognize the university as a seat of true learning, if (though only if) the university's sociality takes a form that echoes the life of the church, and if (though only if) the university schools people in love, joy, peace, patience, kindness, and the rest.

If I abide by the theology sketched in this chapter, then seeking the good of the university—seeking for it to become a truer seat of learning—can only be a matter of discovering how to call it to a deepening of those patterns of sociality so that they become more fully the kind of economy of gift and reception capable of yielding true knowledge; a matter of discovering how to call the university to deepen those patterns of training in the fruit of the spirit without which it cannot claim to be turning out knowers or learners; a matter of

---

[33] For discussions of the practice of Scriptural Reasoning that show one practical form that intellectual hospitality can take, see Mike Higton and Rachel Muers, *The Text in Play: Experiments in Biblical Reading* (Eugene, OR: Wipf and Stock, 2012), pt II.

discovering how to call the university to recognize its proper end, among the many held out to it as desirable, as consisting in wisdom, delight, repair, and lament; a matter of discovering how to call the university to recognize the unity anticipated in all its learning; a matter of discovering how to call the university to worship—and a matter of discovering the ways in which the good life lived, by God's grace, in secular and religiously plural universities can call me and the ecclesial communities of which I am a part into new and deeper ways of understanding the life of Christian discipleship and worship. Whether there is any sense at all to be made along these lines of the contemporary secular and religiously plural university, precisely *as* secular and religiously plural, is the question to which we now turn.

6

The Virtuous University

In Chapter 1, I examined the questing, questioning intellectual life that is visible (however ambiguously and partially) in the emergent University of Paris. I argued that this life was not established over against Christian tradition, devotion, and ecclesial life, but was made possible by them—and that it could properly be understood as itself a form of tradition-formed, ecclesially shaped Christian devotion. At the heart of this devotion lay the sense that one could learn the good ordering of the materials at one's disposal only if, in humility and trust. one took the risk of being called to penitence and transformed understanding by them—called to right order before God by the God-given resistances of one's material, as one placed oneself at God's disposal.

In Chapter 5, I produced my own similar theological account of learning, speaking not as an inhabitant of the thirteenth-century Catholic tradition, but as somebody formed by, and responsible to, twenty-first-century English Anglicanism. Writing as a participant in specific Christian practices of worship and reflection, I argued (among other things) that I am bound to see learning—*all* learning worthy of the name—as a form of discipleship, and to see at its heart a form of participation in the crucifixion and resurrection of Christ by the power of the Spirit: a breaking and remaking of sense inseparable from formation in the various fruits of the Spirit.

In this and subsequent chapters, I ask whether and how it is possible for me, as someone beholden to that tradition, and holding fast to that theology, to contribute to the formation of the intellectual life of the contemporary secular university, a world away from medieval Paris.

There are, in fact, two questions here, pointing in opposite directions. Roughly speaking, there is a question about what I, with my theological account of learning, make of a secular university, and there is a question about what a secular university can in turn make of my attempts to shape its life on theological grounds. Both of these questions are pressing. The first is pressing because I as a Christian can pursue a vocation of love for learning in a secular university only if I can understand such a university as in some degree a context for *real* leaning.[1] Yet, if I can indeed understand the secular university as a context for real learning, that understanding brings with it a set of theological claims about the end that such learning serves, about the character that it must have in order to serve that end well—and about the degree to which it sometimes fails to display that character or serve that end. That in turn means that, precisely to the extent that I can make theological sense of my participation in the university, my participation will be made restless: to know that I belong in such a university will be at the same time to see ways in which it might more completely exhibit the good of which it is capable. And so the other question becomes equally pressing. As someone who has ideas about the good of the university that emerge from my participation in one particular religious tradition, can I call for changes, and hope for that call to be intelligible and attractive, in a secular university where most of the participants do not inhabit my tradition?

In the remaining chapters of this book, I will be trying to demonstrate that the answer to both questions can be a firm 'Yes'. Yes, it is possible for me as a Christian to see what happens in the secular university as good—or as approximating to the good, or as pregnant with the good. And, yes, it is possible for me as a Christian to call such a university to fuller pursuit of that good, and to have some realistic hope as I do so that my voice might be audible and intelligible.

In this and the next two chapters, I will try to provide this demonstration by offering three sets of descriptions of and proposals for university life—descriptions focusing respectively on virtue, sociality, and service of the common good. Each set of descriptions experiments with a discourse that happens to be available, in roughly analogous forms, both to Christian theologians and to secular theorists of higher education, and so to allow a certain mediation between the two. So, on the one hand, I will in each case be pursuing an account of some aspect of university life that will have obvious connections to the theology I set out in the previous chapter; anyone who reads all these chapters together will be able, despite all the differences of idiom, to recognize Chapters 6–8 as an attempt to work out the implications for university life of Chapter 5's Anglican theology of learning. On the other hand, however, I will also be pursuing in each case an account that I hope might be fairly directly recognizable and plausible, and perhaps even attractive, to others—not to every right-thinking human being, but to at least some of my colleagues who do not share my religious tradition, given the sorts of things they happen at present to say and do.[2]

---

[1] I am just about to turn 40, and you can think of this as the mid-life crisis question: Am I really doing any good, here?

[2] I do not have a *theory* of mediation here; rather, I am pursuing a kind of ad hoc apologetics. See above, Introduction, n. 8.

For the reader who inhabits the same tradition as me, I hope that the three sets of descriptions and proposals taken together will lend plausibility to my claim that the secular university truly can be a context for real learning.[3] For the reader who does not inhabit the tradition from which I speak, and for whom my descriptions and proposals therefore come shorn of their foundation, these descriptions and proposals might simply be taken as a buffet of ideas and suggestions that she can take or leave as she sees fit, as and when they prove interesting and plausible in her own terms. However, as I will explain more fully in Chapter 9, my aim is to enable more than buffet-grazing. I hope to contribute to the possibility of serious secular and religious *argument* about university identity, policy, and practice. In particular, I hope that the connection of my descriptions and proposals to the theological foundation set out in Chapter 5 will allow an interlocutor from some other tradition to go beyond the simple acknowledgement of agreements and differences. She might, for instance, try to discover whether any counter-proposal she might offer looks like it could make sense in the terms of my tradition, experimenting with my tradition's discourse even though it is not her own language. Similarly, she might be prompted to see whether my apparently disagreeable claim is one that could make some kind of sense in her own tradition—being spurred to a counter-articulation, parallel to my Chapter 5, of the deeper patterns of her own commitments and formation. She might simply be enabled to dig down within both our accounts to discover the deep reasons for our surface disagreements, and understand how far I might move in her direction and she in mine without betraying those deep reasons. In other words, my hope in providing these three descriptions of university life on the back of the previous chapter's thoroughly theological account of learning is to make possible not consensus but serious disagreement and negotiation.[4]

CHRISTIAN AND SECULAR VIRTUE

The first set of descriptions and proposals that I offer is framed in the language of virtue. That happens at present to be a language in which various secular thinkers have discussed the nature and health of intellectual life, and so to be a plausible language in which to aim at descriptions and proposals recognizable to a secular audience. Because I use that language to reframe my conclusion from Chapter 5, however, I necessarily take it up in distinctive ways—though without necessarily losing that secular audience along the way. I will have

---

[3] The taking-together is important. In particular, the accounts of Ch 6 (on virtue) and Ch. 7 (on sociality) are seriously incomplete without Ch. 8 (on the pursuit of the common good).

[4] For more on this, see below, Ch. 9.

something to say, for instance, about the non-heroic *form* of virtue in a Christian perspective; furthermore, I will give greater prominence than do most secular theorists of intellectual virtue to what might be called 'theological virtues': virtues that, in the sense in which I describe them, are grown in the soil of Christian narratives and practices (scriptural reading, worship, the celebration of the Eucharist),[5] and that accompany the formation of Christ-shaped life in the world. I will be claiming that the modern secular university can be understood as attempting to provide a formation in just this kind of virtue—virtue that is recognizable, in both form and content, *as* virtue to a Christian enquirer.

If such recognition is possible, it follows that the university is a context in which Christians may pursue virtue. Their churches are, after all, themselves incomplete, mixed, and fragile contexts for training in virtue, and, to the extent that the university really does inculcate elements of virtue, there will be something deeply coherent about a Christian worshipper coming from participation in the Eucharistic liturgy on Sunday to work at the university on Monday morning.

However, I will also claim that, if university life is constituted by forms of disciplined practice capable of forming Christian participants more fully for their membership in the Body of Christ, those participants who are not adherents of the Christian tradition are nevertheless also being formed in similar ways. Though they are not members of the Body of Christ, they are nevertheless being formed to echo something of its life.

It also follows that, if Christians who recognize the university as a school of real intellectual virtue therefore labour to make it into a truer school, they might well sometimes find themselves labouring alongside, and collaborating with, others whose labours point in roughly the same direction, even if they rest on different grounds.

More than that, however, it follows that the university can be a context in which Christians might learn more fully something of what real virtue looks like—in terms recognizable within their tradition, but spoken to them from this new context.[6] A Christian may know, for instance, that she is called to honesty—but that does not mean that she knows what the exercise of the virtue of honesty looks like in all contexts. It may be that practices of academic honesty, as they are imperfectly but genuinely sustained in academic communities that own no explicit allegiance to the church, can teach the church more

---

[5] For faith, hope, and charity as theological virtues, see Thomas Aquinas, *Summa Theologiae* 1a2ae.62, in Aquinas, *Summa Theologiae 23: 1a2ae. 55–67: Virtue*, tr. W. D. Hughes (Cambridge: Cambridge University Press, 2006), 137–50.

[6] Secular academic disciplines might therefore join a distinguished line of inadvertent prophets who speak to the people of God from its borders—Balaam's Ass (Numbers 22:21–35) and Cyrus (Isaiah 44:28–45:1) spring to mind.

of what honesty means, and so help the church (itself an incomplete, mixed, and fragile context for training in virtue) to be more fully the church.[7]

I am hinting here at a more general point. The virtues and the vices that Christians learn to recognize and name as they are formed by the worshipping life of their churches are distributed in the world in messy and complex ways, as are the practices and the communities that sustain them. Patient, generous, critical description is needed to map their spread, and the image that emerges is certain to be dappled with all sorts of intensities of grey, rather than resolving into neat maps of black and white. It is true that, as Stanley Hauerwas says, 'no school can do the work of the *polis*',[8] and that by and large universities form students in the values of the state that they serve. It is, therefore, equally true that to hope for universities consistently to anchor a thoroughly counter-cultural virtue, and make possible a thoroughly counter-cultural politics, is wishful thinking. But our *polis* is shaped by fragments and strands of virtue as well as by vice, and it *does* make sense to hope and work for universities to be contexts where some of the real virtues of this *polis* are amplified, and some of its vices weakened. However incomplete may be the formation in virtue that the university sustains, however mixed it might be with other kinds of formation, however fragile might be the basis on which it is sustained, separated as it is from the context that gives those virtues their deepest meaning and widest sway, it nevertheless makes sense to hope for the university to do real, if limited, good.[9]

INTELLECTUAL VIRTUE

The language of virtue is already in play—indeed, is increasingly prominent— in secular discussions of intellectual life.[10] A virtue is 'a deep and enduring

---

[7] Of course, it is not just Christian communities that might stand in such a complex relation to universities. Any tradition that forms its participants in some fairly well-defined system of virtues, and whose participants regard it as the primary context within which their recognition of virtue and vice *should* be formed, is going to be involved in similarly complex negotiations.

[8] Stanley Hauerwas, *The State of the University: Academic Knowledges and the Knowledge of God* (Oxford: Blackwell, 2007), 116.

[9] In Ch. 8 I will face much more directly the question of how the universities can sustain training in such virtues if they are not valued and prepared for in the wider society that those universities serve.

[10] I am thinking specifically of the rise to prominence of virtue epistemology. See, e.g., Abrol Fairweather and Linda Zagzebski (eds), *Virtue Epistemology: Essays on Epistemic Virtue and Responsibility* (Oxford: Oxford University Press, 2001); W. Jay Wood, *Epistemology: Becoming Intellectually Virtuous* (Leicester: Apollos; Downers Grove, IL: IVP, 1998); and Linda Trinkhaus Zagzebski, *Virtues of the Mind: An Inquiry into the Nature of Virtue and the Ethical Foundations of Knowledge* (Cambridge: Cambridge University Press, 1996). For a different perspective on virtue in the university, see Christopher Megone, 'Virtue and the Virtual University', in Simon

acquired excellence of a person'.[11] It is acquired by means of involvement in a practice sustained by a particular community, and is what allows a person to be a good practitioner of that practice. It is skill in pursuit of the good that orientates that practice (and that is itself defined by the practice), and gives the person the capacity and disposition reliably to advance towards that good. A person formed in that virtue has internalized the good of the practice, until that good has become his own good.

I am not directly interested here in virtue as an *accompaniment* to strictly intellectual formation—perhaps as the kind of additional moral training on offer by an educational institution intent upon forming the whole person, not just the mind. Valuable though such breadth is, my focus falls rather more narrowly upon intellectual formation itself: on disciplinary and professional competence, and the various virtues that are constitutive of such competence or required for progress towards it.[12] I am looking, if you like, for an account that would still be of use in the worst-case scenario of a university that has become utterly stripped down to pursuit of narrow curricula—with students simply taking single honours degree courses in Maths, Bioscience, History, or Childhood and Youth Studies, or some such, and without serious emphasis on interdisciplinary integration or on life beyond that curriculum.

Any academic discipline worth the name can properly be understood as a system of virtue. I have in mind something like the 'moral economy of science' described by Lorraine Daston. She insists that 'science depends in essential ways upon highly specific constellations of emotions and values';[13] and that 'not only does science have what I will call a moral economy (indeed, several); these moral economies are moreover constitutive of those features conventionally (and, to my mind, correctly) deemed most characteristic of science as a way of knowing'.[14] A moral economy is 'a web of affect-saturated values that stand and function in well-defined relationship to one another'; it is 'a balanced system of emotional forces'.[15] As such, 'apprenticeship into a science schools the neophyte into ways of feeling as well as into ways of seeing,

Robinson and Clement Katulushi (eds), *Values in Higher Education* (St Bride's Major: Aureus/ University of Leeds, 2005), 117–32. The work of Alasdair MacIntyre looms large in the background, of course; most notably *After Virtue: A Moral Theory*, 3rd edn (London: Duckworth, 2007).

[11] Zagzebski, *Virtues of the Mind*, 137.

[12] I say 'disciplinary *and professional* competence' because I work in a context where the primary reference community for some courses of study is not so much the relevant academic discipline, but a profession. Law is perhaps the most obvious example.

[13] Lorraine Daston, 'The Moral Economy of Science', in Lorraine Daston, *Constructing Knowledge in the History of Science*, Osiris, 2nd ser. 10 (1995), 2–24: 3.

[14] Daston, 'Moral Economy', 3.

[15] Daston, 'Moral Economy', 4. For more on the role of 'emotional forces' in intellectual life, see Mark Wynn, *Emotional Experience and Religious Understanding: Integrating Perception, Conception and Feeling* (Cambridge: Cambridge University Press, 2005).

manipulating, and understanding'.[16] According to Daston, such moral economies draw upon wider societal moral economies, but absorb those more general mores within discipline-specific forms.

Although moral economies in science draw routinely and liberally upon the values and affects of ambient culture, the reworking that results usually becomes the peculiar property of scientists. Traces of the original cultural models—for example, the simplicity, dedication, and humility of Christian saints or the unworldly innocence of the pastoral idyll—lie ready to hand, and can be evoked by the spokesmen of science to win public approval and support. But the ultimate forms that moral economies assume within science, and the functions that they serve, are science's own.[17]

A discipline *is* a moral economy—or a collection of closely related moral economies, interacting and evolving over time. In the article that I have been quoting, Daston traces the evolving economies of the virtues of 'precision' and 'facticity' that have shaped modern science; elsewhere, in an influential collaboration with Peter Galison, she has described at much greater length the economy of the virtue of 'objectivity'. They write that 'objectivity and other epistemic virtues were intertwined with the historically conditioned person of the inquirer, shaped by scientific practices that blurred into techniques of the self'.[18]

Lynn Holt, in his book *Apprehension*, gives a persuasive account of intellectual excellence that meshes well with Daston's, drawing directly on Aristotelian sources.

The ideal knower is one who brings a rich supply of experience and habits of insight, a rich stock of universals and the vocabulary with which to express them, and an ability to deploy this stock in both familiar and novel situations. His experience is formed within the disciplines of practice, but he is able to extend those disciplines in ways which have the potential to transform the practice. It is not the standard-issue equipment—sensory and intellectual mechanisms—which separates those who know from those who do not, but development. There is no 'basic' model of the knower, therefore, but there is a paradigm: one who confronts reality with the full arsenal of tradition.[19]

---

[16] Daston, 'Moral Economy', 5.

[17] Daston, 'Moral Economy', 7. See also Lorraine Daston and Peter Galison, *Objectivity* (New York: Zone, 2007), 40: 'Much of epistemology seems to be parasitic upon religious impulses to discipline and sacrifice.'

[18] Daston and Galison, *Objectivity*, 39.

[19] Lynn Holt, *Apprehension: Reason in the Absence of Rules* (Aldershot: Ashgate, 2002), 70; further page references in text. Holt expands on his comment about the transformation of the practice with a persuasive account of Galileo's repair of Aristotelian physics: he was so immersed in the Aristotelian tradition that he 'could see what physics might become if certain basic elements were transformed, and how a new physics could not only solve some (but not all) of the problems facing the old, but explain why the old physics had to fail' (p. 72).

To confront reality with the full arsenal of tradition means to confront it with a mind formed by 'experience, training, and habituation' (p. 65) to see particular kinds of distinction and connection, and so to apprehend more deeply than can an unformed mind: 'the virtuous will *see things differently*' (p. 47).[20] Academic disciplines are, or should be, communities of such intellectual experience, training and habituation—communities of enquiry in which such fine-grained apprehension is formed (p. 32), and 'the virtuous condition of intellect and character' (p. 112) inculcated.[21] It is a matter of intellect *and character* because virtuous apprehension is bound up with other intellectual and moral virtues such as 'honesty, courage, temperance, and justice' (p. 11); 'perception is indirectly governed by our entire character, directly by the conceptual understanding which has been shaped by our experience' (p. 46).

Disciplines as moral economies, then, are communities of training in virtuous perception, and in the judgement that springs from it.[22] Holt says that 'the paradigm case of apprehension is of a complex intellect confronted with a complex object, in which the intellect understands in a particular context what is "essential" about the object' (p. 31). Perception is not, for Holt, a raw receptivity to be complemented by active intelligence; it is itself an active and intelligent faculty, able to receive the world only because it is trained in making distinctions and seeing relations. If I, as a sighted person, run my fingertips over a line of Braille, I do not simply fail to do some intellectual work with what I have received, perhaps failing to understand what the dots *mean*; rather, I fail at the first hurdle. I do not perceive many of the dots as distinct from one another, and do not perceive the patterns in which they stand. I would need painstaking training and practice to be able to perceive the Braille cells well.

A disciplined form of apprehension is a kind of sensitivity. One could think of an academic discipline, in so far as it is a training in virtuous apprehension, as taking sandpaper to some particular area of one's skin—rubbing it raw,

---

[20] As my colleague, Mark Wynn, suggested to me by email when commenting on this claim, 'the perceptual field of the virtuous person is likely to be differently organized, to have inscribed within it a different pattern of salience'.

[21] Even forms of knowledge frequently thought not to be dependent upon experience work in this way, Holt insists. 'Is the geometer's understanding of triangularity a priori? Only in such an anemic sense as to make it unable to support the claim that the geometer knows triangularity without experience: that *after having acquired* the virtue of understanding, the geometer needs no further experience to judge truly that the sum of interior angles of a triangle is 180. Indeed, we might go so far as to say that such a judgment is analytic. But the key here is that a great deal of geometrical experience is needed in order for it to be understood as analytic' (p. 53).

[22] Being a professional, at least in one way of thinking about it, is precisely a matter of formed apprehension, of having internalized a way of seeing things, and being formed to make judgements. As such it is, or should be, the very opposite of bureaucratization. Think of a bank manager skilled in judging creditworthiness, who knows more than can be captured on any set of forms; a midwife who knows when to whisk the mother to the delivery room, in ways that go beyond combinations of stated procedures and spoken rules of thumb.

until it is unusually, even painfully, sensitive. A discipline *sensitizes*, enabling one to see more in some particular area than is normal: to make finer distinctions, to see things in a finer web of connections.[23]

If this is how intellect works, there will, ultimately, be no 'neutral, impersonal standards of theoretical correctness' because 'the standards of judgment are personal' (p. 13); the standard of excellence for communities of enquiry is the virtuous apprehender. In other words, to find what counts as intellectual excellence, indeed, what counts as excellent knowledge, one needs to find out who knows well—or rather, to become a member of a community that is involved in practices of enquiry within which it is possible to identify who counts as an excellent learner. And such excellent learners are not going to be common: the virtues that Holt is thinking of are excellences that not everyone possesses, because they are acquired only by those with aptitude, and only after serious training (p. 14). Holt's knowers, therefore, are intellectual virtuosi.

The ideal of the virtuous intelligence employed here is not the hero of the Enlightenment, armed with pure reason and rational method alone, stripping away layers of artifice to reveal the thing itself, but someone more akin to the Renaissance *magister*, possessed of a *copia rerum et verborum* and an understanding of the world which is both rooted in his culture yet is more subtle and sophisticated than his peers. (p. 57)

If we follow such authors as Daston and Holt, then, we will see academic disciplines as moral economies or systems of virtue, and see the learning that goes on in universities as primarily a matter of formation in virtue. Such learning will involve a shaping of deep and enduring excellences of person in students, and will show itself in skilled pursuit of the good of some practice of enquiry, in highly specific constellations of emotions and values that fit learners for participation in a specific community of enquiry, and in the forms of apprehension and judgement that such a community sustains.[24]

---

[23] Chris Anderson, *Teaching as Believing: Faith in the University* (Waco, TX: Baylor University Press, 2004), 71: 'All teachers at the university are teachers of reading, whatever else they are.' (He continues 'and what all teachers know is that reading requires community': a point we will come back to in the next chapter.)

[24] In my own university, every module that students take is defined by an official 'module descriptor'. The heart of the descriptor is the list it provides of 'intended learning outcomes', divided into 'module specific skills', 'discipline specific skills', and 'personal and key skills' (see also below, pp. 194–5). The 'discipline specific skills' and 'personal and key skills' are meant to tie back to a 'programme descriptor', which sets out the skills covered by a whole degree programme, and those in turn are meant to tie back to the Subject Benchmark documents produced by the national Quality Assurance Agency. In practice, the requirement to create a list of such skills for every module is mostly experienced as a bureaucratic burden of no real import. It is possible, however (I have seen it done!) to use the process more thoughtfully than that. Imagine a discussion in a department of the core forms of virtue that shape the relevant discipline, and the department's vision of academic life in general. Imagine creating a list, based on that discussion, of core disciplinary practices and core academic practices—and

For those who teach and research in the university, the same description applies. Their currency as academics will fundamentally be a matter of embodied virtue, and they will be academics precisely by virtue of their participation in disciplines that are, to a degree, 'communities of character'.[25] In this view, universities, to the extent that they are contexts for the pursuit of academic and professional disciplines, will be schools of virtue.

This is, I trust, a description of the nature of academic life likely to be recognizable, and perhaps compelling, for a wide range of people in a secular university—and it is a description that, in and of itself, requires no obvious theological commitments from those who champion it.[26] On the other hand, it is couched in terms deeply familiar to me as a Christian theologian, and resonant with much of what I have said in earlier chapters. It chimes, for instance, with the account given in Chapter 1 of the quasi-monastic nature of academic life in Paris, and with the picture of learning as a spiritual discipline, deeply forming the knower's character. It chimes with the theological account in Chapter 5, of learning as a matter of formation in the fruit of the Spirit, a pattern of discipleship in which the person is formed for knowing.

In the next section below, headed 'Apprenticeship', I will experiment with some of the characterizations of academic life that this quite general resemblance makes possible. Going beyond that simple formal resemblance to more substantive matters is more difficult, however. In subsequent sections of this chapter, I will turn away from an account that focuses directly on the virtues that Daston and Holt place centre stage—objectivity and apprehension—and instead suggest an account of academic life that places the focus on virtues that connect more directly to the conclusions of Chapter 5.[27]

---

suggesting that, in future, those filling in these sections of a module descriptor do not need to struggle to invent some plausible flannel simply to get the form through an accreditation committee, but can painlessly adopt and adapt entries from this list. Living with bureaucracy is often a matter of learning to respond to its demands unexpectedly well—and that need not mean creating more work for everyone.

[25] I am playing, of course, on the title of Stanley Hauerwas's *A Community of Character: Toward a Constructive Christian Social Ethic* (Notre Dame, IN: University of Notre Dame Press, 1981).

[26] I am leaving to one side here the question of whether a fully coherent version of this description, all the way down to metaphysical foundations, can be erected on non-theological territory. I am not interested in pursuing that kind of argument in this book.

[27] Each discipline will have its own specific system of virtues—its own specific moral economy. (A historical discipline, for instance, will inculcate a set of virtues pertaining to the handling of historical evidence—recognizable, perhaps, in the tendency to raise certain questions about provenance and transmission, and a sensitivity to anachronism.) Patient ethnographic and historical work will be needed to uncover the systems at work in any given discipline, as well as the forms of fragmentation that threaten to divide it. (Imagine mapping biblical studies, for instance, and registering the differences between those formed in sensitivity to text-critical questions, and those formed in sensitivity to feminist-critical questions.) Although there will be significant overlaps, each discipline will be bound up with its own specific bodies of knowledge; it will be bound up with the mastery of specific techniques and technologies; it will

I should also at this point note that a Christian account of intellectual virtue will need to pull away decisively from the Aristotelian formulations favoured by Holt in at least one important way. In the previous chapter, I spoke of the exemplar of Christian learning as a *saint*, not a master (or a Renaissance *magister*, as in the long quotation from Holt above). Yet the excellence of the saint is somewhat different from the excellence of the master, because, even if it too involves an excellence in apprehension—in seeing truly the world in relation to God and God in relation to the world—it is an excellence that is more thoroughly kenotic in form. That is, the knower as saint is one who is formed to be more fully open to the breaking and remaking of his sense at others' hands, and who has become more fully available as a gift to the whole body. Virtue in the Body of Christ cannot properly be so *heroic* as the Aristotelian virtue that Holt describes, a point with quite serious implications for our vision of academic excellence and of the training appropriate to it—including the implication that this chapter's emphasis on virtue is inseparable from the next chapter's emphasis on sociality.

APPRENTICESHIP

Regardless of questions about the precise content of the systems of virtue involved in academic life, formation in virtue is bound to take the form of *apprenticeship*.[28] As Lynn Holt says, in a system of virtue, excellence is primarily embodied in persons and only secondarily in the products of their virtue (excellent works and judgements) or in codifications of what it is about their works that make them excellent (disciplinary rules and recipes). Even in mathematics, where the products are in one sense utterly rule-governed, excellence consists first of all in the existence of excellent mathematicians, who are capable of producing (in ways that are not themselves simply rule- or

---

privilege specific kinds of question, and sustain patterns of roughly coherent argument about what sort of thing counts as a good answer to such questions. Above all, each discipline will acknowledge different exemplars of good work—and different exemplars of the excellent disciplinary practitioner. It is, however, possible to identify some commonalities that will be nuanced differently in different disciplines, but will be recognizable in some form across all of them—and my account below will try to identify some such commonalities.

[28] The language of apprenticeship is deeply gendered—and not simply because the title 'Master' is so hard to avoid. The language of apprenticeship easily conjures up a picture of paternal authority, guild hierarchy, and corporal punishment, which should make us deeply uncomfortable. My account of 'willingness to judge' and 'openness to being judged below is intended in part to remove some of the baggage that the account of apprenticeship in this section may have dropped on us.

recipe-governed) such products and codifications.[29] Training for disciplinary excellence therefore takes the form, not simply of training in the following of rules and recipes, nor of the production of good works, but in becoming a certain kind of well-formed person.

To put it another way, all university learning properly takes the form of learning a craft—indeed, it takes the form of a craft succession. University education, if it is to be capable of teaching disciplinary and professional excellence, has to involve the formation of extended relationships between masters and apprentices, those more fully formed in the relevant virtues, and those as yet less fully formed who become more fully formed by joining in with the master's practice. It has to involve a fairly lengthy period of formation in which the apprentice learns to internalize the patterns of perception and judgement displayed by his masters, to acquire the practical wisdom that allows such perception and judgement to be exercised well in different circumstances, and so to become himself or herself the master rather than the servant of the formal patterns of the discipline. The apprentice is schooled to become a master himself or herself, moving from following the craft's rules and recipes, to imitation of its virtuous practitioners, to increasingly independent exercise of the perception and judgement in which he or she has been steeped.

Even at this level of generality, to focus on university learning as apprenticeship makes a difference. The nature of apprenticeship as lengthy discipline, for instance, means that one cannot think of university education *simply* in terms of bite-sized chunks, each complete in itself, with the overall process of learning conceived as an accumulation of such chunks. (I am not convinced that anyone really thinks like that, of course; I suspect it is a scary story told by academic parents to their children to keep them behaving well. Nevertheless, it is a useful foil for more interesting ideas.) Modularity needs to be contained within a more carefully designed discipline. For instance, in my university (as in many others), students pick from a range of modules—mostly term-length courses on a particular topic with a particular tutor; they take three or four modules at any one time. Their overall pattern of study is made up of a mixture of compulsory modules and optional modules, with the precise mix depending on the degree that the student is aiming for.[30] This modularity,

---

[29] Not everybody can write a *Principia Mathematica*—you need a Bertrand Russell and an Alfred North Whitehead. Having the persons gets you the book, whereas having the book does not get you the persons.

[30] A typical undergraduate might arrive at 18, having spent the previous two years studying a fairly narrow range of subjects, often clustered within a particular area—maths and a small number of science subjects, perhaps, or a small collection of core humanities disciplines. He or she will then typically spend three years studying a single honours course (Theology, perhaps, or Engineering, or Drama), perhaps choosing all his or her modules from that subject area, perhaps availing himself or herself of the element of allowed modular flexibility and taking a module or two in other subjects along the way.

however, can work only because there is a framework of levels and progression—that is, a system of introductory modules, intermediate modules, advanced modules—with changing styles of teaching, changing class sizes, and changing forms of assessment as the student advances. That encompassing structure means that, whatever freedom students have to choose topics, and to follow their own wishes, they are nevertheless held within a longer-term discipline whose overall shape has been designed for them. Whatever the techniques used to make it happen, with apprenticeship there can be no getting away from that note of *obedience*—of the students following an extended discipline, a form of rigorous training, that in significant part has been laid out for them.

The idea of apprenticeship also provides a way of thinking about two of the popular phrases from recent discussions of academic life: 'research-led teaching' and 'practice-led teaching'. To the extent that apprenticeship is our watchword, we will not take these phrases to mean that teaching can be carried out only by those whose commitment to research is reflected in formal presence of research in their contracts, nor in the recognition of their research outputs in some Research Excellence Framework or tenure process. Rather, we will expect that, in a system of formation by apprenticeship, disciplinary excellence will be taught by those who live and breathe the apprehension and the processes of judgement involved in their discipline, and who show in their own bodies the virtues of their discipline at work. And we can expect that the learning appropriate to their teaching of disciplinary virtue will have a strong component of *imitation* in it—or at least of *participation*: the academic teacher is forming students to participate in her own practice alongside her, to inhabit her own apprehension.

This is not to say that all teaching will have to take the form of seminars and projects, in which shared practice is the dominant mode. Lectures—even to very large groups—might be one of the central elements in such teaching, at least in some disciplines. But such lectures will not (at least, not centrally) consist in the presentation of *results*—but in invitations to follow processes of enquiry and judgement at work: a making explicit of the lecturer's virtuous intellectual working. Any lecturing that systematically hides the labour of thought is problematic. As Karl Jaspers said: 'Lectures are of value when they become a genuine part of a professor's life and work, when they are prepared with care and at the same time inimitably reflect contemporary intellectual life.'[31]

---

[31] Karl Jaspers, *The Idea of a University*, ed. Karl W. Deutsch, tr. H. A. T. Reiche and H. F. Vanderschmidt from the 1946 edition of *Die Idee der Universität* (London: Peter Owen, 1960), 70. Cf. Alfred North Whitehead, 'The Universities and their Function', from *The Aims of Education and Other Essays* (New York: Macmillan, 1929), 97: 'Imagination is a contagious disease...It can only be communicated by a faculty whose members themselves wear their learning with imagination.'

My mention of lecturing 'even to very large groups' suggests another issue: an apprenticeship-based, research-led vision of teaching is likely to have implications for student numbers, or at least for the way in which high student numbers are approached. Apprenticeship will take many different forms, but, because it is a mode of teaching in which the direct relationship between teacher and student is central, it is not straightforwardly compatible with forms of high-volume teaching in which that relationship is inevitably attenuated.[32] In an apprenticeship, the master is not simply held up as a model to apprentices at a distance, but is actively involved in winning the apprentices into her own practice, and in disciplining their untrained efforts. If excellence is embodied primarily in persons, then it is only by forms of intensive interaction with the relevant persons that such winning and disciplining can properly take place. This may mean that in some contexts economics will dictate that the picture of education that I am setting out really comes into its own only at the graduate level, or at best the upper undergraduate level, where student numbers tend to be smaller. Where high student numbers are unavoidable, however, it is still possible to find ways in which something of the intensity of interaction is captured: master classes, in which a large class is not simply invited to watch the teacher, but to watch the teacher engaging intensively with volunteer students; hierarchical arrangements in which small groups are taught by teaching assistants who are themselves being taught by a more experienced teacher; and so on. What matters is that these more complex models are thought through carefully in terms of the patterns of relationship involved, the patterns of imitation and of participation in shared practices of virtue that they allow, and the place they give to those who have been most fully formed in academic virtue. The pursuit of such academic virtue is not going to be compatible with models of teaching that simply emphasize one-on-many teaching, and the mass delivery and distribution of content; it will instead inevitably be a matter of interaction, participation, and imitation. Teaching and learning are fundamentally personal.

The last implication I want to mention is a touchy one. It is that, if teachers are teaching by imitation, embodying for their students the virtues of their discipline, and if one cannot neatly separate out well-defined intellectual or disciplinary virtues from other virtues of courage, honesty, reliability, and courtesy, then we cannot be indifferent to broader questions of virtue and responsibility among the teaching staff—not, again, because a university needs to supply some moral formation *alongside* disciplinary and professional

---

[32] Note that the centrality of the master–apprentice relationship suggests that, where possible, those faculty members most deeply embedded in their disciplines and most fully formed in them, and who most clearly and attractively embody its virtues, should be directly involved in teaching as much as possible—and that *may* mean that senior faculty members need to be more involved in teaching than they sometimes are. There are, however, some non-sequiturs in this argument that require careful attention.

formation (though some universities will claim to do so), but precisely because we claim to supply disciplinary and professional formation. University teaching is inherently and unavoidably a moral endeavour.

OPENNESS TO JUDGEMENT 1: WILLINGNESS TO JUDGE

So much for the most general features of a virtue-centred account. We cannot get any further unless we start thinking about the particular virtues that are required for true learning. Here I am going to take a different tack from those followed by either Holt or Daston, and focus neither on apprehension nor on objectivity, but on a pair of virtues that I think yield a broadly plausible account of academic life, but that also connect very directly to the theology outlined in the previous chapter.[33] Elsewhere I have referred to these virtues as 'boldness and reserve';[34] here, more clumsily, I refer to 'willingness to judge' and 'openness to being judged'. As my account over the next two sections progresses, it will become clear how deeply these connect to the discussion in Chapter 5 of participation in Christ's crucifixion and resurrection.

So, first: willingness to judge. I have had trouble finding the right phrase to use to name this virtue, and 'willingness to judge' captures only very imperfectly what I have in mind. What I have in mind is not simply the virtue of somebody who, growing in the virtue of apprehension, is able to make well-formed judgements. It is, rather, of somebody who has learnt to see herself as *invited and enabled* to make such judgements. This virtue finds its most excellent form in a person who has become an excellent judge—Holt's Renaissance *magister*, perhaps, possessed of subtle and sophisticated apprehension—but who recognizes that this apprehension is not simply and straightforwardly her own, but is an apprehension that has been given to her, into which she has been drawn, that now works through her, and that still calls her to deepen and refine her judgement. For the novice, who is at the beginning of the path towards this goal, this virtue will show itself in the recognition that he has been welcomed into the activity of judging, and is already beginning to be capable of making some well-formed judgements—and that he does so as one who is now caught up in a process that will form those judgements more fully. It will show itself in his being able to give himself over to the process of judging and learning to judge better.

---

[33] I am also not following their lead and looking at the specific configurations of virtue that shape individual disciplines—though such an investigation into the moral economies of particular disciplines is a necessary continuation of the more general analysis I set out here.

[34] Mike Higton, 'Boldness and Reserve: A Lesson from St Augustine', *Anglican Theological Review*, 85/3 (2003), 445–56.

Let me put this more simply. If students are to be formed in virtuous apprehension—in the ability to see distinctions and connections well—and so made ready to judge, it is not enough that their heads be filled with examples of their teacher's judgements. They need to be invited into the process of making such judgements themselves, and that will demand of them that they are willing to be so invited, and willing to take the first risky steps of response.

In humanities disciplines like my own, this invitation can be a difficult one to convey to students who want to know what is expected of them. Students regularly ask, when preparing to write an essay, 'Do you want me to give my own opinions?', and will as regularly claim to have been given different answers by their various teachers: they think they have been told by some that they should keep their own ideas to themselves, by others that they should share them. Both answers are, of course, wrong: we do not want their *opinions*; we want their (increasingly independent, and increasingly well-formed) *judgements*. The difficulty is that many students arrive with plenty of opinions, but not much recognition that they might be invited to judge.

I have sometimes told my students to imagine that they are judges in a court of law, tasked with providing a written judgement. Their job is to summarize evidence and testimony, explain the defence case that is built from that evidence and testimony and the prosecution case built on the same evidence and testimony, and then explain their judgement of the case. To act as judge is not the same as acting as counsel for the defence or for the prosecution, nor is it the same as acting as an expert witness. It means taking responsibility for weighing the cases made, overall and in their details, and giving a clear statement of one's adjudication and of the reasoning that led to it. I tell my students that I am looking for their *own* judgements, certainly—but that this is very different from asking for their opinions.

The invitation to judgement is not an invitation to think that one's judgement is already fully formed. I arrived at university to study mathematics, not theology, and the question of whether I should be giving my own opinion or not was not one that came up a lot, when I was faced with sheets of problems to solve. Nevertheless, some of the same processes were involved. The example seared most deeply into my mind is from the interview I had when applying for a place studying maths. I found myself in a room with two mathematicians, and a blackboard on which was drawn a network dotted with numbers, which my interviewers explained were the maximum loads that each arc of the network could carry. They asked me what the maximum total load was that the network as a whole could carry, from its leftmost to its rightmost nodes. I sat there for some time in silence, trying to work it out, and they were just beginning to offer sympathetic (and probably slightly weary) advice, when I blurted out the right answer. The fact that I had reached the right answer did not, of course, matter at all. What mattered was that the two interviewers then led me to talk through the processes I had gone through in arriving at that answer, helping me to identify the assumptions that I had been making, helping me see that my process of working contained the germ of a general answer to this kind of question, and helping me to identify some potential problem cases and limits. I do not know how well it worked as a diagnostic tool for interview purposes, but in other ways the process was exemplary. I was invited in to a process of judgement-making, and enabled to see how my judgements, naive as they were, were initial, faltering steps on the way to virtuous judgement. Their patience and encouragement, their elicitation of my answer, was crucial—and provided them with the material (my judgement) on which it was then possible to work (training me for more excellent judgement).

As a third example, I want to mention a practice explained to me by Chris Rust.[35] In some of the modules I teach, we have a practice essay—a 'formative assignment'. The mark for this essay does not contribute to the final mark for the module, but the process of preparing it, and the feedback received on it, is supposed to help the students do well in later assignments that do so contribute. One way of handling such a formative assignment is to assign students to small groups, and then to ask each student to mark the formative essays of the other students in that group, providing them with a clear and detailed set of marking criteria, and a template for the kind of feedback that they should provide. The point of such an exercise is not so much the feedback that each student receives from her peers: such feedback is inevitably uneven, and sometimes mistaken. The point is, rather, the student's experience of being invited to judge other people's work with the criteria that will eventually be used to judge her own. The student is, more explicitly than if she had simply received judgements on her own work from a tutor, however lavishly informative that feedback might have been, invited to see herself as a judge whose judgement (and not simply her ability to survive someone else's judgement) is being formed.

If a university is to be a training ground for virtuous judgement, then it needs to be an environment that elicits judgements from students, inviting them in to the process of judgement-making. Such a process requires from teachers a welcoming delight in the apprehensions of their students, such as they are—as well as the forms of correction and critique that are necessary if the students' judgement is to be trained. Students need to be able to recognize themselves as those on the way to well-formed judgement, who have already begun to judge—just as, in the narratives discussed in the previous chapter, the disciples became disciples when they were welcomed to the process of

---

[35] Chris Rust, 'Student Assessment: Lightening the Load while Increasing the Learning', paper delivered at the University of Exeter's 2008 Education Conference on Assessment and Feedback.

discipleship, and saw that their fulfilment as disciples was already visible to their master. To put this another way round, the first rule of teaching is, 'Do not disdain your students.'

This calls, I think, for a learning environment that is, fundamentally, *secure*; an environment that says to the learner: you are welcome, you belong, you are accepted, and you now have the support and the freedom to experiment with judgement. That has implications for our ways of welcoming and including new students and new staff; it has implications for the physical environment in which we work. It is not, for instance, frivolous to spend some of our very limited institutional cash on hospitality for students, on making teaching rooms bearable, on giving students spaces for their own study that are not overtly hostile. We need to balance the need for efficient, cost-effective use of space with the need to provide ecologies within which students can feel that they belong: long-term, habitable, and hospitable niches in which they can put down firm roots. It is not that we need opulence or even great comfort (though looking round the buildings in which I have worked, I do not think that is a danger we need to guard against very assiduously). But we do need an environment that provides individual and communal spaces and facilities within which people can flourish without anxiety. And this is not a peripheral matter, located somewhere at the soft and silly edge of that separable topic, 'student welfare': it has to do with conditions that will allow for learning. It has to do with providing enough basic security that students can have the courage to step out in judgment.[36]

OPENNESS TO JUDGEMENT 2: OPENNESS TO BEING JUDGED

There is, of course, another side to the equation. If judgement needs to be elicited and welcomed, it also needs to be disciplined. An academic discipline is, after all, nothing other than a school of formation in disciplined judgement.

Let me approach this by way of an example. The example is a personal one, and refers to one aspect of my experience of writing a Ph.D. The particular experience I have in mind is that of struggling with the idea that one lengthy part of my Ph.D. should be deleted. My idea had been to combine a theological study of the work of the American theologian Hans Frei with a study of a particular congregation in Cambridge, in order to show that the concepts and arguments with which Frei was working connected in interesting ways to

---

[36] You could say that providing decent rooms is a properly academic matter. A pithier though somewhat more gnomic slogan would be: decent coffee is an epistemological issue.

patterns of practice and habits of thought among 'ordinary' Christians. My commitment to this strange combination was very strong, and I put a great deal of effort into it. Over several years, this effort had become part of my self-perception, and part of my self-presentation: I was a theologian, but not just any kind of theologian—I was a theologian who also did ethnography, a theologian who tried to pay serious attention to the muddles of ordinary Christian practice. And, by the end of the Ph.D., that is simply who I was.

And yet: behind the scenes I was finding it persistently difficult to tie the conceptual knots that would bind together my study of Hans Frei and my study of this congregation. I built various conceptual and argumentative bridges between the two, but never got to the point where I was completely happy that I had established my case. I worked hard at it, and produced various schemes that looked good on paper, but I was, I think, constantly aware at some level that, whenever I had built a bridge that looked firm and usable on paper, I had done so at some loss to the seriousness and attentiveness of my study both of Frei and of the congregation. Those two studies did not want to sit together: they did not want to be made to speak with a common voice, as parts of a single argument—and I felt their resistance as I pushed them together. I did not admit this, of course: I had committed so much time, so much effort, so much of my public image—so much of *myself* to doing the project in this way. I could not admit it to myself, let alone to anyone else. And so eventually, despite my misgivings, it made it into the final Ph.D.; I passed the viva, and was awarded my doctorate. But almost as soon as the viva was over, and one kind of pressure to make the Ph.D. succeed relaxed, I finally admitted that the attempt—interesting though I still think it was—had been a failure. I had ended up misrepresenting Frei, and I had ended up misrepresenting the congregation, in order to make sure that my argument worked—not maliciously, not with any kind of deliberate falsification, but simply because I had not been brave enough to allow the difficulty of my subject matter to overthrow my neat ideas, and make me start again.

Now, it seems to me that one way of describing what happened there is that I failed to *learn*. Of course, I learnt all sorts of things, and picked up all sorts of skills—just as anyone who spends four years doing a Ph.D. must. There is much in my Ph.D. that I still think is pretty good. And actually, there is a more subtle point here. It was only because I learnt all sorts of things—only because I read a ton of ethnographic and social anthropological literature, only because I had read widely and, I hope, deeply in the theology of Hans Frei and in his sources and colleagues and conversation-partners—only because I had accumulated the Ph.D. student's usual bundle of microscopically detailed, massively obscure knowledge—that I was able to register the resistance that threatened to break my Ph.D. in two in the first place. Nevertheless, despite having learnt all that, I still failed to do justice to my subject matter, in one quite fundamental way. And that failure can be described as a failure to be open to being judged. When the realization finally got through to me, it was with a feeling of disillusionment—in the strict sense that I felt an illusion being stripped away: an illusion about my subject matter, but also an illusion about myself. I was left in a far less controllable, far less secure position: determined to rewrite the Ph.D. in the light of this stark realization, dropping the part that had not worked (despite all that I had invested in it)—even though that meant letting go of any very clear idea of where I was headed, and (for quite some time) any very clear idea of what kind of a theologian I was. And I knew that, if I were to avoid a similar failure to learn, I needed to be willing to be overturned, judged, condemned, and remade as I continued to study. I could only learn to the extent that I gave up on security, and on a strong sense of control over my direction.[37]

We only truly learn to the extent that, alongside all the other forms of learning in which we participate, we also open up our ways of thinking and acting to judgement, running the risk of discovering that we are deluded. Learning involves bringing the ways of thinking and acting that we have acquired up against the reality they purport to describe, or against the reality with which they claim to be engaged, and holding open the possibility that our ways of thinking and acting will be broken in the encounter.[38] It is—as my decision to illustrate it with a personal narrative is supposed to suggest—an inherently personal process.

Academic *strength* is directly proportional to academic *vulnerability*. But that simply reinforces the idea I discussed in the previous section, that good learning requires a particular kind of environment—one in which it is safe to make oneself vulnerable in this way. It requires an environment in which it is acceptable to change one's mind, to get things wrong, to get a negative result, to reach an unpopular conclusion. It requires an environment in which one's welcome is not worn out if one tries and fails.[39]

---

[37] I rewrote the material on Frei from scratch, and it was eventually published as *Christ, Providence and History: Hans W. Frei's Public Theology* (London: Continuum, 2004).

[38] We need to keep in mind the words of Oliver Cromwell: 'I beseech you, in the bowels of Christ, think it possible you may be mistaken' (Letter to the General Assembly of the Kirk of Scotland, 3 August 1650, Letter 136 in Thomas Carlyle (ed.), *Oliver Cromwell's Letters and Speeches*, iii (New York: Scribner, Welford and Co., 1871), 18; <www.gasl.org/refbib/Carlyle__ Cromwell.pdf> (accessed 15 June 2010)).

[39] Cf. Hauerwas, *State of the University*, 23. Academic freedom is not a variant of freedom of speech, nor is it a freedom from any form of scrutiny by those who fund academic life. Rather, it is the freedom necessary to our virtues: the freedom to make judgements; the freedom to change one's mind in the face of the evidence (to do what in political life would be the suicide of 'flip-flopping' or 'performing a U-turn'); the freedom to attend for strange lengths of time to difficult matters; the freedom to follow lines of thought and study insistently, however far down the rabbit hole they lead; the freedom to be surprised. If one thinks of academic freedom in this way, then the threats to academic freedom come in multiple forms. Yes, from time to time, the threat takes the form of explicit interference with what academics are allowed to say. But, more often, they are more subtle—and have to do with the ways that the gravitational pull of money distorts the

To be open to judgement requires formation in a number of other virtues. It requires, for instance, clarity. After all, if I am woolly enough and cut corners enough in this book, I may be able to render it all but invulnerable to critique. I may be able to make it spongy and elastic enough to allow me to ride any punch that reviewers can throw at me—spongy and elastic for me to trundle over any obstacle without noticing it.[40] And all I need to do to promote such sponginess and elasticity is to settle back and not try very hard to think. Woolliness seems to be something like a default state for human conduct. On the other hand, I will only say something worth listening to in this book if the proposals I make have enough content to them, and enough structure to them, to allow them to be criticized, to allow me to be called to account by having counter-examples, or gaps in my argument, or alternative ways of seeing things, or disastrous consequences of what I have said, brought to my attention. To clarify our ways of thinking and acting, therefore, can be a way of stiffening the flabby and woolly ways in which we engage with the world, and so of allowing new and deeper ways of opening ourselves up to questioning and testing—to the possibility of discovering that we are heading in a mistaken direction.[41]

In order for this process to work, one also needs to be formed in a virtue we can call integrity.[42] In this context, integrity means ensuring that the justifications that one offers in support of one's judgements fairly represent (as far as is possible) the reasons one truly has for those judgements, such that a critique that tackles those offered justifications is to the point rather than wasted breath. Integrity is a matter of making sure that one is really made available, really exposed, by what one says. Such integrity is not always easy, and may be only very partially possible—after all, knowing one's real reasons for a judgement is a difficult and complex matter. But aiming for integrity, and thereby aiming for vulnerability, is vital if one is to learn.[43]

---

paths that lines of enquiry take, or the ways that inappropriate forms of reward and recognition work against the virtues of patience and openness to judgement. And, even more subtly, they have to do with the spread of cultures of distrust, and of the disappearance of safety in vulnerability. Such threats to academic freedom do not simply make the lives of academics and students less pleasant and less privileged, as if they were a luxury that in austere times we will have to learn to do without: they leach our capacity to learn properly, and our capacity to discern and witness to the truth.

[40] In my experience, many student essays have not yet achieved the status of being wrong, precisely because they have not achieved the right kind of clarity. On the other hand, my friend Rachel Muers reports recently writing on a first-class exam paper, 'everything you say is open to debate and/or further development, but that is a good sign'.

[41] I cannot resist putting this into two slogans. First: 'Knowledge is what enables one to be wrong', and second: 'Only pedants are truly open-minded.'

[42] See Rowan Williams, 'Theological Integrity', in Rowan Williams, *On Christian Theology* (Oxford: Blackwell, 2000), 3–15.

[43] This provides one useful way of thinking about plagiarism. It is not so much a problematic disregard of academic property rights as it is a problematic refusal of academic vulnerability—a

Most fundamentally, the process of opening oneself up to judgement requires formation in attentiveness: the labour of putting oneself in a position to encounter judgement, settling oneself into alertness to the resistances of one's subject matter, and *waiting* to be addressed. Such waiting involves dwelling with one's subject matter in the light of the judgements that one is already involved in making; it involves a willingness to commit time and labour beyond what is necessary, beyond what is expedient, to one's subject matter, in the hope of that address.

At every stage in the process of learning to judge well, one has some machinery of perception and judgement to bring to bear on the object of one's study. One is, however, not exhausted by that machinery, however well embedded it might be in one's ways of seeing, one's ways of being in the world. Attentiveness names the capacity we have for being called out of the current settlement of our ideas and practices by something resembling *loving* attention to their objects—the readiness to register the ways in which they do not match our expectations, and require something else of us if we are to do justice to them.[44]

Such attentiveness takes time. My own experience when writing, for instance, is often of needing to walk away from what I am doing, calm down (and face away from the deadline), and take the time to hear the still, small voice alerting me to some point of resistance in what I have written so far—and then of needing to resign myself to the labour involved in discovering what it would take to do real justice to that problem. There is no telling in advance the scale of the rewriting that will be triggered by attention to the smallest of such resistances.

Efficiency is therefore a dangerous word when it comes to academic work. Often what one needs are not practices that achieve maximum throughput but practices that slow one down, and force one to walk through territory through which it would be all too easy to run.[45] Taking time is, however, difficult for

---

removal of oneself from the line of fire of academic judgement by hiding behind someone else's judgements, someone else's reasons—and without it being clear that one is doing so.

[44] See also Paul Lakeland, 'The Habit of Empathy: Postmodernity and the Future of the Church-Related College', in Stephen R. Haynes (ed.), *Professing in the Postmodern Academy: Faculty and the Future of Church-Related Colleges* (Waco, TX: Baylor University Press, 2002), 33–48, and Denis Robinson, '*Sedes Sapientiae*: Newman, Truth and the Christian University', in Jeff Astley, Leslie Francis, John Sullivan, and Andrew Walker (eds), *The Idea of a Christian University: Essays on Theology and Higher Education* (Bletchley and Waynesborough, GA: Paternoster, 2004), 75–97.

[45] Quite deliberately, for example, I take extensive handwritten notes when reading a book seriously, often copying long passages out verbatim. I might then type up large swathes of those notes in the first stages of writing, before selecting the precise sentences and passages that I am going to quote. This looks like a very inefficient technique if one is simply thinking about transferring the relevant words from their starting place to their destination. It does, however, ensure that those words spend longer in my head on the way through than they might otherwise.

multiple reasons. Academic culture can easily become dominated by short-termism. It is found when students leave their essays until the last minute—perhaps forced by their paid work and by badly thought-through timetables (the bad thinking both theirs and their teachers'). But it also deeply shapes academic research culture. In a UK context, for instance, one of the biggest problems with the Research Excellence Framework (REF)[46] is that it fundamentally skews our perception of time. Even if the number of publications that any one academic needs to submit is small, and the timescale allowed quite long, the process ends up shaping the whole mentality with which we approach research time—and so makes a far more profound difference than its relatively modest targets actually require.

To live with the REF, with its absolute deadlines rolling around every few years, means discovering ways of managing long-term projects—indeed, perhaps more importantly, indeterminate-term projects—in an environment that demands that one publish substantive pieces of work on a predefined timetable. It is certainly possible, but it involves standing to one side of the process. One needs to know the direction in which one wants to head, and the forms of extended engagement that one wishes to pursue, and then to work out how to build a series of short-term projects that will provide contexts in which to spend time with the material, the conversation partners, the thinking that one needs to do. One of my colleagues, David Horrell, set out some years ago on the pathway towards a commentary on 1 Peter, intending to spend at least a decade working with a text of roughly two thousand Greek words. That in itself is an idea that the accounting frameworks in which our research is measured cannot accommodate: there is no credit to be earned for being on the way to such a distant horizon. Nevertheless, with that goal in mind, it is possible to play the system—to discover how to treat it not as a series of hurdles that stand frustratingly between one and one's goal, but as a foundation on which to build stepping stones: projects and publications in which some aspect of that overall project is pursued, and time spent with some subset of the material with which one needs to dwell.

Closely allied to the virtue of patience is the virtue of openness to the unexpected.[47] My current perception of my goals, the current language I have for describing where I am going, is part of what will need to be transformed as I learn. There may simply be no ways in which I can describe now where my learning will take me—no ways that are available to

---

[46] The REF is a periodic centralized review of the research output produced by publicly funded university departments in the UK, and successor to the infamous Research Assessment Exercise. For more on the REF, see below, Ch. 7, pp. 212–14.

[47] Cf. Max Weber, 'Science as a Vocation', in *From Max Weber: Essays in Sociology*, tr. H. H. Gerth and C. Wright Mills (New York: Oxford University Press, 1946), 129–56; <www.ne.jp/asahi/moriyuki/abukuma/weber/lecture/science_frame.html> (accessed 15 June 2010): 'The primary task of the useful teacher is to teach his students to recognize "inconvenient" facts.'

me before I undergo the process of transformation that will lead me there. The process of learning is, at its deepest, a process of unmaking and remaking. And because of that, to put it bluntly, if you know where you are going, you are not learning.

In the learning envisaged in Christian theology, we are not *nearly* complete selves who can examine and understand the gaps in our lives and then cast about for what thing will fill them, what thing will complete us. Learning is not a matter of desire-and-gratification. True learning is tied to a fundamentally different kind of desire: an *incurable* desire—a desire whose pursuit leads not to desire's death but to its growth. True learning involves not the satisfying of desire but desire's redirection and expansion; it involves what has been called a 'steady and endless enlarging of the heart'.[48]

Learning opens us out so that we can see more of what we still need to learn—it draws us into wider conversations that whisper to us of more distant voices that we did not even know we had ignored—and, when we finally hear those voices, they will speak to us of still more distant, still more unexpected, voices waiting on the edges of our perception. We only discover what we are lacking, and therefore discover the shape of our desire, as we learn—and that discovery is as unending as learning.

Learning as gratification is learning that can be surveyed in detachment from its beginning, the whole course seen laid out in front of us leading to clearly visible goals, in a process that does not fundamentally break out of the categories we now have. It is learning that leaves us as we are. It is safe, because it is dead. Real learning, on the other hand, learning bound up with true, incurable desire, overwhelms us and puts us at risk. It is, quite properly, out of our control.

If you can specify exactly where you are going, you are not learning, you are just playing within an existing system; you are putting nothing at risk. Real learning is inherently system-shaking, inherently non-algorithmic. It inherently takes us beyond our existing resources. There is something vertiginous about real learning.

And this has some serious practical consequences. In my university, every course that we put on has to be described on a document called a 'Module Descriptor'. The conceptual centre of the Module Descriptor is a box labelled 'Intended Learning Outcomes'—the glue that holds together the whole vision of learning that those innocent descriptors encode.[49] Assignments should emerge from them; assessment should be testing them; the syllabus should be pursuing them. Yet one must be extraordinarily careful as one pursues this kind of description—careful that one does not design learning out of the system. Because, as I have just said, it is fundamental to the deepest

---

[48] Rowan Williams, *Arius: Heresy and Tradition* (London: SCM, 2001), 243.
[49] See above, n. 24.

kinds of learning—the kinds of learning that we should be most concerned to allow—that they blow the idea of a ready description of intended learning outcomes out of the water. It is the *unintended* learning outcomes that really matter.

CONCLUSION

I have been experimenting with a description of academic life in terms of virtue, attempting descriptions that do not wear their theological origins on their sleeves, and that might therefore be available to those who have approached similar territory from a different direction—but that are nevertheless constructed as riffs on the theological account of learning that I developed in Chapter 5.

The picture I have painted so far is, in effect, of academic disciplines as *spiritual* disciplines. I hesitate to use the word 'spiritual', because it is now so debased—and I have no intention to lead my reader over to the 'Mind, Body and Spirit' shelf in the bookshop, with all the books on crystals and astral projection. I use it because the kind of learning that goes with formation in virtue is not something learners simply do or acquire; it involves processes in which learners are themselves deeply shaped. Indeed, as I have argued, this learning is inherently one in which the learning self is at stake. This kind of learning involves the shaping of emotions and values, of deep orientations, of pervasive ways of seeing. And not just that, but the process of shaping involved is one that involves both being killed and being raised to new life—crucifixion and resurrection. It involves being welcomed into new, virtuous life and discovering that one has that life growing in one; it involves allowing the death of the old patterns of apprehension and judgement that shaped our lives. This is the fundamental shape of a spiritual discipline.[50]

It is because of this that I can see what I am doing—within a secular university focused on disciplinary and professional education, without transgressing the boundaries that such a context properly imposes—as a labour to draw myself and others deeper into something of Christ-like life. It may be concerned only with limited aspects of that life, maybe—but they are real aspects nonetheless. I would not go so far as to say that I am labouring to form disciples (I am not, after all, forming people in intentional devotion to Christ or worship with Christ of Christ's Father), but I am nevertheless seeking to

---

[50] Cf. Parker J. Palmer, 'Toward a Spirituality of Higher Education', in Douglas V. Henry and Bob R. Agee (eds), *Faithful Learning and the Christian Scholarly Vocation* (Grand Rapids, MI: Eerdmans, 2003), 75–85, and J. P. Moreland, *Love God with All Your Mind: The Role of Reason in the Life of the Soul* (Colorado Springs, CO: NavPress, 1997).

develop something proximate to that: a life of openness to judgement that in its own way echoes the dynamic of crucifixion and resurrection that shapes discipleship. I am participating, to the extent that I do my university job well, in something of the person-forming work of the Spirit.

There is much more that still needs to be said, however, and in Chapter 8 I will have a good deal to say about the purpose and public import of all this learning. I will try to do justice to the fact that the formal virtues that I have discussed in this chapter are not themselves enough, without some more substantive connection to pursuit of the good, and to the fact that we cannot talk for long about virtue in the university without talking about how it connects to patterns of virtue in the wider society within which universities sit.

In the next chapter, however, I will return to a hint already dropped in this. A Christian account of virtue, I suggested, is not going to be as *heroic* as the Aristotelian account set out by Holt: it will not so easily have at its heart intellectual virtuosi who stand in isolation as the paradigms of virtue. Rather, virtue will be a matter of formation for the life of the Body of Christ, which means formation for fellowship, or for what Schleiermacher called free sociality. Real learning is inherently social, and the paradigm of learning will be a certain kind of community.

7

The Sociable University

Towards the end of the seventeenth century, a select band of optical pioneers spent an extraordinary number of hours with eyes pressed up to the single lenses of bead microscopes, patiently exploring the world of the very, very small. It takes practice to see anything at all with such lenses, but the resulting magnifications can, it seems, be astonishing. Antoni van Leeuwenhoek, for instance, used such a microscope to prepare drawings of the testicles of fleas; Jan Swammerdam spent months working constantly from half five in the morning until noon, using with almost unimaginable patience and rigour a battery of his own instruments and techniques to prepare a drawing of the ovaries of a queen bee.[1]

On another occasion, when he was dissecting the uterus of a snail, Swammerdam found a collection of tiny oblong worm-like organisms living inside it. On dissecting these worms—worms small enough to live inside the uterus of a snail—he found that each had within it a number of still smaller tadpole-shaped creatures, which could move about independently when placed in water. And when he examined, at the furthest limit of his skill with the lens, one of these tiny tadpoles—a tadpole small enough to live inside a worm itself small enough to live inside the uterus of a snail—he could dimly make out that it was itself composed of elements, which looked like grains of sand against the light. Astonished with each new revelation of detail, he confessed himself brought face to face with his 'ignorance and blindness as to the reason for all of this'.[2] A deeply pious man, he—as one historian puts it—'repeatedly linked the incomprehensibility and inscrutability of insect anatomies to the incomprehensibility and inscrutability of God, and at times explicitly identified his sense of something ungraspable looming before him in the lens with the divine aura still lingering about God's works'.[3] He even found something

---

[1] See Edward G. Ruestow, *The Microscope in the Dutch Republic: The Shaping of Discovery* (Cambridge: Cambridge University Press, 1996); cf. Lisa Jardine, *Ingenious Pursuits: Building the Scientific Revolution* (London: Little, Brown, 1999), chs 2–3; Leeuwenhoek's picture of the bee's organs is reproduced as plate 6 in Jardine's book.

[2] Quoted in Ruestow, *Microscope*, 139.

[3] Ruestow, *Microscope*, 141.

terrible in this wonder, and declared that 'strong, brave men must cleanse themselves of their sin before the aspect of his creatures'.[4] There is something *vertiginous* about real learning, I said in the previous chapter—and Swammerdam provides a near-perfect example: by means of finely honed apprehension (by means, that is, of patient mastery of his techniques and his instruments, and of a mind fitted for their use), he finds himself peering down into a hitherto unimagined depth of complexity, overmastered by a world of such teeming, gratuitous detail—a world that addresses him, and calls him to acknowledgement of his ignorance and his finitude. By means of patient and immensely skilful attention to the world, he hears a word that he could not have said to himself, and is overwhelmed, bowled over by it: made to reshape his ideas in the light of what addresses him.

It is important to notice, however, another aspect of these microscopists' work, which undercuts the impression that they were virtuosi striving in single combat with a world reluctant to give up its secrets, until—by means of their skills and patience—they were led to deeper and deeper levels of personal enlightenment and transformation, the individual recipients of profound epiphanies. It is true that it is not far wrong to imagine the microscopist spending long, solitary hours pressed to a tiny bead through which only one eye can look at once; it is also true that it is not far wrong to imagine him working largely on his own to develop his personal and sometimes secret range of skills and techniques, which will enable him to see what no one else has seen—these men were, after all, pioneers in largely uncharted territory. What one misses if one concentrates on these things, however, is that the learning in which these microscopists were engaged was profoundly *social*.

Some of Leeuwenhoek's first serious observations, for instance, were produced in response to the work of Robert Hooke. Hooke had published a book called *Micrographia* in 1665, containing engravings of things he had seen with his own microscopy equipment; Leeuwenhoek appears to have acquired a copy of the book in Dutch in 1674 and to have set about systematically testing and improving upon Hooke's observations.[5] Leeuwenhoek then sent his findings, and samples of the specimens that he had prepared, back to the Royal Society so that his tests and confirmations of Hooke's works could in turn be tested and confirmed by the circle around Hooke. In 1676, Leeuwenhoek sent to the Royal Society news of his own microscopical discovery: thousands of tiny creatures swimming around in ordinary water (or, to be more precise, ordinary water in which some pepper had been soaked); he sent details of this discovery to the Royal Society so that his observations could be tested and confirmed. It was about a year before the competitive Hooke was able to match

Leeuwenhoek's performance, but as soon as he did he reported back to the society and showed other members how to see these creatures. As an eighteenth-century description of the event puts it: 'They were seen by Sir Christopher Wren, Sir Jonas Moore, Dr Grew, Mr Aubrey, and divers others; so that there was no longer any doubt of Mr Leeuwenhoek's discovery.'[6]

It is an artificial restriction of the story to think of Leeuwenhoek or Swammerdam or Hooke or any of the others pursuing learning in isolation, journeying solo into the secrets of some private world. And I do not simply mean this in the rather banal sense that a serious history of anyone's learning is bound to be a social history. There is a particular sense that the men involved in this explosion of natural philosophical learning in the seventeenth century were engaged in a social learning process. However competitive they were, however obsessed with priority, they were learning from and with and for each other. Many of them seem to have seen themselves as something like members of an emerging clerisy—an emerging caste of learned learners, open to the world in new ways, working together (in cooperation and sometimes fierce competition) to go further into the mysteries of the world than any had gone before. And they seem also to have had a powerful sense that they were learning about a world they shared, to which no one person had esoteric access—and so believed that what they saw could and should be seen by others also, and that what others saw could therefore provide a confirmation or challenge to what they themselves had seen. Their learning was, therefore, thoroughly caught up in networks of exchange and accountability—both testing the work of others and being tested in their turn, and only in that way contributing to a movement of transformation that was of more than personal significance.

This sense of mutual accountability in the face of a single shared world was one of the most important kinds of glue holding together what we now call the Scientific Revolution. More practically, that revolution was held together in large part by the letters and pamphlets and reports and books carrying details of these men's investigations, circulating between scientific practitioners of various kinds—many of them, like Leeuwenhoek's weekly letters to the Royal Society, enabling other practitioners to hear about and test what the sender claimed to have seen or done. To put it only a little too bluntly, without mechanisms for the distribution of mail—without the practical means to pursue their strong sense of mutual accountability in the face of a shared world—the Scientific Revolution could never have happened. The Scientific Revolution was a postal phenomenon.

If you try to give an account of the learning that took place in the Scientific Revolution—the forms of accumulation and vulnerability that made for

---

[6] Quoted in Jardine, *Ingenious Pursuits*, 317.

whatever genuine learning took place—you cannot avoid entering the realm of *sociality*. As you try to describe that learning, you are, of course, going to need to talk about the magnifications that different forms of microscope made possible, and you are going to need to talk about the virtues of individual learners—but you are also going to need to think about all these letters winging back and forward, all that communication, competition, and accountability, all the strident criticism, and so about power relations, about answerability, about honesty and fairness, about friendships, about institutions, about *polity*.[7]

THE SOCIALITY OF LEARNING

In Chapter 1, I argued that, for at least some of the sages of Paris, one could learn the good ordering of one's materials only by participation in a certain kind of communal good: a community involved in the friendly exchange of calls to penitence before God, a community of mutual compunction, and of peaceable but serious disputation. In Chapter 2, I described the Berlin *Wissenschaftsideologie* as, in effect, an attempt to repair a world of Christian learning in which disputation was believed to have degenerated until it was anything but peaceable and serious. The Romantic theorists of *Wissenschaft* dug down to the vision of free, peaceable exchange—the economy of gift and reception in the Body of Christ—that they saw as the Christian world's most positive insight into the nature of learning. The rules of *Wissenschaft* were, they saw—even more clearly than their Parisian forebears—nothing other than the rules of free sociality; *Wissenschaft* lives, if it lives at all, only by means of free, attentive exchange. They then sought to remake the whole world of learning on the basis of that vision, revising or abandoning whatever in the world of Christian learning they could not make to fit with this vision of learning's free exchange of gifts or free sociality.

I suggested, however, that their repair of their religious heritage was undertaken with broken tools. The *Wissenschaftsideologie* speaks of a sociality in which I am free to participate *as myself*, and yet does not mean by that a sociality in which I can participate directly *as* a Christian theologian, one who inhabits and has been formed by a positive, authoritative tradition. The Romantic theorists read the invocation of such a tradition as my bringing to

---

[7] For an extended attempt to see the development and dissemination of theologies and philosophies in these terms, see Randall Collins, *The Sociology of Philosophies: A Global Theory of Intellectual Change* (Cambridge, MA: Belknap/Harvard University Press, 1998).

the academic table of an unavoidably heteronomous authority: an authority that will at some point require me to give answers other than those that I would have given left to the autonomous freedom of my spirit. Obedience to such an authority fundamentally undercuts the freedom of academic sociality, and so is directly and unavoidably destructive of *Wissenschaft*. Here and in Chapter 9, however, I will argue for a different account of free conversation, one that can allow the prior positive formation of the participants to play a decisive role—indeed, one in which the attempted exclusion of that positive formation from the conversation necessarily undercuts the freedom of the sociality generated, and so is itself directly and unavoidably destructive of reason.

Nevertheless, on the central point I am entirely in agreement with those Berlin theorists. Academic life, if it is to promote true learning, needs to take the form of a free sociality—an economy of gift and reception that resembles what Christian theology knows as the life of the Body of Christ. That is simply what learning is, and learning comes in no other form. I said in the previous chapter that we become better as learners the more we discover ways in which our forms of thinking and acting can be opened up to appropriate rebuff. Part of what is involved in learning is our duty to look for the ways in which our claims might appropriately be challenged—and, instead of defending ourselves from those appropriate challenges, heading out to meet them. But appropriate challenges to our ways of thinking and acting do not simply come from the reality that we observe or upon which we act—the reality that may turn out to resist or exceed our ideas and actions in unexpected ways. Appropriate challenges to our ways of thinking and acting also emerge through our attentiveness to others who think about and act towards the same world differently. Appropriate challenges emerge from critiques and reviews, from rejected grant applications and pointed seminar questions. Learning is inherently social.

We cannot be said to be learning in the full sense of the word if our ways of thinking and acting are not being exposed to the ways of thinking and acting of those who differ from us. Learning, if it is to involve growth in appropriate vulnerability, must involve growth in real exposure to other people's ideas—exposure of one's views to them, and of oneself to their views: exposure to their *difference* from oneself. And one might say that real knowledge (right thought and right action, justified belief, however one wants to define it) emerges only out of such processes of interaction; there is no solo route. Until this interaction has taken place, there can be no real knowledge. To put it another way: one academic cannot know anything—or better, no *single* academic can be said to know anything. The smallest unit that can be said to know anything is two academics disagreeing—or, at least, two academics who take seriously the fact that they are different, and learn from that fact; two academics who can hold one another to account.[8]

This inherent sociality of learning provides another meeting ground between my theology of learning and other accounts of university life. There is something ecclesial about good learning, and I can expect that to be recognized by at least some in the university who have no connection to or allegiance to the church—indeed, to some who would regard the church as the very opposite of a community of reason.

On the other hand, of course, from the point of view of my Christian formation, university sociality must look incomplete, ambiguous, and fragile. Nevertheless, I can recognize the university as a context in which Christians may, with caution, further pursue ecclesial sociality—further pursue the life of giving and receiving to which their faith calls them. As I said in the previous chapter, there will be something deeply coherent about coming from partici- pation in the Eucharistic liturgy on Sunday to work at the university on Monday morning.

It follows, however, that the university is made more fully itself to the extent that the freedom of its sociality, and the sociality of its freedom, are tended. The university simply *is* a certain kind of virtuous sociality—a certain kind of moral community—and to care about the university's flourishing must involve caring about the quality of the exchanges that constitute its life, the quality of its collegiality.[9] It therefore makes sense that Christian participants who share something of the theological vision of free sociality that I have set out may labour to make the university more fully sociable (however partial that sociality will necessarily remain), and that they are thereby labouring to make the university more reasonable. Because the vision of the university as a form of sociality is not only a possibility for Christians, however, it is also possible that Christians labouring to tend the university's sociality will find themselves labouring alongside, and collaborating with, others whose labours—though grounded in different ways—point in the same direction, at least some of the time.

Finally, it is therefore possible that universities can be contexts in which Christians might learn more fully something of what true sociality looks like and can be—in terms recognizable within their tradition, but spoken to them from outside. The university displays in its own peculiar, and peculiarly intense, way the dynamics of exchange involved in free sociality: the giving

---

[8] 'Intellectual inquiry ideally takes place within a community of self-transcending friendship founded upon a robust conception of the common good' (Alfred H. Freddoso, '*Fides et Ratio*: A "Radical" Vision of Intellectual Inquiry', in Alice Ramos and Marie I. George (eds), *Faith, Scholarship, and Culture in the 21st Century* (Washington: American Maritain Association/ Catholic University of America, 2002), 13–31: 17).

[9] In this chapter, I focus on the exchanges *within* the university; in the next chapter I pay more attention to exchanges *between* the university and its social environment.

and receiving, the discernment and acceptance, the challenges and invitations. The university therefore reflects back to the church from a particular angle the social life to which it is itself called, and might at times call the church to be more fully itself.

SOCIABLE TEACHING

University life is a conversation, and formation for full participation in it takes the form of a training in civility.[10] In the remainder of this chapter, I simply want to play with the ideas that *teaching* is conversational, and that *research* is conversational—putting off to Chapter 8 questions about interdisciplinary conversation, and to Chapter 9 questions about the university as a conversation about its own good. I am also putting off to Chapter 8 the fact that all these comments take on a political aspect if the extension of sociality to the excluded and oppressed is taken seriously.

'Conversation' and 'civility' may be the wrong words to use: to speak in these terms might suggest that the participants are simply learning to be nice to one another, to avoid giving offence, and to disguise their true disagreements behind a veneer of politeness. The form of sociality that I am describing, however, involves each participant taking the others seriously enough to disagree with them—to criticize, sometimes passionately and forcefully. It does not involve turning a genteel blind eye to intellectual *faux pas*; it is the exchange of informed judgement, and it is likely to issue not in false harmony, but in richer and more interesting disagreement. Nevertheless, its proper functioning *does* require forms of courtesy—forms of acknowledgement, of patient listening, and of painstaking questioning.

In such a conversational context, competition is only a secondary reality. I broadly agree with Michael Oakeshott:

The pursuit of learning is not a race in which the competitors jockey for the best place, it is not even an argument or a symposium; it is a conversation . . . A conversation does not need a chairman, it has no predetermined course, we do not ask what it is 'for', and we do not judge its excellence by its conclusion; it has no conclusion, but is always put by for another day. Its integration is not superimposed but springs from the quality of the voices which speak, and its value lies in the relics it leaves behind in the minds of those who participate.[11]

---

[10] Cf. Jaroslav Pelikan, *The Idea of a University: A Reexamination* (New Haven: Yale University Press, 1992), 55.

[11] Michael Oakeshott, 'The Idea of a University', *Listener*, 43 (1950), 424–6, repr. in *Academic Questions*, 17/1 (2003), 23–30: 25–6. For Oakeshott, the whole of human civilization can be considered a conversation (see Oakeshott, *The Voice of Poetry in the Conversation of Mankind:*

Of course, competition can be very important: think of two labs trying to solve the same problem, racing one another and acquiring extra energy and determination from the competition. But within each lab there will need to be non-competitive exchange in order for the lab to be able to pursue the competition with its rival; and for their results to contribute to the processes of human learning, they will eventually (however long they may be held up by systems of patent and copyright) need to become part of the wider conversational circulation of ideas, open for corporate testing and refinement. Competition is parasitic upon collaboration and conversation: it has its necessary place in academic sociality, but it is not (and cannot be) the final truth about that sociality.

If this is the character of intellectual life, then teaching can be understood as a process of inducting others into this form of sociality. In other words, teaching fits students to take part in the systems of exchange that constitute intellectual life—as both recipients and givers. University education is, fundamentally, a matter of a certain kind of *socialization*—a fact that once again makes it harder to draw sharp lines between the intellectual formation of students and their moral formation.

The attempt to understand teaching as a matter of induction into a certain kind of community can work on multiple levels. It involves the interaction of students with each other; it involves the interaction of students with their teachers; and it involves the interaction of students with the wider community of scholars in their discipline. (I am leaving to the next chapter questions about the interaction of students with scholars of other disciplines, and with communities of enquiry outside the university.)

To illustrate the interaction of students with the wider community of scholars in their discipline, let me quote the student handbook that I produced for a series of evening classes. The section on assessed work and mark schemes and so on is introduced with this preamble, explaining what we are looking for in an essay:

We are looking for evidence that you are able to join in the ongoing conversation we call theology. The mark you get will reflect how well you are managing to join in.

Imagine walking into a room where a conversation is already going on. Even if the conversation is about a topic you already know something about, you would do well to begin by listening carefully. You might then slowly pick up on the different perspectives and approaches being proposed by the speakers in the room. As you

---

An Essay (London: Bowes and Bowes, 1959), and cf. Richard Kyte, 'Conversation and Authority: A Tension in the Inheritance of the Church-related College', in Stephen R. Haynes (ed.), *Professing in the Postmodern Academy: Faculty and the Future of Church-related Colleges* (Waco, TX: Baylor University Press, 2002), 115–30.

become familiar with the conversation, you might *begin* to join in by saying to one or other of the participants, 'So, are you saying that...' and then trying to put *their* thoughts into your *own* words—trying to make sure you've understood where they are coming from. Eventually, you might feel confident enough to make your own positive contribution to the conversation, to state your own case: 'Well, *I* think that ...'.

You wouldn't be joining in, though, if you simply shouted an opinion and left: the others in the room will want to know your reasons—they will want to know how what *you* say relates to what *they* have said, and why you differ from them. And when you have given your arguments and cited your evidence, they may well come back at you, suggesting different interpretations or coming up with counter-arguments. Before you know it, you're in the thick of the conversation.

Keeping something like this image in mind can help when writing an essay, even though many of the voices you'll be arguing with will be in the books you read, rather than in the room around you.[12]

A good deal of what we are looking for in your essay is your ability to listen carefully to a range of authors, and to pick up on some of the different approaches and perspectives that exist. In other words, we're looking for a clear, fair, balanced account of the conversation that has already been taking place.

But we want you to go beyond simply listening: we want you to join in. That is, we're looking for you to build upon the kind of careful, fair listening just described, and then make your own relevant contribution: citing evidence and giving arguments designed to sway the other participants in the conversation. And you should ask yourself, as you make your own contribution: how might the people I'm arguing against respond? What counter-arguments might they have? What awkward evidence might they throw at me? We're not looking for the kind of contribution that brushes awkward evidence under the carpet, or that tries simply to overcome opposition by rhetoric: we're not looking for the kind of arguments put forward by politicians in television interviews. Rather, we're looking for your ability to join the conversation constructively, arguing your corner carefully and in detail, taking your opponents seriously and honestly.

This interaction with the wider community of scholars is inseparable, however, from interaction between students and teachers. I must admit that it was only after I had been using this handbook for some time that I realized that it raised a serious question about the nature of some of my marking and assessing practices. If I am asking my students to treat their essays as a contribution to a conversation, do I use the marking and feedback processes in a way that preserves that sense of conversation—or does any pretence at conversation stop at that point? It is hard to imagine anything *less*

---

[12] It is in this light that I justify two minor dislikes. On the one hand, I dislike the tendency to refer to the items that students find in libraries as 'learning resources'. On the other hand, I dislike Harvard referencing—the kind in which citations of other authors appear as, for example, '(Higton 1997: 27)'. The former makes it sound like books are commodities to be consumed; the second to my ear makes books sound like data sources, the Harvard reference appearing simply as an alphanumeric tag identifying the origin of a particular textual or conceptual fragment. Both seem to me to militate against seeing books as means of engagement with other human beings.

conversational than some ways of marking and returning essays. A student hands in her contribution to the conversation, and—after a long delay—gets back a *number*: 58 per cent. Or her work comes back embellished only with a few ticks. Or, more subtly, her work comes back with the conversation decisively closed: here, her tutor says, is where you were wrong, here is where you were right; end of discussion.

Of course, it is true that this is not an equal conversation. This is an exchange that takes place in an apprenticeship, and the student and teacher exist in a particular asymmetrical relationship that is vital to the learning process. Nevertheless, marking and feedback can still function as a way (one way) of carrying on a conversation or an argument—even though that requires a good deal more effort from the marker.[13] The opportunity is a limited one, of course: it is very often the case that the student has moved on to other topics by the time feedback is received, and that she will never be writing on this particular topic again—but it is often, nevertheless, possible to offer feedback that enables a student to hear how her work sounds to someone else, to understand the kinds of development it would need before it could be heard as a genuine contribution to the ongoing conversation, and to glimpse how the conversation might continue.

I have already said more about the interaction between students and teachers in the previous chapter, when discussing apprenticeship. In the present context, however, it is important to take that model of apprenticeship and insist that, rather than primarily being shaped by apprenticeship to an individual master, students are (or should be) shaped by apprenticeship to a community of teachers—and the virtues in which they are formed are not so much the possessions of individual virtuosi as they are characteristics of an intellectual community. The most memorable lectures from my own time as an undergraduate were those that involved a lively dialogue between two theologians who strongly disagreed—but who modelled in their interactions the nature of serious argument. It became far less easy to understand theology as a matter of the pronouncements of experts, with which one either agreed or disagreed, and far easier to understand it as a dynamic process of ongoing, corporate intellectual labour, and so to imagine that it was possible for me to join in with that process even if it was impossible to imagine myself having achieved the oracular status of my individual lecturers.

Finally, there are questions about the interaction among the students themselves. Do our forms of teaching inculcate, even reward, isolation, and punish interaction and collaboration? This is, of course, a notoriously difficult area, because students quite understandably do not want their grades to be

---

[13] This, by the way, is one of the problems I have with too great a reliance on exams—even when scripts are annotated and returned, the whole dynamic of the exam process seems to militate against anything very conversational going on.

dependent upon the performance of another student, who may not do his or her work well. But learning has to involve intentional training of students for serious exchange with one another—whether it is in seminars or in collaborative projects, or in other contexts—and those forms of exchange need to be prevented from degenerating into yet another context where the only operational relationship is between individual students and their teacher. In part, this can simply be a matter of generating contexts in which such conversation and mutual critique is genuinely encouraged—which means aiming for times, topics, venues, and numbers that do not actively discourage participation. In part, it is a matter of modelling good interaction, and of asking good questions. In part, it can be a matter of partially scripting the interactions: requiring students to ask specific kinds of questions of one another, and to give specific kinds of response (for example, asking a student responding to another's presentation on a set text to point out some passage in the set text to which the presentation did not do justice; asking the presenting student to hazard a reading of that passage). The biggest barrier, however, can sometimes be convincing ourselves as teachers that encouraging the students to interact with each other is not a poor substitute for encouraging them to interact with us.

At a more advanced academic level, one way of describing a Ph.D. is to think of it very much in conversational terms. After all, one way of seeing the Ph.D. student's central task is as the attempt to extend his circle of conversation partners. Conversations with a supervisor, conversations with fellow-students, conversations at conferences and in seminar presentations, conversations with the examiners—but also conversation with the hundreds of people whose books and articles and papers and pamphlets the student reads. The Ph.D. student, normally working on a very focused topic, nevertheless builds a massively extended conversation around that topic, inviting together (in one form or another) all the relevant people that he can find. A Ph.D. is, in that sense, an extended act of hospitality. Sometimes the student is simply playing host; sometimes he is the life and soul of the party; sometimes he is the one who gets to say, to the accompaniment of distant thunder, 'You may be wondering why I called you all here this evening . . .'.

And this hosting of a conversation is a massive extension of vulnerability: you invite all these people into your home, and then allow them to criticize the decor, turn up their noses at the food you serve, pick holes in the things you say. If it were not for the fact that at least some of these conversation partners will be or become friends, this would make a Ph.D. sound like a very bleak prospect indeed.

But this way of describing a Ph.D. is, I think, healthier than that which sees it primarily as the learner making a solitary trek into the jungles of some obscure subject matter, sent out by his tribe on the rite of passage that will either make a man of him, or kill him. Of course, there is something inevitably and properly lonely about a Ph.D., at least in subjects not based in a lab. There is a lot of reading to do, and a lot of writing, and a necessary move into territory that other people have not explored. More prosaically, many undergraduate friends are likely to move away, and there are not likely to be that many people in your immediate vicinity who are interested in the seventeenth-century mathematical instruments of Elias Allen, or the teleological imperative of proto-romanticism, or the Christology and ecclesiology of Hans Frei. But that need not mean that the budding Ph.D. student must nobly say, 'I'm just going outside; I may be some time'—it might instead simply mean that the Ph.D. student has the task of *building* a conversation, a community of interest, of finding the other strange people who are interested in this stuff, and helping others to realize that they could and should be interested. The loneliness of the long-distance Ph.D.-writer is real, but it does not get to the heart of what it means to do postgraduate research.

SOCIABLE RESEARCH

The sociality of learning remains central when we turn from students to their teachers. In the previous chapter, I described the disciplines in which academic staff participate as systems of virtue, and as spiritual disciplines. They can also be described as systems of intensive exchange; they are polities, with attendant forms of civility (which include forms of strident critique). To understand a discipline, one would need to map its conversational ecology, looking at the multitude of forms of interaction that shape departments, collaborative projects, competition between research groups, patterns of publication and reading, conferences, networks of collegial friendship and antagonism, and so on—all the ways in which the discipline's life of exchange is carried on. In fact, on such a map, a discipline might simply be the name for a tangle of networks of exchange of peculiar intensity and interconnectedness.[14]

In fact, the proper form of audit of the health of a discipline or of a department, or of any other academic unit, might be a *conversational* audit—an attempt to map the ecology of ongoing conversations, and of niches for conversation, that constitute the life of that department or discipline. How are conversations sustained? How are new people drawn into them? Where are the conversational connections to other departments and other disciplines? What resources are put into drawing relevant scholars from elsewhere into the conversations that sustain particular projects? What patterns of exclusion shape all those conversations? What virtues enliven and what vices deaden them?

---

[14] It might be possible, for instance, to produce a rough map of disciplines by analysing the patterns of interconnection between academics' Facebook accounts.

Various practical considerations flow from a concern with the quality and intensity of academic conversation. For instance, the achievement of which I am most proud from my years as a head of department in my present university was persuading my colleagues that it was normal—indeed, to a certain extent *expected*—that all those who were available would go together to the common room for coffee each morning. It is not that those conversations were a particularly intense form of exchange of judgement, but they helped sustain the sense of interconnection that made more serious conversations easier. If the life of a department is a conversational ecology, then taking the responsibility for the creation and sustaining of ecological niches for good conversation becomes a core responsibility for all participants, and particularly for those in positions of responsibility.

This is also why academic conferences matter. There is no need to be embarrassed by the fact that their primary purpose is to provide for a certain intensity of sociality or collegiality. Those with responsibility for creating budgets for academic appointments should try to include in them enough to fund the appointee's regular attendance at key conferences—whatever the key conversational loci are in the relevant discipline. Much of the funding available to allow people to go to conferences is tied to formal involvement (giving a paper, for instance), but most of us know that the most fruitful aspects of conferences are the informal conversations and the networks that they sustain. Of course, one cannot guarantee that attendance at a conference will be 'productive'—these things are all but unmeasurable—but one *can* guarantee that non-attendance will tend to isolate. Conferences need not simply be contexts for the formal dissemination and presentation of work; they should offer opportunites for informal exchange, garrulous argument, and the formation and maintenance of friendships—and that is where their real academic value lies.

Having said that dissemination and presentation are not everything, though, it is important to insist that one of the peculiar but essential forms of exchange that shapes academic life is, of course, publication and the reading and criticism of others' publications. Publication in one form or another is an essential feature of healthy academic life. As Jaroslav Pelikan says, "'Publish or perish!' is a fundamental psychological, indeed almost physiological, imperative that is rooted in the metabolism of scholarship as a sacred vocation. For that is how research remains honest, by exposing itself to the criticism and correction of other scholars.'[15] There are, of course, many forms of publication—and a wise conversational audit will not simply look for those that have a traditional halo of prestige. Rather, it will look for the forms of publication that secure the widest and deepest appropriate engagement, that open the work to the widest and deepest appropriate critique, and that do

---

[15] Pelikan, *Idea*, 123–4.

most to enable the conversation to continue. We should not, after all, think of publication simply as the end-point of a project of research—the moment when the polished and finished work is delivered, and the author moves on. That is in some ways a secondary form of publication; the primary form is the kind that allows engagement to reshape what the author is doing, and that stimulate the continuation and expansion of the conversation to which the work is a contribution.[16]

This is one way of thinking about research grants as well, once questions about equipment and other material resources have been set to one side. At least in the humanities, most research grants are opportunities to pay for conversation: to draw a set of conversation partners together over a period of time to exchange well-formed judgements—and our response to the growth in importance of such grant funding need not be to defend ever more precariously our right to work in undisturbed solitude, but an attempt to seize the opportunity it creates for us to immerse ourselves in a wider range of patterns of conversation.

SOLITUDE

The irony has not escaped me that I am writing these words about the inherent sociality of academic life while sitting in what one of my friends has dubbed the Caravan of Seclusion. Following my time as Head of Department, I was granted a period of extended research leave. Fleeing my office on campus, which by now smells ineradicably of management and administration, and reserving for home life those aspects of my work that can weather interruption by small children, I have been given use of some friends' caravan during the day. I have electricity (so can type these words on a laptop), but no Internet connection, no phone, no colleagues to join at coffee. I sit here in academic isolation, looking out at the slopes of Dartmoor, and thank God for the possibility of such solitude.

This solitude is by no means the opposite of conversation, however. I sit here as someone formed by intense tangles of conversation. As I write, I am aware of the voices of friends, colleagues, and critics in my head. I think I know what some of them will say about some of the things I write, and adjust my course accordingly. I spend my time reading and writing—working as a node in a conversational network, albeit one where the patterns of exchange are temporally rather extended. Here in the Caravan of Seclusion, with only the birds and

---

[16] I suspect that changing models of academic publishing, as online publishing comes of age, and economic considerations make traditional publishing increasingly problematic, may have much to offer.

the nearby sheep to hear me, I am thoroughly engaged in academic conversation. In fact, here, away from other distractions, it is easier to listen to some of that conversation than it has been for years, deafened as I have been by the everyday bustle of academic life. If a concern for conversational ecology is to shape the way we conduct academic life, arranging for such solitude will be a life-giving part of it.[17]

Nevertheless, solitude is secondary. Academic life is, or should be, a sociable life—a life in which academic health is proportionate to the degree to which scholars (whether students or teachers) make themselves available to one another, make themselves vulnerable to one another, and take one another seriously enough to disagree.

CONCLUSION

In parallel to Chapter 7's account of virtue, I have here been experimenting with a description of academic life in terms of sociality that does not wear its theological origins on its sleeve, but that nevertheless stands in clear continuity with the theological account of learning that I developed in Chapter 5. I have been painting a picture of academic life that makes it an echo of ecclesial life— of the economy of gift and reception that ecclesial life is called to embody.

Academic learning, then, is good learning to the extent that it resembles the economy of gift and reception that constitutes the Body of Christ. Such a resemblance is, of course, always partial: the networks of exchange are always incomplete, marred by incomprehension, a lack of generosity, a lack of civility—by all the vices, mistakes, and incapacities that distort ordinary sociality.

Nevertheless, as Jacques Derrida has said, to participate in the university is to anticipate a peaceable kingdom—a kingdom of free sociality that is coming, but that has not yet come (though he would also say that it *cannot* come). In the words of Gerard Loughlin: 'The professor is one who promises to keep faith with the university to come, and in promising performs or fabulates the university, in the mode of the "as if". The professor, we might think, is the one who announces the eschaton, if the eschaton is the impossible which is to arrive.'[18]

---

[17] Pelikan, *Idea*, 64–5.

[18] Gerard Loughlin, 'The University without Question: John Henry Newman and Jacques Derrida on Faith in the University', in Jeff Astley, Leslie Francis, John Sullivan, and Andrew Walker (eds), *The Idea of a Christian University: Essays on Theology and Higher Education* (Bletchley and Waynesborough, GA: Paternoster, 2004), 113–31: 128, commenting on Jacques Derrida, 'The University without Condition', in Jacques Derrida, *Without Alibi*, ed. and tr. Peggy Kamuf (Stanford, CA: Stanford University Press, 2002), 202–37.

In this respect too, then, I can see what I am doing—within a secular university focused on disciplinary and professional education, without transgressing the boundaries that such a context properly imposes—as a labour to draw myself and others deeper into life fitted for the Body of Christ. It may be concerned only with limited aspects of the life of the Body, maybe—but they are real aspects nonetheless. I would not go so far as to say that I am labouring to form a church—I am not, after all, forming people by means of liturgies of Word and Sacrament—but I am nevertheless seeking to develop something proximate to that: a life of free exchange and mutual compunction. I am participating, to the extent that I do my university job well, in something of the community-forming work of the Spirit.

Once again, however, this argument is as yet seriously incomplete, and in the next chapter I turn to questions about the overall purpose and public import of all this learning—and try do justice to the fact that the somewhat formal virtues that I have discussed in this chapter and the last are not themselves enough, without some more substantive connection to the common good.

EXCURSUS: THE UK RESEARCH EXCELLENCE FRAMEWORK

To write about publications, research grants, and competition as I have done in this chapter would be incomplete, for someone working in a UK university, without a discussion of the UK Research Excellence Framework (REF). I used to know exactly what I thought about its predecessors—going so far at one point as to write an article entitled 'The Research Assessment Exercise as Sin'.[19] I still stand by much of what I said in that article, but more experience of academic management has made me recognize that we in the UK currently live in a context where there is an inescapable need for government to distribute funds that will pay for academic research activities—and, because the government should itself be accountable, there is therefore an inescapable need for the government to seek assurance that its decisions about that distribution have been fair, that they somehow relate to the quality of the research being done in the funded contexts, that they somehow contribute to the overall health of research in the UK[20]—and that they somehow contribute

---

[19] Mike Higton, 'The Research Assessment Exercise as Sin', *Critical Quarterly*, 44/4 (2002), 40–5.
[20] That is, a concern with appropriate levels of concentration and dispersal, with keeping an appropriate range of subjects alive, and with the promotion of interdisciplinary connections.

to life beyond the academy. I cannot see the set of circumstances within which such demands are inescapable going away any time soon.

Those demands do, however, present us with some serious difficulties. It is not just that, as presently envisaged, the Research Excellence Framework seeks to build a research endeavour that is invulnerable to the charge that money is being wasted, or that poor work is being supported—and that Christian theology has long known that the only form of life that is invulnerable is death. It is not just that the Framework tends to encourage departments, and individuals moving from department to department, to think in terms of accumulating a body of achieved work that is definitively 'ours' or 'mine', a personal store of brownie points that we can bargain for advancement—and that Christian theology has long held that a focus on the accumulation of personal merit is the surest route not to salvation but to damnation.

The bigger problem is more basic. The Framework assumes that it is possible to measure real quality quickly. (Despite what you sometimes hear, *quantity* of research is not really a problem, in the current set-up: taken seriously, the need to produce three or four items of high-quality published research over a five- or six-year period would probably cut down rather than increase most academics' current publishing rates.) But such a measure of quality is simply not possible with any accuracy in the timescales needed—not if one means real generativity and significance, real capacity to shape the field or to have an impact beyond it, which is how the documents describing the Framework tend to phrase things at present.[21] The real generativity and importance of a piece of work emerges only slowly, as the conversation continues—and is almost certain to be controversial to a degree that makes reliance upon the judgement of individual judges, or even small teams of judges, deeply suspect. In fact, generativity and controversy go together: the more important a piece of work is, the more likely it is that quite a few people will dismiss it as of no importance whatsoever.

I have in the past been tempted to say that what is needed instead is something like the conversational audit I described above: some investigation of the patterns of exchange and growth that shape particular disciplines and the connections between them, asking how the conversational ecology has, over time, sustained the production of what has come to be recognized as important work, and asking what kinds of funding are needed to support that ecology. Once one tries to turn such generalized hand-waving into a real system of research review, however, it begins to look very disturbing indeed.

---

[21] 'Outputs will be assessed against criteria of "rigour, originality and significance". By "significance", we mean the extent to which research outputs display the capacity to make a difference either through intellectual influence within the academic sphere, or through actual or potential use beyond the academic sphere, or both' (Higher Education Funding Council for England, *Research Excellence Framework: Second Consultation on the Assessment and Funding of Research* (London: HEFCE, 2009), 10).

It does not take much imagination to envisage the horrors that might be visited upon us by centralized agencies asked to get involved in the detailed terraforming of the academic landscape, designing and reshaping the conversational ecology at every level.

Instead, I think that any system of centralized research review needs to reduce its ambitions to match the data that it can reliably collect. It is simply not possible for it to gather timely data on the real quality or importance of the work being done, and no amount of tweaking of the system is going to change that. But it is possible for panels of competent judges to get a decent sense of whether the samples of work produced in a given context embody core academic and disciplinary virtues—whether they look like the kind of work that has been exposed to judgement, has been grown in the midst of the appropriate kinds of conversational exchange, and has been launched in the right kind of way to make possible further conversation. There is no guarantee that such judgements allow one to spot the really generative work, or to distinguish the excellent from the merely solid—but, since such guarantees are an impossibility, this is a lack that we should simply accept.

Such a form of Research Assessment can only, therefore, be a fairly crude measure of whether a reasonable amount of good-enough work is being done in a department or other unit, relative to the amount of funding it absorbs. Linked to other measures—research grants, graduate student completions—it is perhaps enough to declare in the crudest way that a unit is, in research terms, either healthy, unhealthy, or dead (with the threshold for 'unhealthiness' set at a level that can secure very widespread agreement among academics in the relevant discipline that something is not quite right, and that for 'death' at a level that can secure similar agreement that a unit is not in any serious way research active). It will not be enough to establish any kind of league table of real research excellence[22]—but it might be enough to allow decisions about a very simple allocation of funding. It might also be cheaper than the current ridiculously expensive system.

---

[22] How one can prevent newspapers getting hold of the raw data and establishing spurious league tables is another question.

8

The Good University

Newman considered sound intellectual formation an end in itself, and a 'very tangible, real and sufficient end' at that.[1] He saw such intellectual formation as needing no other utility to make it a good worth pursuing. Irrespective of whether it leads to individual happiness, to social harmony, to the spread of justice, to practical aplomb, or to intellectual influence, it is simply and straightforwardly good to have a mind that is capable of sorting truth from falsehood.

It should be clear by now that—whatever qualifications are introduced by the subordination of intellectual to religious formation in his account— I cannot follow Newman in this regard. Intellectual formation is always already ordered to a higher end: the formation of the peaceable eschatological unity of the Body of Christ, and the fulfilment of all creatures in it. As Nicholas Wolterstorff insisted, it is ordered towards *shalom*.[2] Intellectual formation only becomes itself—only becomes formation rather than deformation, and only becomes truly intellectual—to the extent that it leads towards that end.[3] Understanding is an ingredient of corporate and individual life, and to pursue understanding of any object is to pursue understanding of the ways in which it is possible to live graciously with that object. Of course, the need for delighted contemplation of that object's own way of being, and the attendant refusal to allow the object to be wholly absorbed into the gratification of our desires, are important—but they are important precisely because they discipline and orient our attempts to live graciously with the object in question. To speak of knowledge of something 'for its own sake' can only be a shorthand for such a discipline of disinterestedness, undertaken for the sake of truer ordering of knowledge towards peaceable and flourishing life together.[4] In other words,

---

[1] John Henry Newman, *The Idea of a University Defined and Illustrated*, ed. Ian Ker (Oxford: Clarendon Press, 1976), 97 [103]; see above, Ch. 3.

[2] See above, Ch. 4.

[3] It is, of course, not simply a means to that end, since it is also an ingredient in it; intellectual formation cannot be replaced by some more efficient means of pursuing the same end.

[4] As I understand it, there is no real 'for its own sake' except God. I therefore do not follow Robert Grant, 'Education, Utility and the Universities', in Stephen Prickett and Patricia Erskine-

knowledge is inherently ordered towards God's peaceable kingdom, and there is no 'natural' fulfilment of the human intellect separate from this 'supernatural' fulfilment; there are only penultimate and partial fulfilments that remain incomplete until this final fulfilment is given.[5]

This means, however, that the previous two chapters are incomplete as they stand, however seriously their insistence upon virtue and upon sociality is taken. They leave to one side the question of the end to which intellectual virtue and sociality are ultimately ordered—and so they leave out the deepest and most urgent question that we need to ask about university learning. In this chapter, I reintroduce that question, and answer that intellectual virtue and sociality are ordered to the formation of the flourishing life of all God's creatures together: they are ordered, that is, towards the common good.[6] Without this orientation, the dispositions discussed in Chapter 6 might take the *form* of virtue, but be substantively vicious, and the patterns of exchange discussed in Chapter 7 might take the *form* of flourishing sociality, but be substantively enmeshed in violence—just as, for all their virtue and sociality, the University of Paris was to some degree complicit in the formation of a persecuting society, the University of Berlin in the support of increasingly overbearing state power, and the Catholic University of Ireland in the continued betrayal of the Irish people.[7]

Hill (eds), *Education! Education! Education! Managerial Ethics and the Law of Unintended Consequences* (Thorverton: Imprint Academic/Higher Education Foundation, 2002), 49–71; nor Roger Scruton, 'The Idea of a University' (pp. 73–84 in the same volume); I do not follow Duke Maskell and Ian Robinson, *The New Idea of a University* (London: Haven, 2001); I do not even follow Gordon Graham, *Universities: The Recovery of an Idea*, 2nd edn (Exeter: Imprint Academic, 2008)—though his is the most cogent of these presentations. Graham identifies the common thread holding these accounts together: a belief that the desire to know or understand is 'as basic a feature of human beings as the desire to do or to have' (p. 51), and a belief, therefore, that the fulfilment of such a desire is straightforwardly an element of 'human flourishing' (p. 96). I partly agree with Nicholas Maxwell, *From Knowledge to Wisdom: A Revolution in the Aims and Methods of Science* (Oxford: Blackwell, 1984), 2: 'Granted that enquiry has as its basic aim to help enhance the quality of human life, it is actually profoundly and damagingly *irrational, unrigorous*, for enquiry to give intellectual priority to the task of improving knowledge' (quoted by Mary Midgley, *Wisdom, Information and Wonder: What is Knowledge For?* (London: Routledge, 1989), 20–1). See also Jürgen Habermas, 'The Idea of the University—Learning Processes', *New German Critique*, 41 (1987), 3–22: 13: 'the neo-humanist educational ideal was deformed into the intellectually elitist, apolitical, conformist self-conception of an internally autonomous institution that remained far removed from practice while intensively conducting research'.

[5] To deny this would, it seems to me, mean denying either that we know within various practices or that the ordering of our knowledge is bound up with the ordering of those practices—and so with the ordering of (corporate and individual) life.

[6] In the Conclusion, I will say something about what it means to remember the fuller version of this claim: they are ordered to the formation of the flourishing life of all God's creatures together *before God*.

[7] W. Jay Wood, in his account of intellectual virtue (*Epistemology: Becoming Intellectually Virtuous* (Leicester: Apollos/Downers Grove, IL: IVP, 1998), 46), rightly defines such virtue as 'abiding, reliable traits that allow us to orient our intellectual lives ... *in ways that contribute to human flourishing*' (emphasis added). I have spent enough time talking to my friend and

WHO PAYS?

Stanley Hauerwas has rightly insisted that any attempt to discuss this topic faces a difficult question: *Who pays?*[8] If I want to claim that universities are, or can be, ordered towards creaturely flourishing, who actually asks them to orient themselves in this way, who pays for them to sustain such an orientation, and who values their contribution to such flourishing? Universities do not and cannot exist in isolation: they are the universities *of* specific states, communities, or constituencies, and can sustainably pursue only goods that those states, communities, or constituencies know how to value.[9]

My descriptions and proposals in the previous two chapters have sidled past that question. In effect, I have argued that even if all that is wanted by those who fund the university is for universities to turn out graduates trained for excellence in the various extant disciplines and professions, the university will still need to be committed to the inculcation of intellectual virtue and sociality of the kind I have described. This is not on its own enough, however, and even saying this much involves a gamble. It is not clear that excellence in the various extant disciplines and professions *is* directly valued by those who fund the university. Rather, it might be truer to say it is the employability, the raised earning potential, and the increased economic productivity of those who make their way through university that are most directly valued.[10] Only by historical accident do we currently have societies in which it is widely thought that excellent disciplinary education is a respectable, secure, and reasonably cost-effective means to those ends. It is not hard to persuade oneself to be pessimistic about the potential this strange settlement has for survival—and not hard to be pessimistic about the prospects for a focus on intellectual virtue

colleague David Clough to want to speak more widely of *creaturely* flourishing. Even though we are talking about the apprehension and well-formed judgement of human beings, it is the apprehension and well-formed judgement that they need to live graciously with all God's other creatures, not just other members of their own species. See David Clough, *On Animals: Systematic Theology* (London: Continuum, 2011).

[8] Remember, though, that 'money is but a name for people the university is meant to serve' (Stanley Hauerwas, *The State of the University: Academic Knowledges and the Knowledge of God* (Oxford: Blackwell, 2007), 87).

[9] 'A university able to resist the mystifications legitimated by the abstractions of our social order will depend on a people shaped by fundamental practices necessary for truthful speech' (Hauerwas, *State of the University*, 104). He is drawing on Alasdair MacIntyre, 'The Idea of an Educated Public', in Alasdair MacIntyre, *Education and Values: The Richard Peters Lectures*, ed. Graham Haydon (London: University of London Press, 1987), 15–36.

[10] As I sit on a train revising this chapter, I can look up and see a poster advertising the University of Hertfordshire. It is dominated by the word 'enrich', in a swirly lower-case serif font, bursting with a stylized growth of leaves and bubbles—conveying not businesslike determination but effervescence, joie de vivre, and a passion for life. A severe sans serif font completes the slogan in very much smaller print: 'enrich . . . your employment prospects, with postgraduate study at Hertfordshire'.

and sociality should we see the final triumph of a more hard-nosed insistence upon increasing earning potential by the most efficient and reliable educational means available. It is, after all, not easy to justify Newman's belief that a liberally educated man 'will be placed in that state of intellect in which he can take up any one of the . . . callings I have referred to, or any other for which he has a taste or special talent, with an ease, a grace, a versatility, and a success to which another is stranger'.[11] There may be more direct, more efficient ways to train up virtuosos of the jobs market.

These questions become even more pressing, and even more difficult to answer, when we move beyond the formalities of virtue and sociality to the substantive focus on the common good. To put it crudely: where will the money come from to allow those of us who work in secular universities to make this our focus? Where will our students have gained the initial formation that will have taught them to value such an end, and that will make them or their parents willing to make the investment of time, energy, and money that is required to pursue it? And where will the funding agencies and benefactors be found who will pay for universities to devote themselves to this costly end?[12]

One answer that might sometimes be given, particularly in a context like the UK where state funding has until very recently made up such a high proportion of university income,[13] is that government funding can bring with it an orientation broader than the earning potential of individual students. After all, that funding is ultimately derived from taxes, and the use of taxes to fund universities inevitably brings with it the question of the public good that universities do, over and above the good that they do for those individuals who happen to study and work there.[14] However, that is a harder argument to sustain than it used to be for a writer based in a UK university, who has just seen the dramatic cuts in government funding of university teaching—and where the making of those cuts seems to have been made very much easier by the failure of any widely accepted account of the ways in which universities might genuinely serve the public good.

Nevertheless, tattered elements of such a connection do remain between government funding and the public good served by universities. Quite properly, for instance, debates about funding for research in the UK have recently

---

[11] Newman, *Idea*, 145 [166]. See above, Ch. 3.

[12] William Cavanaugh rightly cautions about any identification of the common good with the state. See William Cavanaugh, 'Killing for the Telephone Company: Why the Nation-State is not the Keeper of the Common Good', *Modern Theology*, 20/2 (2004), 243–74.

[13] For a good brief account of the history of UK university funding, see Graham, *Universities*, 19–21.

[14] Hence the concern voiced so clearly by Stefan Collini in the wake of the range of cuts in government funding announced in 2010: that they represent a failure to understand higher education as a public good. See Stefan Collini, 'Browne's Gamble', *London Review of Books*, 32/21 (4 Nov. 2010), 23–5; <www.lrb.co.uk/v32/n21/stefan-collini/brownes-gamble> (accessed 18 Aug. 2011).

become focused upon the question of 'impact'. The UK Research Councils, who distribute about £1.3 billion of government money annually for research projects in UK universities, define impact as 'the demonstrable contribution that excellent research makes to society and the economy. Economic impact embraces all the diverse ways in which research related knowledge and skills benefit individuals, organizations and nations by fostering economic competitiveness, increasing the effectiveness of public services and public policy, [and] enhancing quality of life, health and creative output.'[15] Right there, in the clause about the impact that the research work of universities has on 'quality of life', there is a route to justifying a focus on the common good.

Except, of course, that this description of 'impact' is very much more ambiguous than that. First, it begins with 'society and the economy', but in the next sentence economy seems to swallow society. Second, economic competitiveness is then the most obvious form of benefit envisaged. Third, it is not the *ends* of public policy and public services that one is invited to research, but their *effectiveness*—and one cannot help suspecting that this is precisely because the primary end has already been stated: economic competitiveness. Fourth, the clause about 'quality of life, health and creative output', reads like a rag-bag of private benefits left over once the public business of economic competitiveness has been dealt with. One does not have to be congenitally cynical to think that there is limited support envisaged for research that might question the very economic model of the public good upon which this definition of impact appears to be based. In other words, there is no obvious support here for what Hauerwas calls a 'university able to resist the mystifications legitimized by the abstractions of our social order'.[16]

---

[15] See, e.g., Research Councils UK, *Pathways to Impact* webpages, <www.rcuk.ac.uk/kei/impacts/Pages/home.aspx> and Arts and Humanities Research Council, *Impact Assessment Position Paper* (London: AHRC, 2006); <www.ahrc.ac.uk/FundedResearch/Documents/Impact%20Position%20Paper.pdf> (both accessed 17 June 2010).

[16] Hauerwas, *State of the University*, 104. Cf. p. 6: 'The university is the great institution of legitimation in modernity, whose task is to convince us that the way things are is the way things have to be.' There are more encouraging official descriptions of 'Impact' available, however. The Research Councils UK document 'Mission and Statement of Expectation on Economic and Societal Impact' (Swindon: RCUK, 2008), <www.rcuk.ac.uk/documents/innovation/missionsei.pdf> (accessed 18 Apr. 2011), begins: 'The Research Councils give their funding recipients considerable flexibility and autonomy in the delivery of their research, postgraduate training and knowledge transfer activities. This flexibility and autonomy encompasses project definition, management, collaboration, participation, promotion and the dissemination of research outputs; this approach enables excellence with impact. In return, the Research Councils expect those who receive funding to: demonstrate an awareness of the wider environment and context in which their research takes place; demonstrate an awareness of the social and ethical implications of their research, beyond usual research conduct considerations, and take account of public attitudes towards those issues; engage actively with the public at both the local and national levels about their research and its broader implications . . .' and so on. There is at least something there to work with.

Of course, there are other sources of funding for universities: businesses, philanthropists, charities, and trusts of various kinds. Their influence varies from context to context, and their purposes (and the values they wish their money to sustain) are diverse. But, however important such sources of funding are as elements of the overall picture, it is hard to get away from the sense that the most successful language available in which to discuss the *public* good that universities serve is economic, whether that language be spoken directly by the state or by those who have been formed as faithful citizens of such a state—and that other attempts to discuss that public good robustly have insufficient weight to keep such economic language in its proper, limited place.[17]

While being realistic (and appropriately suspicious and pessimistic), however, we should not lapse into weary resignation. There is, in fact, no simple answer to the question I posed above: Where will we find students who have been formed to value the common good, and who will be willing to make the investment of time and energy that is required to pursue it? Nor can we give simple answers to similar questions: Where will we find staff with a commitment to such an end strong enough to fund resistance to the blandishments of other, less demanding accounts of the end of university life? Where will we find the government officials, agencies, and ministers who know how to value something beyond economic competitiveness? Where will we find benefactors and philanthropists who are willing to fund endeavours that push against the dominant cultural–economic system? The proper answer to all these questions is not the implied 'Nowhere!', but 'We don't know—but, by the grace of God, we do find them.'

Government is not a monolith; parents and students do not form blocs whose desires and formations can be simply identified. The university is not simply the toy of a uniform ideology in which all value is reduced to economic competitiveness.[18] One of the surprises that attentive Christian learners should be open to is the surprise that there are still many opportunities within the university, even in the state that it is in, to pursue what they, formed by Christian discipleship, can identify as the common good. There are enough colleagues, enough students (and students' parents), enough people in government and in funding agencies of various kinds, enough benefactors,

---

[17] 'Those that run and those that teach in the modern university simply have no idea what or how they might provide an answer to the question of what the university is for or who it is to serve. As a result we are content to comfort ourselves by repeating familiar slogans about the importance of being an educated person who can think critically. Which . . . means that those who have gone to university . . . will have greater earning power' (Hauerwas, *The State of the University*, 76).

[18] 'Universities are not secular through and through any more than universities that claim to be Christian are Christian through and through. I assume, therefore, if a "secular" university is open to the challenge Christians should represent then no Christian should turn down that opportunity' (Hauerwas, *The State of the University*, 8).

who—shaped and sustained by God knows what contexts of formation that are not exhausted by their subordination to the economic order—value something rather broader than simply economic earning potential of the most blatant kind. Concern with the common good is spread more widely and more messily than simplistic accounts might suggest.

In the remainder of this chapter, then, I sketch an account of the ways in which a contemporary secular university might seek to serve the common good. I do not think this account is a description of any secular university as it presently exists—at least, not of any that I have encountered. Neither, however, do I think that this is simply an exercise in futile utopianism. On the one hand, my account does draw on existing examples of university policy and practice—aspects of existing university life that already seem to me good. On the other, my hope is simply that enough of those who are involved in shaping (and paying for) the life of contemporary secular universities might find some such account as this intelligible and valuable, and that some such account as this can, therefore, become one of the discourses that shape the development of universities—one of the voices in the negotiation of university life, strong enough to be worth disagreeing with, arguing with, and settling with.

TENDING PUBLIC REASON

The first step I want to take towards an account of the contribution of a university to the common good is simply to acknowledge the fact that intellectual virtue and sociality are by no means matters for the university alone. The whole society within which universities sit is shaped, in part, by patterns of intellectual activity and exchange, and universities are simply particularly intense loci of such activity and exchange within that broader intellectual landscape. The question of the university's contribution to the common good is, in part, simply a question about the contributory role that universities can play in the sustaining and development of intellectual virtue and sociality across that landscape.

In Chapter 7, I made it clear that intellectual formation should not be seen simply as the acquisition of an individual possession. It is inherently a formation for participation in communities of practice and discourse—shaping people for virtuous participation in such communities, and shaping the communities to sustain such virtue. Except for the occasional half-nod in the direction of the 'professions', however, I have written as if the formation on offer in the university simply fitted people for continued participation in the university, and as if the communities of practice and discourse sustained and developed by the university were simply the academic disciplines themselves. It has not been clear how this formation relates to life beyond the university, including the lives that students will go on to lead once they have left the university.

One standard answer is that, having acquired a stock of intellectual virtue in the university, students will then carry it out into the wider world, and will find both that it contributes to their success as participants in that world, and that they become agents for the diffusion to the general populace of the virtues they have gained. Yet the weight of such an answer is taken precisely by an account of intellectual virtue as the possession of individuals, which they can carry with them from the context in which they acquired it to the very different contexts in which it is needed.[19] If, however, intellectual virtue and intellectual sociality are symbiotic, this answer makes little sense. We cannot think of graduates taking intellectual virtue out into the wider world and living by it unless we are prepared to think of the existence beyond university walls of forms of intellectual sociality, networks, and communities of virtuous intellectual exchange shaped and sustained in part by intellectually well-formed individuals, and in turn sustaining and continuing to form those and other individuals. In other words, if the university's end is broader than individual student success, it has to include an interest in, and an involvement in, society's networks and communities of intellectual exchange.

A society is, after all, itself a hugely complex conversational ecology. It sustains, and is in part constituted by, any number of conversations, arguments, and patterns of chatter, diatribe, approval, and complaint. These conversations are central means by which a society reproduces itself, works on itself, repairs itself, and deludes itself—sets into circulation and conflict and interaction its collected patterns of apprehension and judgement. The cacophony is sometimes sinister, sometimes farcical, sometimes vibrant—and nearly always bewildering and unmanageable.[20]

If the university is tasked with the care of intellectual virtue, then it makes sense for it not simply to send well-equipped individuals out into this maelstrom, but to care about its involvement in this conversational ecology of society more directly, and the contribution it can make to the health of the ecology. Universities properly have an interest in helping their societies to sustain and develop the patterns of intellectual interaction and exchange, the communities of discourse, that allow intellectual virtue to be sustained, and

---

[19] In debates about the public worth of universities and university educations, crude forms of this answer are nicely calculated to generate both incredulity and resentment. Critics are bound to ask whether universities really do turn out conspicuously virtuous students, and whether those without a university education are by the same token conspicuously lacking in virtue. The focus falls all too easily on individuals, and so on invidious comparisons between individuals.

[20] This conversational ecology has both been made more fully visible, and given additional ways of existing, in the online world—particularly since the rise of those developments collectively known as 'Web 2.0', which encourage every user to comment, review, opine, and share, incessantly.

allow such virtue to contribute to the good ordering of society. Universities are, in fact, simply one of the ways that societies have of working upon their own good intellectual ordering.

Such a claim of course relies upon the fact that the university is involved in communities and networks of exchange that stretch far beyond its own walls, on multiple scales. Such involvement might take the form of engagement with government, with non-governmental organizations, with charities, with businesses, with churches, with community groups, with schools, with cultural organizations; it might take the form of involvement in continuing professional development (CPD), in consultancy, or in professional associations; it might take the form of partnerships with other institutions or organizations; it might take the form of research on behalf of other institutions; it might take the form of involvement in the various media that shape popular culture, as content providers, critics, consultants, or presenters. The contemporary university is, thank God, massively entangled in the conversational processes by which society works, and that entanglement is far too complex to allow any simple model of the trickle-down of intellectual virtue to hold sway.

Entanglement itself is not enough, however. What matters is, in the first place, whether those entanglements are used to help sustain and develop the intellectual virtue and sociality of the exchanges and interactions of society, in the senses defined in Chapter 6 and Chapter 7. (We will come back later in the chapter to the further question of the explicit orientation of such virtuous and sociable reactions to the common good.) To concern oneself with the wider exchanges of society means more than being interested in the dissemination of the authoritative results of university research. That might well be a good thing, in many contexts, but it does not by itself make the networks of discourse into which those results are then absorbed any more virtuous or sociable. Beyond dissemination, the university should be seeking to help sustain, develop, and advocate virtuous and sociable intellectual practice wherever it can.

We are, here, in the realm that Newman explored: the world of viewiness and views.[21] For him, it was the incessant chatter of periodical literature that epitomized viewiness, and against which he advocated the patient, virtuous, and sociable formation of views. One of the most visible contexts in which to see this contest in our own day is in the online world. Consider three examples. First, anyone wanting to have optimism about the state of public discourse beaten out of them should make their way to the pages of any online news outlet that allows largely unrestricted public comment on stories. The 'Comment is Free' pages of the online *Guardian* newspaper are the example I know best.[22] To read the comments that accumulate below almost

---

[21] See above, Ch. 3.
[22] See <www.guardian.co.uk/commentisfree> (accessed 18 Aug. 2011).

any controversial topic (which means anything at all to do with politics, the environment, religion, morality, or the wearing of cycle helmets) is to discover what intellectual exchange without virtue or sociality looks like (and how little it deserves to be called either 'intellectual' or 'exchange'). That is not to say that many of the contributors are not intellectually well-formed individuals— indeed, large numbers of them are clearly university graduates—but any virtue they bring with them is all too often lost in a cacophony of misunderstanding, misrepresentation, caricature, personal attack, and conspiracy theory. The format makes it hard for any other kind of exchange to find a foothold; it provides a haven for viewiness.

A rather different example is provided by the *Real Climate* blog.[23] It is run by active academic researchers as a quite deliberate research outreach activity—an attempt to promote real understanding of climate science. The blog is characterized by a firm insistence on the virtues of the discipline (an insistence reinforced by a refusal to allow comments that the editors regard as attacks upon those virtues—comments that refuse to supply reputable evidence for strong claims, comments that indulge simply in *ad hominem* attacks, and so on—and by a policy of didactic online glossing by the blog authors of many of the comments sent in by the public). The authors make the attempt to display the complex patterns of apprehension and judgement actually involved in climate science, and invite their worldwide, very varied audience to see the associated patterns of disciplinary virtue and sociality at work—and to understand, therefore, what is required to make robust claims within that science. It is uphill work, but the resultant blog is a rock in a storm, and it has gathered a community around it just strong enough to preserve its virtue.[24]

A third example is Ben Goldacre's *Bad Science* blog, based on his weekly column for the same *Guardian* newspaper.[25] This is a context whose connections to university life are much more complex; it is not, like *Real Climate*, an outreach activity on the part of university-based researchers. Rather, Goldacre, a doctor, writes a column in which he looks for examples of bad science reporting—whether it is the misreporting of stories about scientific matters, or stories that rely upon or promote pseudoscience of various kinds—and the blog of the column has gathered around it a significant community of like-minded people, at least some of them with a university education in one of the sciences, and a few of them still involved in scientific research. Together they have established patterns of exchange in which some of the virtues and forms

---

[23] See <www.realclimate.org> (accessed 18 Aug. 2011).

[24] It is no accident that the two positive examples are both scientific: on the whole, I suspect that the sciences at present have more tightly defined, and widely accepted systems of virtue and sociality, and that their forms of virtue and sociality are recognizable to a wider public, than most humanities subjects. Cf. Hauerwas, *State of the University*, 131: 'In truth I suspect that the best moral training that occurs in the contemporary university is in the sciences.'

[25] See <www.badscience.net> (accessed 18 Aug. 2011).

of sociality associated with their disciplines are displayed. At least some of the time, evidence gets marshalled, and questioned, and supplemented, and revised; arguments are made, and critiqued, and refined, and abandoned; references get checked (sometimes obsessively), and quotations get qualified by reference to their context. And the community, and its patterns of exchange, are mostly strong enough to handle the comments of those who simply wish to shout, or deal in caricature, misrepresentation, personal attack, and conspiracy theory—and strong enough, at its best, to *train* new participants in at least the rudiments of this kind of discourse. It is, of course, limited in its sphere of virtuous operation—it cannot, on the whole, handle discussions about politics, and certainly cannot handle discussions about religion—but it shows what can happen when the intellectual formation of individuals is combined with the formation of a community in which patterns of appropriate exchange are nurtured.

I am not encouraging, therefore, the simple deployment of university-trained experts, who deliver ready-made solutions (tried and tested within the university) to the outside world. Rather, I am suggesting that the entanglement of universities in the wider society might include (1) the identification of contexts in the wider society where enquiry and exchange are already going on for the sake of social flourishing, or could be going on; and (2) attempts to help sustain or build in those contexts virtuous habits of enquiry and sociable communities of exchange; by (3) drawing on the resources of the relevant academic disciplines, where those disciplines are seen as laboratories for the development of disciplined habits of apprehension and judgement for the sake of such virtuous enquiry and sociable exchange. In this light, an academic discipline is not seen as a closed community, from which results or gains of one kind or another are disseminated to the wider society itself seen as wholly outside the discipline. Rather, an academic discipline is simply a peculiarly intense knot of exchange and enquiry in the tangle of exchange and enquiry that is spread unevenly and messily over a whole society.[26]

It may be on unofficial blogs, it may be in professional associations, it may be in community organizations, it may be in committees of policy-makers; it may deal with refinements of the technologies that shape our society, and the promotion of discussion in and beyond the relevant industries of ways to exploit those refinements to their full potential; it may be an attempt to shape public debate about major challenges like climate change. In any number of ways, however, universities, and the individuals formed in them, should be

---

[26] For this paragraph, cf. Thomas Bender, 'From Academic Knowledge to Democratic Knowledge', in Simon Robinson and Clement Katulushi (eds), *Values in Higher Education* (St Bride's Major: Aureus/University of Leeds, 2005), 51–64: 53–4.

passionately interested in the state of intellectual virtue and sociality across the whole of society.[27]

It is, therefore, entirely proper that grant bodies should ask about knowledge transfer, knowledge exchange, or impact (even if the models they have for identifying those things or quantifying them sometimes need to be questioned)—not, of course, because all university research work can or should be directly engaged with the relevant publics, but because a concern with the health of intellectual virtue and sociality beyond the university is a properly central concern for every discipline.

ARGUING ABOUT THE GOOD

All this is not nearly enough, however. My discussion is still apparently stuck at a formal level, asking about the sustaining and development of proper *forms* of debate—yet we have begun touching upon the role that universities can and do play in substantively shaping public life, and that means that we cannot reasonably avoid substantive questions about whether the changes that universities promote *do any good*—questions about whether and in what way these changes shape society for the better. And that in turn means that we cannot, unless we insist very firmly on turning a blind eye, avoid raising questions about the *nature* of the good or goods that universities hope to promote.

Of course, the problem is that we often *do* insist very firmly on turning a blind eye to such questions. Our disciplines are sometimes very good at claiming that broader questions about the use or impact of our work are not our business—though that in itself is just a symptom. The deeper problem is that debate about the good, about the nature of the society and the forms of individual life at which we can and should be aiming, is perhaps the most notoriously broken form of discourse in our societies. Indeed, we live and work in contexts beset by the widespread tendency to think that real *argument* about the good is not possible: a tendency to regard such questions as lying in the realm of irrational private preference, rather than public discussion.[28] Yet

---

[27] Since writing this chapter, I have discovered Ron Barnett's, *Being a University* (London: Routledge, 2011), and been encouraged by the resonances between my account and his description of the 'ecological university' (in ch. 12).

[28] Alasdair MacIntyre, in 'Catholic Universities: Dangers, Hopes, Choices', in Robert E. Sullivan (ed.), *Higher Learning and Catholic Traditions* (Notre Dame, IN: University of Notre Dame Press, 2001), 1–21: 5–6, argues: 'What the Catholic faith confronts today in American higher education . . . is not primarily some range of alternative beliefs about the order of things, but rather a belief that there is no such thing as the order of things of which there could be a unified, if complex, understanding or even a movement toward such an understanding.'

the implication of my theological account of learning is that we are profoundly mistaken if we think that the transition from the normal subject matter of our academic disciplines to the question of the good is a transition from fact and reason to value and irrational preference. Rather, to ask about the good is the *telos* of reason; it is the context in which reason becomes most fully itself.

It is true, nevertheless, that there is no easy agreement about the good to be had. I am not going to get anywhere if I simply go on saying that the university must serve the good, and expect that to be an answer. Such a claim would leave my claims about the common good vulnerable to capture by discourses focused on economic competitiveness, defence of the nation state, or the loyal pursuit of government policy.[29] In order to avoid that, without simply imposing a predefined understanding of the good, I need to insist that the kind of virtuous and sociable intellectual work I have been describing (whether within the university, or sustained with the university's help in society more generally) urgently needs to include serious, open, inclusive, and critical *argument* about the good.

In part, that simply means keeping alive certain questions. It is possible to envisage, for instance, an insistent, persistent, resistant raising of questions about what is at stake in the changes or stabilities that the university's work promotes or allows; about who benefits and who is harmed, and in what ways; about what kind of society we are thereby becoming, and what kind we want to become or should become; about what idea of the good human life we are assuming; about what counts as success or flourishing in the broadest terms, and how we measure progress towards it or regression from it; about what kind of community with the wider creaturely world we are promoting— and so on.[30]

In order to keep these questions alive, however, it is also necessary to keep alive the belief that they can be discussed with intellectual seriousness—or at least to keep insisting that the claim that they *cannot* be discussed with intellectual seriousness is itself simply one debatable ideology, one that should not be adopted as the unquestioned default stance of the university, and one that is in danger of colluding all too readily with existing dominant ideologies.

If an argument about the good *is* to be intellectually serious, however, it must itself be characterized by intellectual virtue and sociality. It needs, for instance, to be characterized by integrity: by the bringing to argument of the real grounds upon which participants' visions of the good are based, with participants as far as is possible speaking from and articulating the real reasons

---

[29] I am grateful to Jacqui Stewart for pressing this point in conversation.

[30] Tom McCleish, in 'Values and Scientific Research: A Practitioner's View', in Robinson and Katulushi (eds), *Values*, 136–49: 139, speaks of the deepest orientation of the scientific disciplines as being 'towards a healing or reconciliation of broken relationships . . . the reconciliation of humankind with the *physical world*.'

they have for the positions that they hold, and so speaking from and articulating the traditions of moral vision that have formed them. It needs to be characterized by non-coercive attentiveness in the face of the difference that other participants present, and by serious attempts to understand exactly where and why the differences arise. And it needs to be characterized by a search for patterns of peaceable exchange that do not deny or misrepresent these differences.[31]

Otherwise, instead of real dialogue, instead of serious encounter between traditions of thinking about the good well identified and opened up to disagreement, we will either get the violent exclusion of all standpoints other than one claimed by its inhabitants as neutral ground, or the clash of preferences believed to be utterly autonomous and so irrational. There will be no reasons attached to my values (no dependence on a tradition, on a community, on particular patterns of apprehension, argument, and persuasion) and so no possibility of asking, 'Why?' and answering 'Because...' in a way that makes it possible for the conversation to go on, and for the participants to say more, explain more, and argue more.

In fact, therefore, it is *only* if there is a frank acknowledgement and articulation of the particular formations and traditions that shape our commitments, and a bringing of such articulations into argument together, that universities can claim to be conducting an intellectually serious argument about the good—and it is only if universities can claim to be conducting an intellectually serious argument about the good that they can claim to tackle the deepest questions that their work raises, and to be seriously interested in the truth of what they say. In other words, for a university to pursue its task properly—for it to be devoted to true intellectual virtue and sociality, and to the refusal to place hard questions about the common good beyond bounds—it is necessary that it *not* follow those proponents of the *Wissenschaftsideologie* who thought that reason properly required a bracketing of the positivity and particularity of traditional formation. Quite the opposite: for the university to be *fully* reasonable requires that it allow those particular voices to speak as themselves, and to argue seriously with one another. And, given the insistence of the previous section upon the entanglement of the university in the wider conversations of society, this means that universities have a proper concern with the health of such debate across the whole of their societies—and with helping to keep alive in those societies the rumour that serious argument about the good between those formed in multiple traditions is indeed possible.

Before turning to the question of what such argument might look like in practice, however, I want to point out something strange that has happened to

---

[31] Bender, 'Democratic Knowledge', 61, calls for 'less emphasis on achieving consensus, which is usually a form of triumph, but rather on developing a working system of... "non-consensual reciprocity"'.

my argument at this point. I opened this section by saying that something more than a formal commitment to intellectual virtue and sociality was needed: a commitment to the common good. In the face of disagreement about the good, that requirement has now turned out to amount to nothing more than an insistence once again upon intellectual virtue and sociality—or, rather, an insistence that the deepest reasons and highest ends people have for the stances that they take should be brought into virtuous and sociable discourse. That does not mean, however, that I have reduced a substantive commitment to the common good to pure formality, because the formality of my insistence upon virtue and sociality is in reality already substantive: it is itself grounded in a particular vision of the good, and promotes that vision. To secure commitment to this kind of argument about the good that our work serves *is* to secure commitment to a particular, substantive politics—even if is not to secure commitment to the fullness of the theological–political vision that animates my claims.[32] To put this another way: as I see it from the vantage point of my Christian tradition, to secure the commitment of a university to virtuous and sociable argument *about* the common good is already to secure its orientation to something of the common good *itself*—and this becomes particularly clear if we turn our attention directly to the inclusivity proper to such argument.

HOSPITALITY

If true learning involves opening ourselves, as far as is possible, to *all* relevant rebuff, then it ideally involves paying attention to every relevant person— everyone whom we can reasonably expect to have significant insight into what we are trying to talk about.[33] When I was working on my Ph.D. on the theology of Hans Frei, it was relatively easy to work out what that meant: there was a limited set of people to whom I simply had to pay attention, because their work impinged directly on what I wanted to say about Frei. But what if 'everyone relevant' simply means—in principle—*everyone*? If our topic is not the theology of Hans Frei, nor the presence of microscopic animalcules in pepper water, but the common good, who should we leave out?

Learning in relation to the common good is, in other words, a kind of learning that involves opening ourselves, as far as is possible, to *everyone*,

---

[32] See the Conclusion for more on this 'fullness'.

[33] On hospitality, see Aurelie A. Hagstrom, 'Christian Hospitality in the Intellectual Community', in Douglas V. Henry and Michael D. Beaty (eds), *Christianity and the Soul of the University: Faith as a Foundation for Intellectual Community* (Grand Rapids, MI: Baker Academic, 2006), 119–31, and Luke Bretherton, *Hospitality as Holiness: Christian Witness amid Moral Diversity* (Aldershot: Ashgate, 2006).

paying attention to *everyone*—and yet it does not take very long to work out that the 'as far as possible' in this case is 'not very far at all'. It simply makes no sense to think that we could in practice learn with and from everyone, pay serious attention to everyone. And yet, although we cannot imagine how a process of social learning in which all genuinely learn from all could come about in practice, the vision of it can act as a comment upon and a challenge to our actual, finite learning. It can help us to realize that—at least in the deepest and most serious forms of learning to which we can be committed—the question 'Whom have we left out of the conversation?' never goes away. Our learning remains somehow *provisional* because it is learning carried out in the absence of so many of the interested parties. Our knowledge is always *being made*. It is never finished and completed and ready for simple distribution to consumers. At least in the deepest and most serious forms of learning to which we can be committed, there is no point at which we can say, 'It has been seen by Sir Christopher Wren, Sir Jonas Moore, Dr Grew, Mr Aubrey, and divers others; and there is therefore no longer *any* doubt.'[34]

And so widening participation—by which I mean the effort to bring in to the university's conversation (or the conversations that the university helps to sustain) hitherto unrepresented voices—is absolutely essential to the university's purpose. The drive to include other voices, particularly those voices that have normally been ignored in conversations about the goods of our society, is a drive built in to the kind of learning we are called to do. We simply cannot be a university without it. And it is absolutely not a form of *charity*—as if we were giving from the riches of our learning to the poor and needy. Rather, we simply cannot learn properly without them; we need them as much as they need us, perhaps more. We widen participation not so that others can share the learning that we already securely have, but because, if we do not widen participation, none of us is learning as we might.[35]

This is the real unity of *Wissenschaft*, the real unity of reason. That unity involves a unity of disciplines—the kind of interdisciplinarity I will discuss further in the next section.[36] But more than that, it is a unity of people, and so

[34] Of course there are many contexts in which the final settling of some particular question is, indeed, possible. (I began my university education as a mathematician, and I still sometimes hanker for those days when questions could be answered and *stay* answered.) The open-endedness I refer to here characterizes the attempt to identify and pursue the good, or the nature of human flourishing.

[35] 'Only the widest possible participation in the making of knowledge will protect us from our own partialities and consequent blindness' (Thomas Bender, 'Democratic Knowledge', 61). Note that the internationalization of the student body can also be seen in this light—and not simply as a matter of opening new markets and charging exciting fees.

[36] Cf. Karl Jaspers, *The Idea of a University*, ed. Karl W. Deutsch, tr. H. A. T. Reiche and H. F. Vanderschmidt (London: Peter Owen, 1960), 20: 'Oneness and wholeness are of the very essence of man's will to know. In practice this oneness and wholeness is realized only in specialized fields, yet these very specialities are not alive except as members of a single body of

a unity shaped by the involvement of all the traditions, religious and secular, that constitute our world, and a unity shaped by the involvement of the widest possible range of social and cultural groups. A university serious about such unity cannot simply be subordinated to the interests of a current political or economic order since—precisely because it exists to pursue learning, reason, and knowledge—it will have a stake in including in its deliberations those whom the current order silences, ignores, and oppresses, and a stake in making sure that those voices are included in the intellectual sociality of the wider society. That is what 'free sociality' properly means, and Schleiermacher was right: the rules of free sociality *are* the rules of reason.[37]

PRACTISING ARGUMENT ABOUT THE GOOD

I have been speaking at a very high level of generality, and have not done anything to make clear what it might look like in practice for a secular university to sustain such serious argument about the good internally, still less what it might look like to sustain it more generally in society. That is partly because much of the time it is not at all clear to me what it would mean for a university to sustain a broad conversation about anything very much, let alone about the good. The university is not shaped into one overarching conversation, but into a much messier and more complex ecology of conversations, most of which are very much smaller in scale than 'the university as a whole'. The closest that universities tend to get to a common conversation is when there is some cause célèbre—an unpopular piece of university policy, an industrial dispute, a dramatic piece of bad personnel management, or inadequate parking facilities—but even that normally means that there is a very large number of small-scale conversations on a common theme going on, but

learning. Integration of the various disciplines joins them in a cosmos which culminates in the vision of unified science, in theology, and in philosophy.' Cf. p. 57: 'the meaning and creative perpetuation of research can only be preserved if it maintains a lively exchange with the whole of knowledge.' Raymond Langley, in 'Karl Jasper's Three Critiques of the University', in Gregory J. Walters (ed.), *The Tasks of Truth: Essays on Karl Jaspers's Idea of the University* (Frankfurt am Main: Peter Lang, 1996), 23–38: 27, sees this as a regulative idea, 'the inner form and aspiration of every university institution'; Kurt Salamun, in 'The Concept of Liberality in Jasper's Philosophy and the Idea of the University', in Walters (ed.), *Tasks of Truth*, 39–53: 50, insists that, for Jaspers, the unity of *Wissenschaft* can never be finished or realized.

[37] Cf. Gerard Loughlin, 'The University without Question: John Henry Newman and Jacques Derrida on Faith in the University', in Jeff Astley, Leslie Francis, John Sullivan, and Andrew Walker (eds), *The Idea of a Christian University: Essays on Theology and Higher Education* (Bletchley and Waynesborough, GA: Paternoster, 2004), 113–31. He has understood that Newman's 'science of sciences' involves 'not the unity of a general theory of everything, but of a community' (p. 126).

that the forms of exchange between those tiny conversations are sporadic, uneven, and limited. It is not clear that universities as they presently exist have the capacity to generate patterns of exchange between all the tiny conversations that these issues generate, sufficient to produce something like a real, large-scale argument.[38]

Nevertheless, it is possible to imagine some ways in which the conversational ecology of the university can be opened up to include more serious argument about the good. That is, it is possible to attend to the conversational ecology that already exists in the university, to note some knots and strands of conversation that seem to allow for development in this direction, and then to push for that development—and to keep on doing so until it begins to become a norm rather than an exception.

One form of opportunity in the kind of university with which I am familiar is presented by interdisciplinary research projects. Almost any project that has subject matter with the potential to refine, repair, or interrupt the existing patterns of social and individual life in a society, or between societies, cannot but raise questions about the implications and direction of such alterations. However simple the idea or innovation that makes possible the alteration, the alteration itself is very likely to be complex and multifaceted—simply because social and individual life is inherently complex and multifaceted. The proper analysis of any such alteration is therefore interdisciplinary, and that interdisciplinarity can and should extend to ethical and political questions in the broadest sense.[39]

For instance, while I do not imagine that every project in the university that has some engineering or technological pay-off needs to be conducted in explicit interdisciplinary terms with an ethico-political twist, I can imagine that flagship projects, high-impact projects, might well become the foci for such extended attention. I am influenced here by the existence of such projects as the Egenis centre at the University of Exeter—an interdisciplinary research centre 'encompassing a range of perspectives from social science, biology and philosophy' to pursue 'research on the social impact of research in genomic science'.[40] That seems to me to be a model that could be reproduced, or improvised upon, much more widely—and it does not seem impossible to hope that, eventually, most staff and most students should have had some

---

[38] This does suggest, however, that, if one does want to get the whole university talking about something, one should arrange for the central university management to ban it and to fire someone for breaking the ban, for the teaching unions to protest, and for the lawyers hired by the university in defence to requisition one of the university car parks.

[39] Alasdair MacIntyre makes a similar point in 'The Very Idea of a University: Aristotle, Newman and Us', *New Blackfriars*, 91/1031 (2010), 4–19: 15–19.

[40] The ESRC Centre for Genomics in Society (Egenis), 'About us', <www.genomicsnetwork. ac.uk/egenis/aboutus/> (accessed 17 June 2010).

experience of the work of such projects, and so have seen at close quarters what it looks like when serious questions about the good are discussed.

On a somewhat different tack, it is sometimes possible to push for the involvement of varied forms of academic disciplinary attentiveness in a university's internal development of policy and practice—including the attentiveness of those who make questions about the good their special province. This can, of course, simply take the form of protest: the articulate voice in a meeting of the University Senate, say, that complains about the vacuity or destructiveness of some policy decision or document. In my experience, however, such protests normally come too late, and normally serve simply to reinforce narratives already too easily available to those in management positions, about the unrealistic and curmudgeonly obstructiveness of academic staff. Harder but more interesting, and potentially more rewarding, is the attempt to bring these concerns to bear constructively within the processes by which such policy proposals and documents are actually produced. Pushing for serious discussion of the good does not necessarily involve constructing a grandstand from which to pronounce prophetically, but searching for whatever small opportunities for undramatic involvement one's institution allows. Ideally, one wants those in positions of management in the university to come to regard it as normal to include such voices in their deliberations—and to do so not because it is a handy way of neutralizing a potential enemy, but because they have become used to constructive and realistic contributions from such people, and sensitized to the kinds of questions they are likely to raise.

Whom do I mean, though? Who are the people 'who make questions about the good their special province?' There may be people who fit that description in all sorts of disciplinary contexts within the university, but it is likely to refer in particular to some of those called philosophers and theologians (whether or not they are housed in departments of philosophy and theology). I say 'philosophy *and* theology', because it is not enough—if we are seriously going to ask about the public good in the ways I have described—to secure the involvement of some philosophers trained in an abstract discipline called 'ethics'. That assumes a model of public argument about the good that I have been at pains to deny, a model in which public argument about the good can be joined only by those who agree to forget who they are. What we need for such interdisciplinary work really to tackle questions of the common good are people trained in articulating the major religious and secular traditions of thinking about the good that are 'in play' in our society, and who are trained in arguing together.[41] A secular university that took this responsibility seriously

---

[41] It is for this reason that a university that has lost all its philosophers or theologians is in difficulties. In a university in which the various disciplines have become isolated in departmental bunkers, and where interdisciplinary conversation and questioning are a desultory and secondary activity, the axing of a philosophy or theology department may be of symbolic significance,

would appropriately be called a secular *and religious* university, by which I mean a secular and religiously plural university—an appropriate name for a university seeking to be deeply embedded in, and seriously pursuing the good of, a secular and religiously plural society.

THE VALUE OF A UNIVERSITY EDUCATION

Earlier in this chapter, I indicated that I did not wish to focus too directly on the impact that universities have simply by sending graduates out into the wider world. I wanted to avoid the simplistic model that thinks of the university's impact being mediated by intellectual virtue as an individual possession, generated in the universities and then carried out into the wider world in the lives of individual students. Now that I have put in place a rather different framework for thinking about the university's contribution to the common good, however, it is possible to re-focus the discussion on those individual students, on the way they are fitted for life after graduation, and on the contribution they can then make to the common good.

In the first place, it is quite proper—indeed, it is necessary—that the range of university courses on offer includes plenty of forms of professional educa- tion. Karl Jaspers advocates the inclusion of hotel management,[42] Stanley Hauerwas the inclusion of courses on milking cows.[43] As Jaspers and Hauer- was insist, however, this inclusion makes sense only if the circumstances and the form of such inclusions in the university curriculum are right. On the one hand, it matters that this be a genuine form of entanglement in the discourses by which the social world is ordered—it matters, in other words, that hotels or cows play some significant part in the ordering of our world, and that the university's entanglement will have the capacity to sustain and shape the arguments about how this significant part is best arranged. On the other hand, it matters that the university not simply deal with questions of efficiency and technique, with means to the unquestioned ends specified by the profes- sion in question, but that it be able to raise questions about the good of the

---

but it is not likely to have much direct damaging effect on the rest of the university. If, however, we are serious about promoting argument about the good served by the various ideas and innovations that the university develops, the lack of philosophers and theologians in *some* guise is a much more serious problem. To put this negatively: the problem with many of our universities is not that they would consider axing philosophy or theology departments, but precisely that it would do them no significant damage if they did.

[42] Jaspers, *Idea*, 101.
[43] Hauerwas, *State of the University*, 92, 97.

relevant practice[44]—such that students are, in among all the other aspects of their formation, habituated to participate in the virtuous and sociable arguments about that good that the university should be helping to sustain and shape, and to be themselves part of that sustaining and shaping work.[45]

Even for those students whose programmes of study are not so explicitly dedicated to professional training, caring about their employability is still a necessary element of the curriculum, and the spectacle of academic staff with secure contracts and pleasant levels of pay sneering about the idea of concerning themselves with their students' employability should be revolting—and I speak as one who has in the past been revolting in precisely this way. And that does mean that we have a responsibility to give some priority to those aspects of the curriculum that might fairly directly fit students for the world of work—even though the identification of such aspects, and the justification of the claim that they will genuinely be of use, are far from easy. It is not that this direct concern with employability is the sole aim of a university education, nor that it is the primary justification for the courses that students take (such that the *primary* reason for the existence of an English programme for undergraduates would be the fact that it provides them with transferable skills in critical analysis of documents). I do not think either of those things is true. Nevertheless, it should be as unthinkable for us to ignore or downplay this aspect of our provision for students as it would be to refuse to write references for them once they have left. Of course, it is no less important here than it is for students engaged directly in professional training that other students are, in among all the other aspects of their formation, habituated to participate in the virtuous and sociable arguments about that good of their future professions that the university should be helping to sustain and shape, and to be themselves part of that sustaining and shaping work—but that is not the whole of the story, and not the only aspect of employability that it is proper for us to tackle.

Universities are also quite properly in the business of forming citizens. That is, universities are in the business of forming students who are habituated to participate (alongside others) in the virtuous and sociable arguments that the university should be helping to sustain and shape in the public world beyond individual professions—especially arguments about the public good—and to be themselves part of that sustaining and shaping work. We should be forming students ready and able to participate in whatever the equivalents are in their discipline of the Bad Science blog, and less likely to succumb to the unsociable vices that bedevil Comment is Free; students who can help keep the conversations that shape the public world away from what Newman called viewiness;

[44] 'There are also violent and nonviolent ways to milk cows' (Hauerwas, *State of the University*, 92).
[45] Cf. MacIntyre, 'The Very Idea of a University', 15–17.

students who have become habituated to participation in socially inclusive debate about the common good—and so students ready to play a virtuous part in the institutions of democracy.[46]

Once again, however, it is very important not to understand this in too individualistic a way. I am not claiming that universities are good because they produce individual 'wise souls', whose contributions to public discourse (and whose votes) will in general be more worthy than those of the general population—though I would certainly hope that graduates in a particular discipline might be more able than average to avoid talking public rubbish about that discipline. Rather, I am suggesting that there are all sorts of ways in which universities can contribute alongside others to the patterns of discourse that form our society, and help keep those patterns virtuous and sociable, and more deeply and clearly connected to argument about the good. And I am suggesting that we can and should be hoping to turn out graduates ready to participate (alongside many others) in those communal patterns of discourse, and ready by their participation (alongside many others) to help keep those discourses functioning as they should.

Picture an architecture graduate, for instance.[47] She might, in her years at university, have been trained in the many forms of judgement involved in designing safe and practical buildings within tight financial and material constraints, and so be someone who is able to help sustain the discussions in and around her profession about building possibilities and constraints. Her education might help her to be one of those who keep those conversations open to judgement. My hope is that she might also emerge from university habituated to the idea that questions of building design are inextricably bound up with questions about the patterns of flourishing human life that are sustained or obstructed by those buildings. There is no reason to think that

---

[46] I am a little more hesitant about broadening this claim beyond student's involvement in the conversations of public reason. I would like to be able to claim that the virtues that good university education forms also help to make students good citizens in other ways—by making them good neighbours, perhaps, who can recognize their own prejudices and something of how these distort their perceptions and relationships, and who can make and enact informed judgements about the needs of those alongside whom they live. I am not sure, though, how well the virtues that we seek to form, even when the formation works well, transfer to contexts where the forms of attentiveness and patience and judgement are so far removed from the academic disciplines within which the formation takes place. I am grateful to Rachel Muers for discussion on this point.

[47] I have chosen a professional discipline as my example simply for convenience: it is easy to say what I want to say fairly briefly in relation to such a discipline. Nevertheless, I mean these comments to apply just as much to, say, Physics or History. It is just that it takes longer to identify how physics- and history-related discourses are involved in the way our society works, and to discuss how those graduates who do not themselves become professional physicists and historians might nevertheless participate in some aspects of those discourses, and to speculate about how they might do so as people habituated to the idea that those discourses are connected in all sorts of complex ways to questions about the flourishing or good of that society.

she will emerge from her years of university able to offer others priceless pearls of deep wisdom about those patterns of life—but she might still emerge as someone whose work is one small contribution among others to keeping discussions about the deeper purpose and impact of architecture going, within the architectural profession and across those boundaries where architecture is enmeshed in the arguments of the wider society.[48] And that is, perhaps, enough.

CONCLUSION

I argued in Chapter 5 that true knowledge of the world could only be knowledge of the fulfilment that God has for it: knowledge of how to live peaceably and flourishingly together—and knowledge that must, for finite creatures such as us, take the form of both the pursuit of wisdom and the welcoming of delight.

In this chapter, rejecting the idea that knowledge is an end in itself, or that the goal of a public university can be the pursuit of a private indulgence, I have tried to sketch some of the ways in which contemporary secular universities might be orientated towards wisdom, in ways recognizable to one formed by Christian discipleship and worship. I have argued that, for good Christian theological reasons, the orientation to wisdom should take the form not of agreement by university staff and students to pursue a Christian vision of the good, but of widespread and energetic engagement in serious, socially inclusive, religious and secular arguments about the good, in which those speaking from the midst of Christian formation are insistently questioning voices—but by no means the only voices.

Even that is not all, however. Most of what I have said in this chapter has fallen broadly under the heading of wisdom; I have been arguing, in effect, that university learning needs to be orientated towards wisdom—by which I have simply meant, towards argument about the common good or creaturely flourishing. I argued in Chapter 6, however, that wisdom is not everything, and that it needs informing by delight (and by the lament that is delight's partner).[49] Such delight and lament are needed in order to remind us that the world is not best understood in relation to our desire, and that our capacity to

---

[48] If I am to be even more optimistic, I would add that I hope she will emerge from university as someone habituated to the idea that her work as an architect is inextricable from arguments about patterns of human flourishing *and* to the idea that those arguments need to be secular and religiously plural.

[49] Cf. Nicholas Wolterstorff, *Educating for Shalom: Essays on Christian Higher Education*, ed. Clarence W. Joldersma and Gloria Goris Stronks (Grand Rapids, MI: Eerdmans, 2004), 23. Midgley, in *Wisdom, Information and Wonder*, 41, says that 'it is an essential element in wonder

absorb the world into our projects (however worthy those projects) needs regularly to be interrupted by attention to the otherness of that world. Delight and lament are needed to help us register the limits of our interest and control, and to orientate us towards a flourishing in which the good of all creatures is fulfilled, rather than one in which other creatures find their place only in so far as they serve our good. Delight and lament are proper goals of the university— and the development of the capacity to delight and lament a proper good of university education.

This may sound like an implausible claim to make in the light of the question 'Who will pay?', but it is actually one of the aspects of university study that is most visible—and most valued—in the wider world. Documentaries, books of popular science, museums: there are all sorts of contexts in which one can see public fascination with useless knowledge. Yes, the politics of such fascination is often ambiguous, but the fascination is there—and most university teachers know that passionate fascination with the subject matter crops up in the most surprising places among their students, and that it is often a more secure driver of devotion to study than any concern with employability or advancement.[50] Recognizing and feeding an appetite for wonder is a proper goal of university education. The only caveat I would offer, on the basis of my account of delight and of mission in Chapter 6, is that the primary form of this delight is not as a private pleasure—a form of connoisseurship, perhaps—but rather as a delight in sharing delight. A university education should, among other things, be a training in the service of such overflowing delight.

It is, therefore, entirely appropriate, as institutions devoted to the common good, that universities should *also* pursue useless knowledge, knowledge for the sake of delight and lament. One of the first services that knowledge can provide for us, on the way to our fulfilment in the kingdom of God's love and justice, is the constantly repeated demonstration that we are not the whole of the world, that our needs and wants are not the most revealing coordinates against which the world can be plotted, and that our capacity to pursue any end—even that of peaceable community with other creatures in all their manifold difference from us—is radically limited. That insistence does not, of course, sit comfortably alongside my repeated insistence upon the active and deliberate pursuit of practical wisdom, but the two nevertheless belong together. We can expect, not necessarily every individual academic career, but every healthy discipline, perhaps every healthy academic department, to be

---

that we recognize what we see as something we did not make, cannot fully understand, and acknowledge as containing something greater than ourselves.'

[50] This, incidentally, is why involvement in mass media—in television documentaries, radio interviews, books for popular audiences, and the rest—is not (or should not be) a peripheral matter for academics.

caught up in ongoing arguments between those who insist upon the active pursuit of practical wisdom—of *benefit*, in the most direct sense appropriate—and those who champion delight.

To the extent that it is or can be ordered to wisdom and delight, it is possible for me to see my work within a secular university as a labour to draw myself and others deeper into the kind of true knowledge that I described in Chapter 5: knowledge that is more fundamental than the kinds of knowledge that are detached from concern with the good. A university education devoted to wisdom and delight may be concerned only with limited aspects of the true learning that I described in Chapter 5, but they are real aspects nonetheless. University life can properly be a life of service to the peaceable kingdom, the kingdom of love and justice—and that is the main justification we have for thinking that university life might be *good*.

My argument has two more steps to take. In the final chapter, I will turn more explicitly to the fact that my whole account so far is itself a particular and debatable proposal about the good of the university, to be argued about by others who understand that good differently. I will ask what kind of argument the university can conduct about its own life, and whether it is really possible to imagine it taking the secular and religiously plural form I have been describing. In the Conclusion, I will ask what it means for a work in a secular and religiously plural university to be capable of pursuing only a limited aspect of the true learning described in Chapter 5—and, in particular, what it means to remember that true learning is orientated to the formation of the flourishing life of all God's creatures together *before God*.

EXCURSUS: THE VALUE OF THE HUMANITIES

Claims about the public value of higher education in general may not have fared well in public discourse in recent years, but claims about the value of the humanities in particular have fared even worse. Though it has not been my focus in this chapter, nor in the book more generally, an account of the public value of the humanities does nevertheless emerge fairly straightforwardly from what I have said. The humanities disciplines, too, find their goal in the promotion of wisdom and delight—of understanding and forms of judgement that make for more flourishing coexistence with each other and with other creatures. In some cases, the capacity of these disciplines to be orientated to that end will be obvious, as when those disciplines subject the multiple cultural discourses that saturate and shape our present world to multifaceted critical analysis. In some cases, that capacity might be less obvious but no less real, as when those disciplines excavate the memories and traces of the past that shape the negotiations of the present, and subject those memories and traces to historical analysis and testing. In some cases, the orientation to this end might be quite properly indirect, as when those disciplines take forms that lie closer to delight (and lament): the patient discovery of other ways of living in their own integrity, past and present—and, through that, the discovery that our lives are not the only way that life can be, and that we are not the whole of the story.

Humanities disciplines matter because we are ineradicably cultural and ineradicably historical creatures, and the negotiations with each other and with the wider creaturely ecology that have shaped the cultural and historical forms of human life are unavoidably negotiations conducted with patterns of understanding, apprehension, and judgement, with languages and other sign systems, with interpretation and imagination and memory.

All this has been said many times before.[51] The one thing I would add, in the light of the foregoing chapter, is that it is important not to pitch such justifications of the humanities in too individual a register. It can too easily degenerate into the claim that those who graduate from humanities disciplines are able, somehow, to negotiate the world of human culture more gracefully and intelligently than others; that they have acquired an understanding of human meanings and deceptions that makes them conspicuously wise as worldly human agents.

We should insist, rather, that a society is a cultural and historical reality, and that it includes multiple ways by which it takes account of its own cultural and historical nature, and subjects it to discussion, argument, analysis, and critique. There is a whole ecology of such intellectual activity stretching across any society. Universities are one important niche in that ecology, and can play a significant part in sustaining the whole thing—but they are neither its only sources nor its only home, and the patterns of entanglement and involvement by which they are connected to that wider ecology have to do with much more than the production of well-formed graduates. Of course, we may hope that graduates well formed in particular disciplines will be less likely than average to talk rubbish about matters that fall within those disciplines—but that is only one of the ways in which universities contribute to the self-reflexivity of society, and in and of itself it will not necessarily look like wisdom.

---

[51] See, e.g., Nigel Biggar, 'What are Universities for? A Christian View', in Mike Higton, Jeremy Law, and Christopher Rowland (eds), *Theology and Human Flourishing: Essays in Honour of Timothy J. Gorringe* (Eugene, OR: Wipf and Stock, 2011), 238–50. See also Rowan Williams, *Why Study the Past? The Quest for the Historical Church* (London: DLT; Grand Rapids, MI: Eerdmans, 2005), and John Webster, '"There is no Past in the Church, so there is no Past in Theology": Barth on the History of Modern Protestant Theology', in Mike Higton and John C. McDowell (eds), *Conversing with Barth* (Aldershot: Ashgate, 2004), 14–39.

9

The Negotiable University

In the second part of this book, I have been offering a construal of university life based on the theology set out in Chapter 5, and have articulated that construal by means of claims about virtue, sociality, and the common good. Such a bid to construe the life of universities is possible because, in one sense, there is no fixed 'idea' of the university. The university is not the implementation of a blueprint, nor has its life evolved in such a way as to mimic the kind of reality created to a plan.[1] Rather, universities are—and always have been—meeting places for *multiple* ideas about their nature, their proper functioning, and their ends.

THE CONVERSATION OF CONSTRUALS

University life is shaped by the interaction between multiple ideas about the nature and good of higher education. Such ideas or construals are not necessarily explicit or articulate; they are rather habits of mind and practice, likes and dislikes, patterns of recognition and bafflement or rejection, fragments of stories and metaphors and half-remembered conversations. To say that someone has a stance or a construal of university life is simply to say that she has some malleable, evolving, quite probably incoherent, but nevertheless characteristic way of negotiating her way through that life. It will be revealed in the grumbles that she can be relied upon to express in committee meetings, in the preference she shows for extensive handwritten comments on student essays, in the predictable reaction she has to proposed library reorganization, in the talk she gives year after year to new undergraduates about plagiarism. It will probably be more plausible to describe this construal in relation to her field or discipline or department—to the intellectual and practical context in which

---

[1] Few people, casting a critical eye over the empirical evidence provided by university life, are going to be tempted to campaign for 'intelligent design' to be taught as a serious option in courses on university history.

she spends the majority of her time, which is organized around the particular sources of her academic inspiration and vocation, and which does most to shape her sense of the possibilities and challenges of academic life—but to the extent that she participates in, comments on, thinks about, and moves through the wider structures of her university, and of the higher-education sector more broadly, it will also be a construal of the university more generally.

University life is built from the interaction of such construals: they feed one another, shape one another, react against one another, collude and collide in any number of ways. In places, university life will be sustained by patches of agreement between construals, of varying scales. In places, it will be made up of ongoing disagreements between construals—disagreements sustainable enough to count as part of how this life works, for now. In places, the patterns by which these construals or stances interact to form university life will be stranger, as when there are persistent patterns of misrecognition or misunderstanding that also somehow become part of how this corporate life works, how it sustains itself over time. Ask, for instance, how the distinction between 'managers' and 'academics' sustains itself over time in a university like mine, even when most of the managers were academics until they crossed the divide, and, as well as answers relating to unspoken dress codes, changed responsibilities and conversation partners, and petty power dynamics, you are likely to need answers that have to do with the power of patterns of incomprehension to persist and to contribute backhandedly to the organizing of a sustainable life.

The interactions by which construals form university life and are formed by university life do not often take the form of clearly articulated arguments; they are mostly not arguments at all. Human beings—even students, academics, and managers—have endless ways of adjusting their paths in response to one another, or falling into step with one another, or asserting themselves against one another, or riding roughshod over one another, or misunderstanding one another. University life is shaped by all of these.

The university is, then, an evolving settlement between such construals, in which the construals themselves are reshaped. By 'settlement', I simply mean that the life so formed has enough practical consistency and persistence to be recognizable today as roughly the same institution that it was yesterday, and to be a context in which at least some ongoing practices can be sustained, and in which it will be possible tomorrow to pick up the threads of some of the conversations that I left unfinished today.[2]

The university is not, therefore, to be mistaken for the account that the dominant management discourses gives of it, though those discourses might play an important role in shaping the settlement that the university is. The

---

[2] See my account of settlements in Mike Higton and Rachel Muers, *The Text in Play: Experiments in Biblical Reading* (Eugene, OR: Wipf and Stock, 2011), ch. 10.

university is not to be mistaken for *any* single ideology or political theory, however heavily it may lean in the direction of one or another from time to time. Most of the people who make the university what it is walk through it trailing tatters of all sorts of ideological formations, even if the colouring of such fragments is such as to give the view of the university from a distance an apparently consistent hue. The attempt to step back and set out *the* epistemology or *the* ontology of the contemporary university is an attempt to throw important sets of fragments into relief—it is a tool, a ruse, for the commentator on university life, and, however important and illuminating it might be (and it can be both), it is secondary to the more patient discovery of the rougher texture that university life has up close.

Any attempt to speak into this context so as to make some kind of difference—to rally colleagues around some vision for the future, to hold university leaders to account for some betrayal or failure, to push some policy change through a fine mesh of committees—involves (unless it is an act of sheer imposition) some kind of attempt to elicit recognition for what one says from the participants in this messy life. That is, it involves laying out some kind of articulated construal of a university's life, in the hope that one's listeners will find a home in that articulation for at least some elements of their own construal: they will recognize it as, at least in part, a description of *their* university, even if their own construal or stance is altered by their adoption of this articulation. This sort of thing is going on all the time, with more and less success; writing a book about university life is, in this light, simply a heavy-handed and possibly perverse way of pursuing the ordinary means by which such life is shaped.

To the extent that what I have said provides a recognizable description of university life, it seems to me that the Jamesian 'hotel-corridor' model cited by George Marsden,[3] described in Chapter 4 above, is deeply implausible— implausible, that is, as a description of what in fact goes on in universities. I have not mentioned the word 'reason' in my description so far, but I have been assuming that it is an important part of what is included under the heading 'university life'—and am simply unpersuaded that university life is shaped by clear, more-or-less universal agreements about what counts and what does not count as appropriate participation, established prior to the negotiations of university life, and providing the accepted context for those negotiations. That the *idea* of such a hotel-corridor agreement is prominently in play in many universities, and that it has some practical heft in the shaping of university policy and practice, I do not doubt; that the actual processes of reasoning together in universities are closely described by any such account seems much less plausible. Rather, there is an ongoing negotiation, mostly

---

[3] George M. Marsden, *The Outrageous Idea of Christian Scholarship* (New York: Oxford University Press, 1997), 46; see above, p. 113.

unspoken or inarticulate—an ongoing interaction of construals, including construals of the proper nature of university reasoning, of what counts as a good reason in the various different argumentative contexts that a university provides (from seminar rooms to senate chambers, coffee shops to laboratories). And such negotiation goes on not first of all at the level of the university as a whole but in those smaller-scale contexts where collective passions are organized around some problem or project: in fields or disciplines, perhaps, but also in management groups and leadership teams. In such contexts, and then emerging from them into the wider negotiation of the university, there are differing (though overlapping) ideas in play about what constitutes excellence in argument, about the virtues that good reasoners will display, about the people who can be taken as exemplars of reasoning practice, about the practices and forms of sociality by which lives of reason are appropriately formed, and about the good that such excellence serves. The university is, in part, an argument about its own nature and good.

TRADITION-SHAPED VOICES

To say this—that is, to say that a 'hotel-corridor' model is 'prominently in play', but that I do not recognize its descriptive claims—serves to highlight the fact, already mentioned above, that even in this chapter I am not offering a neutral description of university life. Even here, my construal of the nature of university life is one shaped by my participation in a particular tradition, and it is one with which other participants in the university will disagree. I will think they do so wrongly, of course, but they might persist in thinking that I am the one who is wrong. My construal of university life in this chapter is not meant to be a view from nowhere, any more than were the construals offered in the previous three chapters, however strongly I may harbour the fantasy that it will be found immediately and wholly convincing by all university practitioners the moment they read it.

This partiality of view does not mark me out from other participants in university life, however. Each of the construals in play in university life can, with some important caveats, be described as having been shaped by a particular tradition of moral formation (just as many of the authors introduced in Chapter 4 insisted). I am not sure I can describe university life in terms of a clash of world views, mostly because I am not convinced that people *have* world views, but it does seem clear that a construal receives its shape and force in part from a person's passage through particular social contexts beyond the university in which ideas about virtue, sociality, and the good are given at least an initial slant. The university is, in part, constituted by the interaction between traditions.

This picture of the university as a negotiation between voices already formed by numerous traditions does need qualifying, of course. In the first place, the university (and more especially the smaller-scale contexts within it that focus people's passions and vocations) is a context of its own, and, however much it comes to reflect the ideas present in the culture around it, it also has its own density and momentum: it is not *simply* the repetition of the traditions from which its practitioners come.[4] In the second place, I am aware that the word 'tradition' in this context has become uncomfortably baggy. In one direction it is stretched to cover the sometimes rather shapeless moral formation that occurs on a passage through a culture mediated by a particular family history, schooling, job, and other involvements and social locations. In the other, it is being used to refer to something more readily identifiable, even if hard to describe well—as when I say that I am writing from within the English Anglican tradition. It is worth at least being aware of the metaphorical stretching at work in these descriptions. In the third place, I do not want my appropriation of the language of tradition to bring with it the assumption that any given university could convincingly be assigned to a single dominant tradition, or provided with a single genealogy—or that this book is an attempt to enthrone a new single tradition as the dominant framework for academic life. My emphasis here falls as much on the word 'negotiation' as on the word 'tradition'.

University life can be seen as a settlement between practitioners who arrive already shaped by different traditions of moral and intellectual formation, however much they then go on to be reshaped by university life itself. The 'rules of the academic game' are the product of the ongoing process of settlement, the ongoing negotiation (implicit and explicit) between these differing practitioners. Those rules emerge as a set of provisionally agreed rules of thumb within this activity of settlement, and are (however subtly) subject to constant renegotiation. That there are some such rules is indicated by the possibility of speaking out of turn in any given university, saying or doing the wrong thing, or not acting in a way that makes recognizable sense. That the rules are subtle and shifting is indicated by the difficulty of identifying with any clarity just where the boundaries of acceptable university behaviour lie, and of the possibility of discovering that what makes sense in one institution gains no purchase in another.

Of course, some of my university colleagues (as I would describe it, and as they would probably not) may have received moral and intellectual formations within traditions that lead them to think it a mistake to try speaking to the university as a whole from within a particular tradition of formation; they might think it a form of obscurantism unlikely to be capable of contributing to

---

[4] Cf. the quote from Lorraine Daston above, Ch. 6, n. 17.

properly university-wide, properly *public* conversation about the good of secular university life. Some of them will think, perhaps, that we should begin by discussing the neutral rules of engagement that are needed if people of different traditions are to talk to one another. To clarify and secure such procedural commitments will seem to them the high road to sustaining and promoting university reason. Others of them might think, perhaps, that we should begin by looking at the way in which some field of study or discipline or object of study has on its own a sufficient gravitational pull to organize a life of reason around itself, reshaping its investigators more or less regardless of their prior formations. Attending to those particularities, and to the vocations that they generate, will seem to them the high road to renewing and deepening university reason. My conviction, however, is that my theological tradition can provide a rather different answer both to questions about the nature of public argument between people of differing traditional formations, and to questions about how best to understand the captivating pull of particular contexts and objects of study, and what such captivations add up to—and that approaching those questions from the direction of my tradition does not obviously involve giving up on seriousness about public reason or on the nature of the modern research university as secular and religiously plural.

Of course, I do not expect everyone in the university to agree with this conviction of mine. I expect to be thought wrong (and possibly incoherent), just as I will think many of my interlocutors wrong (and possibly incoherent). The first thing to say about such disagreement is that it is not in itself necessarily a fatal problem for university life. I am pretty sure that, even while we disagree, we will still be able to contribute to the ongoing evolution of shared practices together, with just about good enough agreement on what I will call (though my interlocutors may not) excellence, virtues, exemplars, and disciplines—just about good enough, that is, to allow us to carry on teaching students together, sitting on committees together, discussing university parking provision together, and so on. That may possibly be because our practice, our *operative* construal of university life, does not match our antagonistic theoretical pronouncements, but it may simply be that there is enough overlap between the implications of our differing theoretical positions to allow a pragmatic accommodation. The outcome of our arguments does not need to be consensus, but sustainable patterns of shared action, habits of shared life, that are understood differently by the differing participants, and in which the patterns of our ongoing disagreements are acknowledged and negotiated. There may come a time when such possibilities of shared action evaporate, but I do not think such a time is close in my own context.

The second thing to say, though, about the disagreement that I expect is that (on theological grounds that I have already made clear) I hope that such a disagreement can, at least in some contexts, become a real *argument*—and a virtuous and sociable argument at that. To justify that claim, however, requires some kind of indication of the *kind* of argument I think possible between those working within different traditions—working as they do with different assumptions about what *counts* as a good argument.

ARTICULATION AND ATTENTIVENESS

Such conversation is, I think, made possible first of all by articulation and attentiveness—forms of the virtues already discussed in Chapter 6. Articulation is a matter of trying to stop murmuring, of trying to become articulate and explicit about one's own construal of university life. This is not simply, however, a matter of learning to raise a voice so as to assert one's distinctiveness. Rather, it involves trying to become articulate about the patterns of *reasoning* involved in one's construal—giving reasons for the faith that is in one (whether or not one's reasons involve appeal to grounds shared by others in the university). I say that this process involves *trying* to become articulate because one may in fact not be a good observer of the nature and roots of one's own construal. The connections one makes to the patterns of reasoning of one's tradition may be artificial, or one's identification of those patterns may be inadequate. Any attempted articulation can only be provisional and questionable. Nevertheless, it is important to make the attempt.

Alongside such articulation, attentiveness to the articulations of others is needed—or, where such articulations are missing, assistance for others to become articulate or attempts to become articulate on their behalf. Such articulations will be no less provisional than one's own, of course, and part of the task of attentiveness will be a suspicious nose for misrepresentations and non sequiturs—not yet in order to ask whether this person's articulate construal of the good of university life is *true*, but simply in order to understand whether this person's articulation is a fair description of the patterns of reasoning by which her construal is in fact shaped.

The way in which articulation and attention make argument possible may be clearer if I discuss an example. In Chapter 4, I described Steve Holmes's case for academic freedom in a Baptist University.[5] What he provides is, precisely, an articulation: it not only sets out his convictions about academic freedom, but shows the patterns of reasoning by which those convictions are connected to some of the deepest commitments of his Baptist tradition. And it seems to me to be a fairly plausible articulation: I cannot see any obvious reason to doubt that it represents key lines in the broader structure of thinking within which his convictions about academic freedom sit. That does not mean

[5] See above, Ch. 4, n. 51.

that this is necessarily the route by which he first arrived at his convictions about academic freedom, but that this articulation aptly describes the way he has now made sense of those convictions in the light of his theological allegiances—and of his theological allegiances in the light of his beliefs about academic freedom. I cannot, either, see any obvious reason to doubt that this articulation provides a fair description of the way Holmes's priorities now run—such that convincing him that a rather different view of academic freedom would be more securely based on those same Baptist foundations will be likely to change his approach to academic freedom rather than to change his Baptist allegiance.

Now I am not a Baptist theologian. The deep Baptist commitments that drive Holmes's argument are not *my* commitments, and, however valid the argument that Holmes makes from them to his conclusions, it cannot compel agreement from me. That does not mean, however, that I am reduced to silence by Holmes's articulacy. Nor are my responses confined to a simple comparison of his views with mine, nor to the pursuit of some purely pragmatic agreement that takes for granted (unargued) the shape of his convictions and the shape of mine, and looks for overlaps big enough to build shared projects on.

Holmes's articulacy, even though it articulates a tradition not my own, actually makes argument possible. Because he has made it articulate for me, I can experiment in his discourse (even though I can do so only as an amateur, a provisional apprentice): I can argue with him about what really follows from the commitments he has exposed; I can see whether I can argue on *his* grounds towards something that looks more like what *I* would want to say about academic freedom. I can ask him what, on his grounds, he can say about various aspects of academic freedom that he has not covered, and try to provoke him to envy by expounding the things that I think I can say, from within my tradition, about those things. At a deeper level, because his articulation includes some sense of the relative priority of the various Baptist commitments that he discusses, I can argue with him about the coherence and plausibility of those commitments. And, if I have managed to become as articulate about my Anglican commitments and their connection to my account of academic freedom, he can do all these same things with my articulation in return.[6]

Such argument, made possible by our articulation and attentiveness, can have many possible results. It might lead to one or both of us changing our minds about the nature of academic freedom; indeed, it might lead to us

---

[6] It is worth noting, of course, that our reasons for engagement in this kind of argument, our descriptions of what we are doing as we so engage, and the precise styles of our engagement, may well differ, because there may well be differing Baptist and Anglican construals of such argument.

significantly extending the area within which our conclusions about academic freedom resemble one another. It might, on the other hand, lead to our understanding more deeply the nature of our disagreement, and so the limits upon our possible cooperation—if, for instance, I understand precisely *why* some of my convictions about academic freedom are not reproducible on Holmes's grounds. And it can (and almost certainly will) lead to both of us amending our articulations. They were both only *attempts* at articulacy in the first place, and it is hard to imagine a serious conversation between the two of us that would not show us routes to better articulations: more faithful identification of our commitments as Baptist and Anglican, more careful explanation of how those commitments relate to questions about academic freedom, more precise delineations of the limits and uncertainties of our conclusions about that freedom. In other words, this process of arguing could lead to the securing of extended agreement, to richer and more interesting disagreement, and to deeper mutual understanding and deeper self-understanding—and on the basis of all that, to the discovery of new patterns of shared and unshared action, a new shape of academic life together.

This is a fictional example. Steve Holmes and I do not significantly disagree about academic freedom, and the argument that I have described is not one that we have had—though we have been friends and colleagues for a long time, and have had arguments like this on other topics in the past.[7] However, my understanding of this kind of argument has been shaped more recently by the example of arguments between Jewish, Christian, and Muslim scholars in the context of a practice called Scriptural Reasoning. I have described that practice in greater depth elsewhere, but it involves scholars from the three traditions meeting in small groups to engage in intensive discussion of each other's Scriptures together—not on the assumption that we already agree about the meaning, authority, or appropriate use of those Scriptures, nor on the assumption that the arguments will be such as to create consensus, but simply because such argument is possible, and transformative. A Scriptural Reasoning discussion can be understood as a laboratory for articulation and attentiveness: a context in which the various participants learn to articulate more clearly the ways in which their convictions are shaped by the ways Scriptures are read in their traditions, and also learn to attend to the articulations of others. And, just as in the fictional example above, such articulacy and attentiveness lead not simply to comparison or to the identification of areas of pragmatic overlap, but to the securing of some kinds of deeper agreement, to the development of richer and more interesting disagreement, and to increases in mutual

---

[7] That we are friends is by no means the least important condition for the possibility of such arguments, of course, as Ch. 7 suggested.

understanding and in self-understanding (all, once again, in the context of friendship).[8]

Grasping the possibility of argument like this between traditions (which is not simply a matter of attempted 'out-narration') is important if you are to understand my aim in writing this book. The theological account of learning I articulated in Chapter 5 led me on to claims about virtue and sociality in Chapters 6 and 7. I may hope for the triumph of my understanding of virtue and sociality over other views of the nature of reason, but I cannot consistently hope for a vicious and unsociable triumph. Whatever may be my ultimate hope for university life (or for life in general), it can only properly be approached by way of a penultimate hope: a hope for a virtuous and sociable engagement with those who think about the university differently, in pursuit of the university's good.[9] My hope is, therefore, for an *argument*, in which my Christian theological voice vies critically with other religious voices, and with secular voices. I will participate in that argument for Christian theological reasons, construing the nature of the argument itself in Christian theological ways, and arguing seriously for the truth of my Christian theological construal of higher education. I trust that the secular and other religious participants will have their own reasons for serious argument, and their own construals of what such argument involves—and that there will be enough rough overlap between these varying construals to allow us to join in a common argumentative practice. In other words, I am not looking to re-found the Christian university, but to help secular and religiously plural universities take seriously their secular and religiously plural nature. I think I can do something to work positively and actively towards that penultimate goal; what the ultimate outcome of the argument will be is not for me to predict.

NEGOTIATING THE UNIVERSITY

To speak about the life of the university on Christian theological grounds, indeed on Anglican grounds, is not to abandon serious argument—argument capable of making a real difference.[10] The understanding of the life of the

---

[8] See Higton and Muers, *Text in Play*, pt 2. See also Nicholas Adams, *Habermas and Theology* (Cambridge: Cambridge University Press, 2006), esp. Ch. 11.

[9] See Rachel Muers, *Keeping God's Silence: Towards a Theological Ethics of Communication* (Oxford: Blackwell, 2004), 86–8, discussing the section 'Ultimate and Penultimate Things' in Dietrich Bonhoeffer, *Ethics*, Dietrich Bonhoeffer's Works (ed. Clifford J. Green) 6, tr. Reinhard Krauss, Charles C. West, and Douglas Scott (Minneapolis: Fortress, 2005).

[10] It does mean that 'securing universal consensus' cannot be the primary goal—but, as university life does not work by that kind of consensus, and few arguments of any kind produce it anyway, this does not seem like a heavy price to pay.

university that I have proposed is one in which such articulation is seen not as a form of violent self-assertion, but as a way of opening oneself up to interaction, to questioning, to challenge, and to change; it is seen as a form of vulnerability rather than violence, one that calls forth attention, and makes real argument possible—including argument with those who understand the nature of argument, its virtues, excellencies, exemplars, and disciplines, somewhat differently.[11]

To make such a proposal, however, is only one step in the real work of negotiating the shape of university life, or of promoting the development of an articulate and attentive, socially inclusive, secular, and religiously plural argument within the university about its own nature and good. Such negotiation takes place not primarily in the pages of books, but in endlessly particular interactions in specific times and places: talking to colleagues over coffee, serving on committees, sending an email to the Vice-Chancellor, asking questions at seminars, trying to get slogans (and jokes about other people's slogans) into circulation—seizing the opportunities that one must trust will present themselves, and working with those people, practices, and discourses, expected and unexpected, that—despite the inimical ideologies that may circulate around them—might prove allies of, or seriously articulate and attentive opponents of, the kind of convictions about university life that I defend.[12] In the words of Timothy Jenkins, discussed in Chapter 4, the work of negotiating the university will properly take the form of a series of experiments in providence.[13]

---

[11] It is very hard to say in advance what limits there might be on the capacity for me, understanding argument in my way, to argue with someone who understands argument very differently. Clearly, faced with someone who understood argument as a process of hitting one another with big sticks (and there are such people in the university), I should probably just run away.

[12] I do not find I have much use for the claim that the university is in crisis, except as a way of persuading others that my writing of this book is timely. I worry that a focus on crisis undercuts the ability to cultivate the kind of patient hope that experiments in providence demand. On the clash between hope and the 'myth of declension', see Rodney J. Sawatasky, 'Prologue: The Virtue of Scholarly Hope', in Douglas Jacobsen and Rhonda Hustedt Jacobsen (eds), *Scholarship and Christian Faith: Enlarging the Conversation* (Oxford: Oxford University Press, 2004), 3–14: 5.

[13] See above, Ch. 4, n. 96.

Conclusion

Stanley Hauerwas wrote that '[a]ny attempt to justify Christian participation in the university as we know it is an invitation to self-deception'.[1] That is a risk that, in writing this book, I have decided to run.

I began with the emergence of the University of Paris, and argued that at least some of those who shaped that emergence understood it as a new form of corporate spiritual discipline. The life of reason was, for them, a life of Christian devotion, in which learners experience compunction in the face of the reality that they are invited to know, but as yet misrecognize. Later in the book, I developed my own retrieval of this theme in an account of intellectual virtue centred on the virtues of openness to being judged and openness to judgement, echoing the dynamics of crucifixion and resurrection that are at the heart of Christian discipleship.

I moved on to the creation of the University of Berlin, and argued that the theorists of *Wissenschaft* who set the initial tone for that university were not engaged in as straightforward a rejection of their Christian heritage as is sometimes assumed. Instead, their rejection of the subordination of reason to the Christian tradition's heteronomous authority was itself grounded upon an account of free sociality that drew heavily, and explicitly, on the Christian tradition's vision of the Body of Christ. The rules of *Wissenschaft* were, for them, the rules of free sociality—and there was something ineradicably ecclesial about their vision of free sociality. Later in the book, I sought to retrieve this vision of the sociality of reason, without the exclusion of particular, positive formation that, as I see it, threatens to defeat it. I developed an account of the inherent sociality of university learning, drawing on my own theological understanding of the economy of gift and reception that animates the Body of Christ.

From Berlin, I crossed the Channel to Oxford and the Irish Sea to Dublin. I argued that Newman's account of the nature of university life drove too sharp a division between intellect and religion, and allowed intellect too

---

[1] Stanley Hauerwas, *The State of the University: Academic Knowledges and the Knowledge of God* (Oxford: Blackwell, 2007), 106.

autonomous a province of its own—albeit a province made stable and prosperous by its alliance with the far stronger empire of religion. In response, later in the book, I developed my own account of the end that intellectual development, simply as intellectual, serves—and argued that it always already serves a supernatural end. The end of all learning is the peaceable kingdom—the flourishing of all God's creatures together—and to know some object properly means to know all the ways in which its life contributes to that kingdom, and all the ways in which we may live graciously with it, including all the ways in which it is not exhausted by our projects and desires. I developed, therefore, an account of university learning as inherently ordered towards the public good—but argued that, in the context in which the university finds itself, that ordering will primarily take the form of a commitment to raising the question of the good (of flourishing and peaceable coexistence), and to arguing about the good in socially inclusive debates in which those formed in diverse secular and religious traditions can acknowledge their formation.

Finally, having examined various recent writings in which Christian writers talked about making an explicitly and avowedly Christian contribution to their universities, or seeking to sustain and develop explicitly and avowedly Christian institutions, I developed my own account of the way in which a Christian participant might contribute to the life of a secular and religiously plural university—by working in whatever ways present themselves to promote virtue, sociality, and the pursuit of the common good, and by seeking to encourage and sustain a rigorous religious and secular argument in the university about the university's nature and purpose.

The book has been animated by three overlapping convictions. First, that university learning is, at least in part, real learning. It has something of the character of discipleship, ecclesiality, and orientation to the common good that constitute real learning according to someone formed in my tradition. Real learning is often missed, marred, ignored, and misrecognized, and where it flourishes the flourishing is fragile—but it nevertheless makes sense for someone called to pursue real learning to do so within a university, and to do so without despair.

Second, universities can and should serve the public good—and can and should articulate more clearly the ways in which they serve it. They do not simply contribute to GDP, or improve the earning power of individual students; they do not simply provide individual students with learning as a personal possession and an end in itself; they do not simply display the health of their host society by their pursuit of properly useless knowledge. Rather they are (or can be, and should be) vital parts of the intellectual ecology by which a society takes stock of itself and its position in the world, and subjects its existing patterns of apprehension and judgement to analysis and criticism. A university is (or can be, and should be) one of the agencies by which a society becomes more virtuous and sociable, and keeps alive the question of its orientation to the good.

Third, universities can and should host open and serious arguments about their own nature and purpose, and should be able to do so in ways that include explicitly religious voices as well as voices formed within multiple secular traditions. Indeed, in order to be as virtuous, as sociable, as orientated to the good as they can be, universities desperately *need* to play host to such arguments. Universities, precisely because they are institutions for reason, for *Wissenschaft*, for rigorous intellectual endeavour, should take the form of complex secular and religiously plural, multidisciplinary and interdisciplinary, socially inclusive conversations.

All these claims involve both an affirmation of what universities are already, at their best, and a desire to work on those universities until they become better at what they properly do. I have argued, along the way, that there are indeed multiple avenues along which it appears to be possible, at present, to pursue that desire—ways of working for the good of the university that are realistic about the kinds of institutions universities presently are. At times, the book has no doubt come dangerously close to degenerating into an offering of homespun wisdom, as I have tried to illustrate my abstract claims about the nature of university life with descriptions of some of the ways in which I see those claims worked out in the ordinary practices and decisions of the institutions in which I work. That is, however, the level at which ideas of the university primarily live: in small changes, unremarkable decisions, ordinary habits. The large-scale decisions of policy-makers and managers matter too, of course—but they matter precisely because of the ways in which they impinge upon, restrict, or open up the scope for the real decisions and practices of academic life. And it is only if we know what we love at the level of ordinary academic practice that we will know what we are fighting for when the opportunity arises, as it sometimes does, for campaigning on a larger scale.

In concluding, I want to note two important limitations upon what I have said. In the first place, it is important to note that the good that a secular and religiously plural university pursues, or that can properly be pursued for a secular and religiously plural university, is limited. The university is not, after all, the church. It might be capable of forming people in dispositions that Christians can recognize as Christian virtues, in sociality that echoes the sociality of the Body of Christ, and in a pursuit of the world's flourishing that Christians can recognize as a true orientation to the good. Indeed, it might be that socially inclusive, secular, and religiously plural universities can sometimes be contexts in which the Christian participant can learn *more* about virtue, sociality, and the common good than they have done in church. But it does not directly form people for worship and discipleship—and yet worship and discipleship are the deepest, fullest forms that all true learning properly takes.

Just to the extent that the learning taking place in the university is real learning, it is learning that remains incomplete without worship and discipleship—learning that would be made more fully itself were it to be united to worship and discipleship.

This does, however, mean that worship and discipleship are entirely fitting accompaniments to life in the university—indeed, that they are the *most* fitting accompaniments. Study and worship belong together, and worship makes study more fully itself: it makes the disciplined use of reason more fully itself, it makes intellectual virtue and sociality more fully themselves. We might say, therefore, that nobody belongs on campus more fully than a chaplain, that no student organization makes more sense than a Christian union, or that a chapel completes a college—however deep the patterns of misrecognition and incomprehension might be that confuse those relationships. The chaplain, the Christian union, the chapel: *if* they do their job properly, they call the university to its highest good at the same time that they witness to that good's penultimate nature.

The second limitation that I want to register is simply that labour for the good of the university is fragmentary, frustrating, and marked by frequent disappointment. For most of us who work in universities, and for much of the time, it will be a matter of paying attention to the life of the university one is in, learning its ways, and looking out for those opportunities to nudge it in the right direction—and to build whatever alliances are possible for such nudging. It will be a matter of what I have described in Chapter 4 as a making available of oneself for the unforeseen work of God, putting oneself in its way, and listening carefully for the rumour of its coming.

The university is going to remain an ambiguous and ambivalent institution. Its life is going to remain a negotiation between multiple discourses, many of which (including many of the most dominant) are deadening or destructive. Nevertheless, it is also likely to remain a place where a difference can be made by exercises of virtue, by experiments in sociality, and by carefully placed questioning about the good of what we do—and a place where real learning flourishes in unexpected places, however heavy the odds against it. Labour for the good of the university will mean avoiding the constant low murmur of grumbling and the deliberate cultivation of isolation and of unsullied purity by which so many academics beg to be ignored, and ensure all too effectively their own powerlessness. It is likely, instead, to take a series of unheroic but hopeful forms: a seat on a dull committee, an attempt to find a way of filling in a bureaucratic form gracefully, a squirrelling into the procedures of Quality Assurance of questions about conversational ecology, a letter of thanks to the senior management when they say something sensible, a well-timed protest. It is likely to require refusal to give way to despair or to disdain, and instead a commitment to patient labour with humour and hope—combined with a willingness to live in the ambiguous and unfinished muddle of the present.

Bibliography

Abelard, Peter, *Historia calamitatum*, in *The Letters of Abelard and Heloise*, ed. and tr. Betty Radice and M.T. Clanchy, rev. edn (London: Penguin, 2003), 3–46; Latin text available at <www.thelatinlibrary.com/abelard/historia.html> (accessed 27 Aug. 2009).

——, *Sic et non*, prologue, tr. W. J. Lewis; <www.fordham.edu/halsall/source/Abelard-SicetNon-Prologue.html> (accessed 2 Sept. 2009).

Adams, Douglas, *The Hitch Hiker's Guide to the Galaxy* (London: Pan, 1979).

Adams, Nicholas, *Habermas and Theology* (Cambridge: Cambridge University Press, 2006).

Albisetti, James, McClelland, Charles E., and Turner, R. Steven, 'Science in Germany', in *Science in Germany: The Intersection of Institutional and Intellectual Issues*, *Osiris*, 2nd ser. 5 (1989), 285–304.

Allgemeines Landrecht für die Preußischen Staaten (ALR) II.12; <www.smixx.de/ra/Links_F-R/PrALR/PrALR_II_12.pdf> (accessed 27 Nov. 2009).

Anderson, Chris, *Teaching as Believing: Faith in the University*, Studies in Religion and Higher Education, ed. Michael Beaty, Jean Bethke Elstain, Stanley Hauerwas, Stephen R. Haynes, 2 (Waco, TX: Baylor University Press, 2004).

Anrich, Ernst (ed.), *Die Idee der deutschen Universität* (Darmstadt: Hermann Gentner Verlag, 1956).

Anselm of Canterbury, *Truth, Freedom and Evil: Three Philosophical Dialogues*, ed. and tr. Jasper Hopkins and Herbert Richardson (New York: Harper & Row, 1967).

——, *The Major Works*, ed. Brian Davies and G. R. Evans, Oxford World's Classics (Oxford: Oxford University Press, 1998).

——, *Proslogium; Monologium; An Appendix in Behalf of the Fool by Gaunilo; and Cur Deus Homo*, tr. Sidney Norton Deane (Chicago: Open Court, 1903); <www.fordham.edu/halsall/basis/anselm-intro.html> (accessed 3 Sept. 2009).

Applegate, Celia, 'Culture and the Arts', in Jonathan Sperber (ed.), *Germany 1800–1871*, Short Oxford History of Germany (Oxford: Oxford University Press, 2004), 115–36.

Aquinas, Thomas, *Summa Theologiae 23: 1a2ae. 55–67: Virtue*, tr. W. D. Hughes (Cambridge: Cambridge University Press, 2006).

Arts and Humanities Research Council, *Impact Assessment Position Paper* (London: AHRC, 2006); <www.ahrc.ac.uk/FundedResearch/Documents/Impact%20Position%20Paper.pdf> (accessed 17 June 2010).

Ashby, Eric, 'The Future of the Nineteenth Century Idea of a University', *Minerva*, 6 (1967), 3–17.

Astley, Jeff, Francis, Leslie, Sullivan, John, and Walker, Andrew (eds), *The Idea of a Christian University: Essays on Theology and Higher Education* (Bletchley and Waynesborough, GA: Paternoster, 2004).

Bahti, Timothy, 'Histories of the University: Kant and Humboldt', *Modern Language Notes (MLN)* 102/3 (Apr. 1987), 437–60.

Baldwin, John W., 'Masters at Paris from 1179–1215: A Social Perspective', in Robert L. Benson and Giles Constable (eds), *Renaissance and Renewal in the Twelfth Century* (Cambridge, MA: Harvard University Press, 1982), 138–72.

——, *Masters, Princes and Merchants: The Social Views of Peter the Chanter and his Circle* 1: *Text* (Princeton, IL: Princeton University Press, 1970).

Barnett, Ron, *Being a University* (London: Routledge, 2011).

Beales, A. C. F., 'The Modern University in the Light of Newman's Idea', in H. J. Parkinson (ed.), *Some Centenary Addresses on Newman's Idea of a University* (London: Newman Association, 1953), 34–51.

Bender, Thomas, 'From Academic Knowledge to Democratic Knowledge', in Simon Robinson and Clement Katulushi (eds), *Values in Higher Education* (St Bride's Major: Aureus/University of Leeds, 2005), 51–64.

Benson, Robert L., and Constable, Giles (eds), *Renaissance and Renewal in the Twelfth Century* (Cambridge, MA: Harvard University Press, 1982).

Bernstein, Richard J., 'Religious Concerns in Scholarship: Engaged Fallibilism in Practice', in Andrea Sterk (ed.), *Religion, Scholarship and Higher Education: Perspectives, Models and Future Prospects. Essays form the Lilly Seminar on Religion and Higher Education* (Notre Dame, IN: University of Notre Dame Press , 2002), 150–8.

Biggar, Nigel, 'What are Universities for? A Christian View', in Mike Higton, Jeremy Law, and Christopher Rowland (eds), *Theology and Human Flourishing: Essays in Honour of Timothy J. Gorringe* (Eugene, OR: Wipf and Stock, 2011), 238–50.

Bonhoeffer, Dietrich, *Ethics*, Dietrich Bonhoeffer's Works (ed. Clifford J. Green) 6, tr. Reinhard Krauss, Charles C. West, and Douglas Scott (Minneapolis: Fortress, 2005).

Borges, Jorge Luis, *Ficciones*, ed. Anthony Kerrigan, tr. Emecé Editores (New York: Grove Press, 1964).

Brentano, Clemens, *Universitati Litterariae: Kantate auf den 15ten October 1810* (Berlin: Julius Eduard Hitzig, 1910); facsimile available at <www.archive.org/details/5471646> (accessed 3 Dec. 2009).

Bretherton, Luke, *Hospitality as Holiness: Christian Witness amid Moral Diversity* (Aldershot: Ashgate, 2006).

Brock, M. G., and Curthoys, M. C. (eds), *The History of the University of Oxford*, vi. *Nineteenth-Century Oxford, Part 1* (Oxford: Clarendon Press, 1997).

Broman, Thomas, 'The Habermasian Public Sphere and "Science *in* the Enlightenment"', *History of Science*, 36 (1998), 123–49.

Brown, Catherine, *Contrary Things: Exegesis, Dialectic, and the Poetics of Didacticism*, Figurae: Reading Medieval Culture, ed. Daniel Boyarin et al. (Stanford, CA: Stanford University Press, 1998).

Bruford, H., *The German Tradition of Self-Cultivation: 'Bildung' from Humboldt to Thomas Mann* (Cambridge: Cambridge University Press, 1975).

Burke, Peter, *The Art of Conversation* (Ithaca, NY: Cornell University Press, 1993).

Burtchaell, James, *The Dying of the Light: The Disengagement of Colleges and Universities from their Christian Churches* (Grand Rapids, MI: Eerdmans, 1998).

Burwicke, Roswitha, 'From Aesthetic Teas to the World of Noble Reformers: The Berlin Salonière (1780–1848)', *Pacific Coast Philology*, 29/2 (1994), 129–42.

Cabezón, José Ignacio, 'Introduction', in José Ignacio Cabezón, *Scholasticism: Cross-Cultural and Comparative Perspectives*, Toward a Comparative Theology of Religions, ed. Paul J. Griffiths and Lauri L. Patton (Albany, NY: SUNY, 1998), 1–17.

——, *Scholasticism: Cross-Cultural and Comparative Perspectives*, Toward a Comparative Theology of Religions, ed. Paul J. Griffiths and Lauri L. Patton (Albany, NY: SUNY, 1998).

Cahoy, William J., 'A Sense of Place and the Place of Sense', in Stephen R. Haynes (ed.), *Professing in the Postmodern Academy: Faculty and the Future of Church-related Colleges*, Issues in Religion and Higher Education, ed. Michael Beaty and Stephen R. Haynes, 1 (Waco, TX: Baylor University Press, 2002), 73–111.

Campolo, Anthony, 'The Challenge of Radical Christianity for the Christian College', in Douglas V. Henry and Bob R. Agee (eds), *Faithful Learning and the Christian Scholarly Vocation* (Grand Rapids, MI: Eerdmans, 2003), 139–57.

Carpenter, Joel A., 'The Mission of Christian Scholarship in the New Millennium', in Douglas V. Henry and Bob R. Agee (eds), *Faithful Learning and the Christian Scholarly Vocation* (Grand Rapids, MI: Eerdmans, 2003), 62–74.

Carruthers, Mary, *The Craft of Thought: Meditation, Rhetoric, and the Making of Images, 400–1200* (Cambridge: Cambridge University Press, 2000).

Carson, D. A., 'Can There Be a Christian University?', *Southern Baptist Journal of Theology*, 1/3 (1997), 20–38.

Cavanaugh, William, 'Killing for the Telephone Company: Why the Nation-State is not the Keeper of the Common Good', *Modern Theology*, 20/2 (2004), 243–74.

Charlton, Bruce, 'Audit, Accountability and All That: The Growth of Managerial Technologies in UK Universities', in Stephen Prickett and Patricia Erskine-Hill (eds), *Education! Education! Education! Managerial Ethics and the Law of Unintended Consequences* (Thorverton: Imprint Academic/Higher Education Foundation, 2002), 13–28.

Chenu, Marie-Dominique, *Nature, Man and Society in the Twelfth Century: Essays on New Theological Perspectives in the Latin West*, tr. Jerome Taylor and Lester K. Little, 2nd edn (Chicago, IL: University of Chicago Press, 1968).

Church of England, *Common Worship: Services and Prayers for the Church of England* (London: Church House Publishing, 2000).

Clanchy, M. T., *Abelard: A Medieval Life* (Oxford: Blackwell, 1999).

Clark, William, *Academic Charisma and the Origins of the Research University* (Chicago, IL: University of Chicago, 2006).

Clough, David, *On Animals: Systematic Theology* (London: Continuum, 2011).

Coad, Dominic, 'Creation's Praise of God: An Ecological Theology of Non-Human and Human Being', unpublished Ph.D. thesis, University of Exeter, 2010.

Cobban, Alan B., *The Medieval English Universities: Oxford and Cambridge to c.1500* (Aldershot: Scolar Press, 1988).

——, 'Reflections on the Role of the Medieval Universities in Contemporary Society', in Lesley Smith and Benedicta Ward (eds), *Intellectual Life in the Middle Ages: Essays Presented to Margaret Gibson* (London: Hambledon, 1992), 227–41.

Colish, Marcia, L, 'Systematic Theology and Theological Renewal in the Twelfth Century', *Journal of Medieval and Renaissance Studies*, 18.1 (1988), 135–56; repr. in Colish, *Studies in Scholasticism*, §I.

——, 'Abelard and Theology', in Stephanie Hayes-Healy (ed.), *Medieval Paradigms: Essays in Honour of Jeremy duQuesnay Adams*, The New Middle Ages, ed. Bonnie Wheeler (New York: Palgrave Macmillian, 2005), i. 3–12; repr. in Colish, *Studies in Scholasticism*, §VII.

——, *'Studies in Scholasticism*, Variorum Collected Studies CS838 (Aldershot: Ashgate, 2006).

Collini, Stefan, 'Browne's Gamble', *London Review of Books*, 32/21 (4 Nov. 2010), 23–5; <www.lrb.co.uk/v32/n21/stefan-collini/brownes-gamble> (accessed 18 Aug. 2011).

Collins, Randal, *The Sociology of Philosophies: A Global Theory of Intellectual Change* (Cambridge, MA: Belknap/Harvard University Press, 1998).

Colvert, Gavin T., 'The Spirit of Medieval Philosophy in a Postmodern World', in Alice Ramos and Marie I. George (eds), *Faith, Scholarship and Culture in the 21st Century* (Washington: American Maritain Association/Catholic University of America, 2002), 32–56.

Copleston, William James, 'Memoir of Edward Copleston, DD Bishop of Llandaff', *The Christian Remembrancer*, 23 (1852), 1–29.

—— (ed.), *Memoir of Edward Copleston* (London: John W. Parker and Son, 1851).

Cromwell, Oliver, *Oliver Cromwell's Letters and Speeches*, ed. Thomas Carlyle (New York: Scribner, Welford and Co., 1871), <www.gasl.org/refbib/Carlyle__ Cromwell.pdf> (accessed 15 June 2010).

Cronin, Ciaran, 'Kant's Politics of Enlightenment', *Journal of the History of Philosophy*, 41/1 (2003), 51–80.

Cullen, Christopher M., *Bonaventure*, Great Medieval Thinkers, ed. Brian Davies (Oxford: Oxford University Press, 2006).

Culler, A. Dwight, *The Imperial Intellect: A Study of Cardinal Newman's Educational Ideal* (New Haven: Yale University Press, 1955).

Curzon, Robert, 1215 Statutes of the University of Paris, in Henricus Denifle (ed.), *Chartularium Universitatis Parisiensis*, i. *1200–1286* (Paris: Delalain, 1889), 78–80; <www.archive.org/details/chartulariumuniv01univuoft>, tr. Dana Carleton Munro in *Translations and Reprints from the Original Sources of European History* 2 (Philadelphia, PA: University of Pennsylvania Press, 1896), 3.12–15; <www.archive.org/details/translationsrepr02univiala> (accessed 30 Sept. 2009).

D'Costa, Gavin, *Theology in the Public Square: Church, Academy and Nation*, Challenges in Contemporary Theology, ed. Gareth Jones and Lewis Ayres (Oxford: Blackwell, 2005).

D'Onofrio, Giulio (ed.), *History of Theology*, ii. *The Middle Ages*, tr. Matthew O'Connell (Collegeville, MN: Liturgical Press, 2008), 164–70.

Dale, P. A., 'Newman's "The Idea of a University": The Dangers of a University Education', *Victorian Studies*, 16/1 (1972), 5–36.

Daston, Lorraine, 'The Moral Economy of Science', in Lorraine Daston, *Constructing Knowledge in the History of Science*, *Osiris*, 2nd ser. 10 (1995), 2–24.

—— and Galison, Peter, *Objectivity* (New York: Zone Books, 2007).

Daum, Andreas W., '*Wissenschaft* and Knowledge' in Jonathan Sperber (ed.), *Germany 1800–1871*, Short Oxford History of Germany (Oxford: Oxford University Press, 2004), 137–61.

Davies, Oliver, *The Creativity of God: World, Eucharist, Reason*, Cambridge Studies in Christian Doctrine, ed. Colin Gunton and Daniel W. Hardy (Cambridge: CUP, 2004).

Davis, H. Francis, 'Our Idea of a University', in H. J. Parkinson (ed.), *Some Centenary Addresses on Newman's Idea of a University* (London: Newman Association, 1953), 1–17.

Denifle, Henricus (ed.). *Chartularium Universitatis Parisiensis*, i. *1200–1286* (Paris: Delalain, 1889), 78–80; <www.archive.org/details/chartulariumunivolanivuoft>, tr. Dana Carleton Munro in *Translations and Reprints from the Original Sources of European History* 2 (Philadelphia, PA: University of Pennsylvania Press 1896) 3.12–15; <www.archive.org/details/translationsrepr02univiala>.

Derrida, Jacques, 'The Principle of Reason: The University in the Eyes of its Pupils', tr. Catherine Porter and Edward P. Morris, in *Diacritics*, 13/3 (Autumn 1983), 3–20.

——, 'Mochlos; or, The Conflict of the Faculties', tr. Richard Rand and Amy Wygant, in Richard Rand (ed.), *Logomachia: The Conflict of the Faculties* (Lincoln, NE; London: University of Nebraska Press, 1992), 1–34.

——, 'The University without Condition', in Jacques Derrida, *Without Alibi*, ed. and tr. Peggy Kamuf (Stanford, CA: Stanford University Press, 2002), 202–37.

Dockery, David S., *Renewing Minds: Serving Church and Society through Christian Higher Education* (Nashville, TN: B&H Academic, 2007).

The ESRC Centre for Genomics in Society (Egenis), 'About us', <www.genomicsnetwork.ac.uk/egenis/aboutus/> (accessed 17 June 2010).

Evans, C. Stephen, 'The Calling of the Christian Scholar–Teacher', in Douglas V. Henry and Bob R. Agee (eds), *Faithful Learning and the Christian Scholarly Vocation* (Grand Rapids, MI: Eerdmans, 2003), 26–49.

Evans, G. R., *Old Arts and New Theology: The Beginnings of Theology as an Academic Discipline* (Oxford: Clarendon Press, 1980).

——, *Anselm*, Outstanding Christian Thinkers, ed. Brian Davies (London: Geoffrey Chapman, 1989).

Fairweather, Abrol, and Zagzebski, Linda (eds), *Virtue Epistemology: Essays on Epistemic Virtue and Responsibility* (Oxford: Oxford University Press, 2001).

Falls-Corbitt, Margaret, 'Prolegomena to Any Postmodern Hope for the Church-related College', in Stephen R. Haynes (ed.), *Professing in the Postmodern Academy: Faculty and the Future of Church-related Colleges*, Issues in Religion and Higher Education, ed. Michael Beaty and Stephen R. Haynes, 1 (Waco, TX: Baylor University Press, 2002), 49–71.

Ferruolo, Stephen C., *The Origins of the University: The Schools of Paris and their Critics, 1100–1215* (Stanford, CA: Stanford University Press, 1985).

Fichte, Johann Gottlieb, 'Concerning the Only Possible Disturbance of Academic Freedom', in G. H. Turnbull, *The Educational Theory of J. G. Fichte: A Critical Account, Together with Translations* (Liverpool: University of Liverpool; London: Hodder and Stoughton, 1926), 263–5.

Fichte, Johann Gottlieb, 'Deduced Scheme for an Academy to be Established in Berlin (1807)', tr. G. H. Turnbull in G. H. Turnbull, *The Educational Theory of J. G. Fichte: A Critical Account, Together with Translations* (Liverpool: University of Liverpool; London: Hodder and Stoughton, 1926), 170–259; German original, 'Deduzierter Plan einer in Berlin zu errichtenden höheren Lehranstalt', in Ernst Anrich (ed.), *Die Idee der deutschen Universität* (Darmstadt: Hermann Gentner Verlag, 1956), 125–217.

——, 'The Theory of the State', extracts tr. in G. H. Turnbull, *The Educational Theory of J. G. Fichte: A Critical Account, Together with Translations* (Liverpool: University of Liverpool; London: Hodder and Stoughton, 1926), 265–83.

——, *Addresses to the German Nation*, ed. George Armstong Kelly, tr. R. F. Jones and G. H. Turnbull, European Perspectives, ed. C. Black (New York: Harper and Row, 1968).

Ford, David F., *Self and Salvation: Being Transformed* (Cambridge: Cambridge University Press, 1999).

——, *The Future of Cambridge University*, Lady Margaret's Sermon, Commemoration of Benefactors (Cambridge: Cambridge University Press, 2001).

——, 'Faith, Universities and Wisdom in a Religious and Secular World: A View from Cambridge', lecture at the University of Lund, 2004.

——, 'Knowledge, Meaning, and the World's Great Challenges' (The Gomes Lecture, 2003), *Scottish Journal of Theology*, 57/2 (2004), 181–202.

——, *Christian Wisdom: Desiring God and Learning in Love*, Cambridge Studies in Christian Doctrine, ed. Daniel W. Hardy (Cambridge: Cambridge University Press, 2007).

——, 'God and the University: What Can We Communicate?', paper delivered at the National Convention on Christian Ministry in Higher Education, no date.

——, and Hardy, Daniel W., *Jubilate: Theology in Praise* (London: DLT, 1984) = *Praising and Knowing God* (Philadelphia, PA: Westminster, 1985).

Francis of Assisi, 'A Letter to Brother Anthony of Padua', in Francis of Assisi, *Early Documents* (ed. Regis J. Armstrong, J. Wayne Hellman, and William J. Short), i. *The Saint* (Hyde Park, NY: New City, 1999), 107.

Frank, Manfred, 'Metaphysical Foundations: A Look at Schleiermacher's *Dialectic*', tr. Jacqueline Mariña, in Jacqueline Mariña (ed.), *The Cambridge Companion to Friedrich Schleiermacher* (Cambridge: Cambridge University Press, 2005), 15–34.

Freddoso, Alfred J., '*Fides et Ratio*: A "Radical" Vision of Intellectual Inquiry', in Alice Ramos and Marie I. George (eds), *Faith, Scholarship and Culture in the 21st Century* (Washington: American Maritain Association/Catholic University of America, 2002), 13–31.

Frei, Hans W., *Types of Christian Theology*, ed. George Hunsinger and William C. Placher (New Haven: Yale University Press, 1992).

Gabriel, Astrik L., 'The College System in the Fourteenth-Century Universities', in Francis Lee Utley, *The Forward Movement of the Fourteenth Century* (Columbus, OH: Ohio State University Press, 1961), 79–124.

——, 'The Ideal Master of the Mediaeval University', *Catholic Historical Review*, 60/1 (1974), 1–40.

Garland, Martha McMackin, 'Newman in his own Day', in John Henry Newman, *The Idea of a University*, ed. Frank M. Turner, Rethinking the Western Tradition, ed. David Bromwich et al. (New Haven: Yale, 1996), 265–81.

Gierl, Martin, '"The Triumph of Truth and Innocence": The Rules and Practice of Theological Polemics', tr. William Clark in William Clark and Peter Becker (eds), *Little Tools of Knowledge: Historical Essays on Academic and Bureaucratic Practices*, Social History, Popular Culture and Politics in Germany, ed. Geoff Eley (Ann Arbor: University of Michigan Press, 2001), 35–66.

Gilley, Sheridan, 'What has Athens to do with Jerusalem? Newman, Wisdom and the *Idea of a University*', in Stephen C. Barton (ed.), *Where Shall Wisdom Be Found? Wisdom in the Bible, the Church and the Contemporary World* (Edinburgh: T&T Clark, 1999), 155–68.

di Giovanni, George, 'Translator's Introduction' [to *Religion within the Boundaries of Mere Reason*], in Immanuel Kant, *Religion and Rational Theology*, ed. Allen W. Wood and George di Giovanni, *The Cambridge Edition of the Works of Immanuel Kant*, ed. Paul Guyer and Allen W. Wood (Cambridge: Cambridge University Press, 1996), 41–54.

Goodman, Dena, *The Republic of Letters: A Cultural History of the French Enlightenment* (Ithaca, NY: Cornell University Press, 1994).

Grafton, Anthony, 'Polyhistor into *Philolog*: Notes on the Transformation of German Classical Scholarship, 1780–1859', *History of Universities*, 3 (1983), 159–92.

Graham, Gordon, *Universities: The Recovery of an Idea*, 2nd edn, Societas: Essays in Political and Cultural Criticism (Exeter: Imprint Academic, 2008).

Grant, Edward, *God and Reason in the Middle Ages* (Cambridge: Cambridge University Press, 2001).

Grant, Robert, 'Education, Utility and the Universities', in Stephen Prickett and Patricia Erskine-Hill (eds), *Education! Education! Education! Managerial Ethics and the Law of Unintended Consequences* (Thorverton: Imprint Academic/Higher Education Foundation, 2002), 49–71.

Gregory, Frederick, 'Kant, Schelling and the Administration of Science in the Romantic Era', in *Science in Germany: The Intersection of Institutional and Intellectual Issues, Osiris*, 2nd ser. 5 (1989), 16–35.

Griffiths, Paul J., 'Scholasticism: The Possible Recovery of an Intellectual Practice', in José Ignacio Cabezón, *Scholasticism: Cross-Cultural and Comparative Perspectives*, Toward a Comparative Theology of Religions, ed. Paul J. Griffiths and Lauri L. Patton (Albany, NY: SUNY, 1998), 201–35.

——, *Intellectual Appetite: A Theological Grammar* (Washington: Catholic University of America Press, 2009).

Habermas, Jürgen, 'The Idea of the University—Learning Processes', *New German Critique*, 41 (1987), 3–22.

Hagstrom, Aurelie A., 'Christian Hospitality in the Intellectual Community', in Douglas V. Henry and Michael D. Beaty (eds), *Christianity and the Soul of the University: Faith as a Foundation for Intellectual Community* (Grand Rapids, MI: Baker Academic, 2006), 119–31.

Hahn, Barbara, 'A Dream of Living Together: Jewish Women in Berlin around 1800', in Emily D. Bilski and Emily Braun (eds), *Jewish Women and their Salons: The Power of Conversation* (New Haven: Yale University Press, 2005), 149–58.

——, *The Jewish Pallas Athena: This Too a Theory of Modernity*, tr. James McFarland (Princeton: Princeton University Press, 2005).

Hardy, Daniel W., *God's Ways with the World: Thinking and Practising Christian Faith* (Edinburgh: T&T Clark, 1996).

Hart, Daryl B., 'Christian Scholars, Secular Universities, and the Problem with the Antithesis', *Christian Scholar's Review*, 30/4 (2001), 383–402.

Hatch, Nathan O., 'Christian Thinking in a Time of Academic Turmoil', in Douglas V. Henry and Bob R. Agee (eds), *Faithful Learning and the Christian Scholarly Vocation* (Grand Rapids, MI: Eerdmans, 2003), 87–100.

Hauerwas, Stanley, *A Community of Character: Toward a Constructive Christian Social Ethic* (Notre Dame, IN: University of Notre Dame Press, 1981).

——, *Christian Existence Today: Essays on Church, World and Living in Between* (Durham, NC: Labyrinth Press, 1988).

——, *The State of the University: Academic Knowledges and the Knowledge of God*, Illuminations: Theory and Religion, ed. Catherine Pickstock, John Milbank, and Graham Ward (Oxford: Blackwell, 2007).

——, 'More, or a Taxonomy of Greed', in Mike Higton, Jeremy Law, and Christopher Rowland (eds), *Theology and Human Flourishing: Essays in Honour of Timothy J. Gorringe* (Eugene, OR: Wipf and Stock, 2011), 199–2011.

Haugen, Kristine Louise, 'Academic Charisma and the Old Regime', *History of Universities*, 22/1 (2007), 199–228.

Haynes, Stephen R., 'A Review of Research on Church-related Higher Education', in Stephen R. Haynes (ed.), *Professing in the Postmodern Academy: Faculty and the Future of Church-related Colleges*, Issues in Religion and Higher Education, ed. Michael Beaty and Stephen R. Haynes, 1 (Waco, TX: Baylor University Press, 2002), 1–30.

Haynes, Stephen R. (ed.), *Professing in the Postmodern Academy: Faculty and the Future of Church-Related Colleges*, Issues in Religion and Higher Education, ed. Michael Beaty and Stephen R. Haynes, 1 (Waco, TX: Baylor University Press, 2002).

Hays, Richard B., 'The Palpable Word as Ground of *Koinonia*', in Douglas V. Henry and Michael D. Beaty (eds), *Christianity and the Soul of the University: Faith as a Foundation for Intellectual Community* (Grand Rapids, MI: Baker Academic, 2006), 19–36.

Heidegger, Martin, 'The Self-Assertion of the German University [1933]', tr. Karsten Harries, *Review of Metaphysics*, 38/3 (1985), 470–80.

Henry, Douglas V. and Agee, Bob R. (eds), *Faithful Learning and the Christian Scholarly Vocation* (Grand Rapids, MI: Eerdmans, 2003).

—— and Beaty, Michael D. (eds), *Christianity and the Soul of the University: Faith as a Foundation for Intellectual Community* (Grand Rapids, MI: Baker Academic, 2006).

—— —— 'Introduction', in Douglas V. Henry and Michael D. Beaty (eds), *Christianity and the Soul of the University: Faith as a Foundation for Intellectual Community* (Grand Rapids, MI: Baker Academic, 2006), 9–15.

Herrad of Landsberg, *Hortus Deliciarum* in *Herrad von Landsperg, Aebtissin zu Hohenburg, oder St. Odilien, im Elsass, im zwölften Jahrhundert und ihr Werk: Hortus deliciarum*, ed. Christian Maurice Engelhardt (Stuttgart: J. G. Cotta, 1818);

selected plates reproduced online at the Bibliothèque Alsatique <bacm.creditmutuel.fr/HORTUS_DELICIARUM.html> (accessed 26 Aug. 2009).

Hertz, Deborah, 'Salonières and Literary Women in Late Eighteenth-Century Berlin', *New German Critique*, 14 (1978), 97–108.

Higher Education Funding Council for England, *Research Excellence Framework: Second Consultation on the Assessment and Funding of Research* (London: HEFCE, 2009).

Higton, Mike, 'The Research Assessment Exercise as Sin', *Critical Quarterly*, 44/4 (2002), 40–5.

——, 'Boldness and Reserve: A Lesson from St. Augustine', *Anglican Theological Review*, 85/3 (2003), 445–56.

——, *Christ, Providence and History: Hans W. Frei's Public Theology* (London: Continuum, 2004).

——, 'The Fulfilment of History in Barth, Frei, Auerbach and Dante' in Mike Higton and John C. McDowell (eds), *Conversing with Barth*, Barth Studies, ed. John Webster, George Hunsinger, and Hans-Anton Drewes (Aldershot and Burlington, VT: Ashgate, 2004), 120–41.

—— *Vulnerable Learning: Thinking Theologically about Higher Education*, Grove Ethics, 140 (Cambridge: Grove, 2006).

—— and McDowell, John C. (eds), *Conversing with Barth*, Barth Studies, ed. John Webster, George Hunsinger, and Hans-Anton Drewes (Aldershot and Burlington, VT: Ashgate, 2004).

—— and Muers, Rachel, *The Text in Play: Experiments in Biblical Reading* (Eugene, OR: Wipf and Stock, 2012).

——, Law, Jeremy, and Rowland, Christopher (eds), *Theology and Human Flourishing: Essays in Honour of Timothy J. Gorringe* (Eugene, OR: Wipf and Stock, 2011).

Hofstetter, Michael J., *The Romantic Idea of a University: England and Germany 1770–1850*, Romanticism in Perspective: Texts, Cultures, Histories, ed. Marilyn Gaull and Stephen Prickett (Basingstoke: Palgrave, 2001).

Hogg, David S., *Anselm of Canterbury: The Beauty of Theology*, Great Theologians, ed. John Webster, Trevor Hart, and Douglas Farrow (Aldershot: Ashgate, 2004).

Holmes, Arthur F., *Building the Christian Academy* (Grand Rapids, MI: Eerdmans, 2001).

——, 'The Closing of the American Mind and the Opening of the Christian Mind: Liberal Learning, Great Texts, and the Christian College', in Douglas V. Henry and Bob R. Agee (eds), *Faithful Learning and the Christian Scholarly Vocation* (Grand Rapids, MI: Eerdmans, 2003), 101–22.

Holmes, Stephen R., 'Awesome Hospitality: On the Absurd Idea of a Baptist University', in Stephen R. Todd (ed.), *The Baptist University* (Waco, TX: Baylor University Press, forthcoming).

Holt, Lynn, *Apprehension: Reason in the Absence of Rules* (Aldershot: Ashgate, 2002).

Hooke, Robert, *Robert Hooke's Micrographia* (Lincolnwood, IL: Science Heritage, 1987).

Hoover, Jeffrey, 'Introduction to "Toward a Theory of Sociable Conduct"', in Ruth Drucilla Richardson (ed.), *Friedrich Schleiermacher's* Toward a Theory of Sociable

Conduct *and Essays on its Intellectual–Cultural Context*, New Athenaeum/Neues Athenaeum, 4 (Lewiston, NY: Edwin Mellen, 1995), 9–19.

Howard, Thomas Albert, *Protestant Theology and the Making of the Modern German University* (Oxford: Oxford University Press, 2006).

Huber, Victor Aimé, *The English Universities* (ed. and tr. Francis W. Newman) II/1 (London: William Pickering; Manchester: Simms and Dinham, 1843).

Hugh of St Victor, *The Didascalion of Hugh of St Victor: A Medieval Guide to the Arts*, tr. Jerome Taylor (New York: Columbia University Press, 1961).

Hughes, Kevin L., 'Remember Bonaventure? (Onto)Theology and Ecstasy' *Modern Theology*, 19/4 (2003), 520–45.

Hughes, Richard T., 'Christian Faith and the Life of the Mind', in Douglas V. Henry and Bob R. Agee (eds), *Faithful Learning and the Christian Scholarly Vocation* (Grand Rapids, MI: Eerdmans, 2003), 3–25.

Humboldt, Wilhelm von, *The Sphere and Duties of Government (The Limits of State Action)*, tr. Joseph Coulthard (London: John Chapman, 1854); <files.libertyfund. org/files/589/0053_Bk.pdf> (accessed 27 Nov. 2009).

——, 'On the Spirit and the Organisational Framework of Intellectual Institutions in Berlin', *Minerva*, 8 (1970), 242–50; German original, 'Über die innere und äussere Organisation der höheren wissenschaftlichen Anstalten in Berlin', in Ernst Anrich (ed.), *Die Idee der deutschen Universität* (Darmstadt: Hermann Gentner Verlag, 1956), 375–86.

Illich, Ivan, *In the Vineyard of the Text: A Commentary to Hugh's Didascalion* (Chicago, IL: University of Chicago Press, 1993).

Jacobsen, Douglas and Jacobsen, Rhonda Hustedt, 'More than the "Integration" of Faith and Learning', in Douglas Jacobsen and Rhonda Hustedt Jacobsen (eds), *Scholarship and Christian Faith: Enlarging the Conversation* (Oxford: Oxford University Press, 2004), 15–31.

——— (eds), *Scholarship and Christian Faith: Enlarging the Conversation* (Oxford: Oxford University Press, 2004).

Jaeger, C. Stephen, *The Envy of Angels: Cathedral Schools and Social Ideals in Medieval Europe, 950–1200* (Philadelphia, PA: University of Pennsylvania Press, 1994).

Jardine, Lisa, *Ingenious Pursuits: Building the Scientific Revolution* (London: Little, Brown, 1999).

Jaspers, Karl, *The Idea of a University*, ed. Karl W. Deutsch, tr. H. A. T. Reiche and H. F. Vanderschmidt (London: Peter Owen, 1960).

Jenkins, Roy, 'Newman and the Idea of a University', in David Brown (ed.), *Newman: A Man for Our Time: Centenary Essays* (London: SPCK, 1990).

Jenkins, Timothy, *Religion in English Everyday Life: An Ethnographic Approach* (Oxford/New York: Berghahn, 1999).

——, *An Experiment in Providence: How Faith Engages with the World* (London: SPCK, 2006).

Kant, Immanuel, 'An Answer to the Question: What is Enlightenment?', in Mary J. Gregor and Allen W. Wood (eds), *Practical Philosophy, The Cambridge Edition of the Works of Immanuel Kant*, ed. Paul Guyer and Allen W. Wood (Cambridge: Cambridge University Press, 1996), 11–22.

——, *The Conflict of the Faculties*, in Immanuel Kant, *Religion and Rational Theology*, ed. Allen W. Wood and George di Giovanni, *The Cambridge Edition of the Works of Immanuel Kant*, ed. Paul Guyer and Allen W. Wood (Cambridge: Cambridge University Press, 1996), 233–327.

——, *Religion and Rational Theology*, ed. Allen W. Wood and George di Giovanni, *The Cambridge Edition of the Works of Immanuel Kant*, ed. Paul Guyer and Allen W. Wood (Cambridge: Cambridge University Press, 1996).

Kelsey, David H., *Eccentric Existence: A Theological Anthropology* (Louisville, KY: WJK, 2009).

Kennedy, Arthur L., 'The University as a Constituting Agent of Culture', in Gregory J. Walters (ed.), *The Tasks of Truth: Essays on Karl Jaspers's Idea of the University* (Frankfurt am Main: Peter Lang, 1996), 97–115.

Ker, Ian, 'Editor's Introduction', in John Henry Newman, *The Idea of a University Defined and Illustrated*, ed. Ian Ker (Oxford: Clarendon Press, 1976), pp. xi–lxxv.

——, *John Henry Newman: A Biography*, Oxford Lives (Oxford: Oxford University Press, 1988).

Kyte, Richard, 'Conversation and Authority: A Tension in the Inheritance of the Church-related College', in Stephen R. Haynes (ed.), *Professing in the Postmodern Academy: Faculty and the Future of Church-related Colleges*, Issues in Religion and Higher Education, ed. Michael Beaty and Stephen R. Haynes, 1 (Waco, TX: Baylor University Press, 2002), 115–30.

Lakeland, Paul, 'The Habit of Empathy: Postmodernity and the Future of the Church-related College', in Stephen R. Haynes (ed.), *Professing in the Postmodern Academy: Faculty and the Future of Church-related Colleges*, Issues in Religion and Higher Education, ed. Michael Beaty and Stephen R. Haynes, 1 (Waco, TX: Baylor University Press, 2002), 33–48.

Langley, Raymond, 'Karl Jaspers's Three Critiques of the University', in Gregory J. Walters (ed.), *The Tasks of Truth: Essays on Karl Jaspers's Idea of the University* (Frankfurt am Main: Peter Lang, 1996), 23–38.

Lawler, Edwina, 'Neohumanistic–Idealistic Concepts of a University: Schelling, Steffens, Fichte, Schleiermacher and von Humboldt', in Herbert Richardson (ed.), *Friedrich Schleiermacher and the Founding of the University of Berlin: The Study of Religion as a Scientific Discipline*, Schleiermacher Studies and Translation (Lewiston, NY: Edwin Mellen, 1991), 1–44.

Leff, Gordon, *Paris and Oxford Universities in the Thirteenth and Fourteenth Centuries: An Institutional and Intellectual History*, New Dimensions in History: Essays in Comparative History, ed. Norman F. Cantor (New York: John Wiley & Sons, 1968).

Levinger, Matthew, *Enlightened Nationalism: The Transformation of Prussian Political Culture 1806–1848* (Oxford: Oxford University Press, 2000).

——, 'The Prussian Reform Movement and the Rise of Enlightened Nationalism', in Philip G. Dwyer, *The Rise of Prussia 1700–1830* (London: Longman, 2000), 259–77.

Lotz, Denton, 'Christian Higher Education and the Conversion of the West', in Douglas V. Henry and Bob R. Agee (eds), *Faithful Learning and the Christian Scholarly Vocation* (Grand Rapids, MI: Eerdmans, 2003), 123–38.

Loughlin, Gerard, 'The University without Question: John Henry Newman and Jacques Derrida on Faith in the University', in Jeff Astley, Leslie Francis, John Sullivan, and Andrew Walker (eds), *The Idea of a Christian University: Essays on Theology and Higher Education* (Bletchley and Waynesborough, GA: Paternoster, 2004), 113–31.

——, 'The Wonder of Newman's Education', *New Blackfriars*, 92/1038 (2011), 224–42.

MacIntyre, Alasdair, 'The Idea of an Educated Public', in Alasdair MacIntyre, *Education and Values: The Richard Peters Lectures*, ed. Graham Haydon (London: University of London Press, 1987), 15–36.

——, 'Catholic Universities: Dangers, Hopes, Choices', in Robert E. Sullivan (ed.), *Higher Learning and Catholic Traditions* (Notre Dame, IN: University of Notre Dame Press, 2001), 1–21.

——, *After Virtue: A Moral Theory*, 3rd edn (London: Duckworth, 2007).

——, 'The Very Idea of a University: Aristotle, Newman and Us', *New Blackfriars*, 91/1031 (2010), 4–19.

Makdisi, George, 'Madrasa and University in the Middle Ages', *Studia Islamica*, 32 (1970), 255–64.

——, 'The Scholastic Method in Medieval Education: An Inquiry into its Origins in Law and Theology', *Speculum*, 49/4 (1974), 640–61.

——, *The Rise of Colleges: Institutions of Learning in Islam and the West* (Edinburgh: Edinburgh University Press, 1981).

——, *The Rise of Humanism in Classical Islam and the Christian West, with Special Reference to Scholasticism* (Edinburgh: Edinburgh University Press, 1990).

Mariña, Jacqueline (ed.), *The Cambridge Companion to Friedrich Schleiermacher* (Cambridge: Cambridge University Press, 2005).

Markham, Ian, 'The Idea of a Christian University', in Jeff Astley, Leslie Francis, John Sullivan, and Andrew Walker (eds), *The Idea of a Christian University: Essays on Theology and Higher Education* (Bletchley and Waynesborough, GA: Paternoster, 2004), 3–13.

Markowski, Michael, 'Peter Abelard's *Sic et Non*: The Master Key to Wisdom' (2005), <people.westminstercollege.edu/faculty/mmarkowski/Hall/Abelard.htm> (accessed 23 July 2009).

Marsden, George M., *The Soul of the American University: From Protestant Establishment to Established Nonbelief* (New York: Oxford University Press, 1994).

——, *The Outrageous Idea of Christian Scholarship* (New York: Oxford University Press, 1997).

Marshall, Bruce D., *Trinity and Truth*, Cambridge Studies in Christian Doctrine, ed. Colin Gunton and Daniel W. Hardy (Cambridge: Cambridge University Press, 2000).

Marty, Martin E., 'The Church and Christian Higher Education in the New Millennium', in Douglas V. Henry and Bob R. Agee (eds), *Faithful Learning and the Christian Scholarly Vocation* (Grand Rapids, MI: Eerdmans, 2003), 50–61.

——, 'Foreword', in Douglas Jacobsen and Rhonda Hustedt Jacobsen (eds), *Scholarship and Christian Faith: Enlarging the Conversation* (Oxford: Oxford University Press, 2004), pp. vii–ix.

Maskell, Duke, and Robinson, Ian, *The New Idea of a University* (London: Haven, 2001).

Matheson, P. E., *The Life of Hastings Rashdall D.D.* (Oxford: Oxford University Press; London: Humphrey Milford, 1928).

Mathewes, Charles, *A Theology of Public Life*, Cambridge Studies in Christian Doctrine, ed. Daniel W. Hardy (Cambridge: Cambridge University Press, 2007).

Maxwell, Nicholas, *From Knowledge to Wisdom: A Revolution in the Aims and Methods of Science* (Oxford: Blackwell, 1984), 2.

McCleish, Tom, 'Values and Scientific Research: A Practitioner's View', in Simon Robinson and Clement Katulushi (eds), *Values in Higher Education* (St Bride's Major: Aureus/University of Leeds, 2005), 136–49.

McClelland, Charles E., '"To Live for Science": Ideals and Realities at the University of Berlin', in Thomas Bender (ed.), *The University and the City: From Medieval Origins to the Present* (New York: Oxford University Press, 1988), 181–97.

McClelland, Vincent Alan, *English Roman Catholics and Higher Education 1830–1903* (Oxford: Clarendon Press, 1973).

McFarlane, Andrew, 'The Human Person as an Epistemic Agent: The Contours of Creaturely Cognition in Karl Barth's Church Dogmatics', unpublished Ph.D. Thesis, University of Edinburgh, 2008.

McGrath, Fergal, *Newman's University: Idea and Reality* (London: Longmans, 1951).

——, *The Consecration of Learning: Lectures on Newman's Idea of a University* (Dublin: Gill and Son, 1962).

Megone, Christopher, 'Virtue and the Virtual University', in Simon Robinson and Clement Katulushi (eds), *Values in Higher Education* (St Bride's Major: Aureus/University of Leeds, 2005), 117–32.

Midgley, Mary, *Wisdom, Information and Wonder: What is Knowledge For?* (London: Routledge, 1989).

Milbank, John, 'The Conflict of the Faculties: Theology and the Economy of the Sciences', in John Milbank, *The Future of Love: Essays in Political Theology* (London: SCM, 2009), 301–15.

—— and Pickstock, Catherine, *Truth in Aquinas*, Radical Orthodoxy, ed. John Milbank, Catherine Pickstock, and Graham Ward (London and New York: Routledge, 2001).

Moreland, J. P., *Love God with All Your Mind: The Role of Reason in the Life of the Soul*, NavPress Spiritual Formation, ed. Dallas Willard (Colorado Springs, CO: NavPress, 1997).

Muers, Rachel, *Keeping God's Silence: Towards a Theological Ethics of Communication*, Challenges in Contemporary Theology, ed. Gareth Jones and Lewis Ayres (Oxford: Blackwell, 2004).

Nathanson, Stephen, *The Ideal of Rationality* (Atlantic Highlands, NJ: Humanities Press International, 1985).

Newman, John Henry, *The Office and Work of Universities* (London: Longman, Brown, Green and Longman, 1856).

——, *My Campaign in Ireland*, ed. W. Neville, i: *Catholic University Reports and Other Papers* (Aberdeen: A. King, 1896).

Newman, John Henry, *Loss and Gain: The Story of a Convert* (London: Longmans, 1906).

——, *Parochial and Plain Sermons* (London: Longmans, Green and Co., 1907), v.

——, *Parochial and Plain Sermons* (London: Lomgmans, Green and Co., 1908), vii.

——, *Sermons Preached on Various Occasions* (London: Longmans, Green and Co., 1908).

——, *Historical Sketches* (London: Longman, Green, 1909).

——, *Oxford University Sermons* (London: Longmans, Green and Co., 1909).

——, *The Letters and Diaries of John Henry Newman*, xiv. *Papal Aggression*, ed. Charles Stephen Dessain and Vincent Ferrer Blehl (Oxford: Clarendon Press, 1963).

——, *The Letters and Diaries of John Henry Newman*, xv. *The Achilli Trial*, ed. Charles Stephen Dessain and Vincent Ferrer Blehl (London: Thomas Nelson, 1964).

——, *The Idea of a University Defined and Illustrated*, ed. Ian Ker (Oxford: Clarendon Press, 1976).

Nietzsche, Friedrich, 'On Truth and Lying in a Non-moral Sense', tr. Ronald Speirs, in Nietzsche, *The Birth of Tragedy and Other Writings*, ed. Raymond Geuss and Ronald Speirs, Cambridge Texts in the History of Philosophy, ed. Karl Ameriks and Desmond M. Clarke (Cambridge: Cambridge University Press, 1999), 139–53.

Nockles, P. B., 'An Academic Counter-Revolution: Newman and Tractarian Oxford's Idea of a University', *History of Universities*, 10 (1991), 137–97.

O'Neill, Onora, 'The Public Use of Reason', *Political Theory*, 14/4 (1986), 523–51.

Oakeshott, Michael, *The Voice of Poetry in the Conversation of Mankind: An Essay* (London: Bowes and Bowes, 1959).

——, 'The Idea of a University', *Listener*, 43 (1950), 424–6, repr. in *Academic Questions*, 17/1 (2003), 23–30.

Palmer, Parker J., 'Toward a Spirituality of Higher Education', in Douglas V. Henry and Bob R. Agee (eds), *Faithful Learning and the Christian Scholarly Vocation* (Grand Rapids, MI: Eerdmans, 2003), 75–85.

Parkinson, H. J. (ed.), *Some Centenary Addresses on Newman's Idea of a University* (London: Newman Association, 1953).

Paton, David M., *Blind Gudies? A Student Looks at the University* (London: SCM, 1939).

Paulsen, Friderich, *Die deutschen Unversitäten und das Universitätstudium* (Hildesheim: Georg Olms, 1966 [1902]), 40–52.

Pelikan, Jaroslav, *The Idea of a University: A Reexamination* (New Haven: Yale University Press, 1992), 55.

Percival, Edward France, *The Foundation Statutes of Merton College, Oxford* (London: William Pickering, 1847).

Peterson, Jonathan, 'Enlightenment and Freedom', *Journal of the History of Philosophy*, 46/2 (2008), 223–44.

Pinkard, Terry, *Hegel's Phenomenology: The Sociality of Reason* (Cambridge: Cambridge University Press, 1994).

Powicke, F. M., 'The Medieval University in Church and Society', in *Ways of Medieval Life and Thought: Essays and Addresses* (London: Oldhams, 1949), 198–212.

Pozzo, Riccardo, 'Kant's *Streit der Fakultäten* and Conditions in Königsberg', *History of Universities*, 16/2 (2000), 96–128.

Prickett, Stephen, and Erskine-Hill, Patricia (eds), *Education! Education! Education! Managerial Ethics and the Law of Unintended Consequences* (Thorverton: Imprint Academic/Higher Education Foundation, 2002).

Rae, Murray, 'Learning the Truth in a Christian University: Advice from Søren Kierkegaard', in Jeff Astley, Leslie Francis, John Sullivan, and Andrew Walker (eds), *The Idea of a Christian University: Essays on Theology and Higher Education* (Bletchley and Waynesborough, GA: Paternoster, 2004), 98–112.

Ramos, Alice and George, Marie I. (eds), *Faith, Scholarship and Culture in the 21st Century* (Washington: American Maritain Association/Catholic University of America, 2002).

Rasch, William, 'Ideal Sociability: Friedrich Schleiermacher and the Ambivalence of Extrasocial Spaces', in Ulrike Gleixner and Marion W. Gray (eds), *Gender in Transition: Discourse and Practice in German-Speaking Europe 1750–1830* (Ann Arbor: University of Michigan Press, 2006), 319–39.

Rashdall, Hastings, *Ideas and Ideals: Comments on Theology, Ethics and Metaphysics*, ed. H. D. A. Major and F. L. Cross (Oxford: Basil Blackwell, 1928).

——, *The Universities of Europe in the Middle Ages* (ed. F. M. Powicke and A. B. Emden), i. *Salerno, Bologna, Paris* (Oxford: Oxford University Press, 1936).

Research Councils UK, 'Mission and Statement of Expectation on Economic and Societal Impact' (Swindon: RCUK, 2008); <www.rcuk.ac.uk/documents/innovation/missionsei.pdf> (accessed 18 Apr. 2011).

Richardson, Ruth Drucilla (ed.), *Friedrich Schleiermacher's* Toward a Theory of Sociable Conduct *and Essays on its Intellectual–Cultural Context*, New Athenaeum/Neues Athenaeum, 4 (Lewiston, NY: Edwin Mellen, 1995).

Ridder-Symoens, Hilde de (ed.), *Universities in the Middle Ages*, A History of the Universities in Europe, ed. Walter Rüegg, 1 (Cambridge: Cambridge University Press, 1992).

Robinson, Denis, '*Sedes Sapientiae*: Newman, Truth and the Christian University', in Jeff Astley, Leslie Francis, John Sullivan, and Andrew Walker (eds), *The Idea of a Christian University: Essays on Theology and Higher Education* (Bletchley and Waynesborough, GA: Paternoster, 2004), 75–97.

Robinson, Simon and Katulushi, Clement (eds), *Values in Higher Education* (St Bride's Major: Aureus/University of Leeds, 2005).

Rothblatt, Sheldon, *The Modern University and its Discontents: The Fate of Newman's Legacies in Britain and America* (Cambridge: Cambridge University Press, 1997).

——, 'An Oxonian "Idea" of a University: J. H. Newman and "Well-Being"', in M. G. Brock and M. C. Curthoys (eds), *The History of the University of Oxford*, vi. *Nineteenth-Century Oxford, Part 1* (Oxford: Clarendon Press, 1997), 287–304.

Rouse, Richard H. and Rouse, Mary A., '*Statim invenire*: Schools, Preachers, and New Attitudes to the Page', in Robert L. Benson and Giles Constable (eds), *Renaissance and Renewal in the Twelfth Century* (Cambridge, MA: Harvard University Press, 1982), 201–25.

Rowan, Frederica (ed. and tr.), *The Life of Schleiermacher as Unfolded in his Autobiography and Letters* (London: Smith, Elder and Co., 1860), i.

Royal, Robert, 'Introduction', in Alice Ramos and Marie I. George (eds), *Faith, Scholarship and Culture in the 21st Century* (Washington: American Maritain Association/Catholic University of America, 2002), 1–10.

Rüegg, Walter, 'Themes', in Hilde de Ridder-Symoens (ed.), *Universities in the Middle Ages*, A History of the Universities in Europe, ed. Walter Rüegg, 1 (Cambridge: Cambridge University Press, 1992), 3–34.

Ruestow, Edward G., *The Microscope in the Dutch Republic: The Shaping of Discovery* (Cambridge: Cambridge University Press, 1996).

Runcie, Robert, 'Theology, the University and the Modern World', in Paul A. B. Clarke and Andrew Linzey (eds), *Theology, the University and the Modern World* (London: Lester Crook Academic Publishing, 1988), 13–28.

Rust, Chris, 'Student Assessment: Lightening the Load while Increasing the Learning', paper delivered at the University of Exeter's 2008 Education Conference on Assessment and Feedback.

Salamun, Kurt, 'The Concept of Liberality in Jasper's Philosophy and the Idea of the University', in Gregory J. Walters (ed.), *The Tasks of Truth: Essays on Karl Jaspers's Idea of the University* (Frankfurt am Main: Peter Lang, 1996), 39–53.

Sawatasky, Rodney J., 'Prologue: The Virtue of Scholarly Hope', in Douglas Jacobsen and Rhonda Hustedt Jacobsen (eds), *Scholarship and Christian Faith: Enlarging the Conversation* (Oxford: Oxford University Press, 2004), 3–14.

Schelling, Friedrich Wilhelm Joseph, *On University Studies*, tr. E. S. Morgan, ed. Norbert Guterman (Athens, OH: Ohio University Press, 1966); German original, 'Vorlesungen über die Methode des akademischen Studiums', in Ernst Anrich (ed.), *Die Idee der deutschen Universität* (Darmstadt: Hermann Gentner Verlag, 1956), 1–124.

Schiller, Friedrich, 'What Is, and to What End do We Study, Universal History?', tr. Caroline Stephan and Robert Trout; <www.schillerinstitute.org/transl/Schiller_essays/universal_history.html> (accessed 27 Nov. 2009); German original 'Was heißt und zu welchem Ende studiert man Universalgeschichte', *Der Teutsche Merkur*, 4 (1789), 105–35; <de.wikisource.org/wiki/Was_heißt_und_zu_welchem_ Ende_studiert_man_Universalgeschichte%3F> (accessed 27 Nov. 2009).

Schleiermacher, Friedrich D. E., *Occasional Thoughts on Universities in the German Sense, with an Appendix Regarding a University Soon to Be Established (1808)*, tr. Terrence N. Tice with Edwina Lawler, EMTexts (Lewiston, NY: Edwin Mellen, 1991); German original, 'Gelegentliche Gedanken über Universitäten im deutschen Sinn', in Ernst Anrich (ed.), *Die Idee der deutschen Universität* (Darmstadt: Hermann Gentner Verlag, 1956), 219–308.

——, 'Towards a Theory of Sociable Conduct', in Ruth Drucilla Richardson (ed.), *Friedrich Schleiermacher's* Toward a Theory of Sociable Conduct *and Essays on its Intellectual–Cultural Context, New Athenaeum/Neues Athenaeum*, 4 (Lewiston, NY: Edwin Mellen, 1995), 20–39.

——, *Dialectic or, The Art of Doing Philosophy: A Study Edition of the 1811 Notes*, tr. Terrence N. Tice, American Academy of Religion Texts and Translations, ed. Terry Goodlove, 11 (Atlanta, GA: Scholars Press, 1996).

Schwinges, Rainer Christoph, 'Student Education, Student Life', in Hilde de Ridder-Symoens (ed.), *Universities in the Middle Ages*, A History of the Universities in Europe, ed. Walter Rüegg, 1 (Cambridge: Cambridge University Press, 1992), 194–243.

Scruton, Roger, 'The Idea of a University', in Stephen Prickett and Patricia Erskine-Hill (eds), *Education! Education! Education! Managerial Ethics and the Law of Unintended Consequences* (Thorverton: Imprint Academic/Higher Education Foundation, 2002), 73–84.

Sewell, William, *Thoughts on the Admission of Dissenters to the University of Oxford: and on the Establishment of a State Religion* (Oxford: D. A. Talboys, 1834).

Shaffer, Elinor S., 'Romantic Philosophy and the Organization of the Disciplines: The Founding of the Humboldt University of Berlin', in Andrew Cunningham and Nicholas Jardine (eds), *Romanticism and the Sciences* (Cambridge: Cambridge University Press, 1990), 38–54.

Simms, Brendan, 'Political and Diplomatic Movements, 1800–1830: Napoleon, National Uprising, Restoration', in Jonathan Sperber (ed.), *Germany 1800–1871*, Short Oxford History of Germany (Oxford: Oxford University Press, 2004), 26–45.

Slee, Peter, 'The Oxford Idea of a Liberal Education 1800–1860: The Invention of Tradition and the Manufacture of Practice', *History of Universities*, 7 (1988), 61–87.

Smith, James K. A., *The Devil Reads Derrida, and Other Essays on the University, the Church, Politics and the Arts* (Grand Rapids, MI: Eerdmans, 2009).

Smith, Steve, 'Where is the Government's Mandate to Change the World of Higher Education?', *Guardian*, 19 Oct. 2010; www.guardian.co.uk/education/2010/oct/19/universities-change-world-government-funding (accessed 18 Aug. 2011).

Sommerville, John, *The Decline of the Secular University* (Oxford: Oxford Univeristy Press, 2006).

Southern, R. W., 'The School of Paris and the School of Chartres', in Robert L. Benson and Giles Constable (eds), *Renaissance and Renewal in the Twelfth Century* (Cambridge, MA: Harvard University Press, 1982), 113–37.

——, 'The Changing Role of Universities in Medieval Europe', *Historical Research*, 60/142 (1987), 133–46.

——, *Scholastic Humanism and the Unification of Europe*, i. *Foundations* (Oxford: Blackwell, 1995).

——, *Saint Anselm: A Portrait in a Landscape* (Cambridge: Cambridge University Press, 2000).

Sperber, Jonathan (ed.), *Germany 1800–1871*, Short Oxford History of Germany, (Oxford: Oxford University Press, 2004).

Steffens, Heinrich, *Vorlesungen über die Idee der Universitäten*, in Ernst Anrich (ed.), *Die Idee der deutschen Universität* (Darmstadt: Hermann Gentner Verlag, 1956), 309–74.

Steffens, Heinrich, *The Idea of the University*, tr. Gordon Walmsley, *Copenhagen Review*, 2 (2008); translation of Lecture 1 from Steffens, *Idee der Universitäten*; <www.copenhagenreview.com/two/the%20university.pdf> (accessed 27 Nov. 2009).

Sterk, Andrea, 'Preface', in Andrea Sterk (ed.), *Religion, Scholarship and Higher Education: Perspectives, Models and Future Prospects. Essays form the Lilly Seminar on Religion and Higher Education* (Notre Dame, IN: University of Notre Dame Press, 2002), pp. xiii–xviii.

Sterk, Andrea (ed.), *Religion, Scholarship and Higher Education: Perspectives, Models and Future Prospects. Essays form the Lilly Seminar on Religion and Higher Education* (Notre Dame, IN: University of Notre Dame Press, 2002).

Stock, Brian, *The Implications of Literacy: Written Language and Models of Interpretation in the Eleventh and Twelfth Centuries* (Princeton: Princeton University Press, 1983).

Thiessen, Elmer John, 'Objections to the Idea of a Christian University', in Jeff Astley, Leslie Francis, John Sullivan, and Andrew Walker (eds), *The Idea of a Christian University: Essays on Theology and Higher Education* (Bletchley and Waynesborough, GA: Paternoster, 2004), 35–55.

Ticciati, Susannah, *Job and the Disruption of Identity: Reading beyond Barth* (London: Continuum, 2005).

Tice, Terrence N., 'Dedicatory Preface', in Friedrich D. E., Schleiermacher, *Occasional Thoughts on Universities in the German Sense, with an Appendix Regarding a University Soon to Be Established (1808)*, tr. Terrence N. Tice with Edwina Lawler, EMTexts (Lewiston, NY: Edwin Mellen, 1991), pp. i–iv.

Turnbull, G. H., *The Educational Theory of J. G. Fichte: A Critical Account, Together with Translations* (Liverpool: University of Liverpool; London: Hodder and Stoughton, 1926).

Turner, R. Steven, 'The Prussian Universities and the Concept of Research', *Internationales Archive für Sozialgeschichte der deutschen Literatur*, 5 (1980), 68–93.

——, 'The Great Transition and the Social Patterns of German Science', *Minerva*, 25 (1987), 56–76.

Turpin, K.C., 'The Ascendancy of Oriel', in M. G. Brock and M. C. Curthoys (eds), *The History of the University of Oxford*, vi. *Nineteenth-Century Oxford, Part 1* (Oxford: Clarendon Press, 1997), 183–92.

Verger, Jacques, 'Patterns', in Hilde de Ridder-Symoens (ed.), *Universities in the Middle Ages*, A History of the Universities in Europe, ed. Walter Rüegg, 1 (Cambridge: Cambridge University Press, 1992), 35–74.

Vial, Theodore, 'Schleiermacher and the State', in Jacqueline Mariña (ed.), *The Cambridge Companion to Friedrich Schleiermacher* (Cambridge: Cambridge University Press, 2005), 269–85.

Walker, Andrew, and Wright, Andrew, 'A Christian University Imagined: Recovering Paideia in a Broken World', in Jeff Astley, Leslie Francis, John Sullivan, and Andrew Walker (eds), *The Idea of a Christian University: Essays on Theology and Higher Education* (Bletchley and Waynesborough, GA: Paternoster, 2004), 56–74.

Walters, Gregory J. (ed.), *The Tasks of Truth: Essays on Karl Jaspers's Idea of the University* (Frankfurt am Main: Peter Lang, 1996).

Ward, Benedicta, 'Introduction', in *The Prayers and Meditations of Saint Anselm, with the Proslogion* (London: Penguin, 1973), 25–86.

Ward, Graham, 'The Emergence of Schleiermacher's Theology and the City of Berlin', in Mike Higton, Jeremy Law, and Christopher Rowland (eds), *Theology and Human Flourishing: Essays in Honour of Timothy J. Gorringe* (Eugene, OR: Wipf and Stock, 2011), 108–26.

Weber, Max, 'Science as a Vocation', in *From Max Weber: Essays in Sociology*, tr. H. H. Gerth and C. Wright Mills (New York: Oxford University Press, 1946), 129–56; <www.ne.jp/asahi/moriyuki/abukuma/weber/lecture/science_frame.html> (accessed 15 June 2010).

Webster, John, '"There is no Past in the Church, so there is no Past in Theology": Barth on the History of Modern Protestant Theology', in Mike Higton and John C. McDowell (eds), *Conversing with Barth*, Barth Studies, ed. John Webster, George Hunsinger, and Hans-Anton Drewes (Aldershot and Burlington, VT: Ashgate, 2004), 14–39.

——, 'Curiosity', in Mike Higton, Jeremy Law, and Christopher Rowland (eds), *Theology and Human Flourishing: Essays in Honour of Timothy J. Gorringe* (Eugene, OR: Wipf and Stock, 2011), 212–23.

Weckel, Ulrike, 'A Lost Paradise of Female Culture? Some Critical Questions Regarding the Scholarship on Late Eighteenth- and Early Nineteenth-Century German Salons', tr. Pamela E Selwyn, *German History*, 18/3 (2000), 310–36.

Werpehowski, William, 'Ad Hoc Apologetics', *Journal of Religion*, 66/3 (1986), 282–301.

Whitehead, Alfred North, *The Aims of Education and Other Essays* (New York: Macmillan, 1929).

Willard, Dallas, 'How Reason can Survive the Modern University: The Moral Foundations of Rationality', in Alice Ramos and Marie I. George (eds), *Faith, Scholarship and Culture in the 21st Century* (Washington: American Maritain Association/Catholic University of America, 2002), 181–91.

Williams, George H., *Wilderness and Paradise in Christian Thought: The Biblical Experience of the Desert in the History of Christianity and the Paradise Theme in the Theological Idea of the University*, The Menno Simons Lecture 1958 (New York: Harper and Bros, 1962).

Williams, Rowan, *On Christian Theology*, Challenges in Contemporary Theology, ed. Gareth Jones and Lewis Ayres (Oxford: Blackwell, 2000).

——, *Arius: Heresy and Tradition* (London: SCM, 2001).

——, 'Faith in the University', in Simon Robinson and Clement Katulushi (eds), *Values in Higher Education* (St Bride's Major: Aureus/University of Leeds, 2005), 24–35.

——, *Why Study the Past? The Quest for the Historical Church* (London: DLT; Grand Rapids, MI: Eerdmans, 2005).

——, 'What is a University?', 2006; <www.archbishopofcanterbury.org/698> (accessed 17 Mar. 2010).

——, Oxford University Commemoration Day Sermon, 2004; <www.archbishopofcanterbury.org/1205> (accessed 17 Mar. 2010).

——, 'Faith, Reason and Quality Assurance: Having Faith in Academic Life', 2008; <www.archbishopofcanterbury.org/1644> (accessed 17 Mar. 2010).

Wilson, F. M. G., *Our Minerva: The Men and Politics of the University of London 1836–1858* (London: Athlone, 1995).

Wolterstorff, Nicholas, *Educating for Shalom: Essays on Christian Higher Education*, ed. Clarence W. Joldersma and Gloria Goris Stronks (Grand Rapids, MI: Eerdmans, 2004).

Wood, W. Jay, *Epistemology: Becoming Intellectually Virtuous*, Contours of Christian Philosophy, ed. C. Stephen Evans (Leicester: Apollos; Downers Grove, IL: IVP, 1998).

Wynn, Mark, *Emotional Experience and Religious Understanding: Integrating Perception, Conception and Feeling* (Cambridge: Cambridge University Press, 2005).

Zagzebski, Linda Trinkhaus, *Virtues of the Mind: An Inquiry into the Nature of Virtue and the Ethical Foundations of Knowledge* (Cambridge: Cambridge University Press, 1996).

Ziolkowski, Theodore, *German Romanticism and its Institutions* (Princeton: Princeton University Press, 1990).

Index

Index

Printed in the USA/Agawam, MA
November 12, 2013

581900.061